COVER: Miles Fullman leads into an Arctic sunset on pitch 18 of Memento Mori, a new route on the south tower of Mt. Asgard on Baffin Island, Nunavut, Canada. See page 66. *Sam Stuckey*

ABOVE: Zdeněk Hák traverses the western flank of the south spur of Batura V between camps 1 and 2, en route to the first ascent of Muchu Chhish in Pakistan. See page 258. *Jaroslav Bánský*

Julia Niles
Mapuche Territory
Cochamó, Chile
Photo: Tara Kerzhner

ARC'TERYX

CONTENTS

Alexis Rojas on the fifth ice pitch during the first ascent of Odissea on the south face of Cerro Tronco in Chile. **See story on page 213.**
Gonzalo Robert

CLIMBS + EXPEDITIONS

The American Alpine Club
710 10th St., Golden, Colorado, 80401
E-mail: aaj@americanalpineclub.org
publications.americanalpineclub.org
ISBN (paperback): 979-8-9874576-7-2
ISBN (hardcover): 979-8-9874576-8-9

Printed in South Korea on FSC-certified materials.

MIX Paper | Supporting responsible forestry FSC® C147056

PHOTO: Cody Winckler during the first ascent of Yashkuk Sar I in Pakistan. See story on page 34. *August Franzen*

THE AMERICAN ALPINE JOURNAL

THE AMERICAN ALPINE CLUB

OFFICIALS FOR 2024–2025

AAC member Zach Lovell

2024 GREAT RANGES FELLOWSHIP

A-B
Anonymous Donors
Peter Ackroyd
Russell Adams
Alpenglow Foundation and the John Hobby Catto Family
Mark Andreasen
Conrad Anker
Michael and Matthew Ashley
Alex Balkanski
George Basch
Jessica Bauer
Maureen and Brian Beck
Gordon A. Benner MD
John Berry
John Bird
Jim Bodenhamer
Stephen Bonowski
Steve Bott
Ryan Bouldin
Philip Boyer
Tanya Bradby and Martin Slovacek
Michael Brandt
Samuel Britton
Jennifer Bruursema
Will Butcher

C-D
Brandon Cambio
Mitch Campbell
Ward Chewning
Richard Clawson
Jerry Clayton
Dan and Ilene Cohen
John Connor
Kevin Cooney
Billy Cox
Lori Coyner
Christopher Croft
Mary Cullinane
Rupert Dance
Joseph Davidson
Lee Davis
Scott Davis
Laura Dawson
Elle De Bell
Michael Declerck
Rob DeConto
Alvin DeMaria
Richard and Martha Draves
The Duckworth Family

E-F
Jim Edwards and Michele Mass
Stuart Ellison
Philip Erard
Timothy Erickson
Frank and Margaret Fickeisen
Carla Firey
Keith and Liz Fleischman
Charles and Lisa Claudy Fleischman Family Fund
James Frank
Bruce Franks
Alexander Friedman
Jim Frush

G-H
Ben and Christa Gabriel
Pete Gallagher
James Garrett and
Franziska Garrett, MD
Ryan Gellert
David Gerstenberger
Garth Gherardini
Michael Gibbons
Caroline Gleich and Rob Lea
David Goeddel
Jonathan Gopel
Eric Green
Wayne and Cynthia Griffin
Till Gross
Allyson Gunsallus
Robert B. Hall and Sheila Matz
Rick Hanheide
Travis Hays
Rocky Henderson
Kailey Herrmann
Scot Hillman
Michael Hodges
Jennifer and Marley Hodgson
Richard E. Hoffman MD
Holdfast Collective
Hornbein Family Charitable Fund
Robert Horton
William Hudson
Rob Hutchinson
Minh Huynh

I-K
Alex Intermill and Lisa McKinney
Joe Jakowski
Zhen Jian
Dylan Johnson
Didier Jourdain
Cody Kaemmerlen
Kelson Foundation
Adam Kilgus
Mark and Samskriti King
Laine Kline
Mark Kroese
Paul Kuchu

L-M
Phil Lakin Jr.
David Landman and Marian Hawley
Jesse Laniak
The Lasky-Barajas Family Fund
Ryan Lauth
John Lee
Austin Lee
Pedro Lemos
Erik Letko
Brody Leven
Dave Lonack
George Lowe III
Howard and Ann Lukens
Chris Lynch
Liam Mac Sharry
Brent Manning
August March
Troy Martin
Bridget Martin
Katie Massey
Ann Mathieson
Thomas McCarthy
Michael McClelland
Heidi McDowell
Gary McElvany
Mackenzie McGrath
Craig McKibben and Sarah Merner
Brad and Melissa McQueen
Richard Merritt
Hari Mix
Jim Morrison
Paul Morrow

N-P
Alan Nagel
Dennis Nelms
John and Alicia Nicholson
Sean O'Brien
Cyril F. and Marie O'Neil Foundation
Jeanne OConnell
Bob Palais
Joyce Palmese
John Parsons
Charles Peck
Allen Peery
Jeff Phillips DDS
Michael Plunkett
Keenan Pope
Melissa and Jim Prager

R-S
Chuck Reid
John Reppy
Jessica James Reynolds
Jodi Richard
T. Scott Richards
Mark and Teresa Richey
David Riggs
Michael Riley
Joel Robinson
Taylor Rodriguez
William Rougeux
Sage Summit Advisors
Naoe Sakashita
Raymond VJ Schrag
Steve and Paula Mae Schwartz
Ellen Sebastian
George Shaw
Stephen Shiboski
Will Shillito
Samuel Silverstein MD
Curt Simonson
John Sirois
Cody J Smith
James Sneeringer
Steven Sorkin
Kate Sparks
Spitzer Family Foundation
Katelyn Stahley
Brian Steers
Rob and Jennifer Stephenson
Emerson Stewart and Parisa Tabriz
Barbara Straka
Theodore "Sam" Streibert
Bob Strode
Duncan Stuart
Pavan Surapaneni
Steve Swenson and Ann Dalton

T-V
Geoffrey Tabin
Jack and Pat Tackle
John Taladay
Eddie Taylor
Keith Thomajan
Steffen Thompson
Greg Thomsen
Andrew Tomko
John L. Townsend
Jay Underwood
Alexander Uy

W-Z
Nick Valencia
Travis Van Overbeke
Genevieve Walsh
Winston Warme
Robert Weggel
Steve Whitaker
Ryan Whitted
Tracy and Bruce Wilhelm
Nathan Wilhelm
Nina Williams
Mark Woodard
Graham Zimmerman
Jane Zimmerman

OR
OUTDOOR
RESEARCH
Rooted.
BORN IN THE ELEMENTS
BUILT ON THE TRAIL

FRIENDS OF THE AAJ

The following people helped make this year's AAJ possible with a gift of $250 or more between January 2024 and April 15, 2025. Thank you!

Peter Ackroyd
Mark Andreasen
Gordon A. Benner MD
Carla Firey
Jim Frush
Richard E. Hoffman MD
Holdfast Collective
David Landman and Marian Haw
Dougald MacDonald
Mark and Teresa Richey
David Riggs
Samuel Silverstein MD
Theodore "Sam" Streibert
Jack and Pat Tackle

Patrick Gephart moves along the east ridge of Tengkangpoche in Nepal. **See page 316.**
Pat Perry Johnson

patagonia®
Built for the Cleanest Line

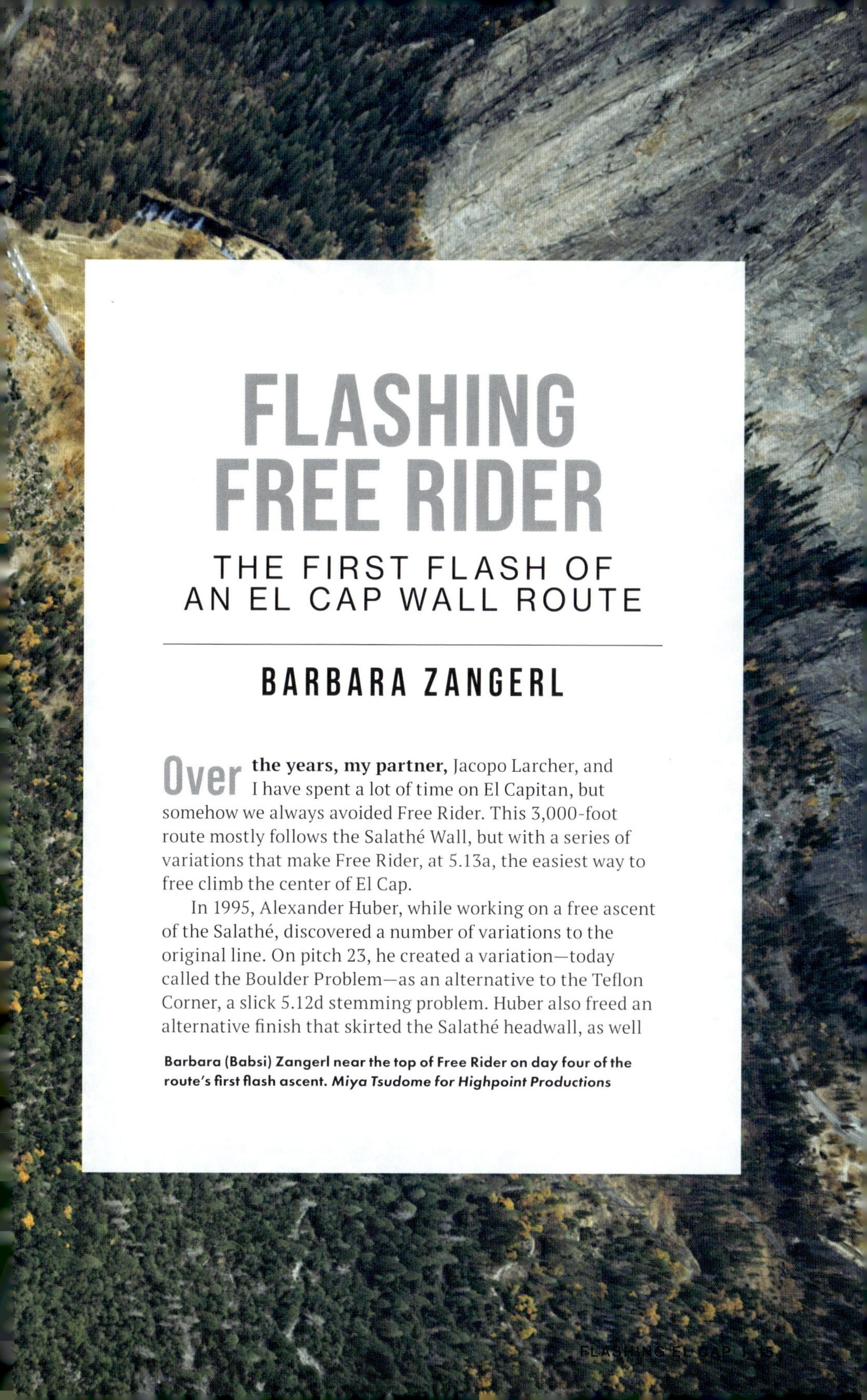

FLASHING FREE RIDER

THE FIRST FLASH OF AN EL CAP WALL ROUTE

BARBARA ZANGERL

Over the years, my partner, Jacopo Larcher, and I have spent a lot of time on El Capitan, but somehow we always avoided Free Rider. This 3,000-foot route mostly follows the Salathé Wall, but with a series of variations that make Free Rider, at 5.13a, the easiest way to free climb the center of El Cap.

In 1995, Alexander Huber, while working on a free ascent of the Salathé, discovered a number of variations to the original line. On pitch 23, he created a variation—today called the Boulder Problem—as an alternative to the Teflon Corner, a slick 5.12d stemming problem. Huber also freed an alternative finish that skirted the Salathé headwall, as well

Barbara (Babsi) Zangerl near the top of Free Rider on day four of the route's first flash ascent. ***Miya Tsudome for Highpoint Productions***

SO CLOSE...

A QUARTER CENTURY OF EL CAP ONSIGHT AND FLASH ATTEMPTS

Prepared by Matt Samet

1997

Japanese climber Yuji Hirayama goes for the Salathé Wall (VI 5.13b) onsight over two days. He takes one fall on the 5.12d Teflon Corner (pitch 23), pulls his rope, and onsights the adjacent Huber Pitch (5.12d at the time)—today known as the Boulder Problem. He falls on each of the crux headwall pitches, but redpoints them to free the full Salathé.

1998

Leo Houlding and Patch Hammond (both U.K.) attempt El Niño (VI 5.13c) ground-up and onsight, one month after the first ascent by Alex and Thomas Huber. Houlding, age 18 at the time, grabs a quickdraw on the route's third pitch (the first 5.13) to avoid a 70-footer and pulls on a draw on the first bolt of the next pitch to suss the initial holds. He redpoints those pitches and onsights the rest of the route's six 5.13 pitches, and he seconds all of Hammond's leads cleanly.

2003

Hirayama goes for El Niño onsight, taking two falls—one on pitch four, one on pitch 15—before next-go redpointing those pitches. He onsights the rest of the route in four days total, with a day on the Valley floor in the middle of the ascent.

2004

American twins Mark and Mike Anderson climb Free Rider, swinging leads, with the second climbing free and Mike taking no falls, including leading the Boulder Problem (5.12d at that time). The catch? The brothers had aided the Salathé Wall two years earlier, though they felt this added no useful beta for their flash attempt. They also returned to the Valley floor twice before jugging back up their ropes for their final, three-day push—once so Mike could fly home to Salt Lake City to take final exams for his master's degree in robotics.

(continued on page 18)

as a long offwidth to avoid a 5.13 lead above the Ear on the Salathé route. He kept all this quiet until he could return to the wall with his brother, Thomas, three years later. The two redpointed Free Rider in 1998 in only 15 hours and 25 minutes.

Among the hard pitches on Free Rider, the Monster Offwidth was the one that seemed to me like an almost impossible challenge: a mythical beast, running 200 feet up to El Cap Spire on pitch 20. In fact, Jacopo and I had never attempted Free Rider, the Salathé, or Golden Gate mainly out of fear of the Monster, which is shared by all three of those climbs. For us, offwidth climbing felt so hard that we couldn't imagine climbing in that style for 200 feet.

Instead, Jacopo and I focused on other free lines on El Cap that better suited our style—thin, technical, bouldery, and sustained routes like El Niño (VI 5.13c, 2015), Zodiac (VI 5.13d, 2016), Magic Mushroom (VI 5.14a, 2017), PreMuir (VI 5.13d, 2019), The Nose (VI 5.14a, 2019), and El Corazón (VI 5.13b, 2023, by me and Lara Neumeier). Every time we left Yosemite, we were already dreaming up our next adventure on the wall.

The idea of trying to flash Free Rider was first suggested to us a few years ago by Kolin Powick, a good friend and former product director at Black Diamond. Back then, it seemed unrealistic, but the seed was planted. We felt it might be something we'd attempt one day. [*See sidebar at left and on the next spread for a list of El Capitan onsight and flash attempts, including on Free Rider.*]

In 2023, the idea began to take firmer shape, and the more we thought about it, the more the challenge intrigued us. Could we really climb all those pitches without falling even once? It seemed impossible, especially considering how tricky even the easier pitches on El Cap can be. We decided our main goal would simply be to see how far we could get without taking a fall.

Over time, we had improved our Yosemite crack-climbing skills, even though we were always quite slow on big-wall ascents. We took our time to figure out the hardest pitches and solve the individual sequences, spending five to 11 days to free each route on El Cap. We weren't deliberately preparing for flashing Free Rider, but these climbs brought us closer.

Our final preparation began in the fall of 2024, when Jacopo and I both climbed the single-pitch trad route Magic Line, the thin 5.14c layback by Vernal Falls in Yosemite, less than two weeks apart in late October and early November. That's when the decision was made—it was time to try Free Rider.

Zangerl leading Magic Line (5.14c) in Yosemite Valley. She and partner Jacopo Larcher each redpointed this trad climbing testpiece in the fall of 2024, which helped convince them they were ready to attempt a flash of Free Rider. *Jacopo Larcher*

To prepare for Free Rider's wide cracks, we dedicated four days specifically to offwidth climbing, tackling old-school Yosemite 5.10s like Generator Crack, Twilight Zone, and Ahab. These routes pushed us to our limits but also helped us overcome our biggest worry about Free Rider.

On our first offwidth day, we set the goal of top-roping Generator Crack two times, back to back, before trying Twilight Zone—which I did on lead and which was one of my hardest onsights ever! (It felt scary and insecure—like wrestling with myself for 40 minutes.) On the second day, we could barely get out of bed, with our muscles hurting all over. We needed half a day off before we got back to the next offwidth. But every day felt easier, and when we returned to Generator Crack on the last day of our offwidth clinic, it felt way more enjoyable.

I also had a good day of preparation by climbing Astroman and the Rostrum back to back, which I did with Laura Pineau on November 10. (Jacopo was trying Magic Line that day.) Covering so many pitches of different crack sizes in a single day was excellent training. Still, I wasn't sure such limited preparation would be enough. Thoughts of falling in key sections lingered.

First was the Freeblast, the first ten pitches of the Salathé Wall; here, the climbing involves notoriously slick and difficult friction. Then there was the dreaded Monster. In the days leading up to the attempt, Jacopo and I sought advice from friends: Emily Harrington gave me special beta for the crack, including using double shoes on one foot—a larger shoe over a smaller one for more secure jams—and recommended elbow pads and kneepads. Alex Honnold shared a crucial piece of beta: If we got too tired, we should lean outward to the right, resting off a jammed left leg. This would turn out to be very helpful.

To better understand the moves on the Boulder Problem—

2006
American Alex Honnold does Free Rider over two days (11 years before his famous solo). Having already done the Freeblast—the lower ten slab pitches, graded 5.11—Honnold wasn't attempting a flash of Free Rider, but, he says, "I tried my hardest the first time." He fell on the Boulder Problem crux and then redpointed the pitch next go, though, he noted, "it's worth adding that the crux was much easier back then [at 5.12d]—a jug broke off later and forced the karate-kick maneuver."

2009
Swiss climber Ueli Steck leads every pitch free on Golden Gate (VI 5.13b) over four days, onsighting the climb's three 5.13 and four 5.12 pitches. The only fall he takes is on the 5.11c hand crack above El Cap Spire, having slipped on wet rock.

Cédric Lachat, also from Switzerland, onsights every pitch of Free Rider, but with a few "asterisks": He had already onsighted the Freeblast ten days earlier during an aborted attempt on Golden Gate, and he skipped these pitches during the Free Rider ascent, jumaring up to Heart Ledges. Lachat also fell off the Boulder Problem (newly upgraded to 5.13a since the key hold broke), then onsighted the Teflon Corner; he led every other hard pitch onsight during the three-day effort.

2012
Leo Houlding climbs Free Rider mostly onsight over two days—minus the Freeblast, which he had previously climbed—with just one fall on the Boulder Problem, which he quickly redpoints before scampering to the top.

2014
In late spring, American climber Ethan Pringle attempts to flash Free Rider. Climbing with Walker Emerson in a 36-hour push, Pringle takes one fall on the Boulder Problem, then redpoints the pitch, before taking the route to the top with no further falls.

In May, U.K. climbers James McHaffie and Dan McManus set out to climb the Salathé, with McHaffie ultimately making a ground-up free ascent, after some falls on the headwall pitches. En route, both climbers flash the Boulder Problem, with beta from Valley local James Lucas, and McHaffie flashes the Enduro Corner (5.12). Had they taken a left below the headwall onto Free Rider, it's likely McHaffie would have achieved the first El Cap flash.

the V7/5.13a technical crux on pitch 23 (originally climbed at 5.12d by the Hubers; a hold later broke)—we watched the video of Alex climbing this sequence in the film *Free Solo*. (We never planned to try the Teflon Corner or have it as a Plan B; for us, it was always clear that if we fell on the Boulder Problem, our flash was over.) We could have prepared more thoroughly for other pitches, but diving in with minimal beta felt less stressful. Other than the Monster Offwidth and the Boulder Problem, we'd be improvising.

On the day we began—November 19—I was nervous but excited. Our original plan was to start climbing at 4 a.m., but the forecast had changed, with clouds and possible snow for the first two days, and then even worse. Our upcoming flight home to Europe meant it was now or never, so we decided to wait until 8 a.m., but it was still freezing cold at the start. Somehow the poor forecast took the pressure off—we knew that if it started to snow or rain, it would be over, so we took an attitude of "Let's see how far we get." With numb fingers and toes, I overgripped every hold on the first pitch, and was glad when the

Free Rider (VI 5.13a) on El Capitan, with (1) the Monster Offwidth, (2) the Boulder Problem, and (3) the Enduro Corner and Round Table traverse. Larcher and Zangerl climbed the route in 32 pitches. ***Chris Falkenstein***

day eventually began to warm up.

On pitch four, a 5.11b slab, a bolt up and left lured me off route. It felt steeper and harder going that way, so I downclimbed a couple of moves and took a rightward detour, skipping that bolt. Later, Eric Bissell, who was filming our ascent, told me that going right and skipping the clip is the standard way to climb that section. Luckily, I realized my mistake in time. Above, the 5.10 corner/chimney of the Half Dollar pitch was wet, and Jacopo and I were both relieved when we got through this and finished Freeblast.

We continued that same day over to Lung Ledge at the base of the Hollow Flake, having swung leads all day. (As with our previous El Cap climbs together, Jacopo and I planned to trade leads on most of Free Rider. For the hardest pitches, I led the Monster and Scotty Burk offwidths, both of us led the Boulder Problem, Jacopo led the first pitch of the Enduro Corner while I led the harder second pitch, and Jacopo led the

That October, U.K. climber Pete Whittaker tries to flash Free Rider, taking a fall on the Boulder Problem, then redpointing it, and then onsighting the 5.12d Teflon Corner next door. Whittaker and partner Tom Randall had previously climbed the Freeblast, and they left the wall after day one on Free Rider because of crowds around Heart Ledges, returning the next morning to continue up the route.

2016
U.K. climber Calum Coldwell-Story makes a one-fall ascent of Free Rider, coming painfully close to the flash before falling off the last move of the Boulder Problem. He redpoints that pitch next try and either leads or seconds every other pitch with no falls.

2018
Czech climber Adam Ondra attempts the Salathé (VI 5.13c while linking the two headwall pitches) onsight in a one-day push, supported by Nico Favresse (Belgium). Ondra fires through the Boulder Problem but falls on the headwall in the mid-day heat. As with McHaffie four years earlier, Ondra might well have fired an El Cap route first try if he'd opted for the Free Rider finish.

2021
After focused training, Josh Wharton (USA) makes it to the end of the Boulder Problem on Free Rider, sticking the ninja-kick move, only to have his foot slip before finishing.

2022
Czech climber František Bulička comes painfully close to flashing Free Rider, as he fires through the Boulder Problem with beta from partner Tim Greenwood, only to fall higher up, on the Enduro Corner, when his foot slips on a sling attached to a fixed Hexentric.

2024
Jacopo Larcher (Italy) nearly flashes Free Rider along with Babsi Zangerl. He falls once on the Boulder Problem, then redpoints the pitch and continues to the top without falls.

SOURCES: *Climber accounts, published reports (including the AAJ), and correspondence with the climbers.*

5.12 pitch to the Round Table.) Early the next morning, we tackled the Hollow Flake. Jacopo led the pitch, which felt like climbing three pitches in one. First, you downclimb about 100 feet, then traverse to the flake, and then climb back up 165 feet. It felt endless and physically demanding.

After that, the climbing became more enjoyable, with easier terrain that allowed us to move faster. Before long, we reached the Ear, pitch 18. I led this 5.7 chimney, which was nerve-wracking at first. It felt exposed, and placing gear was difficult. But as I climbed higher, more holds appeared, and the chimney wasn't as bad as I'd initially thought. When I reached the belay, though, my nerves spiked again—there it was, the Monster Offwidth. It looked even more intimidating and endless than I had imagined, this smooth, dark crack splitting the blank granite. But I couldn't wait to start!

The hauling up to that point had been tough. On Freeblast, we hauled one heavy bag that constantly got stuck. At Heart Ledges, we picked up a second haulbag with our portaledge that we had pre-hauled two days earlier, using fixed lines that drop straight from Heart Ledges to the ground. We had enough gear and supplies for four days. As we climbed higher, the bags got lighter and the wall got steeper, making the hauling easier.

The Monster Offwidth was my lead. Within ten feet, I was already out of breath. I used every trick I had learned: double shoes on my right foot (a borrowed size 41 TC Pro from my friend Nemo over my size 37 TC Pro), an elbow pad and kneepad for my left side, and Alex's leg-jam-and-lean resting technique. None of it made the climbing easy, but it made it possible. I focused on one move at a time, trying not to think about how much farther I had to go. When I finally reached the belay, roughly 30 minutes later, I was overwhelmed with relief. One of the hardest sections was behind me, but it had taken everything.

We pushed on to El Cap Spire and, in the dark, climbed two more pitches, fixed them, and then slept at the Spire. That night marked our lowest point in terms of energy—we were totally wasted after the Monster Offwidth, and we could have used a rest day. Still, we were both thrilled to have climbed this far without falls, and that night rested as best we could.

WE WERE TOTALLY WASTED AFTER THE MONSTER OFFWIDTH, AND WE COULD HAVE USED A REST DAY. STILL, WE WERE BOTH THRILLED TO HAVE CLIMBED THIS FAR WITHOUT FALLS.

We allowed ourselves a later start, letting the sun warm the stone. We didn't talk much about the next pitches, only setting it up so that Jacopo would try the Boulder Problem first, since I had led the hard pitches the day before. Normally, we talk a lot about the cruxes and beta and plans, remembering all the moves and footholds. But on Free Rider it was different—we just focused on moving upward.

As a warm-up, the 5.10 crack below the Boulder Problem pitch was already demanding. By the time I reached the belay I was nervous, and the crux looked as intimidating as I had imagined—slightly overhanging and complex, with a confusing array of bad footholds.

Jacopo seemed to be pretty chill when he started. It was hard to see the pressure he felt (and about which he only told me afterward). He climbed very smoothly, making it look easy up to the infamous "ninja kick." There, he started to struggle. It seemed like he wanted to mantel up on

Zangerl approaching the crux moves of the Boulder Problem, traversing toward the breadloaf hold to set up for the ninja kick. *Eric Bissell for Highpoint Productions*

the "breadloaf" pinch, which didn't work, and then he missed a tiny undercling pocket that helps queue up the kick move. One second later, he was hanging on the rope—and all was over! After the fall, there was no noise of frustration or shouting; Jacopo just said, "Luckily I had a rope. And now all the pressure is gone."

Jacopo's fall dealt a blow to my confidence. He is stronger than me, and if he wasn't able to do it, how could I?

Still, I had the advantage of seeing his attempt, getting his beta, and adjusting my approach based on what I'd learned—that I could use the undercling pocket to set up for the kick, and that the hold after the kick was positive. I reminded myself to focus on giving my best on every single move, and to let go of what I couldn't control.

AS SOON AS I STARTED TO CLIMB, THE PRESSURE DISSOLVED AND I IMMEDIATELY GOT INTO FIGHT MODE.

As soon as I started to climb, the pressure dissolved and I immediately got into fight mode. I used the same beta as Jacopo, but my height made the sequence more challenging. I couldn't reach the breadloaf before the kick move from the same footholds. Realizing this, I climbed back to rest on a good crimp, and then looked for a different solution. That adjustment drained me, and by the time I set up for the ninja kick, I was pumped.

When I finally committed, the kick felt completely out of control. For a brief moment, I was sure I was going to fall. But miraculously, my foot stuck to the dihedral wall. That moment—when everything hung by a thread—was one of the most intense of my climbing career. And when it all clicked, it was one of the best feelings I've ever experienced on a wall.

Jacopo's fall meant his chance to flash Free Rider was gone, though he did redpoint the pitch right after I sent it. I could see how much the fall—his only fall on the route—hurt him. It is such a fine line between sending and failing on a flash attempt, and there is no second chance. We had never had those feelings before on El Cap. Still, despite his disappointment, Jacopo cheered me on. His unwavering support made everything easier, and I couldn't have done it without him.

After the Boulder Problem, I felt an incredible surge of energy and euphoria. I wanted to ride that high and climb as far as possible that same day. (I'd found I could stay focused during the climbing, but it felt harder to manage my nerves in the portaledge at night.) Our original plan had been to bivy before the difficult Enduro Corner to save energy, but I had the feeling it would be better to continue all the way to the sloping ledge of the Round Table, beyond the Enduro Corner.

Jacopo led the 5.11 first pitch of the Enduro Corner, pitch 26, and I followed. The climbing was tough, with bad hand jams and tricky layback sections. Leading the upper corner, a 5.12 pitch, I opted to layback the entire section. It was exhausting and more physical, but it felt safer than jamming. The corner was pumpy, and I had to climb quickly and place minimal protection to avoid burning out.

Afterward, we moved into the long 5.12 traverse to the Round Table. While seconding, at the start of that pitch, I had to stretch dynamically to reach a hold, barely catching it with my second hand to stop the swing. It felt wild and out of control, but I didn't hesitate, which saved me from falling.

At the Round Table, we took a short break to rest and eat, and then I decided to climb another pitch before stopping for the night. To my surprise, it was harder than I'd expected—and harder than the 5.11d hand crack indicated in the topo. I hadn't brought enough cams or a tagline, and the crack near the top was wet and slippery, which stressed me out. When I finally reached the belay, I was exhausted.

That night on the Round Table wasn't restful, with the 5.10d Scotty Burk Offwidth still looming above—the last true battle. If I could make it up that pitch, I had the feeling the flash would be in the bag. When Jacopo fell asleep, it was completely silent up there. I looked up at the sky, just thinking about how it would all be over in 24 hours. *Will I have sent or will have I fallen? And how will that feel?* I'd been telling myself at every moment on the wall that I should be proud to have made it so far. I could have fallen on the Freeblast or the Monster. At the same time, so close to the flash, it was hard to feel satisfied with anything less than success.

Larcher and Zangerl at their bivy at Round Table Ledge, the last night on the wall. Hauling gear and supplies added to the difficulty of their four-day ascent, but the two had plenty of wall experience—they had already free climbed five different El Cap routes together. *Miya Tsudome for Highpoint Productions*

The next day, I battled my way up the Scotty Burk, and then came the final chimney, pitch 32, a 5.9. I climbed with my left side in first, pushing upward, but when I reached the overhanging section, I couldn't exit. With my back stuck to the wall, the good holds were out of reach. I had to downclimb, reposition myself with my right side in first, and then climb up again.

This time, I grabbed the good holds and executed the chimney. That was the very last little hurdle. From there, it was easy terrain to the top.

When we finally reached the summit of El Capitan, I was overwhelmed with emotion. The experience felt surreal—after all the effort, fear, and doubt, it was done. Standing there with Jacopo, looking out over Yosemite Valley, I could barely believe I had flashed the Free Rider.

SUMMARY: No-falls first-try ascent of Free Rider (VI 5.13a) on El Capitan in Yosemite Valley, California, by Barbara Zangerl, November 19–22, 2024. This was the first flash of any of El Cap's main wall routes. Zangerl spoke about this ascent on the Cutting Edge podcast.

ABOUT THE AUTHOR: Born in 1988, Austrian Barbara (Babsi) Zangerl started climbing at age 14. In addition to numerous free ascents of El Capitan routes, she has redpointed 5.14d sport climbs as well as the Yosemite traditional climbs Meltdown and Magic Line (both 5.14c).

Spencer Gray leading the first pitch of Kaqur Kangri's headwall, at 6,500 meters on the southwest arête. Kande Hiunchuli (6,627m) is on the horizon. *Ryan Griffiths*

CHARMED IN MUGU

THE SOUTHWEST ARÊTE OF KAQUR KANGRI IN NEPAL

SPENCER GRAY

I was not expecting so much delight.

Ryan Griffiths, Matt Zia, and I had come to the sparsely populated Mugu District in western Nepal to attempt a tall line on the south side of Kaqur Kangri (a.k.a. Kanti Himal, 6,859m), a majestic butte of a peak on the border with Tibet. We had pictures of half the mountain and an old, almost Victorian description of the south face from *The Himalayan Journal*. We would take our best shot at the obvious sharp prow in the photos—the unclimbed southwest arête—but we had a more or less cheerful willingness to fail. We figured we'd get up something or another, and, if nothing else, roustabout for a month in a remote valley that, as far as we knew, hadn't seen climbers in a quarter century.

Matt and I had met in Patagonia in 2016 and climbed in the Chaltén massif, where we discovered a good chemistry. We have since shared the rope in Montana—my home state and where Matt and Ryan both live now—and in India. They are professional guides: ice in winter, alpine rock in the summer, and Ryan in Alaska in the spring. I'm based in Seattle, work in public policy in the energy sector, and climb when I can.

I approached Matt in March 2024 about returning to the Himalaya, my fifth expedition to the region, and he suggested that Ryan round out our ideal team size. We roped up once as a group, when Matt and Ryan visited me in Squamish. There, we uncovered a shared mid-pitch propensity for breaking into a contagious twang and delivering laconic country wisdom: "You know what they say," delivered in a deadpan drawl, followed by a pause, "you can't pickle a possum without gettin' vinegar on your britches."

Kaqur Kangri was our preferred kind of objective: high enough to require extra effort, low enough to still let you reliably pull hard, and relatively off the radar. The southwest arête appeared to stick to the best rock on the south side and mostly avoid the impact zone of two shelves of active seracs that loom over the rest of the south face—one about halfway up, the other just below the summit. It's still hard for me to believe there is a mile-thick hunk of stone that good just sitting out there minding itself, evading the paparazzi.

The mountain is in the far north tip of Shey Phoksundo National Park, which spans a wide range of ecosystems, including the rain shadow north of the Kanjiroba massif. That area includes much of the Kanti Himal mountains, of which Kaqur Kangri is the most prominent peak. Kaqur was first climbed by a Japanese team from the alpine club of Doshisha University in Kyoto, led by Toyoji Wada, in September 2002. The eight-member team (including three Sherpas) approached from Tibet and summited by the east ridge after fixing lines.

Japanese expeditions from the Osaka Alpine Club had reconnoitered the Nepalese side several years earlier. Sadao Yoshinaga, the leader, described their first view of Kaqur Kangri in 1997, from a border peak to the north, in the 2001 *Himalayan Journal* (paraphrased slightly): "[A] tall gigantic peak dominating others came into their sight....The shape of the peak was just like a big vaulting box piled up to a 1,000m height with snow and ice."

In 1998, a team of four Japanese and 20 porters hacked through thick shrubbery to reach the south side: "The awful south face of 1,800m high was standing in front of them," the same article reported. "The south face itself is composed of [a] lower half of rock precipices and upper half of overwhelming hanging glaciers with numerous huge ice cliffs, defending against the raiders into the face.... It seemed to be impossible to find a feasible route to the summit. They tried to seek for [an] alternative route on the east ridge, west face, and northwest ridge. Their hard work for a week, however, ended in vain."

When I first read these grandiloquent words, I half expected a dragon to make an appearance. Naturally, we had to give it a go.

The only pictures of the south face we could find were taken by trekkers from a distant pass—Chyargo La, eight miles away—and by a handful of climbers on other peaks, and none of them showed our entire route. A few photos showed a promisingly compact headwall above the south face. But the lower half of the mountain was cut off, leaving it to our imagination. Geologic maps were inconclusive: In this region, some granitic rock had been exposed, but huge stretches of flaky schist and other metamorphic rock were mixed in, sometimes on the same mountain. We kept our hopes in check.

A FEW PHOTOS SHOWED A PROMISINGLY COMPACT HEADWALL. BUT THE LOWER HALF OF THE MOUNTAIN WAS CUT OFF, LEAVING IT TO OUR IMAGININATION.

Kaqur is in a tick-list desert. The closest 8,000-meter summit (Dhaulagiri) is almost 90 miles away as the chough flies. Gurla Mandhata (7,694m) is about the same distance in the opposite direction, in Tibet. There are only two 7,000-meter peaks in western Nepal (Api and Saipal). One effect of having few headliners is sparse regional traffic from climbers and trekkers. Reconnaissance reports by Paulo Grobel, Julian Freeman-Attwood, and others have raised western Nepal's profile in past editions of the *AAJ* (2015 and 2019, for example), but still relatively few people climb there.

In Kathmandu, en route to our launching point of Gamgadhi, Mugu's capital, we hired two brothers-in-law, Devendra (Deven) and Buddhi Tamang, as our on-the-ground fixer/translator and camp cook, respectively. They are Tamang

The view from Chyargo La toward the border with Tibet and the south side of Kaqur Kangri, in the center. The 6,859-meter peak, also known as Kanti Himal in Nepal, had only been climbed once, in 2002, by the east ridge, approached from Tibet. *Spencer Gray*

Nepalese from a village in the Rolwaling region. Their help was essential while negotiating for mules and supplies, and for navigating the basic local infrastructure.

From Gamgadhi, we walked with nine mules and their handler, Kali, for eight days to base camp, including four days spent improving six miles of an existing path so the mules and their wide loads could pass. This side trail departed the main trail, which connects Mugu and Dolpo, at the Takla Khola, in a Fangorn Forest–like vale of huge Himalayan birches, their trunks bent wildly and leaves yellowing. We continued up a tributary of the Mayongthan Khola and set up base camp in an alpine meadow at 4,700 meters, with a view of the upper third of Kaqur Kangri.

The side trail we improved is used seasonally by hunters and collectors of *yarsagumba* (*Cordyceps sinensis*). This parasitic fungus grows in some alpine grasslands of the Himalaya out of the heads of infected moth larvae. The fungus fruiting body, attached to the larval corpse, is hand-harvested in late spring, like a tiny carrot, and sold as a prized ingredient in traditional Tibetan and Chinese medicine. It has purported immune-boosting and Viagra-like properties (it has in fact shown promising pharmacological results in preclinical testing). *Yarsagumba* has been overcollected in many places, damaging local ecosystems like the Takla and Mayongthan valleys, both of which we camped in. The market demand is overwhelming: In recent years, *yarsagumba* has sold for more than $20,000 per kilogram in Nepal and makes up more than half the annual income for some families who collect it.

We would be climbing above a mycological gold rush, with Shey Phoksundo National Park clearly showing the knock-on effects: fire pits, cast-off clothing, playing cards, and hundreds of

The 1,670-meter southwest arête of Kaqur Kangri (6,859m), with bivouacs shown. The summit is hidden behind. The team descended along the northwest ridge (left). ***Spencer Gray***

food wrappers scattered about the larger meadows, which were largely devoid of wildlife. Our first afternoon in base camp, I scooped water out of a pond recharged by a side channel of the river, and then slowly dumped it back out when I noticed a dozen tiny squiggles wriggling out of the sediment, perhaps new settlers left behind by the fungus harvesters.

"Delightful," I said, turning to Matt and Ryan. "Worms."

From the moment we scrambled to the base of Kaqur's south face at 5,200 meters, we could see the rock was excellent. The same high-quality granitic gneiss (so it seemed) that we had found while acclimatizing on a neighboring 6,226-meter peak extended to the summit of Kaqur—information that could only be gleaned in person. Most of the basin and side valleys below Kaqur, apart from discrete contact zones with neighboring schist, seemed to have similar rock. It could have come straight off Mt. Moran in the Tetons.

We spent a week scoping the southwest arête from various angles and at different times of day, formulating our plan for bivouac sites and tactics. In base camp one morning, we saw a giant serac fall from the mountaintop, creating a huge debris zone across the bottom of the south face and confirming our choice to hug the arête. The two biggest puzzles were the middle rock section, with obvious snow-covered ledges but smooth, compact rock in between, and the upper headwall—the steep crown lording over the subrange. We grew convinced that there were enough features to pull it off.

We joked that our basic tactic would be Heavy and Slow, rather than Light and Fast. We each packed 11 pounds of food, plenty for five to seven days. We prioritized selecting the best bivy sites to stay well rested for the upper headwall, the obvious crux, rather than climbing until dark each day to gain meters. We hoped this would give us three relatively flat places to sleep: a thin, shaley ledge, which would probably fit a tent, after we raced up the lower slabs, and the diggable (we hoped) bottom and top of the snowfield separating the headwall from the lower serac band, with a Dyneema ice hammock supplementing whatever ledges we could chop.

My feet and Ryan's are within one size of each other, so we'd share rock shoes for leading, although we anticipated climbing mostly in boots. To reduce weight, we packed a single synthetic quilt for two people, with a nylon floor that Ryan had sewed on to retain warmth, plus one hoodless sleeping bag. We had a small double rack, with extra pitons and nuts for rappel anchors. Ryan has a taste for homemade metal: I'm still not sure whether he found some of his pitons in a back-alley smithy in Thamel or yanked them off street signs at home in Bozeman.

On day one, October 15, we three soloed about 1,500 feet of fourth- and low-fifth-class ramps and short steps to reach an overhanging chimney at the first cliffband. While an easier path lay through a drainage gully 50 yards right,

Gray on beautiful rock at about 6,000 meters, below the hanging snowfield that separates the south face's serac bands. *Ryan Griffiths*

it was exposed to serac fall, whereas the chimney was shielded by a buttress. Ryan led two pitches at stiff 5.10 in the rock shoes, including a laser-cut offwidth that had us laughing in disbelief at its high quality. As we followed, Matt and I skated off overhanging and crimpy sections in our double boots.

A couple of hundred feet above was a sloping band of red talus at 5,800 meters, where we stopped for the night after chopping out the frozen ground to fit the tent. The next morning, our MSR Reactor stove (a veteran of several trips at high altitude) failed catastrophically, apparently because of a thermal trip, an internal mechanism to prevent overheating that cannot be field-repaired once triggered. Fortunately, we had stashed a spare, if dinky, PocketRocket stove at the base, but getting it would require descending over 600 meters and fixing ropes to facilitate a return trip that same day. We had three more days of a bluebird forecast before an unsettled pattern moved in—losing a whole day could jeopardize this summit window. But no stove, no go. We bit the bullet and spent the day yo-yoing down and back up.

Staying attuned to your own motivations and risk tolerance is the only way to return repeatedly to big-mountain environments. While we were in base camp and acclimatizing, we had received the news that Michael Gardner, a fellow guide and a friend of Matt and Ryan's, had passed away in a fall on Jannu East, in far eastern Nepal. His death deeply affected our team. Now, up on the mountain, Matt was discovering that, at that particular moment, his compass was not pointing toward Kaqur Kangri. I'm grateful that reaching that difficult conclusion deepened rather than strained our friendships. "Would something make the difference to change your mind?" I asked. Matt reflected, quiet, and then replied, "Maybe just time."

ABOVE: The second bivouac site, at the bottom of the hanging snowfield, at about 6,200 meters. An ice hammock enhanced the ledge. ***Ryan Griffiths***

LEFT: Ryan Griffiths at about 6,000 meters, with unnamed and unclimbed Peak 6,226m (6,145m on some maps) in back to the west. ***Spencer Gray***

After we retrieved the spare stove, Matt returned to base camp to explore side valleys and alternative objectives, while Ryan and I continued upward.

To begin our third day, I led perhaps ten pitches (up to 5.9) in boots, steep and occasionally loose enough to warrant pitching it out. We zigzagged up run-out edges and ledges on a triangular panel at the corner of the west face, pulling through several roofs and stacked blocks that moved us past overhanging cliffs. It was amazingly fun, moderate rock climbing, mostly in the sun in bare hands.

After the surface turned to plastered névé and ice, we put on crampons and Ryan took over for a block. We simul-climbed until sunset, at about 6,200 meters, at the base of the hanging snowfield on the south side of the arête, then hacked out a ledge from bullet ice. The first serac band was now below us.

The next day, Ryan led a simul block up solid névé with small penitentes glued to blue ice, just to the right of the plunging edge of the arête. Our calves burned. At the top of the snowfield, we reached a shallow ice cave at 6,500 meters, with a small rock roof, and enlarged it into a luxurious, flat bivy, right at the base of Kaqur's spectacular crux headwall.

"Morning, sunshine," Ryan said saccharinely, waving at me from the opposite corner of the tent. We brewed coffee and watched the distant summits of the Dhaulagiri group glow in the first light.

Kaqur's headwall showed several potential lines. While there seemed to be obvious ledges and corners to the right, they were closer to the upper seracs and had some blank sections. We stuck to the arête, along a semicontinuous weakness.

We had planned to complete the headwall in one long day, but the only appreciable precipitation of the expedition arrived while we were on the crux pitches, with six sticky inches falling over 36 hours. Already-sustained dry-tooling became somewhat more sustained as we swept and blew snow off pick slots and frontpoint divots. We completed the headwall in eight mixed pitches over two days.

To start off, I got lucky with the route's best pitch, a glorious corner that would be a classic at any mixed crag: My bare right hand jammed up gear-swallowing cracks while my left hand threw an ice tool over a series of umbrella bulges of water ice. I could only giggle in the sunshine and shake my head. I said to Ryan, "I think that pitch is in the new Kaya guide to Ouray, isn't it?"

As the weather moved in, I led into twilight on what turned out to be the crux pitch, up 60 feet of offwidth and chimney, with unprotectable ice in the back. The bottom of this feature flared open, with no footholds. We were stuck momentarily. After three abortive free attempts, and not wanting to break my ankles, I hammered in a knifeblade. I could step on it only after chocking my left hand behind an ice jam and cocking a drop-knee. The rest of the pitch ("pretty fucked," Ryan recalled fondly the next morning) required similar scrounging, arm-barring, and tenuous high-steps.

Griffiths leads an ice hose through Kaqur Kangri's upper headwall at about 6,700 meters on the southwest arête. The eight mixed pitches of the headwall took two days to climb. *Spencer Gray*

I belayed Ryan from a sloping nook beneath another icy chimney and dihedral. After the prior block of leads and five days on the face, I was fried, so when Ryan arrived, he took over digging most of the bivy. A sharp piece of ice sliced the tensioned ice hammock as we loaded it. Then one of our tent poles snapped. But we still had enough room to curl tightly on our sides.

Ryan led the next day, clawing his way with occasional aid up two overhanging, brittle pitches of ice and then traversing around a final overhang. We exited the headwall on a ramp of moderate water ice, in light snowfall and heavy spindrift, and camped on the summit plateau. It was -5°F, and the wind blew steadily at about 25 mph all night.

On the morning of October 21, we left our packs and walked for an hour in sunshine up the snowy summit ridge, reaching the top on our seventh day on the mountain, most likely only the second team of climbers to stand there. The edge of Indian Kumaon, nearby Tibet, and central Nepal defined the horizon. For ten brief minutes, we savored this very involved approximation of walking on the moon and then began our descent.

We reached the base in one day via the northwest ridge and a west-facing slope below the north col, mostly downclimbing and making about a dozen rappels. This descent line would make a lovely fast ascent in the right conditions.

Matt, a mensch, left a headlamp lit for us at the base and waited all evening to meet us with extra food. Two days later, six mules returned to base camp and we all started walking out.

Objectives like the southwest arête of Kaqur Kangri used to be what most climbing was: trying something kind of hard, an inconvenient distance from home, and relying on imagination as much as effort to turn a thing dreamt into a thing done. There are still plenty of places to contrive that same experience. We just have to look harder—and be willing to court risk in an unpredictable operating environment.

Our team didn't have what we'd consider a close call, but in debriefing, I still counted 23 discrete times when the risk ticked up. A mule nearly broke my knee with a kick when I tried to bring it into camp one morning. On our first day of climbing, we hustled up a ramp that was probably at the outside edge of the ricochet zone of the upper serac band. Two days later, Ryan and I both simultaneously realized that we were pushing our unroped luck on low-angle but hard-frozen talus above the west face. "If we slip here, it's to the bottom, eh?" I said.

Of four minor rockfall incidents, we mitigated two by our choice of protected belays and bivvies. Another was friendly fire: On rappel, I chucked a baseball-sized rock so the ropes wouldn't dislodge it. But I misaimed, and the rock bounced down the snow slope and nailed Ryan in the shoulder. I reasoned that Ryan had probably done something in a prior life to deserve getting punched in the clavicle. He was less sure.

On day three, below the snowfield, we pulled through suspended, stacked blocks in a roof that would have chopped the rope had they dislodged. On the upper headwall, my ice tool tethers got tangled behind a cam after I had campused out a diagonal rail. I couldn't reverse the move, and I couldn't continue until I had unthreaded the tools. Half growling, half screaming, I locked off on one arm, frontpoints screeching, and freed myself. When he followed, Ryan simply lowered out and jugged.

On the descent, Ryan and I had probably our riskiest moment when we crossed a 40-foot-wide wind slab partway down the upper northwest face. It appeared suddenly, a shallow pocket of cross-loaded danger in an otherwise stable snowpack. The tension on the slope and the soft, hollow *thump* as our boots and ice tools pressed through the snow put us both on edge. But with no other signs of failure or propagation, and a morning of downclimbing a similar aspect and angle above us, we each judged it safe enough to proceed.

An hour before we regained the base of the mountain, fed up with navigating the messy corners of the final glacier, we briefly but obtusely committed to soloing steep glacial ice, embedded with crushed pebbles, as we traversed 15 feet above the bottom of a closed crevasse. We were spurred on by Matt's tiny light in the distance and the promise of fresh Snickers. Perhaps a week on the mountain and the tedious descent had dulled our nose for risk.

Three days later, we stopped at Chyargo La on the trek back out and took in our final view of Kaqur. I crouched beneath fluttering prayer flags to lounge against a rock, my fingers getting sticky pulling globs of *gulab jamun* out of a can we'd saved until now for a treat. Kaqur's summit seracs glinted in the mid-day sun from what seemed like a very long ways away. Matt and Ryan laughed as I passed them the can for a shot of syrup to wash it all down.

SUMMARY: First ascent of the southwest arête of Kaqur Kangri (6,859m, 29.766N, 82.750E), Mugu District, Nepal, by Spencer Gray and Ryan Griffiths, with support from Matt Zia. The ascent (1,670m, ED+ M7 WI5 A0, with 5.10 rock and steep snow) was from October 15 to 21, 2024, with descent via the northwest ridge on the final day.

ABOUT THE AUTHOR: Spencer Gray is an American climber who holds lowball butt-scrapers and alpine choss in equally high regard. He works in public policy related to energy and natural resources, and is based in Seattle.

Griffiths rappelling the northwest ridge of Kaqur Kangri, with the icefall on the southeast side of Peak 6,226m behind. The team exited to skier's left off the glacier below and rappelled back into the valley of their advanced base camp. *Spencer Gray*

UP, UP, AND AWAY

THE FIRST ASCENT OF YASHKUK SAR I IN THE KARAKORAM

DANE STEADMAN

Crashhhh! rang through the perfectly still night. *To say this woke up August Franzen, Cody Winckler, and me would be a lie: How could we sleep? We were camped below the biggest objective of our lives, on our first trip to Pakistan, alone in the Yashkuk Yaz valley aside from our two cooks and a liaison officer back at base camp, surrounded by the most beautiful, terrifying, inspiring, and chaotic mountains we'd ever seen. Now, on the glacier beneath Yashkuk Sar I (6,667m), about a mile past our advanced base camp, I poked my head out the tent door to see a gargantuan avalanche roaring down the peak's north wall, its powder cloud billowing toward us.*

Dane Steadman about 1,300 meters up the north pillar of Yashkuk Sar I at the end of the second day on the route. Sax Sar, climbed during acclimatization, is at far right. ***August Franzen***

"Should we run?" asked August.

"I think we're good—there's no way any chunks can make it over that moraine," I replied.

I watched, mesmerized, as the powder cloud grew taller, closer, taller, closer, then I zipped the door shut in the nick of time. The maelstrom rocked our tent, and we all sat up to brace the poles against the wind and driving snow. When the blast finally subsided, we shook the snow from the tent, unzipped the door, and looked back out to see Yashkuk, silent and brooding again, its seracs and ice walls glistening under the full moon.

A month earlier, on August 16, I'd sat at the Jones Social bar in the Hamad International Airport in Doha, Qatar. To my right sat Cody. He had moved to my hometown of Cody, Wyoming, a couple of years earlier, and we had been primary climbing partners ever since. To Cody's right sat August, with whom, aside from five quick minutes on the Kahiltna Glacier that spring—him half hidden under a parka and glacier glasses—I had never spent any time. I'd heard August's story from friends, and it was one filled with tragedy: His girlfriend, Kalley Rittman, had passed away in a climbing accident near his home in Valdez, Alaska, four years earlier, and he had lost a string of other close friends in the year that followed.

Our trip had come about from a shared desire to fulfill a lifetime dream: to climb in the Karakoram, the greatest mountains on Earth in all of our eyes. I had stumbled upon Yashkuk Sar on Google Earth a year earlier, while perusing the more remote reaches of the Karakoram, and it seemed the perfect objective: unclimbed, minimally explored, high enough but not too high, hard enough but (hopefully) not too hard, with an aesthetic and objectively safe line up and then a logical way to traverse the mountain and descend a different route, adding to the adventure. We each ordered a Tiger beer and clinked bottles beneath a mirror inscribed with "Up, Up, and Away," toasting the trip to come.

On August 18, together with our liaison officer, Khan Zada, and our trip organizer, Ali Saltoro, we stepped down onto the tarmac in Skardu. We were picked up by one of Ali's jeeps, and after meeting our cooks, Ali and Idrees, along with another jeep filled with base camp supplies, we set off along the Karakoram Highway.

In the afternoon of our second day on the road, we turned into the Chapursan Valley. The farther we drove, the more it seemed we went back in time. As we passed rows of mudstone houses, terraced wheat fields lined with poplars, and free-roaming sheep and yaks, it was easy to imagine we were back in the days when, per the local lore, Genghis Khan rode in over a pass to the north, or when weary travelers carried silk through the valley on the backs of camels. Only the occasional car or motorbike disrupted the illusion.

Our destination was the Pamir Serai, a guesthouse owned by a bearlike, blue-eyed, stony-faced man named Alam Jan, whose booming laugh and stories of mountain adventures filled our last evening in civilization. The next morning, we started our walk toward base camp, heading southwest along the Yashkuk Yaz Glacier. Two mellow days of hiking with our 25 porters and one donkey would bring us, along with Ali, Idrees, and Khan Zada, to base camp at 4,000 meters, eight miles up the glacier.

To the best of our knowledge, only three climbing teams had visited this valley, about ten miles from the border

August Franzen (front) and Cody Winckler en route to Sax Sar (ca 6,200m), the final acclimatization climb before Yashkuk Sar I. The team's new route spiraled around Sax Sar, starting from the southeast, probably only the mountain's second ascent. The high peak closest in back is Yashkuk Sar II. ***Dane Steadman***

with Afghanistan, and the most recent had been 18 years earlier. The first two teams—one Japanese (2001) and one Russian (2005)—had aspirations to climb Yashkuk Sar I, as we learned from the locals later. But no one had made significant progress up its imposing north wall, which is split by a 2,000-meter central buttress that we hoped to climb. In 2006, Markus Walter and Bruce Normand, who'd shared valuable information with us before we left, climbed three of the lower 6,000-meter peaks in the valley after bailing from an attempt on nearby Batura II.

After one night in base camp, we established advanced base a mile up the west fork of the Yashkuk Yaz, beneath the noisy north wall of unclimbed Yashkuk Sar II, the lower, eastern summit of the twin-peaked Yashkuk massif. Fortunately, there were huge mounds of rocky rubble on the glacier to shield us from its rumblings. The next morning, we got our first close-up view of our peak.

Plastered with fresh snow and with the summit veiled by clouds, the north wall was intimidating, though the central buttress looked safe. The mist-cloaked upper headwall was still a big question mark. It was only on the first of our acclimatization climbs—a 5,300-meter subpeak of the 6,000er across from Yashkuk II—that we finally glimpsed the upper slopes. The headwall looked hard, but discontinuous white streaks up its center gave us hope there would be dots to connect. On our second warm-up climb, of the 6,200-meter Sax Sar, via a new route that spiraled up the mountain from its southeast corner, we were rewarded with a perfect view of Yashkuk Sar I's north wall, framed by a sea of jagged peaks. We were floating in the sky, higher than we'd ever been, in the heart of Central Asia. Our objective was beautiful; our bodies were ready.

The alarm rang at 3 a.m. on September 19, just three hours after we'd witnessed the massive avalanche on Yashkuk Sar I. We dusted the snow off our bags, packed up, and set off across the glacier. The

avalanche had been intense, but it wasn't the first we'd seen off Yashkuk, and it wasn't particularly concerning: The central buttress's 2,000 meters of gray ice and black stone protruded from the serac-crowned wall, protecting us, we assumed, from the monstrous avalanches that regularly swept the face.

By noon, we had already finished our daily goal of 500 vertical meters. August had led two long simul-blocks—up an initial ice couloir and then left, across broken gneiss veiled by deep powder, to reach a system of ice runnels that bypassed the monolithic lower buttress. The big snowfield above had just gone into the shade, so up, up, and away we continued.

Across the snowfield we gained a broad couloir, just left of the buttress crest, that glistened with ancient blue ice. Partway up the couloir, at around 5,600 meters, with the shadows lengthening, we looked for a place to spend the night.

"What about that snow arête?" I asked, pointing left when Cody and August arrived at my belay. "We'll be safe from anything that falls, and it doesn't look too hard to get to—just eight meters across that bit of rock."

An hour and a half later, I laughed sardonically at my words as I desperately brushed snow aside in search of the tiniest ripple for my frontpoint in the black gneiss. The last 20 meters—not eight—had offered a distressing combination of loose yet compact slab traversing, hammering in beaks, and stuffing cams behind frozen blocks. Now my calves were on fire, though I was just a body length from good ice. Finally, I unveiled a slanting edge, just enough to rock up and left and reach the ice.

As the sun set, we began to arrange our first bivy. After a strenuous hour of trying to hack a flat spot out of the arête, we broke out our secret weapon: a Russian ice hammock. After another hour and a half of faffing, chopping, tensioning, and swearing, the tent was pitched, with only six inches hanging over the ledge. Inside its green walls, we set about making water, eating, and trying in vain to sleep.

At dawn, I was stirred by a crash and a hiss. I looked out the tent door to see an immense avalanche roaring down the northeast face a couple of hundred meters away, the billowing snow illuminated pink as it raced down to the glacier 1,000 meters below. Safe on our ice arête and pleased with the previous day's progress, we packed up leisurely in the warm morning sun, then set off up interminable ice slopes.

Cody led that day—up, to the right, up more, then back left, on calf-burning, lung-searing, steely-blue ice. As the sun sank toward the peaks of the Hindu Kush, he traversed to a ridge festooned with bulging snow mushrooms.

"This isn't gonna work for a bivy!" he called back from the first, innocent-looking (from our perspective) mushroom. "I don't know what's holding this thing on, and there's an overhanging wall on the other side!"

"What about higher?" I called back. "I'm sure we can get the tent up on one of those mushrooms! And isn't there a traverse ledge on the other side?" I recalled spotting a white line that cut left across the arête to an ice gully, but I wasn't sure Cody was near it.

"I don't know, dude—it's pretty wild over here! I could bring you guys over."

"Is there a good anchor?"

"Ummmm..."

As we deliberated, I felt a primal fear of the impending darkness. This had been the "surefire good bivy," and if the whole arête was as marginal as Cody's stance, we were in for a rough night.

ABOVE: Yashkuk Sar I (6,667m) and the line of Tiger Lily Buttress (left) on the north pillar. The team descended the upper west face and north face (right). ***Dane Steadman***

OPPOSITE PAGE: Franzen starting up the route on September 19. The climbers angled left up an icy couloir to reach a leftward traverse and moderate mixed terrain, skirting the monolithic rock wall on its left. ***Dane Steadman***

Cody investigated higher. The next mushroom was equally precarious, but then he spotted one just below it that might work. He climbed off the back side of the higher mushroom, lassoing it and adding some screws for a belay.

It was a wild spot, a blade of snow perched at around 5,900 meters, directly below the headwall we'd spent nearly a year fretting about. Bounded by rocky arêtes, the headwall looked steep, but it was well protected by those arêtes from the looming seracs on either side. Our best way through, we figured, would be an icy dihedral splitting the wall.

After many brews and a dinner of ramen thick with life-sustaining peanut butter, we crawled into our shared sleeping bag. Not ten minutes later, we heard another crash: *Not to worry,* I thought. *It must be from one of the seracs to our left.* We almost didn't bother to look, but when Cody unzipped the door, we were horrified to see a huge avalanche, lit by the full moon, roaring down the dihedral we intended to climb the next day, though well to the left of our knife-edge bivy. A big mushroom must have collapsed, and dozens more like it threatened our line.

Bivy perch just below the north pillar headwall, not long before an avalanche forced the team to reevaluate their route. ***August Franzen***

Our world turned upside down: I knew we couldn't climb up that deadly corner. Failure seemed imminent.

"Well, what do you guys think?" I asked into the gloom. Awkward silence.

I frantically scrolled through photos of the headwall on my phone, comparing angles and features. The center line was clearly out, and the monolithic rock towers crowning the western edge of the headwall, to our right, looked too hard. But maybe there, on the left edge of the wall, a couple of hundred meters from the dihedral, was a way. Through a rock band, up an ice arête, then up a chimney that cut through another rock band below a wild mushroom ridge. We all agreed it was worth a shot.

At dawn, after a left-diagonaling rappel off the ridge, August led a long block up the ice arête, toiling through deep snow in the hot sun. By early afternoon, we had reached the headwall. It was time to answer all those questions.

The first rope length—my lead—was tenuous: A compact slab of jet-black gneiss with little for hooks or protection led to a thin dribble of delaminated ice. After a few body lengths of delicate tip-tapping, I stepped left, onto a hanging snow arête, aiming for a vertical, snow-plastered rock band. Shattered but well-frozen gneiss made for good hooks, abundant gear, and quick progress.

"Rock!" I yelled as one of my ropes dislodged the unfrozen block I'd just worked so carefully to avoid. "Rock... ROCK...*ROCK!!!*"

Defying the logical fall line, the block was somehow skipping toward the arête where August and Cody were belaying, exposed and vulnerable, a solid vertical mile above the glacier. A white poof of down shot into the air as the rock hit Cody's right shoulder.

"ARE YOU OKAY?!" I screamed.

"Yeah...I'm...good," he grunted.

I continued, this time more gingerly. Half an hour later, I had a five-piece rock anchor and stood on an outrageous snow mushroom on a knifeblade arête where we could maybe, just maybe, pitch the tent. I brought up August and Cody, and as the sun set, we settled into the airiest bivy of our lives. While a good six inches of tent hung off each side of the arête, the inside of our little green haven felt safe enough—until you shifted and felt the void beneath a cheek. The altitude here at 6,200 meters was killing our energy and appetite.

On the morning of September 22, we didn't bother with breakfast. After coffee and a couple of rounds of electrolytes, Cody traversed back onto broken gneiss as the moon set and the sun rose. A rope length higher, we were back in the shade of the cold headwall. Cody fought through a heavy blanket of snow as he scratched up the rock beneath. I glanced nervously between the three-beak anchor, the dizzying exposure beneath the mushroom on which we stood, and Cody as he dug sideways, beneath a cornice, trying to regain the crest.

The next pitch climbed the rocky arête itself, across which Cody eventually traversed right and out of sight below a mushroom. For the next half hour, the rope inched out slowly and snow poured down. Seconding, I saw what had taken

Winckler early on day four, the second day on the headwall of Yashkuk Sar's north pillar. *Dane Steadmn*

so long: Around the corner, the wall overhung slightly, with the whole north face sweeping below, while hooks and protection came solely in the form of questionable, jutting blocks. When we arrived at the belay, Cody still looked exhausted from his lead.

I continued up and right, weaving through the most surreal snow features I'd ever seen—otherworldly, Dr. Seussian blobs. "We've gotta be almost there—I bet that was the last hard pitch," August said when he reached the belay. I chuckled at his optimism as I set off toward more cartoonish mushrooms and an alabaster band of marble capping the headwall. While trying to get over a mushroomed arête, I heard a whoompf and felt my right foot drop. I watched the mushroom accelerate silently, then cascade over the headwall with a crash.

"Okay, I think that was the last hard one," August repeated at the next belay. The ice runnel above didn't look bad, but something told me this was deceiving, and soon I found myself stemmed wide and clearing out pockets of snow from overhanging, honeycombed ice. I sliced through the cornice topping the runnel, certain I'd poke through to sunlight on the summit ridge, only to find more shade, blue ice, and another cornice.

"That has to be the ridge up there," we all agreed at the next belay, pointing to the skyline. I pulled through the next cornice. Still in the shade. Finally, half a rope length of trenching through snow deeper than myself brought me into the light.

The imagined joyful victory stroll across the summit ridge was anything but. Our lungs screamed as we trudged through knee-deep snow, illuminated gold by the setting sun, while a bitter west wind stung our faces. Our plan had been to sleep on the summit, but halfway up the windswept ridge we dashed into a wide crevasse. While it proved more of a wind funnel than a wind block, we were thrilled to finally have somewhere flat to bivy.

THE IMAGINED JOYFUL VICTORY STROLL...WAS ANYTHING BUT. OUR LUNGS SCREAMED AS WE TRUDGED THROUGH KNEE-DEEP SNOW.

We awoke from our half-sleep to an inch of snow covering everything inside the tent. It had accumulated overnight from the tiny breathing hole we'd left in the door. The mood was grim as we brewed up and choked down a few bites of whatever we could stomach: half a Clif Bar for me, a Gu packet for August, and, in classic Cody fashion, a sugary drink for him.

It had been a rough night and everything was wet, but we knew the summit was close. If we were lucky, we'd be off the mountain that day.

As the sun rose, we left the tent with only parkas and water bottles in our packs. After 30 minutes of walking—and four days on the wall—we could go no higher. We hugged, cheered, and marveled at the incredible view, surrounded by four of the greatest mountain ranges on Earth (the Karakoram, the Himalaya, the Hindu Kush, and the Pamirs) spread across four countries (Afghanistan, Pakistan, China, and Tajikistan). Then we dropped a couple of meters off the east side of the summit to a flat, wind-sheltered plateau that would have made a perfect bivy. *Oops.*

From his pack, August produced a little Ziploc bag filled with some of Kalley's ashes. Cody and I each laid a hand on his shoulder as he threw the ashes up into the wind, which swept them across the Karakoram toward China. We stood silently as August let the tears flow, then we sat, taking it all in, beneath a deep-blue sky.

An hour later, we collected our gear

from the crevasse bivouac, crossed the hanging glacier below the summit pyramid, and began rappelling the broad ice gully splitting the mountain's west face. Some 600 meters lower, we tied back in and traversed up and left to where we could cross the west ridge and drop back down toward the West Yashkuk Glacier cirque. One thousand meters passed in a blur of Abalakovs and downclimbing; that evening, we made our final rappel over the bergschrund. Our hackles stayed up as we weaved through the gaping crevasses of the upper glacier basin, giving wide berth to seracs over its western edge.

Franzen (in back) and Winckler on the summit ridge late in the fourth day of the climb. The team bivouacked 30 minutes below the summit in a windy crevasse. *Dane Steadman*

Before the sun set on September 23, we crossed beneath the final debris field and coiled the rope, safe on the rocky, dry glacier. At the first stream on the bare ice, we knelt to suck thirstily at the trickle, savoring the sweetness of the water.

Three weeks later, the three of us sat again beneath the "Up, Up, and Away" mirror in the Qatar airport bar, clinking three Tiger bottles together to celebrate two incredible months in Pakistan. We named our climb Tiger Lily Buttress, inspired by the Tiger Team moniker that our exuberant cook, Idrees, had given us at base camp upon our successful return. The trip wouldn't have been the same without Idrees's "Tiger Style," and after our ascent of Yashkuk Sar I, none of us would be, either.

SUMMARY: First ascent of Yashkuk Sar I (6,667m) in the northern Batura Muztagh of the Karakoram, Pakistan, by August Franzen, Dane Steadman, and Cody Winckler (all USA), September 19–23, 2024. The trio climbed the mountain's north pillar and named it Tiger Lily Buttress (2,000m, AI5+ M6 A0). They descended by the upper west and lower north faces. They also climbed a new route from the southeast on Sax Sar (ca 6,200m); details are at the *AAJ* website.

ABOUT THE AUTHOR: Born and raised in Phoenix, Dane Steadman now calls Cody, Wyoming, his home. Between expeditions, he works as a guide and field tester.

Tom Livingstone on the opening pitch of the west ridge of Gasherbrum III. In back is the final pyramid of Gasherbrum I (8,080m), seen from the north. The standard Japanese Couloir route finishes up the sunlit slopes on the left. *Aleš Česen*

EDGE OF ENTROPY

THE FIRST ASCENT OF GASHERBRUM III'S WEST RIDGE

TOM LIVINGSTONE

For many years I've asked myself, *What would be the most difficult route you could climb, at the highest altitude?* Could I take the challenge of places like the Alps, Alaska, and the Canadian Rockies, then supercharge that to the world's tallest mountains, somewhere around 8,000 meters? That would be a real beast.

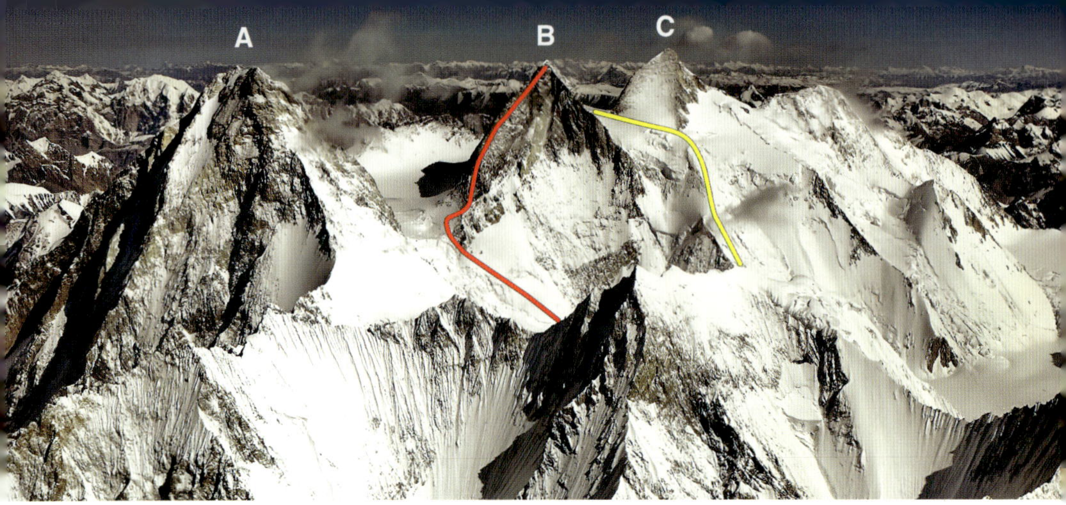

Aerial view of the Gasherbrum group from the southwest, taken in October 2006, showing (A) Gasherbrum IV (7,925m), (B) Gasherbrum III (7,952m map elevation), and (C) Gasherbrum II (8,035m). The foreground ridge holds the summits of Gasherbrums VI and V. The 2024 route up the west ridge is shown in red; the final part of the ascent was behind the ridge. The yellow line shows the descent, starting with ten rappels down the east face (hidden), then down along the normal route for Gasherbrum II. ***Jacek Wiltosiński***

Gasherbrum III (7,952m on maps) is often ranked as the world's 15th-highest peak and had only been climbed twice, both times from the east. Aleš Česen invited me to try the unclimbed west ridge in 2022. A few years earlier, we had made the second ascent of Latok I together, along with Luka Stražar, but Gasherbrum III was more than 800 meters higher. Of course, we knew it wouldn't be possible to climb quite as hard as we could at lower elevations, but Aleš and I were keen to explore the possibilities.

The west ridge's 950-meter spine of dark granite looked appealing. We wanted a route that would be difficult, but not overly so. The line seemed as if it would be quite safe objectively, since it's mostly on an arête. The rock appeared solid, unlike on many of the Gasherbrum peaks made of crumbly marble and limestone. And the descent would be down the normal route of neighboring Gasherbrum II. The line looked psycho—but not *too* psycho.

The west ridge of Gasherbrum III had been attempted only once, in 1985, by Scottish climbers Geoff Cohen and Des Rubens. [*The Scots called this feature the southwest ridge, but the majority of the ridge runs westward.*] Cohen and Rubens put in an impressive effort, reaching about 7,700 meters on their second day on the ridge, but then bailed due to poor weather and slow progress—they had left their bivy kit lower down, hoping to summit and return the same day.

Our attempt in 2022 explored the balance between desire and rationality. Camped near the start of the ridge at around 7,000 meters, we watched and listened to extremely strong winds ripping over our objective. I mean "rip" literally, in the sense that a tearing sound emanated from the mountain. We really wanted to climb the ridge, but it seemed likely we would be blown off the peak. Rational thought prevailed, so we contoured around to the northwest side of Gasherbrum III, hoping for shelter. We climbed for two days up easy snow and mixed steps until, at about 7,650 meters, we hit a 100-meter-high granite tower. This formation reminded me of a smaller version of Tengkangpoche's northeast pillar, a line I had climbed a few months earlier, taking seven days and lots of aid. Aleš and I felt we'd be out of our depth to attempt such a difficult tower at that height, so, again, rationality prevailed.

Climbing with Aleš is great fun, and I trust him completely. After three big trips, I don't think we've ever argued. Planning a rematch in the summer of 2024, we reflected on our experiences together, including Latok and our prior attempt on G-III. We figured we'd only have one shot to climb Gasherbrum III, because we would be wasted by the altitude and effort after a single try. Patience would be key because, with base camp located at 5,000 meters, we knew we would recover very slowly from our acclimatization forays. We planned a trip lasting two months, in order to give us the best chance of success.

To reach base camp, shared with climbers aiming for Gasherbrums I and II, you walk up the Baltoro Glacier for six days, covering 112 kilometers. Once there, over the course of about three weeks, we made three trips some ways up G-II's normal route, the southwest ridge, to acclimatize. (We planned to use the same route to descend from Gasherbrum III if we made it to the summit.) During this period, there were always strong westerly winds at high altitude. G-II is just over 8,000 meters, and about 40 people per year attempt it. They usually jumar fixed ropes that are installed every season, use supplementary oxygen, and have a lot of Sherpa support. There are exceptions to this, and we didn't use any of this assistance during acclimatization.

TOP: Aleš Česen contemplates the rocky west ridge of Gasherbrum III, seen in profile, from the South Gasherbrum Glacier. The ridge gains about 950 meters from the G-III/G-IV col.

BOTTOM: Česen holds a coiled rope found near the bottom of the west ridge, abandoned nearly 40 years earlier, in 1985, by Geoff Cohen and Des Rubens, who reached 7,700 meters in the only previous attempt on the ridge. *Tom Livingstone (both photos)*

Poor weather meant our first two acclimatization trips were shorter than we'd have liked, so we planned a third trip to be sure we'd be prepared. On July 20, our 30th day in Pakistan, we spent one night at 7,000 meters. Unfortunately, in the morning, Aleš became very dizzy; he felt the spins as we descended to Camp 1 and then on to base camp the next day. It was impressive that he was able to keep it together during this descent. The cause of his dizziness was uncertain, but we suspected an inner ear issue.

We rested for a week and tried to find some medicine that might be helpful. There was a pleasant scene in base camp, thanks to a neighboring group of Austrian climbers and some American skiers. Aleš improved gradually. We missed a good weather window during this time, and afterward the conditions deteriorated somewhat. But when Aleš had recovered sufficiently, we decided to take our one shot.

Leaving base camp on July 31, we slept at Camp 1 for Gasherbrum II, at almost 6,000 meters, a spectacular site in the middle of the South Gasherbrum Glacier, surrounded by enormous peaks. On our second day out, we climbed a long icefield to reach the basin between Gasherbrums IV and III, skirting the nasty icefall that plunges from the basin by scaling the icefield to the right. [*This icefall is where, later in August, three Russian climbers*

Česen follows a traversing pitch at roughly 7,700 meters on the second day on the west ridge. In back is the unclimbed east face of Gasherbrum IV. The right skyline is the upper northeast ridge, the route of the peak's first ascent, in 1958, by Walter Bonatti and Carlo Mauri; the traverse between the north top (right) and the main summit on the left was one of the cruxes of their climb. At left is the southeast ridge, attmpted in 2023 by Dmitry Golovchenko and Sergey Nilov; their attempt ended in tragedy when Golovchenko fell from a bivouac site below the rocky headwall. *Tom Livingstone*

were hit by an ice avalanche while searching for the body of Dmitry Golovchenko, who fell from the southeast ridge of Gasherbrum IV during an attempt in 2023. His climbing partner on that attempt, Sergey Nilov, died in the avalanche on August 17, 2024, and two others were injured and required a rescue.]

Aleš and I camped that night at around 7,000 meters, at the foot of G-III's west ridge. Our packs were quite heavy and our throats already dry.

On August 2, our first real climbing day, we started up the west ridge. About 100 meters up, piled under some rocks, we found a coiled rope that the Scots had left during their descent, 39 years earlier. It felt fantastic to be really climbing after so much time acclimatizing. We pitched steep rocky slabs, thankfully with plenty of holds, then climbed snowy mixed ground, each of us leading a bunch of good pitches, including a dinosaur-spine arête. In midafternoon, at 7,485 meters, we stopped to bivy amid some rocks.

For breakfast, we launched onto the upper ridge. In falling snow and light winds, we tried to keep moving up, climbing thrutchy chimneys and steep steps. Above, we could see a headwall near the end of the ridge. Although perhaps only five big pitches high, it looked quite menacing, so we eyed a potential bypass to the left. In late afternoon we stopped to bivy beneath this wall, at 7,800 meters. Unfortunately, we were unable to cut a platform big enough for the tent and were forced into an open, sitting bivy. The cold kept us awake, as did the snowfall piling onto our double sleeping bag. I'm sure we fried a few brain cells that night. Alpinism is such a beautiful trap, a constant struggle between what you want and what you need. Part of us simply wished we could be somewhere else, more comfortable, but somehow we needed to keep climbing.

In the morning, without much discussion, we started traversing left to bypass the headwall. In hindsight, it's possible we took not only a longer route but also maybe a harder one. The rock slabs coated with fresh powder snow were quite difficult and insecure. Deep, collapsing snow also took a lot of energy. A final difficult pitch stopped us at around 7,900 meters. It had about 15 meters of steep, awkward climbing and no protection. After seconding the pitch, Aleš said, "I don't know how you climbed that." It feels impossible to grade such a pitch at that height—maybe about M6?

On the summit, we felt knackered but also very relieved the route had worked out. Our two inReach devices and watch all recorded 7,958 meters. There was no evidence of other life on top, human or otherwise. Nothing we could see, as far as the horizon, implied life could even exist in such places. It's hard to describe, but it had felt as though we'd become slightly less human the higher we climbed. If being human is having conscious thoughts and experiencing emotions, we certainly weren't all there at some points during the climb.

We made about ten rappels down the east side of the mountain, descending the line of the only two previous ascents of Gasherbrum III (first climbed in 1975 by Alison Chadwick-Onyszkiewicz, Janusz Onyszkiewicz, Wanda Rutkiewicz, and Krzysztof Zdzitowiecki). Then we traversed over to the normal route of G-II and bivvied at Camp 4 (7,400m). The next day, we continued down along the many fixed ropes abandoned after the 2024 attempts and earlier seasons on G-II. Stylistically, it would have been preferable not to use these ropes, as we had avoided them while we were acclimatizing. It would have felt completely contrived, however, to make our own V-threads right next to other climbers' anchors and ropes. On August 6, we retraced the familiar steps down the South Gasherbrum Glacier to base camp. A few days later, happy but hungry, we trekked over the Gondogoro La and down to Hushe, the nearest village, where we feasted on eggs and chapatis.

OPPOSITE PAGE: Česen navigates rocky steps and spindrift on the third climbing day. ***Tom Livingstone***

ABOVE: Livingstone starts a mixed pitch just below the summit. On the upper half of the west ridge, the snow was "unhelpful"; Livingstone had to clear most of the snow from the groove above him to find useful holds. ***Aleš Česen***

It had been very satisfying and interesting to achieve my long-term goal of experimenting with climbing technical pitches at high altitude. I think we learned a great deal about how depleting the altitude can feel, yet how it's still possible to function and climb, thanks, in part, to a good partnership. It's also true that high-altitude climbs take a lot of time, energy, and money, and, for now, more difficult climbing at lower elevations occupies most of my thoughts. However, I'm still very curious about pushing this other aspect of alpinism. And besides, my original idea had been to climb to "around 8,000 meters," so there's obviously still room for improvement!

SUMMARY: First ascent of the west ridge of Gasherbrum III (7,958m GPS), by Aleš Česen (Slovenia) and Tom Livingstone (U.K.), with descent by the original 1975 route on the east face, then down the southwest ridge (normal route) of Gasherbrum II. The round trip from base camp took seven days (July 31–August 6); the pair spent three of those days climbing the 950-meter west ridge and descending the east face.

ABOUT THE AUTHOR: Tom Livingstone is a British climber who lives in Chamonix, France. He wrote a feature article for *AAJ 2020* about the first ascent of the northwest face of Koyo Zom in Pakistan's Hindu Raj. About this year's expedition, he said, "This climb was a very rewarding experience with a great friend. Cheers, Aleš."

ALPINE EDUCATION

CHALLENGING NEW ROUTES IN PERU AND PAKISTAN

YUDAI SUZUKI

These days, becoming a great alpine climber undoubtedly requires high-level physical fitness and proficiency across various climbing styles. However, as others have said before, alpine climbing isn't just a sport—it feels more like an art form. Physical strength is undoubtedly an asset, but no amount of athletic training will lead you to a striking mountain with limited information or to develop an eye for beautiful and climbable lines. Exceptional ability on short rock or ice climbs does not necessarily give you the composure to

Keisuke Ohkura moves up the labyrinthine southeast ridge of Quitaraju on day four of the 2024 ascent. The team had expected the south spur, at the start of their climb, to be the crux, but the ridge proved to be difficult and consequential. ***Yudai Suzuki***

deal calmly with unexpected challenges, nor the communication skills to work well with porters. For me, alpine climbing is an extension of travel and adventure, a form of exploration where the puzzles of the unknown are solved step-by-step.

I began serious mountaineering around 2013 as a member of the Waseda University Alpine Club in Tokyo. For many in Japan, joining a university club is a gateway to serious climbing. It's not uncommon for motivated students to bond across universities, forming climbing partnerships. With only about 10 to 15 alpine climbers under age 30 in Japan who actively pursue overseas expeditions, it's a small community where news travels quickly.

As a student, I primarily undertook long expeditions in the Japanese Alps, which, though only 3,000 meters tall, are close to the sea, resulting in harsh winter weather. The approaches often are very long, and university expeditions typically are in the mountains for 12 days—much longer than my international climbs, which rarely exceed four or five bivouacs. I can confidently state that Japan is among the best places to gain experience in tough winter camping and climbing.

Simultaneously, I pursued climbing overseas, in the Dolomites, Yosemite, and Patagonia. In 2017, I participated in the first ascent of Lajo Dada (6,426m) in Nepal, which, although technically easier than my recent expeditions, involved a grueling 26-hour summit push. That climb instilled in me a deep appreciation for adventurous mountaineering without prior information, so different from the Everest "shopping mall."

In the summer of 2022, I embarked on my first Karakoram expedition, targeting the unclimbed 7,000-meter peak of Gasherbrum VI. We only reached 6,000 meters, in part because our three-person team didn't train together enough, and we lacked the mutual trust to support one another in an emergency.

Since then, I've placed greater emphasis on building strong relationships and training with partners—such as practice with simul-climbing on big routes and bivying on uncomfortable ledges—even if it means climbing less for myself. To prepare for our expeditions in 2023, Kei Narita and Yuu Nishida—two friends from my university alpine club connections—and I spent 30 days in the mountains together. The result was two big new routes: the first ascent of the north face of Ausangate (6,384m) in Peru, with Narita, and the first ascent of the northwest ridge of Ghamubar Zom V (6,400m) in Pakistan, with both Narita and Nishida.

WITH ONLY ABOUT 10 TO 15 ALPINE CLIMBERS UNDER AGE 30 WHO ACTIVELY PURSUE OVERSEAS EXPEDITIONS, IT'S A SMALL COMMUNITY.

Standing on the summit of Ghamubar Zom V in September 2023, we watched an unforgettable sunset illuminating the peaks of the Hindu Raj. Among them was Thui II, one of the most rugged and alluring mountains in the range. We quickly decided to return to this area one year later, with the aim of climbing Thui II.

While Kei, Yuu, and I planned our trip to Pakistan in the fall, I longed for another expedition. Returning to the relatively affordable Peruvian Andes seemed like a good option. Coincidentally, Keisuke Ohkura and Kazumasa Otsubo were also considering a trip to Peru. Kei and Yuu lacked the funds for an extra trip, and although I'm certainly not well-off, I decided to go anyway, banking on the momentum from recent successes. I was 29 and well aware that the chances of finding partners for overseas expeditions soon might dwindle; these days, a lot of Japanese people quit expeditionary climbing around age 30 as they get married, have kids, or gain responsibility at work. Ohkura and Otsubo were close to my age, and we had already climbed together; leading up to the expedition, we scheduled a few sessions to practice climbing systems and team coordination.

I had climbed in southern Peru in 2023 but had yet to visit the Cordillera Blanca. Seeking a potential new line, we discovered that the south spur of Nevado Quitaraju (6,036m) was unattempted. The lack of massive overhanging seracs in the upper sections, a common feature in Peruvian mountains, added to its appeal.

The line of Dream House on the south spur and southeast ridge of Quitaraju (6,036m). The ascent took five days, and the climbers descended by the north face during the fifth day. *Yudai Suzuki*

The proposed line promised a mix of rock and ice on the lower face, a series of adventurous snow mushroom formations on the buttress itself, and a finish on the complex southeast ridge, above 5,750 meters. I found vague information suggesting that a 250-meter section of the southeast ridge had been climbed more than 50 years earlier, but I assumed the ridge's conditions had changed significantly due to global warming. [*The south spur of Quitaraju is on the right side of the steep south face, which has had two ascents, both to the left of the spur: by Slavko Svetičič and Žarko Trušnovec from Slovenia, in 1986, and by Nick Bullock and Al Powell from the United Kingdom, in 2001. The upper southeast ridge (confusingly called the south ridge in the original report) was climbed in 1969 by the remarkable German expedition of Klaus Schreckenbach, Bernd Schreckenbach, Hans Saler, Klaus Süssmilch, Hartmut Schmidt, and Wolfgang Weinzierl, who also climbed new routes on Artesonraju, Alpamayo, and Ausangate, as well as the first ascent of Chaupi Orco in Bolivia and various lower peaks. On Quitaraju, in a five-day traverse, they climbed the east face and upper southeast ridge and descended the west ridge.*]

We began by acclimatizing on Quitaraju's north face. Though this is one of the range's most commonly climbed routes, the 60°–70° ice slopes were challenging under the intense sun. We headed down a little before reaching the summit.

Afterward, we returned to the town of Huaraz to regroup, then trekked back to Laguna Jatuncocha, at about 3,880 meters, to set up base camp. From there, we carried loads through thick vegetation and up scree slopes, eventually establishing an advanced base camp beyond Laguna Quitacocha at 4,800 meters. The south side of Quitaraju was markedly different from the approach to Quitaraju's north side and popular Alpamayo, with no visible signs of human activity. Cutting through the head-high vegetation with heavy loads was grueling.

Early on June 25, under the light of the moon and headlamps, we climbed a couloir on the right side of the south spur for about 30 minutes until the angle steepened, requiring us to rope up. Otsubo led the first pitch on brittle, crackless rock, progressing slowly and carefully. It was an anxious belay, and hearing his call from the next anchor was a relief. Carrying five days of supplies, I felt the difficulty as I followed. Otsubo's skillful lead in the dark set the tone for our expedition.

For much of the bottom section, all three of us tied into a single half rope, with one follower tied in at 50 meters and the other at the end of the rope. We climbed in blocks, alternating leads every two pitches. The system worked well, as the rock had too few cracks to set proper anchors every 60 meters efficiently, and often we'd have to clean the belay anchor and climb together until the next safe belay point. The seconds followed almost everything on the route, only jumaring one crux section on the upper ridge.

THE SECONDS FOLLOWED ALMOST EVERYTHING ON THE ROUTE, ONLY JUMARING ONE CRUX SECTION ON THE UPPER RIDGE.

After an easy pitch, a steepening snow slope led to a mixed wall, and I took over the lead. The vertical corner above looked easy, but the holds were obscured by fresh snow, creating a challenging M6 wide section, with sugar snow complicating the mantel at the top. Even after the hard section, there were no proper placements, so I had to place some sketchy Peckers and pins as an anchor, which took time to set up. Again, we resolved to simul-climb as much as possible.

The next pitch was primarily a snow slope, but it ended with about three meters of vertical snow and ice. Despite searching carefully for protection, there was no choice but to run it out for 20 meters. I hammered in a piton—better than nothing—but it only went in halfway. This section would earn an R/X grade. With no other options, I steeled myself and climbed over the unstable vertical snow and ice.

We resumed climbing simultaneously, gaining about 120 meters in elevation. At that point, I handed the lead to Keisuke. From a distance, the next section had looked easy, but most of it was loose, powdery sugar snow. Keisuke advanced by digging for handholds, tackling some M5 mixed climbing, steadily gaining altitude. We continued rotating leaders, and to be honest, each leader's slow progress, caused by the exertion at over 5,000 meters and the relentless snow clearing, probably made the belayers impatient. But for the leaders, the climbing was so engrossing they would lose track of time.

In the final stretch of the day, Keisuke led a long section of simul-climbing, weaving past seracs and onto a narrow ridge. We had gained about 13 to 15 rope lengths. Internally, I felt a sense of satisfaction, thinking, *The technical crux is now behind us.* However, it turned out the lower rock wall was merely the appetizer.

After sunset, we crawled into our tent, about a quarter of which was suspended over empty space, with our feet and heads dangling. We were so exhausted we managed to get some sleep despite the discomfort.

The second day saw the terrain shift

to a steep ridgeline, similar to my experience the year before on Ghamubar Zom V. The 50°–70° snow mushrooms and the difficulty seeing the way ahead in low-angle terrain made route-finding arduous. The photos we had taken from base camp were of little help. Sugar snow was even more plentiful than on the face below.

In the afternoon, I navigated two otherworldly ice tunnels and a narrow ridge before encountering an impassable slab. After descending eight meters and traversing, we found a snow slope that just might go. Keisuke traversed a full rope length to the right and found a miraculous half-cave of ice, where we were able to set up our bivouac just before sunset. Though we had managed only six pitches all day, we were grateful for the chance to rest.

We needed to complete the complex south buttress and connect to the southeast ridge by the end of the third day, as our food and physical energy would not last much longer. Keisuke began our efforts, dancing through two delicate traverse pitches to reach a beautiful ice cave belay. Otsubo took on the third and fourth pitches. Although the snow slope appeared straightforward, it turned out to be utterly untrustworthy 70° snow. In the thin air, he painstakingly and patiently connected the line. The tension of constant route-finding never let up.

TOP: Ohkura starting yet another vertical wall of soft ice and snow on Quitaraju's upper southeast ridge, on day five of the climb. *Yudai Suzuki*

BOTTOM: The first night's bivouac on Quitaraju, with a quarter of the tent hanging in space. *Yudai Suzuki*

As I took over the lead again, the slope felt steeper than 80°, but the snow was firm and ice screws were solid for once, allowing steady progress. At the end of this section, I cleared a tunnel in the soft ice, crossing back to the opposite side of the ridge. The struggle with soft sugar snow continued, but finally we managed to reach the southeast ridge. After a bit of nighttime climbing, we found a bivouac site beneath a serac—the only feasible spot—and stopped there.

The next day, we hoped to cover distance quickly by simul-climbing, but day four turned out to be the hardest of the climb. First thing in the morning, as I was climbing over a mushroom, the snow and ice supporting my hands and feet gave way simultaneously, resulting in a five-meter fall. This was shocking,

Starting day four on Quitaraju, moving up the complex mushrooms and ice walls of the southeast ridge. *Kazumasa Otsubo*

as I had never fallen on a winter alpine wall. There had been no warning—all four points just gave way. A poor ice screw thankfully held.

Regathering my focus, I tackled the next pitch. Placing gear in a chossy rock wall, we traversed directly beneath a massive snow mushroom. Of course, I would have preferred to avoid such a dangerous section, but it was the best option. With some grade V rock moves, I forced my way along the fragile rock. We had already come so far on the ridge that summiting and descending the opposite side was by far the best option. It began to feel more like an escape attempt than a climb.

After two easier pitches, we faced a vertical mushroom. Keisuke quickly realized his axes weren't holding in the soft snow and ice, so he abandoned the direct approach and opted for a wide detour. Through trial and error, he connected the line, allowing us to make good progress again—only to be stopped by another massive mushroom.

This time, I was in the lead and targeted what seemed to be the most promising section of the mushroom, about 20 meters high. The wall felt vertical. I abandoned any thoughts of free climbing and equalized two okay screws to create an intermediate anchor. From there, I placed another screw and carefully eased my weight onto it, then another, and then slowly cleared the soft, shifting snow and ice near the top of the mushroom. Suddenly, I was violently ejected backward.

My mind went blank as I plunged. I saw the two highest screws pop out, but then stopped in midair after falling 15 meters. I assumed I had injured myself. However, after cautiously moving my body, I realized I was unharmed—a stroke of incredible luck. A sprain or worse in that location could have been catastrophic. What had saved me was the equalization of the final anchor and the fall through empty space, which prevented my legs from hitting solid ground.

The atmosphere was serious as Otsubo tied into the dangling rope and headed back up. I had been trying to climb a direct line for the benefit of the two followers, but Otsubo instead angled toward the right edge of the mushroom, progressing slowly, using aid on snow stakes. He eventually manteled onto the far side of the ridge and disappeared from sight, bringing an indescribable sense of relief—our line had connected. Fortunately, just beyond this, we found the flattest tent site of the entire route, providing an ideal place to bivy.

On day five, only 130 meters of elevation difference remained to the summit, though it still appeared distant. After eating the last 40 grams of freeze-dried rice, we set off, with Keisuke leading a long stretch of simul-climbing. He gained three rope lengths but was stopped again by a vertical mushroom. Here, he too fell unexpectedly due to unstable ice and was stopped by the belay anchor. This was a mountain of too many narrow escapes. Regaining composure, Keisuke managed to break through on the next attempt.

The lead passed to me, and I miraculously discovered a 60-meter gully of high-quality ice between the mushrooms, which allowed me to climb efficiently to just under the summit. At the very top, I made one unforgettable move on sugar snow to get over a meter-wide crevasse. Just before noon, I drove in two snow pickets on the summit and brought the other two to the top.

Including the simul-climbing, our ascent totaled over 40 rope lengths—a very long climb. The joy we felt on top was fleeting, as we immediately began our descent via the north face. Fatigued to the point where downclimbing was a struggle, we carefully made V-threads in the sunlit ice and rappelled. Twice, we left webbing in the ice—the only gear we left on the mountain. Frequent rockfall made the entire descent harrowing.

The line followed in September 2024 for the first ascent of the west face of Thui II (6,523m). The face is about 1,450 meters high. After a final bivouac on the summit, the climbers rappelled the ascent route during their fourth day on the mountain. *Yudai Suzuki*

Climbing up to the high camp between Quitaraju and Alpamayo was excruciating, and by the time we reached the saddle it was pitch black, but the way down the glacier on the other side was familiar from our acclimatization. At Alpamayo's base camp, we were too exhausted to pitch our tents, instead collapsing in a vacant hut. The next day, still in our high-altitude boots, we trekked down to our south face base camp.

When we looked up at the line we had drawn, all the tension and pain we had felt in the mountains transformed into beautiful memories. We called the route Dream House, after the inexpensive lodge where we stayed in Huaraz as well as the miraculous bivouac spots scattered along Quitaraju's complex ridges.

My mind had already turned toward Pakistan. I returned to Tokyo on July 13, and just over five weeks later, on August 19, I headed to Islamabad. During the short time in between, I focused on regaining climbing fitness at the gym and crags, replenishing nutrition, and relaxing. By the time I left, I felt in excellent condition for alpine climbing.

The first ascent of Thui II was on August 4, 1978, by a British team climbing the southeast ridge, after three prior attempts that began in 1969. In the 46 years since the first ascent, no ascents of the mountain were recorded. Based on Google Earth imagery, the west face of Thui II appeared to consist of ice and rock suitable for mixed climbing all the way to the summit. We had decided to

The climbers gained more than 800 meters of elevation during the long first day on Thui II. After rapidly simul-climbing the lower face, they reached much more technical terrain. Here, Kei Narita avoids sparse, rotten ice by jamming up a steep crack packed with ice. ***Yudai Suzuki***

ON THE FOLLOWING PITCHES, WE WERE SHOWERED BY ICE MELT. LUCKILY, THERE WERE CRACKS NEXT TO THE ICE THAT COULD BE DRY-TOOLED AND JAMMED.

spend all of September in Pakistan's remote northwestern frontier, just as we had for Ghamubar Zom V.

There was only a little information about the approach to Thui II's west face via the Risht Glacier, starting in the Yarkhun Valley. A French team had visited the area a few years earlier in spring, combining skiing with climbing a mountain they called Risht Peak (ca 5,960m; *see AAJ 2020*).

We traveled by jeep for two days from Chitral toward the Afghan border, eventually arriving at Shost village in the Yarkhun Valley, which divides the Hindu Raj from Afghanistan's Wakhan Corridor to the north. Beyond Shost, a rough dirt road extended another 30 minutes, and our skillful driver got us up a 35° slope to a tiny settlement, where a family generously allowed us to stay in their home. One family member, a university student, was particularly curious about us, and we shared many conversations. Their support and kindness made a lasting impression.

From the road, we hiked south up the Risht valley for six or seven hours to find a grassy spot suitable for base camp, with flat ground and a small water source, at an altitude of 4,300 meters. Four days of rain kept us resting at camp. When the weather cleared, we enjoyed a ten-day window of good weather, during which we did a five-day trip to an unnamed 6,000-meter point and spent two nights at a 5,740-meter col just north of Risht Peak.

During these acclimatization climbs, we observed Thui II and sketched out a potential route up the west face, which would gain nearly 1,500 meters. The lowest fifth of the face consisted of snowfields, followed by near-vertical ice and rock pitches, with the crux seeming to be close to the summit at 6,200 to 6,400 meters.

Back at camp, we received an inReach notification that an impending storm would last over 12 days. We entered "base camp mode," passing time by bouldering and watching movies. At its worst, heavy snowfall buried the kitchen tent, and we briefly considered worst-case scenarios. However, as the sun eventually returned, the snow melted and revealed patches of grass. We couldn't observe the conditions on the upper part of our planned route from base camp, and we were slightly worried about avalanches, but on September 20 we climbed to advanced base camp at 5,000 meters to launch our attempt.

Narita leading the M6 corner soon after the second bivouac on Thui II, at about 6,300 meters. ***Yudai Suzuki***

We set off with four and a half days of food, two half ropes, and a small rac3k of cams, nuts, and pitons. We quickly climbed the initial snowfield, just above advanced base camp, then simul-climbed two long pitches, totaling about eight rope lengths, at a good pace, until reaching steeper rock and ice. The actual climbing began with melting, suspect ice. I managed it using a 30-centimeter streak of verglas and a corner. The flaring cracks seemed like they'd spit out my Tricams. I'd rate this section M4+ R.

On the following pitches, we were showered by ice melt. Luckily, there were cracks next to the ice that could be dry-tooled and jammed. Both Narita and I have climbed up to M11+ in Japan, but this pitch was rough. Above, the crack widened more than our largest cam, a number 3, but we managed. Subsequent pitches featured stacked-block rock climbing and thin ice mantels—Nishida's leads were impressive. The last five meters seemed too rough to follow with heavy packs, and we decided on hauling.

By sunset, we had gotten to 5,810 meters. We extended a flat spot with a snow hammock to set our first bivy. We had climbed about 15 rope lengths, including the simul-climbing at the bottom. A good start.

Day two began with simul-climbing three rope lengths on snow bands before being sucked into couloirs of steep ice and mixed, where we started pitching it out. The ice was solid in the morning, and we ascended seven pitches of steep, technical climbing with some hanging belays. One pitch involved climbing a vertical chimney with no ice or snow, requiring barehanded free climbing on brittle rock—around 5.8 or 5.9, with no proper gear placements.

At the end of this weak spot in the amazing headwall, we reached a slanting mini-ridge, where we decided to stop and bivy, given the accumulated fatigue and effects of altitude. Again, we expanded the spot with a snow hammock, and we retired at dusk. Even with our heads and feet not on solid ground, being able to lie flat at 6,250 meters gave us hope for the next day. It had been about 25 rope lengths up to this point.

The final 300 meters remained uncertain. We debated leaving gear at the bivouac site, in hopes of making it back that night, but chose to carry everything, as the wall looked to get even steeper. In the end, this was the right decision.

Narita got the first lead, which had a nasty downclimb with a traverse. The second pitch was a corner covered with thin verglas. Protecting the ice didn't work, but small cracks to the side took cams. I followed the pitch and still remember the axe-torquing move at the top—roughly M6. Narita commented that doing torquing moves at 6,300 meters felt like a dream.

After climbing a short snow slope, we had the option to go left or right. Heading left would have brought us directly to a couloir and snowfield leading to the summit, but this felt unappealingly straightforward, and Nishida decided to take a peek to the right, toward the sheer wall. What initially appeared to be a sea of blank rock miraculously revealed firm, juggy holds. Nishida dry-tooled this section. At over 6,300 meters, every move was exhausting, leaving me with a headache and gasping for breath. Pitch four was another 80° mixed pitch of three-star quality. The fact that the line was connecting felt unbelievable.

NISHIDA DECIDED TO TAKE A PEEK TO THE RIGHT, TOWARD THE SHEER WALL. WHAT INITIALLY APPEARED TO BE A SEA OF BLANK ROCK MIRACULOUSLY REVEALED FIRM, JUGGY HOLDS.

On pitch five that day, I took over the lead. The nature of the wall changed drastically—I could see no corners or weak points, just a big slab. I climbed up to the base of the slab to investigate and discovered a single thin crack, running from thin hands to pinkie finger width. Traversing around it would have been challenging, so I decided to gamble and follow the thin crack.

Despite some sunlight, the cold at 6,400 meters made barehanded jamming painful, yet gloves were out of the question. About halfway up, all the footholds disappeared, forcing me to remove my crampons and transition to aiding, carefully placing small cams and Tricams. Where the crack disappeared, I free climbed short sections. Ultimately, the crack ended entirely, but there was a very thin flake about a meter to the left. Stretching my arm to its limit, I placed a 0.2 Camalot and clipped into it with a sling, cautiously shifting my weight onto it. Clearing away sugar snow and pressing against fragile rock, I manteled onto a small terrace, where I decided to end the pitch. I must have wrestled with it for

over an hour at this point. Even now, I find it incredible that such a thin, hidden crack allowed us to climb directly up the slab.

I could see a good flake directly above, but I had no idea what lay beyond it. *Maybe if I can't see anything, it means the slope might ease?* I climbed about five meters using good holds and saw an expanse of ice waiting ahead. It was clear this would be "blue ice torture," but it would lead to the summit.

By now it was already past 3 p.m. Swinging our axes with full force into the hard ice, we progressed painfully slowly, but we were over 6,400 meters and couldn't go any faster. After four pitches of this, as Nishida led, the opposite side of the mountain suddenly dropped away and he emerged into the narrow summit. The sky turned deep orange as we stood at 6,523 meters.

Battered by strong winds, we took an hour and a half to prepare for a summit bivouac. Narita and Nishida leveled the ground while I worked on melting snow. This was the flattest bivouac site of the entire climb, but the combination of intense climbing, high altitude, strong winds, and the freezing cold after sunset made for a miserable night. In total, we had climbed 32 to 34 rope lengths, with the simul-climbing included. Tomorrow we would only need to descend.

Waking on day four, we saw majestic Ghamubar Zom V, the peak we had ascended last year, towering to the southeast. We could clearly see our line, and it struck me how much longer the ridge was than I remembered. It was a moment of deep reflection.

Around 8 a.m., in a continuing cold wind, we began

Yudai Suzuki on the final rock pitch of Thui II's west face. Although he couldn't see it yet, the summit icefield was just above. *Kei Narita*

rappelling our ascent route. In fact, we were thankful for the relentless westerly wind, as it seemed to have blown away the heavy snow that accumulated during the storm at base camp. Using V-threads, rock horns, and a couple of pitons, we made about 23 rappels to reach the top of the initial simul-climbing section.

At this point, it was already past 7 p.m., and the sky was completely dark. However, the snow had hardened, and there were no falling rocks, so we continued, downclimbing simultaneously on one rope, reversing our ascent. Black ice appeared in places, but we carefully placed screws and cams, calmly dealing with each section. At 10 p.m., we reached the Risht Glacier. It had been a very long descent requiring full concentration.

In less than an hour, we had trekked back to ABC, where we finally removed our harnesses for the first time in four days, overwhelmed with an indescribable sense of fulfillment. We slept deeply in the denser air until 10 a.m. the next morning.

This climb reaffirmed for me how all-encompassing, free, and extraordinary alpine climbing can be. What made me especially happy was that we had managed to ascend a beautiful unclimbed wall in a single, calligraphic brushstroke from base to summit. We named the route Spider's Thread, after the lines of ice on the wall and the countless big spiders living around the base camp.

The past three years have taught me important lessons about alpine climbing in unexplored terrain and allowed me to grow as an alpinist. What did I learn on the two big climbs in 2024? There are too many things to list here, but if I were to name three, they would be:

1. Believe the route connects and keep climbing. On routes like the labyrinthine mushroom ridge of Quitaraju or the precarious aid section at 6,400 meters on Thui II, the cruxes were often hidden from below. If I had hesitated, I wouldn't have been able to push through. Once you take a step forward, you are committed and you must trust yourself to find the route.

2. Be realistic. Conversely, it's important to remain calm and imagine the worst-case scenario. Risks must be carefully and realistically assessed. When I suffered the 15-meter fall in Peru, I was lucky to escape without injury—I should have chosen a more cautious line.

3. Cultivate the initiative to find good unclimbed lines and go try them. I've had the opportunity to experience first ascents on five 6,000-meter peaks. But I can say it is not easy to identify good objectives. Living in Japan, far from the highest mountains of Asia or South America, I have to leverage tools like the internet and Google Earth to identify objectives and imagine unclimbed lines. After that, the important part is having

the maximum commitment to go and see what's there. You won't know what it's like until you try.

Drawing on the invaluable experiences I gained from climbing Quitaraju and Thui II in 2024, I hope to continue discovering and pursuing creative alpine routes and expanding my understanding of the unknown.

Narita follows a thin crack up the steep slab at 6,400 meters on Thui II, a key to the route. He is carrying two packs because the leader, Suzuki, had left his pack below the crux of the pitch. *Yudai Suzuki*

SUMMARY: New route up the south spur and southeast ridge of Nevado Quitaraju (6,036m) in the Cordillera Blanca, Peru, June 25–29, 2024, by Keisuke Ohkura, Kazumasa Otsubo, and Yudai Suzuki, Japan. The route is called Dream House (1,240m, VI M6 AI5+ R/X A2); the descent was by the north face. New route up the west face of Thui II (6,523m) in the Hindu Raj of Pakistan, September 21–24, 2024, by Kei Narita, Yuu Nishida, and Yudai Suzuki, with descent by the same line. They called the route Spider's Thread (1,450m, ED+ M7 A2).

ABOUT THE AUTHOR: Born in 1994 in Tokyo, Yudai Suzuki works, climbs, and skis as much as he can when not on expeditions. He works as a coach for Waseda University's alpine club, as an athlete for The North Face, and as a ski guide, mountain cameraman, and lecturer.

This story was translated from Japanese by Heikki Ruuska.

UNTIL ONLY THE MOUNTAIN REMAINS

THREE MODERN AID ROUTES ON BAFFIN ISLAND

MILES FULLMAN

"Just **drill something already,** damn it," I mutter under my breath as Brandon hooks farther and farther above the belay ledge. Sam and I listen anxiously to every creaking adjustment of steel on stone, willing the placements to hold. CRACK! The rock breaks under a hook and sends Brandon flying. One beak after another rips out.

The fall is long enough for us to wonder if anything is going to hold. Suddenly the rope pulls tight and catches Brandon a few feet above the ledge. He's staring at Sam and me with a rack of beaks clipped to the lead rope, sitting in a heap against his harness. A single rivet from the hardware store had kept him from hitting the ledge. I light a cigarette and pass it over.

For Brandon Adams, Sam Stuckey, and me, big walls are one of the main reasons we fell in love with climbing. Each of us was drawn like a moth to a flame to the crucible of American rock climbing, Yosemite Valley. While steadily honing our craft on the soaring granite walls, we each harbored the same dream of establishing first ascents on Baffin Island, a mythical arena of massive walls rearing out of the sea, ice, and rugged valleys.

Some of Baffin's biggest and remotest walls were climbed in the 1990s, a time when helicopters were used for certain approaches and the typical strategy relied on extensive fixed ropes and capsule-style siege tactics to put up new routes in the harsh and unpredictable environment. Nowadays, lighter and more advanced gear, reliable weather forecasting, and modern Yosemite tactics like short-fixing and simul-climbing make such cumbersome approaches unnecessary. A modern hard-aid rack consists of a healthy assortment of beaks and hooks instead of the traditional sawed angles, knifeblades, copperheads, and nuts.

Today's focus on free climbing has pushed hard big-wall climbing out of the spotlight. But that doesn't mean it isn't still being done at cutting-edge difficulty.

Sam Stuckey leading an A3+ pitch, with 200 feet of beaks and hooks, on Ragnarok (2,500′, VI 5.11 A5), a new route on the west face of Frigga I. The route was completed and descended in four and a half days, compared with 17 days for the only other route on the face. ***Miles Fullman***

Moving loads up the Weasel River Valley. Even with gear cached near the top of the valley in advance of the expedition, it took six days of hiking under haulbags weighing up to 90 pounds to reach the team's first base camp. *Miles Fullman*

On El Cap, people had been saying for years there were no big unclimbed lines left to do, but Brandon established two new routes recently, in 2018 and 2021. These routes are prime examples of modern hard aid: pushing the latest gear available to its absolute limit.

This kind of big-wall climbing satisfies not only creative problem-solving but also aesthetic exploration. In *Rock and Ice* 24, Dale Bard espoused his perspective on wall climbing: "Then you get into what I was eventually doing—going up on El Capitan for the location. While sitting in El Capitan's Meadow and staring up at the wall, I'd see something real pretty. Over by Iron Hawk, there's a beautiful orange swirl that looks like it's painted on the wall. I wanted to go up there, so I did." To the big-wall climber, the most outrageously steep, blank, and direct aspect begs the question: Can we go up there?

Brandon and I met in the Valley in 2018 when I was a climbing steward and he was a climbing ranger. Brandon approaches everyday life with a bumbling bear sweetness that disappears as soon as he enters the vertical, revealing maniacal intensity and hyperactive focus. He climbs every pitch like it might be his last, with a beak tattooed across his chest and Tool blasting on his phone.

Over the years, we've shared many days roped together, setting speed records on El Capitan and exploring the High Sierra. Many of my climbing firsts have been with Brandon, from learning how to drill a bolt to discovering the laborious process of establishing new routes. While descending from the Incredible Hulk in the summer of 2022, he asked if I was interested in climbing on Baffin Island. The seed was planted.

I first heard about Sam when he made a rare repeat of Jolly Roger (Cole-Grossman, 1979), an A4+ R testpiece on El Cap. Sam is another fanatic for hard aid routes, having climbed over 100 desert towers, including nearly everything in Utah's Fisher Towers. When Brandon partnered with Sam to climb Continental Drift on El Capitan (Anker-Gerberding-Thaw, 1997), he asked

Sam if he too was interested in going to Baffin.

In the fall of 2023, the three of us committed to planning the expedition. Sam and I roped up for the first time in Yosemite in the spring of 2024. We climbed well together and quickly bonded over his encyclopedic knowledge of obscure film and music. The Baffin team was forged.

In March, the three of us gathered in Salt Lake City to compile the necessary supplies to be shipped to Pangnirtung and cached in advance beside Summit Lake, about 30 miles up the Weasel Valley, when snow machines could still access the valley. We packed two lead lines, one haul line, a double rack of cams, a couple of dozen beaks, a pile of bolts and bits, and a fistful of rivets. We loaded buckets with food, consisting mostly of couscous, the king of expedition grains. Entangled in a labyrinth of shipping manifestos, spreadsheets, and Canadian import restrictions, we held our breath as the gear shipment cleared customs—then lamented our nonrefundable flights when our food shipment was rejected at the border.

To save us from hundreds of miles of backbreaking load-ferrying, Sam flew to Ottawa at the last minute and frantically acquired food in Canada, then shipped it on to Pangnirtung. Without Sam's commitment, I have no doubt that our expedition would have been vastly less successful. All of our gear and food made it to local outfitter Peter Kilabuk in Pangnirtung to be cached at Summit Lake.

On July 6, we landed on a dirt runway, relieved to see that the remaining sea ice in Pangnirtung Fjord had been blown out by strong winds the day before our arrival, allowing us boat passage to the end of the fjord, where it meets the Weasel River. We then spent six days hiking with nearly 90-pound haulbags, enjoying the pleasure of every variety of post-holing along the way: boggy tundra, river crossings, quicksand, moraine, talus, sand dunes, and deep snow. Brandon joked that falling

Brandon Adams plows the trail to base camp on the Turner Glacier. Traveling light, by Baffin standards, the team brought no shovels and had to dig out their tent site with food buckets. *Miles Fullman*

into a crevasse would merely be the ultimate post-hole.

With 24-hour daylight, we would hike until we were deliriously crippled and then sleep until we could walk again, losing track of the calendar days. Almost a week of toil brought us to our first base camp, a couple of miles up the Turner Glacier, below the northwest face of Frigga I (1,264m). Using the buckets from our gear shipment as snow shovels, we excavated a platform for the tent. From here we could see up the Parade Glacier, an offshoot of the Turner that lies between the west face of Frigga I and the east face of Mt. Asgard (2,015m), and the striking east face of Mt. Loki (1,920m) a few miles farther away, guarding the head of the Turner Glacier.

On July 15, we hiked our gear up to the menacing west face of Frigga, which persistently overhangs and tapers to a point like a sword. There is only one other route on this formation: Slith the Frightful (Barker-Rzeczycki, 1996), on the left side of the west face. In 1998, Japanese climbers attempted to climb the right side of the west face (*AAJ 1999*). Unsure of their line's exact location, we aimed for an obvious natural system of sweeping corners and splitter cracks skirting the right edge of the face.

We started climbing on July 16. Sam led us off the snow, and we strained against the heavy bags. Brandon quested above the belay ledge, with delicate hooks on fragile flakes and baby beak placements in friable rock, a true master of his craft. While I was cleaning the pitch, it started raining heavily and I got soaked to my skin hammering out beaks in a waterfall. I pried loose a large flake that Brandon had hooked across—it hung directly above the ledge where we had just belayed. As I levered it outward, it sheared off a significant plate of the wall. We watched, transfixed, as it obliterated the belay ledge. Our vulnerable position, 60 miles from Pangnirtung, began to sink in.

Climbing the next pitch, we encountered hangerless bolts, discovering that the line we had scoped overlapped in places with the aborted Japanese attempt. At our first bivouac, we almost set the portaledge on fire while priming the stove in our homemade hanging kit for the first time.

To conserve our limited anchor hardware, we strove to make every pitch a full rope length, drilling anchors with one rivet and one bolt. Carrying everything on our backs into the mountains had necessitated spartan choices about equipment, but using the bare minimum of gear to accomplish our goals also became one of the most engaging challenges of the expedition. We had just enough of everything to see us through our objectives with a thin margin for error.

USING THE BARE MINIMUM OF GEAR TO ACCOMPLISH OUR GOALS BECAME ONE OF THE MOST ENGAGING CHALLENGES OF THE EXPEDITION.

The climbing continued to be engaging, alternating between soaring beak seams and splitter cracks. Leading the offwidths with sparse protection was especially exciting while bypassing delicately perched chockstones, which could easily have killed the belayer if dislodged.

We reached what was clearly the Japanese attempt's high point—a reported 300 feet from the summit—and continued up for about 800 feet more climbing. On the fourth day we pushed for the summit, leaving our haulbags on a ledge halfway up the wall.

Unencumbered by hauling, we moved more efficiently. The leader would often be short-fixing the next pitch while the follower finished hauling and the third person tagged up gear or drilled another bolt at the anchor for the descent. The Japanese attempt had taken 27 days, and Slith the Frightful was established over 17 days. With the advantages of modern tools and tactics, we would climb and descend our route in four and a half days.

The climbing to the summit turned out to be some of the best: A steep and exposed pitch accessed a perfect headwall, where rope-stretching beak seams led to a final pitch of free climbing over wet, creaking plates. We sat on the snowy ridgeline and marveled at the majestic frozen panorama.

We spent July 21 to 23 shuttling everything to a new base camp on the moraine below the east face of Mt. Loki. We were relieved to relocate, as the rapidly melting glacier was turning our first camp into a lake. As we were shuttling our gear up the Turner Glacier, we noticed a system of corners splitting the captivating eastern

Approaching the 2,500-foot west face of Frigga I. The arrow marks the start of Ragnarok, which continued directly up the right side of the face (see the *AAJ* website for a route photo and topo). The only prior route up the west face was Slith the Frightful, on the left side, climbed in 1996 by Wally Barker and John Rzeczycki. *Miles Fullman*

The line of Fenrir on the east face and upper southeast ridge of Mt. Loki. The initial 1,500-foot wall was unclimbed before 2024; the southeast ridge had been climbed by Dave Nettle and Reuben Shelton in 2013. *Expedition Photo*

wall on Loki. This aesthetic peak, sometimes called the Matterhorn of Baffin Island, had three existing routes: the west ridge (Baird-MacCallum-Morton-Paul, 1965), the south buttress (Lee-Parker, 1982), and the southeast ridge (Nettle-Shelton, 2013). But the steep east face was unclimbed.

Stormy weather kept us tentbound for a week. To pass the time, we made crosswords for each other with words from a book of Norse mythology. We learned the stories behind the names of the mountains surrounding us, such as Asgard: hall of the Aesir, the warlike Norse gods. The Inuktitut names for the formations were more literal, Asgard being named Qattaujannguaq, which translates to "looks like a barrel."

In *Arctic Dreams*, Barry Lopez writes, "Language is not something man imposes on the land. It evolves in his conversation with the land." As we lived on the glacier surrounded by these enormous walls, we learned the names for the peaks that had evolved out of the people's relationship with them, logical in their referential description, and the names that had been bestowed on them by wayward adventurers. Somewhere in the intersection of these two relationships with place, one as an inhabitant and the other as a pilgrim, we formed our own connection with these wild mountains.

A brief lull in the weather allowed a reconnaissance of Loki. Hiking past the toe of the southeast ridge, we scrambled along a talus field slanting up below the east wall to the highest point, where a sweeping system of splitters rose up the smooth buttress. While we waited for the storm to break, we free climbed the corners and cracks at the start of our line and fixed three pitches.

On August 1, we ascended our fixed lines and continued to the summit of Mt. Loki. Brandon pushed the rope up the lower wall while I freed the pitches on Micro Traxion. The most memorable section involved thoughtful face climbing into a striking finger crack; I fell on the pitch but estimated it would go free in the 5.12 range. We named this pitch Gleipnir, after the unbreakable, ropelike material the Norse gods used to bind Fenrir the wolf, Loki's child, until he escapes during Ragnarok, the foretold end of the world in Norse mythology. Maybe someone will get inspired to repeat our route and free Fenrir from his unbreakable bonds.

At the top of the 1,500-foot wall, we traversed left below a large overhang to join the southeast ridge, then followed this for another 3,000 feet or so, mostly soloing and simul-climbing a few sections. From the summit, the view to the northwest over the Penny Ice Cap extended incomprehensibly. Massive snow domes slumped surrealistically atop bristling formations in every direction. We descended to the south, making 13 rappels down the south buttress, and stumbled over crevasses to base camp in the early hours of the following morning.

The good weather continued, and we knew we had to make the most of it, so the next day we ferried loads across the Turner Glacier and fixed ropes at the bottom of the

south tower of Mt. Asgard. We had scoped a line up the blankest stretch of wall between Sensory Overload (Lavigne-Papert-Walsh, 2012) and The Bavarian Direct (Bruckbauer-Grad-Guscelli-Reichelt-Schlesener, 1996); the latter was freed in 2012 by Alex and Thomas Huber, with a set of variations, discovered in 2009, known as The Belgarian (VI 5.13c).

We started climbing where the rock meets the glacier, a ways to the right of Sensory Overload. On August 4, we hauled our last loads off the glacier and committed to the wall.

That first day we climbed over 1,000 feet, making a hanging bivy following a hard and consequential pitch that Brandon later named "No Parachute, No Ground," after a concept in the meditation book he was reading. A fitting description of the mental game of dangerous aid climbing, if you ignore the very real ledge Brandon nearly hit while ripping the pitch. After a few drags and a slap on the helmet, Brandon re-racked all of the beaks piled on the lead line, pulled back up to the single rivet that had caught his fall, and started tapping beaks back into the same placements.

The wall was unrelenting, interweaving thin seams and flakes. Every rope length was slow going and hard won, a sustained puzzle requiring ingenuity and delicacy. By this point the three of us had merged into one organism, the rhythms of wall climbing feeling familiar and instinctual. We each tacitly set to our respective tasks, confident in the knowledge that everyone was doing their part. After two successful ascents, we felt more at ease in the Arctic environment, and the looming wall began to seem more like an old friend than a menacing adversary. It

Using a Micro Traxion on a fixed rope, Miles Fullman works to free the aid pitches climbed earlier on the lower east face of Mt. Loki. The hardest of these pitches is estimated to be free climbable at 5.12+. In back are the north (left) and south towers of Mt. Asgard. Farther back on the left is the top of the Frigga massif. ***Sam Stuckey***

The south tower of Mt. Asgard from the west, showing the approximate lines of (1) Porter Route on north tower (Charlie Porter, solo, 1975), (2) Ratatoskr (Golovchenko-Nilov, 2017), (3) Sensory Overload (Lavigne-Papert-Walsh, 2012), (4) Memento Mori (Adams-Fullman-Stuckey, 2024), (5) The Belgarian variations (2009, yellow lines), (6) The Bavarian Direct (Bruckbauer-Grad-Guscelli-Reichelt-Schlesener, 1996), and (7) Direct West Face (Bagley-Barbella-McCarthy-Redfern, 1987). ***Expedition Photo***

felt like we could keep going forever, climbing walls that never ended until the sun circled below the horizon and the polar night froze us to the rock. Steadily we pieced together the imaginary line, upward through the myriad uncertainties.

We shared smokes at belays to calm frazzled nerves, taking in the long waves of light spilling over the glaciers in great amber swaths. Clouds encircled us and danced in wreaths around the summit of Loki; great wisps of fog swirled below, above, and around us. The Arctic stillness made the rhythm of the hammer all the more piercing.

At a long belay, Brandon asked if I had thought of any good names for the route, and I suggested Memento Mori: "Remember you must die." It seemed appropriate, a reminder of the experience we had been sharing on this huge wall, a reminder of the inevitability of our own mortality and a call to make the most of our fleeting time.

We checked the forecast and learned that our weather window would be closing soon, so we pushed hard, constantly unsure if there would be enough climbable features, to reach a big bivy ledge and then charge for the summit. Above the ledge, we continued up a corner and then Sam brilliantly traversed rightward to the base of an immaculate crack system, reminiscent of the Shield headwall on El Capitan. I fixed one aesthetic pitch and looked up before descending for the night to see the splitter extending to the heavens.

The next morning, anxious to stand on top and descend before the weather hit, I started short-fixing from the top of the fixed lines and pushed the rope up the final thousand feet in just four hours. The rock was impeccable, and the climbing and position phenomenal. We reached the top just after noon and spent another four hours relaxing in the sun on the uncannily flat summit, admiring rock crystals and reveling in how strange it felt to stand atop one of the mountains of our dreams.

As I gased over at Frigga I's magnificent west face and the route we had called Ragnarok, the name's apocalyptic significance in Norse mythology seemed fitting from this perch: The beginning is the end, and the end is the beginning.

The next day we rappelled thousands of feet with core-shot ropes. We returned to base camp and crawled into the tent just as the skies unleashed.

We endured the storm contentedly, in disbelief at all we had just experienced. Our tent was sinking into the glacier, pulling the roof close to our faces. The glacier shuddered, making ominous pops and growls. Wind and ice hissed against the walls. Mere millimeters of synthetic fabric and a pile of down feathers kept us sheltered from the harsh elements. When the storm cleared, we hiked off the glacier and into the valley, elated to see signs of life and thaw in the warmth of the sun.

Stuckey cleans a pitch midway up Asgard. The team's rack was exceptionally light for hard first ascents on huge walls: a double set of standard cams, one number 5 cam, a fistful of hooks, around 30 beak pitons, and some bolts. *Miles Fullman*

The comedown from such an intense experience unfolded in stages. I returned to Yosemite with no motivation to climb. Soon after arriving, someone close to me passed away in a climbing accident. Downloading from the expedition while processing the sudden loss was intensely jarring. I was reminded once again that nothing lasts forever. The more I reflect on the name we chose for our route on Asgard, the more it seems appropriate. We are fragile creatures. We ought to make the most of every moment in this life while we ever so briefly have it.

The epigraph of the *Insight Meditation* book Brandon carried with him offers a short poem by the Chinese poet Li Bai. We spent much time pondering its significance in the cramped quarters of our tent during the storms, peering through the vestibule to steal glances at Asgard. I find it very fitting:

The birds have vanished down the sky.
Now the last cloud drains away.
We sit together, the mountain and me,
until only the mountain remains.

SUMMARY: Three new routes in Auyuittuq National Park, Baffin Island, Nunavut, Canada, by Brandon Adams, Miles Fullman, and Sam Stuckey (all USA). First ascent of Ragnarok (2,500′, VI 5.11 A5), on the west face of Frigga I, July 16–20, 2024. New route Fenrir (4,500′, with 1,500′ new, V 5.11 A2) on the east face of Mt. Loki, August 1, after fixing three pitches. First ascent of Memento Mori (3,600′, VI 5.10 A5), west face of the south tower of Mt. Asgard, August 4–8, after fixing two pitches. Topos for these routes are at the *AAJ* website. An interview with all three climbers is on the Cutting Edge podcast.

ABOUT THE AUTHOR: Miles Fullman calls Yosemite Valley home. A lover of mountains and books, he says climbing for him is a literary pursuit and an integral aspect of his quixotic journey of self-realization.

> "THE EFFORT WAS PHYSICAL, TECHNICAL, BUT ABOVE ALL MENTAL, IN MANAGING STRESS AND EMOTIONS. THE MOST DIFFICULT ASPECT...WAS TO STAY FULLY CONCENTRATED FOR SO MANY HOURS A DAY AND TO LOWER THE STRESS IN COMPLICATED SITUATIONS, TO STAY LUCID TO TAKE GOOD DECISIONS."

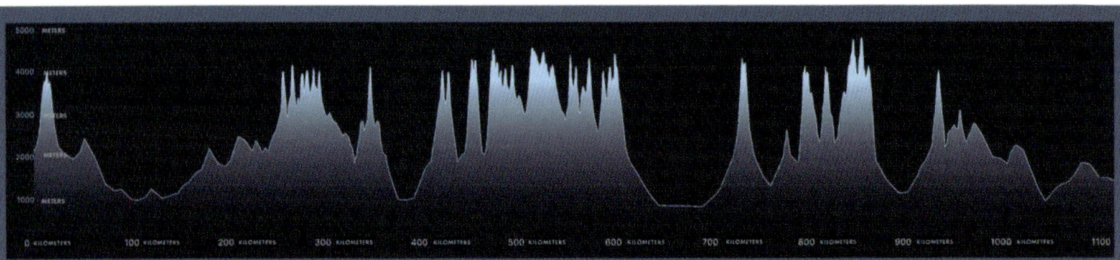

"The connections [were] rooted in the aesthetics of the routes, in the idea that once I reached a mountain range, I would stay up there, linking summits, moving continuously or resting in refuges, until all the peaks were linked."

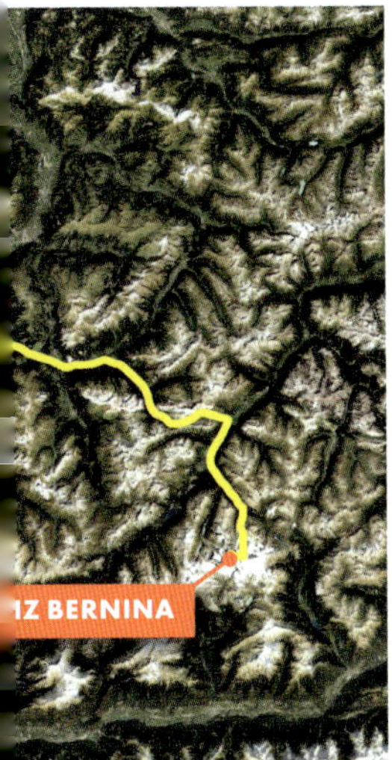

ALPINE CONNECTIONS

KILIAN JORNET'S 19-DAY TRAVERSE OF THE ALPS' 4,000-METER PEAKS

From August 13 to 31, Kilian Jornet Burgada traversed the Alps from east to west by foot and bicycle, reaching all 82 of the 4,000-meter-plus summits. The previous fastest time for this link-up, using no motorized transportation, was 60 days. Dubbed Alpine Connections, Jornet's 19-day adventure—with one weather-related rest day—involved more than 160 alpine routes. He partnered with various friends but reached more than half of the peaks alone. Jornet posted a detailed report at his website soon after finishing; these excerpts and data are drawn from that account, his daily Strava posts, and Coros.com. ***—Dougald MacDonald***

BY THE NUMBERS

DISTANCE: 1,207km+ by foot and bike
ELEVATION GAIN: 72,233m (236,985′)
LONGEST DAY: 34 hours
AVERAGE SLEEP: 5 hours, 17 minutes
CALORIES BURNED: 8,300/day avg.

Past 4,000er Link-Ups

1993: Simon Jenkins and Martin Moran link 75 peaks in 52 days by foot and bike; later that year, the UIAA creates an "official" list of 82 peaks.

2004: Patrick Berhault and Philippe Magnin link 65 peaks on foot and skis before Berhault dies in a fall on April 28.

2007: Miha Valič attempts to climb the 82 peaks in 82 winter days, using a van between climbs; he finishes in 102 days.

2008: Diego Giovannini and Franco Nicolini climb the 82 peaks in 60 days with no mechanized transport.

2015: Ueli Steck links the peaks in 62 days, using a paraglider for some descents.

2024: Christian Maurer and Peter von Känel make extensive use of paragliders to summit the peaks in 51 days.

DAY 3 — A
BERNESE ALPS
99KM, 6 SUMMITS

ALETSCHHORN: After a couple of hours of sleep, Jornet looped over five peaks in about ten hours, then descended off the Jungfrau and headed to Aletschhorn. Heavy rain fell as he approached the north spur. "It was going to be dark soon.... I was completely soaked. So I decided to change plans and go to the south face, hoping the rain would stop.... The way out the Aletsch Glacier was insanely long." About 24km and 1,400m lower, he started climbing again. A ten-minute nap on the floor of the Oberaletsch hut revived him just enough to continue. "I reached the summit just after sunrise.... I could see just under me in the north the place where I stood 12 hours ago in the rain. It was a long detour, but with those conditions I believe it was the right call." In all, Jornet climbed 7,890m (25,886′) on this very long day.

DAY 15 — B
MONT BLANC MASSIF
24KM, 4 SUMMITS

VERTE TO DROITES TRAVERSE: Warned by guides that conditions had seriously deteriorated in this part of the rapidly warming range, Jornet felt a sense of dread. "I knew the risks I would be taking that day would be high. It felt a bit like I was going to the slaughterhouse." On the Moine Ridge, headed to the Aiguille Verte, "The arête I remembered didn't exist anymore. The multiple rockfalls and collapses had changed its shape." The traverse to the Aiguille du Jardin was like "playing Jenga with the rocks." On Les Droites, he was left hanging by one hand after rocks collapsed. The decision to continue did not make him proud: "I mean, the small decisions of where to abseil, how to downclimb, or how to protect myself had been good, and that's what kept me alive, but the decision...to keep going was something I wasn't happy about."

LEARN MORE: *To read Jornet's in-depth personal blog on the traverse, search "Petite Balade Alpine."*

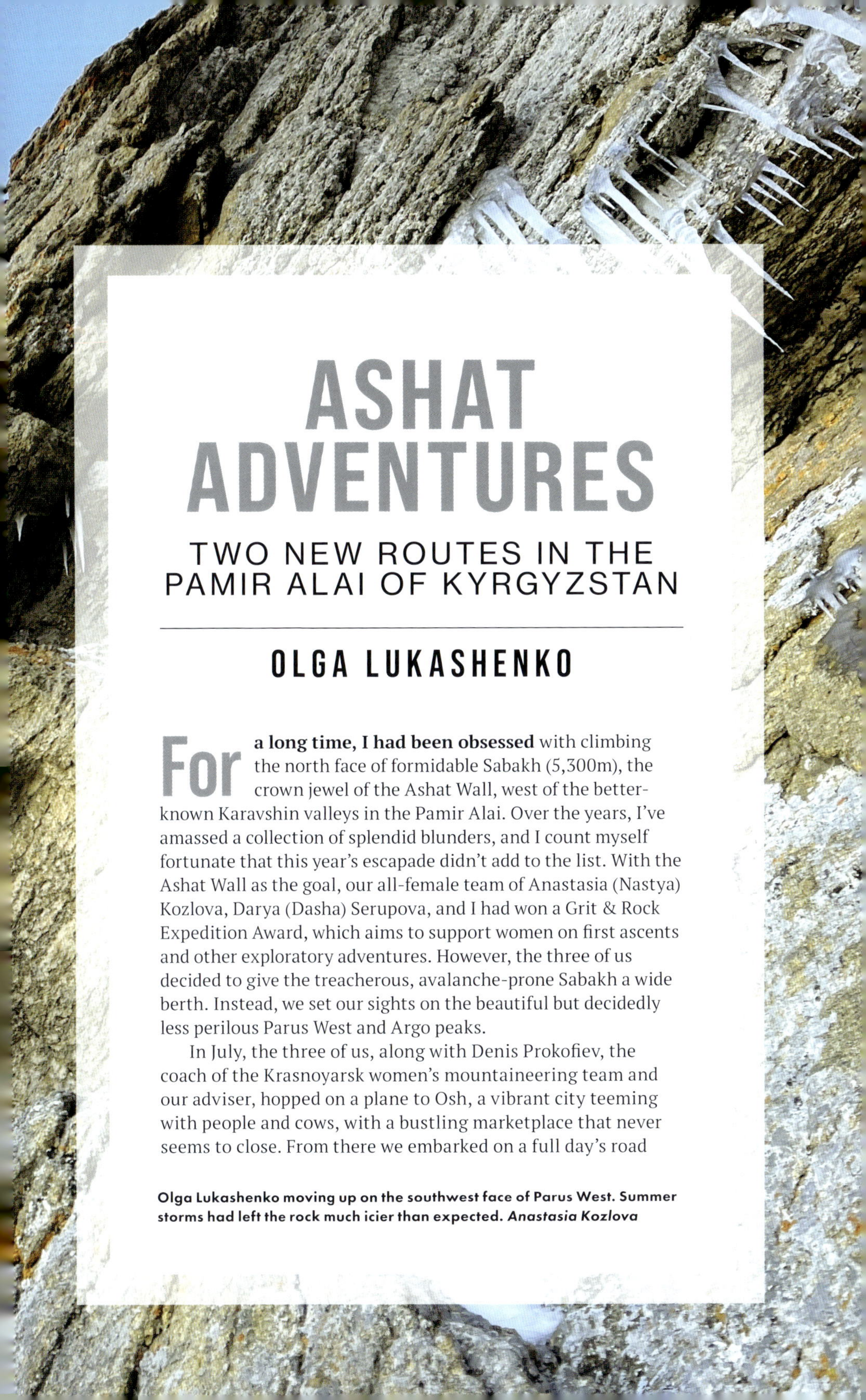

ASHAT ADVENTURES

TWO NEW ROUTES IN THE PAMIR ALAI OF KYRGYZSTAN

OLGA LUKASHENKO

For **a long time, I had been obsessed** with climbing the north face of formidable Sabakh (5,300m), the crown jewel of the Ashat Wall, west of the better-known Karavshin valleys in the Pamir Alai. Over the years, I've amassed a collection of splendid blunders, and I count myself fortunate that this year's escapade didn't add to the list. With the Ashat Wall as the goal, our all-female team of Anastasia (Nastya) Kozlova, Darya (Dasha) Serupova, and I had won a Grit & Rock Expedition Award, which aims to support women on first ascents and other exploratory adventures. However, the three of us decided to give the treacherous, avalanche-prone Sabakh a wide berth. Instead, we set our sights on the beautiful but decidedly less perilous Parus West and Argo peaks.

In July, the three of us, along with Denis Prokofiev, the coach of the Krasnoyarsk women's mountaineering team and our adviser, hopped on a plane to Osh, a vibrant city teeming with people and cows, with a bustling marketplace that never seems to close. From there we embarked on a full day's road

Olga Lukashenko moving up on the southwest face of Parus West. Summer storms had left the rock much icier than expected. ***Anastasia Kozlova***

ABOVE: The new route up the southwest face of Parus West (4,850m). Prior routes climbed the southwest ridge (left of the 2024 route) and south-southwest buttress (just beyond the right skyline). ***Olga Lukashenko***

LEFT: Anastasia Kozlova on the southwest face of Parus West, with part of the north-facing Ashat Wall behind. ***Darya Serupova***

THE FINAL SECTIONS WERE PACKED WITH SNOW AND ICE, AND WE'D LEFT OUR ICE TOOLS AND CRAMPONS IN BASE CAMP.

journey to the village of Uzgurush. Upon arrival, we loaded 200 kilograms of equipment and provisions onto donkeys and horses, and the real fun began—a two-day hike through rugged terrain. When the horse wranglers left, we were completely alone in the wilderness.

The mountains were draped in fresh snow. We waited patiently for two days, giving the faces a chance to shed their icy cloaks. We established base camp about two to three hours from the Ashat Wall, near a reliable water source. Our advanced base camp (ABC) would be just a 40-minute trek away, the perfect staging ground for our main objective: the north face of Argo.

First, though, Nastya, Dasha, and I decided to warm up and acclimatize on a logical line up a giant dihedral on the southwest face of the rocky Parus West (4,850m), which really looks like the "sail" for which it is named on the side we would climb. The terrain looked promising, with beautiful granite. On July 15, after approaching the wall and checking out conditions, we decided to start climbing late that same afternoon and we bivouacked low on the face.

The next day, Dasha took the lead, and we confidently made progress, climbing excellent rock pitches. However, it soon became evident that Parus wasn't as rocky as advertised. The final sections were packed with snow and ice, and we'd left our ice tools and crampons in base camp. I found myself leading ice and mixed terrain with nothing but a rock hammer, which I had to use to carve steps in the hard snow and ice for about 100 meters. This was either incredibly innovative climbing or a nod to the early climbing trailblazers—certainly not a lack of planning or foresight!

We bivouacked midway up the wall, sitting on our packs and the rope, and then again near the summit. Starting down on the morning of July 18, we stumbled upon the belay anchors left in 2012 by Yury Koshelenko and Vasily Kolisnyk on the south-southwest buttress, and we used two of them that were in good condition.

While I was rappelling and searching for a spot to set up an anchor, I noticed a rock the size of a melon hurtling down from above. I was about to shout "Nice try, but you missed!" when it didn't, smacking my hand. I howled in frustration as we continued down, either from the useless painkillers or from the thought that we might not be able to climb Argo. Luckily, my hand wasn't broken, just bruised and bloodied.

All in all, our route had been an ideal warm-up, designed to fool us into thinking that the ascent of Argo (4,750m) would be a breeze. For a couple of days, we gorged on food—borscht, stew, and so on—rolling from one plate to another, and at the same time we managed to sort through the equipment and stuff it back into the packs, preparing for our main objective.

The first time we saw Argo and the Ashat Wall, during a reconnaissance, they were completely covered with snow and the wall looked huge, powerful, harsh, amazing. Thinking of the legends who had climbed here before was intimidating.

After our second approach, we discovered that the ice runnels in the center of Argo's north face were about to melt; our intended route essentially did not exist. Fortunately, we found some ice on the far right side of the wall, to the right of the Petrov Route (1989, 6A), one of two existing routes on the face.

TOP: The new route on Argo. The 1989 Petrov Route is just to the left, but completely independent. *Olga Lukashenko*

BOTTOM: Darya Serupova, day three on Argo. *Olga Lukashenko*

On July 22, we started up an ice gully (which had completely melted out by day five as we rappelled down). The warmth made the ice unstable and sketchy, so I opted for mixed climbing, even though the ice would have been quicker and easier to climb. The three screws I placed in the rotten ice were just for my sanity. Nonetheless, we managed to gain the first 500 meters—nearly half the route—quite quickly, completing it in one day.

The second half of the wall became significantly steeper.

The formidable north-facing wall at the head of the Ashat Gorge. From left to right: Dioskuri (at least 4,800m), Argo (4,750m), and Svarog (5,000m). The 2024 route climbed the right side of Argo, then traversed left to the top. Sabakh, the highest peak of the group, is off-picture to the right. ***Olga Lukashenko***

The main challenges? Oh, just the usual: slippery, ice-filled cracks, loose rock and rockfall hazards, and weather that seemed to think it was auditioning for a disaster movie, with frequent thunderstorms, hail, and snowfall. Hauling our heavy equipment was a real endurance test. As if that weren't enough, we had brought a well-worn portaledge that clearly was designed to test our willpower and sense of humor. Without these, the daily two-hour wrestling match to assemble the ledge would have been unbearable.

WE HAD BROUGHT A WELL-WORN PORTALEDGE THAT CLEARLY WAS DESIGNED TO TEST OUR WILLPOWER AND SENSE OF HUMOR.

A storm was forecast for our second day on the route, and our plan was to ride out the storm but still try to make a little progress. While my two climbing partners battled through a few pitches, the sky darkened and hail and snow began to fall. I stayed behind to guard the house, eating everything I could reach and rolling from side to side to appear busy.

The next two days were intense, pushing us to 7b (French) on the rock. Nastya tackled an incredible frozen chimney with fearless precision. Dasha took on a stunning wide crack stretching several pitches; these ideally would have been protected with a number 6 Camalot, but since we had only a single number 4, protecting this crack turned into a thrilling exercise in creativity with chockstones and other features. At one point, we ended up on a full rope length of vertical scree—huge, disconnected blocks where removing a piece of protection might trigger a cascade of failure, possibly damaging the rope. I felt a tremendous relief at having overcome this demanding aid section (up to A3+).

On July 25, we reached the saddle between Argo and Svarog, with a stunning view into the mountains of Tajikistan. We set up the portaledge there and decided to go for the summit right away, leaving behind the ledge, sleeping bags, and other gear. The upper west ridge had enjoyable climbing, passing pillars of granite interspersed with mixed climbing. After four more pitches, we reached the top and then descended back to the saddle for our fourth bivouac.

Rappelling from the saddle went smoothly—the ropes didn't get stuck even once. There were many free-hanging rappels, which, with heavy packs, became excellent exercises for the core and back muscles. At the last anchor, we unclipped the portaledge and watched as it limply bounced and rolled down the slope. The three of us relished the spectacle, savoring a blissful moment of sweet revenge.

Returning to base camp after five days on the wall felt like coming home after months away. We recalled the lively debates at the end of our first day on the rotten ice—whether to rappel or to continue up. Now we felt drained yet delighted. I have no doubt these are landmark routes for the three of us, and we'll remember this trip as a significant turning point. As for where this will lead us, well, we will see.

TOP: Kozlova leading the first pitch after the third bivy on Argo. The team's camo climbing pants are not military—just inexpensive! *Olga Lukashenko*

BOTTOM: Lukashenko, Serupova, and Kozlova (left to right) on the Ashat Wall. *Olga Lukashenko*

SUMMARY: Two new routes in the Ashat Gorge, Pamir Alai, Kyrgyzstan, by Anastasia Kozlova, Olga Lukashenko, and Darya Serupova from Russia—these were the first climbs by a women's team in this valley.

The trio first climbed the southwest face of Parus West (4,850m), July 15–18, 2024. Their new route was graded Russian 5B (ED- 6c M3 A2), with 28 pitches and 1,460 meters of climbing distance (1,150m vertical). They rappelled the south-southwest buttress.

From July 22 to 26, they completed a new route on the north face of Argo (4,750m), to the right of the Petrov Route (1989, 6A) and completely independent of that line. The 29-pitch route gained 950 meters, with 1,250 meters of climbing, and was rated Russian 6A (ED 7b M5 A3+). They descended the climbing route, placing two bolts for rappel anchors. No bolts were placed during the ascents.

ABOUT THE AUTHOR: Educated in Russia and Switzerland, Olga Lukashenko lives in Germany and France while working full-time in information technology for a Czech company. Adding to her overflowing plate, she's training to become an IFMGA guide.

RYU-SHIN

A RETURN TO THE MIRROR WALL OF EAST GREENLAND

SEÁN VILLANUEVA O'DRISCOLL

It **had been a 50-day odyssey** to get from Oban, Scotland, to the massive shield of granite called Mirror Wall on the Renland peninsula of East Greenland. Those seven weeks included sailing through rough seas, vomiting with seasickness, dodging storms in the Faroe Islands and Iceland, lots of hangboarding, waiting for the sea ice on Greenland's east coast to clear up, ice-floe slaloming, and, finally, 12 days of ferrying heavy loads over 19 miles of endless moraines and treacherous glaciers to reach the wall.

On August 6, 2023, three tiny specks—the American climber-photographer Ben Ditto, the bold British headpointer Franco Cookson, and I—stood on the crevasse-sewn Edward Bailey Glacier, getting our first look at the cold, impenetrable, northwest-facing mirror. Our hearts sank. Though two routes had been established on the wall's flanks and one in left-center, our plan was to find a free line directly up the center of the 1,000-meter wall. However, it seemed completely blank, with no obvious features and no clear possibilities for natural protection.

Our options were either to repeat one of the three existing lines or to try a different, easier mountain. But Mirror Wall is by far the biggest, steepest, most eye-catching rock face in that region. And we weren't here to climb a sure thing.

As the sun slowly emerged from behind the wall, a line of abstract shadows suddenly appeared, suggesting flakes and seams and igniting a spark of excitement. "We don't need to succeed," I said. "We just need to try our best!"

Just before we committed, our fourth teammate, Nicolas Favresse, rejoined the team. During our first day of hiking loads, a big granite block had slid from under Nico's foot; he fell into a pool of icy water and deeply gashed his upper shin. To avoid infection, he'd been forced to stay on the sailboat, rest, and keep his wound clean while the three of us continued to ferry loads.

Seán Villanueva O'Driscoll stems up the difficult corner on pitch 13 that halted his attempt in 2023. Returning in 2024, he was able to push through, allowing the team to complete the route. ***Julia Cassou***

Navigating the tortured glacier below Mirror Wall. ***Julia Cassou***

Once on the wall, we spent nine days slowly fighting our way up a mix of hard free climbing, long, committing runouts, and precarious aid on skyhooks and birdbeaks. Most days, we were on the verge of bailing. About halfway up, we reached a right-facing dihedral, one of the few distinct features on the wall's lower half. The corner, however, was completely closed, with no possibilities for pitons, beaks, or even copperheads; plus, the rock was flaky, exfoliating, and sandy.

Using friction with my palms and feet, I pushed my way up the corner for about 20 meters, placing the odd piece of marginal gear. Finally, with no more possibility for protection, I carefully set a hook on a micro-edge and hand-drilled a bolt. Four meters higher, out to the right, I could see a flake that clearly would take a cam.

Up I went, pushing the two walls apart, the gritty rock crackling under my feet, swimming deeper and deeper into a dark sea of uncertainty. However, no matter how hard I tried, I just couldn't reach that flake. At one point I even stayed in the corner and climbed past the flake—but with nothing to aim for, I had to take the ten-meter fall. For two days I tried this section, taking frightening fall after frightening fall. On one, I hyperextended my right foot, leaving my ankle swollen and blue.

Above us, an obvious crack system looked to lead to the summit. But I was unable to free climb to it, and we'd run out of aid tricks. Additionally, we were slowly running out of food, time, and—more importantly—toilet paper.

Maybe if I aided up high on the bolt and placed another bolt, I could reach the flake. *But where*, I pondered, *should one draw the line?* Even the blankest of walls can be climbed with a bolt ladder. Before starting up, we knew we would have to place bolts, but we had agreed there had to be a certain distance between them, requiring either free climbing or hard aid to bridge the gap. Maybe this call is rather subjective—very dependent on skill, strength, and courage. But you must draw a line if you want to keep the challenge alive.

As we retreated, gutted, I started making plans to return.

Nico, Ben, and Franco made other plans for 2024, so I had to find a new team. The Wide Boyz crack expert Pete Whittaker came to mind—he's just handsome enough that his reflection on the smooth granite meant we wouldn't be looking at ugly stuff! "I'm not sure if it will go—there is a possibility that we make it to the 2023 high point and have to bail again. But I need to go back to find out," I told Pete over the phone in February. One year earlier, we had spent a fun month together in Patagonia, managing a couple of first free ascents.

"Well, if there wasn't uncertainty, it wouldn't be an expedition, would it?" Pete said.

It felt like a stroke of genius when I thought of inviting the Japanese trad-master Keita Kurakami, with whom I'd bonded at Camp 4 in Yosemite through our shared enjoyment of playing the flute. With his rope-solo free climb of the Nose of El Capitan in 2018 and his many committing trad climbs, he'd always inspired me with his philosophical approach and loyalty to style. When I warned him of the magnitude of the challenge, he humbly said, "It sounds like the wall that will test a human's mental strength. I'm really looking forward to it!" Meanwhile, the French climber-photographer Julia Cassou, who had joined Pete and me on some of our climbs in Patagonia, decided she couldn't miss out either.

Pete Whittaker leads pitch nine, one of the difficult face climbing pitches in the first half of the new route. Eventually, Whittaker redpointed this "razor blade slab" at 8b/5.13d R. *Julia Cassou*

And then we received a devastating blow, just two weeks before the expedition—a shocking, three-word message from Keita's friend Takemi Suzuki, who'd been slated to join as the team photographer: "Keita has passed." I hoped it was just a translation mistake, but tragically we learned that Keita, while hiking on Mt. Fuji to train for Greenland, had died when his heart stopped, the result of an underlying heart condition. He was only 38.

Understandably, Takemi could not join this trip. After a few days of contemplating, Pete, Julia, and I decided to continue, and we strengthened the team with the experienced El Cap aid climber Seán Warren from the U.K., who, on very short notice, managed to get the green light from his boss and girlfriend (not the same person). We laminated a photo of Keita to carry with us, a close-up portrait by Drew Smith, Keita's broad smile radiating happiness. Even though he was gone, Keita would be coming with us in print and in spirit. If we managed to carry this snapshot all the way up the wall for a summit picture, it would surely bring a smile to Keita's close friends and family.

TOP: Mirror Wall, showing (1) Midnight Solarium (2012), (2) Reflections (2015), (3) Ryu-Shin (2024), and (4) Ledgeway to Heaven (2012). ***Matt Pycroft | Coldhouse Collective | Berghaus***

ABOVE: The photo of Keita Kurakami that was carried up Mirror Wall. Kurakami wrote in *Alpinist*: "The rock we climb is a mirror, and in it, we see the silent reflections of dialogues that have taken place between climbers across many decades—and also within ourselves." ***Drew Smith***

On July 29, we set out on the sailboat *Cornelia* from Ísafjörður, Iceland. In charge was Captain Mike Brooks from the United Kingdom and the first mate, Trevor Green, from Canada. On August 2, we lowered anchor in Skillebugt Fjord, the drop-off point for Mirror Wall. We got straight to business ferrying loads and managed to get all the gear and food to advanced base camp, on the glacier about three hours from the wall, in only seven days. Our pickup was arranged for September 5, aboard the sailing vessel *Caval'ou*, skippered by Vicente Soto.

I had raved to my teammates about the famous "Arctic high," and how the previous year we had only had two days of rain during our 30-day stay. But there would be no such luck this time: It ended up being overcast with at least some rain or snow on most days. We only had two days of pure blue skies on the whole trip.

Starting up the wall in wet conditions, Pete and I made quick work of the relatively easy first 300 meters. The next day, August 12, we hauled gear and food, committing to a push that would go on for 18 days. We took advantage of every little weather window to advance toward the dihedral, last year's high point, 600 meters up. Seán Warren, with the agility of a cat, took care of the difficult aid, sometimes on wet, snowy rock.

"I never knew aid climbing could be so graceful!" Julia exclaimed, pointing her lens.

"You are a pretty good aid climber for a free climber!" Seán W shouted down as he repeated some of my delicate hooking from the previous year.

Pete stepped up for the hard, run-out free sections. On pitch nine, I was attentively belaying as Pete delicately tick-tacked up small edges ten meters above his last piece. All of a sudden, he let out a scream as a crimper crumbled under his fingers. I saw him sagging backward, almost falling, and my heart skipped a beat. Somehow, clinging with just two fingers, Pete reached out to a good hold.

"That was close!" he said.

As Seán W and Pete took most of the hard leads, I shouted up beta, while Julia took care of the photos and rope management. It was all part of Pete's master plan: "Let Seán W and I do the leading," he told me. "Then, when we get to the dihedral, you will be fresh for the rematch!"

On day seven, August 18, we reached pitch 13, the notorious corner.

I was curious: Was it really impossible, like it had felt a year ago? Would anything be different this time? I prepared to just give it my best, without any attachment to the

Seán Warren, the team's aid climbing specialist, redpointing pitch ten (6c+ R), just below the second portaledge camp on the wall. *Julia Cassou*

outcome. If I tried my hardest, I could accept failure without regrets.

"I'm just going to take a look," I said.

"Yes. Just ease into it," Pete coached. "Take a few falls, slowly build up your confidence, and then smash it out!"

Julia and Seán W watched from below as the silent air filled with shared excitement. I thought of Keita, and how he would have loved to be here; I thought about how life is fragile, and how it can be taken at any moment. I put Keita's photo in my chest pocket, feeling it give me strength.

Back in the corner, I moved with precision, my feet confidently smearing, my palms pushing on the nothingness. There I was, far above the bolt, that old, familiar place. I had visualized this moment so many times over the past year. I looked to my right: The flake was within reach! I couldn't believe it. I threw in a cam and gently shifted my weight onto it. A hollow cracking sound reverberated as the flake expanded. A fall from here, with the bolt five meters below and to the left, could create an ugly swing into the dihedral—but the flake held. I continued up with a mix of aid and free climbing, finally reaching better rock and protection.

"It goes, boys and girl!" I hollered. We all cheered in joy.

A steep but featured black basalt dike brought me to a vertical face without protection, where I placed a bolt for an anchor. The next 30 meters looked like intricate aid on flakes and seams. So I called up Seán W, speculating it was probably the last section

Villanueva O'Driscoll on the complex and pumpy pitch 12: A2+ beaks and hooks to a pendulum, followed by 8a/5.13b free climbing. ***Julia Cassou***

where he could make his aid skills shine. Fortunately, the wall was at its steepest, as Seán put a few big holes in the air. "I haven't taken this many falls on any of the hard aid on El Cap," he shared. Eventually, he reached the promising crack system that looked to stretch clear to the summit.

The next 30 meters were a seam on which Seán W made his funny birds sing. I named this pitch the "Magic Salathé Flame," since it looks like the single-pitch trad line Magic Line (Vernal Falls, Yosemite), but with the exposure of the Salathé headwall (El Capitan), in an alpine setting similar to Eternal Flame (Trango Tower, Pakistan). The seam turned into a finger crack, and Pete and I started switching leads, free climbing pitch after pitch of spectacular, quality cracks, high on the headwall of Mirror Wall. As we drifted in this ocean of granite, the views broadened and the tip of the ice cap appeared behind the surrounding peaks; the glacier below now seemed very distant.

One evening, as I was sorting out the anchor before zipping down the fixed lines to our portaledges, the photo of Keita fell out of my pocket. It hung for a second, floating in an updraft, before I quickly grabbed it and put it back into my pocket.

"We still need you!" I said.

On August 22, day ten on the route, we committed to a summit push. Taking the sharp end, Julia delicately weaved her way up, dodging ice and snow, until she liberated us with a cry of "SUMMIT!" After some big, emotional hugs, I pulled out the photograph of Keita for the group picture. We sat on the summit couch, our feet dangling over 1,000 meters of air, enjoying the view of the endless ice cap and basking in a rare bit of sunshine.

The next day, back at our portaledges, we finally took a much-needed rest day. I was reading in the portaledge when shutterbug Julia, hanging on a rope above,

ABOVE: Cassou, Whittaker, Villanueva O'Driscoll, Warren—and Kurakami—on top. ***Seán Warren***

LEFT: High camp on Mirror Wall, which saw only about three hours of sun per day. ***Julia Cassou***

asked me to stick out my head for a picture. Reluctantly, I sat up. As I fumbled through the ledge opening, the photograph of Keita, which I'd been using as a bookmark, fell out. It started to spin extraordinarily fast as it floated in the breeze, giving the photo a flickering effect, Keita just smiling his big, infectious smile. Then, almost as if to say he was no longer needed, Keita flickered away from us.

As Keita wrote in his story "A Thousand Days of Lapis Lazuli" in *Alpinist* 56, "The rock we climb is a mirror, and in it, we see the silent reflections of dialogues that have taken place between climbers across many decades—and also within ourselves. Out of all this action and conversation, something greater emerges that is transmitted from generation to generation, forming a kind of collective intelligence, an influence that might still flicker across great spans of time and space, mere fragments of dreams of the billions of lives that come into the world—and leave the world."

During his life, Keita had the *shakuhachi* flute player's name of Ryu-shin, which translates to "Heart of the Dragon." This climb is named in his memory.

SUMMARY: First ascent of Ryu-Shin (1,000m, 8b R A2+) on the northwest-facing Mirror Wall, Renland, East Greenland, by Julia Cassou, Seán Villanueva O'Driscoll, Seán Warren, and Pete Whittaker, August 11–29, 2024. They reached the summit on August 22.

During the descent, the team stayed on the wall for seven additional days, aiming to redpoint various pitches that had not gone free during the first ascent. These included the run-out "razor blade slab" of pitch nine (Whittaker, 8b R); pitches eight and ten, leading to the second portaledge camp (Warren, 7b+ R and 6c+ R, respectively); the pitch 13 dihedral (Villanueva O'Driscoll, 7c+ R); and the pitch 16 finger crack (Whittaker, 7b+). A detailed topo of the route is at the *AAJ* website.

Villanueva O'Driscoll writes: "I tried my hand at the Magic Salathé Flame, pitch 15, laybacking the thin, offset seam above the wildest exposure possible, my feet smearing, every move feeling nails and low percentage. In the end, we managed to free all but that pitch and pitches 11, 12, and 14. I do think these four pitches will someday go, providing a spectacular free wall. But for us, with the time we had left, they were just way too difficult."

ABOUT THE AUTHOR: Seán Villanueva O'Driscoll was born and raised in Belgium, with Irish-Spanish roots. He has been climbing challenging big walls in ranges around the world for the past 20 years.

ODYSSEA BOREALIS

A 35-DAY WILDERNESS ADVENTURE IN GREENLAND

SILVAN SCHÜPBACH

A **first ascent** is not about the what, but the how. New territory is a finite resource, and that's why I want to climb new routes as cleanly as possible. I prefer to climb without bolts and to approach the mountain under my own steam on an expedition. In a real adventure, success is uncertain; the mountain has a chance of not being climbed. I like that.

Matteo Della Bordella, Alex Gammeter, Symon Welfringer, and I reached Tasiilaq in East Greenland in mid-July. Our climbing goal was the huge, unclimbed northwest face of Drøneren (1,867m), near the head of South Skjoldungen Fjord (Inugsuarmiut Fjord). The mountain is more than 300 kilometers southwest of Tasiilaq by air and much farther by sea. Our plan was to kayak there and back, adding significant uncertainty to our adventure.

Although the Skjoldungen area has been settled at various times, it has had no residents for more than 50 years. The climbing history in the area centers on American Mike Libecki, who made six journeys to Skjoldungen by motorboat, from 2002 to 2017, and completed first ascents on various formations, some solo and some with partners. During his final trip, Libecki and friends started up a very steep wall on the northwest face of Drøneren, which he had labeled Granddaddy Tower, but had to abandon the attempt after 300 meters and switch to a smaller objective because of poor weather and lack of time—sea ice had delayed their journey to the fjord by ten days.

The team encountered four polar bears during the trip, some of them too close for comfort. ***Silvan Schüpbach***

Unfortunately, the conditions were similarly bad for our planned approach. Record pack ice blocked many East Greenland settlements when we arrived, making navigation impossible. We waited for days in Tasiilaq.

I had paddled a kayak to climbs in East Greenland during three previous expeditions (*see AAJs 2015, 2017, and 2022*), and, ironically, I had always said this was much better than being on a classic Himalayan expedition, because there is no downtime. In the Himalaya, the base camp is reached quickly, with the support of local helpers, and if the weather is bad, you just wait it out and let the cook spoil you. But when you're kayaking in Greenland, you have to cook for yourself, look for a suitable camp every evening, and even in bad weather keep paddling toward your destination. There is always something to do—though only, of course, when the sea ice permits you to travel.

A *piteraq*, a katabatic storm from inland, finally relieved us and pushed the pack ice away from the coast. Knowing that the ice could close again at any moment, we opted to begin our journey by motorboat, starting on July 23 from Isortoq, about 60 kilometers west of Tasiilaq, and reaching a launch point for our kayaks another 90 kilometers down the coast on July 24.

We were finally alone in the wilderness! Long days at sea followed as we slowly paddled south. Huge glaciers and barren mountains lined the coast, while massive icebergs crowded the ocean.

Nothing was given to us; every day at sea was a surprise. One day, as we traversed a large fjord, the water's surface started freezing. Soon, we couldn't break the ice layer. With everyone pushing the leader's kayak, we barely managed to get back to shore—escaping a long night out on the water. Another time, we were almost crushed by ice floes as the tide changed. After the sixth day of paddling, a storm pinned us in the tent for 60 hours, all of which we spent hoping the nylon wouldn't tear. The wind even sent small rocks flying through the air. Just before the storm's peak, we built a small platform under an overhanging rock—the most sheltered spot we could find.

We started each morning with the open question of what surprise the day would bring. Nobody thought about the climbing to come—the sea and the Greenlandic wilderness had a firm grip on us.

With no designated leaders, our team functioned like a small democracy, with all its advantages and disadvantages. Even deciding where to take the next pee break could lead to long discussions. We were an intense group, with strong opinions and slow decision-making processes. It didn't always make for a good atmosphere, but it was the key to our success and safety in this punishing environment. I look back with pride at the decisions we made. They were painstakingly discussed, and always good and focused.

After ten days and 300 kilometers of kayaking, we finally reached our destination. At the head of Skjoldungen's twin 45-kilometer fjords is Dronning Marie Dal (Queen Marie Valley), which is like an oasis compared with the barren landscape we had been passing; now we saw lush vegetation, clear streams and rivers, and beautiful mountains—a picture-postcard idyll. Relieved, we beached the boats, set up base camp close to the water among a handful of big boulders, and turned our thoughts toward climbing.

Drøneren—the peak's name on the official Danish map, meaning "Drummer," perhaps referring to the sound of falling ice and rock—is a huge, complex massif. The northwest face is hidden in a side valley, invisible from our camp, and we were impatient to ferry our gear over and see the wall up close. The approach through the flat valley floor had its own special charm. To keep our clothes dry, we waded naked through rivers and swamps, getting stung by thousands of sand flies. Farther up, we

climbed over moraines and firn fields to the glacier below the wall. As if to welcome us, shortly after our arrival, a huge boulder fell from the left part of the wall and crashed spectacularly at its foot. After this, we quickly agreed to stick to the central pillar for our climb.

To save space and weight, we had packed only two inflatable portaledges and a few ropes for fixing, including our tagline and dynamic ropes. On the last half day of predicted good weather, on August 6, Matteo and Symon fixed the first five pitches. This first part was mainly easy but sketchy ground on semi-solid rock. Subsequently, the weather became very unsettled. We usually had one day of good weather followed by two days of rain.

On another day, we climbed up to fix the last of our ropes. This time, Alex and I reached a point on the pillar where there were no more cracks. Inspecting photos of the wall we'd taken from below, I saw a small crack appearing ten meters left of our position. I was very keen on this challenge—a hard but logical crux across a run-out traverse.

At first, I tried to climb free and onsight, but I soon realized the Pecker I'd placed wouldn't be good enough, so I aided for one meter. The rock was flaky, and I ended up linking up four shallow Peckers, with the equation that "four times bad equals one times good." After some hesitating, I decided to go all in and free climb the traverse. Although there were some nice crimps, the rock was crumbly. Right before the crack, a foothold broke. With a last, panic-driven effort, I caught the crack and placed a good cam. Even though it was only a few meters long, this crux pitch will forever be written in my climbing memory book.

Matteo checked out the pitch on second, did some cleaning and ticking, and gave all the beta to Symon, who freed the pitch

TOP: Entering the north arm of Skjoldungen Fjord, with an impressive unnamed, unclimbed peak in back. *Silvan Schüpbach*

BOTTOM: The author near base camp with an arctic char. Fishing was a welcome distraction during the long waits for good weather. *Alex Gammeter*

with ease. We proposed a grade of 7b R for this crux pitch.

By now we had fixed around ten pitches, using every meter of rope we had.

We'd had our hands full ever since leaving Tasiilaq—exactly what I like about these expeditions. Unfortunately, after these first efforts, there was no weather window in sight to finish the climb. During one rainy day, a cruise ship came by, breaking the tedium at base camp. Armed to the teeth for defense against polar bears, the guide and well-heeled guests visited us briefly, saying they would soon have to return to the ship to eat in one of the three restaurants on board. Unfortunately, we weren't invited, but at least they left a case of beer for us to enjoy in camp.

We knew the base camp bouldering very well by now, and Matteo had perfected the technique of catching fish with an ice tool. Nevertheless, our motivation decreased with each day we spent waiting to climb.

In the meantime, it snowed a lot in the mountains—the peaks around us looked ready for ski season—forcing us to abort one attempt early. During another attempt to move beyond the fixed ropes, a vicious storm came roaring in, catching us by surprise. We were already high on the ropes when small rocks started to fall. After a fridge-sized rock passed by, we retreated again. One of our fixed ropes had been cut by falling rocks.

Running low on food and time, we had a decision to make: Either we would bail on the climb and start the return trip by kayak now, or we'd allot our remaining time to climbing and call the motorboat operator to arrange a pickup closer to base camp. We opted for one last chance to climb, giving up the plan to kayak all the way back.

RUNNING LOW ON FOOD AND TIME, WE HAD A DECISION TO MAKE. WE OPTED FOR ONE LAST CHANCE TO CLIMB, GIVING UP THE PLAN TO KAYAK ALL THE WAY BACK.

On August 15, we abandoned a third attempt due to rain. It was only on our fourth attempt, on August 17—pushing right up against our deadline for leaving the fjord—that we were able to give a real effort.

When we finally reached the end of the fixed ropes again, Symon and Matteo climbed quickly into the new terrain. Meanwhile, Alex and I carried the gear. Our climbing strategy was: one leader and one follower with Jumars, and then the second party following with Jumars and hauling. It was great to finally be on the wall and giving it our best shot! Challenging pitches on good rock were followed by ledges and sloping terrain with scree and brittle rock. A steep pillar offered complex climbing with great exposure. Late in the evening, we reached a ledge that we had scoped as a bivouac site. Unfortunately, it was sloping, and we had to dig in the scree and snow to find a place to sleep. The mood was finally good, though, and motivation remained high.

The next day, Alex and I climbed ahead. It was cold, and the higher we got, the more snow we found. Steep, snowy gullies led us to the left. Although the terrain became easier, the conditions got worse and worse. Alex climbed some mixed pitches—without crampons or an ice axe. A final headwall of about 100 meters towered above. Fortunately, we found a corner that was largely free of snow. Overhanging climbing with maximum exposure led to the foot of the impressive ice cap overlaying the summit plateau. What a way to finish the wall!

A hundred meters later, we stood on the summit. Drøneren is a high, free-standing mountain with commanding views: We could see the vast Greenlandic ice sheet, the many impressive mountains around us, and the Arctic Ocean off in the distance, shimmering like silver.

We rappelled to the bivouac in the last light of the day. That night, we had the best summit party, reveling in our success as the northern lights danced above.

The same day that we reached base camp, tired and satisfied, we received bad news via our satellite phone: Our hoped-for motorboat ride back out of Skjoldungen Fjord was not possible, due to its distance from Tasiilaq. So, we packed our things and loaded the kayaks. We still had enough food for four days and wanted to make it at least half of the 300 kilometers back north, within range of a boat pickup.

Just as we were getting into the kayaks, a very curious polar bear appeared right behind us. Alarmed, I took out my rifle and fired a warning shot. The bear continued toward us. I fired a second time. Finally, the bear retreated, and we hurried to get into the kayaks and say goodbye to our base camp oasis.

During the following days at sea, we had mostly good weather but decided to keep night watch in case of more bear visits. After four days and paddling 150 kilometers, we set up our last camp and waited for the boat. But no one came. It wasn't until evening that we learned no one was prepared to pick us up! Many panicked phone calls later, we managed to arrange another boat.

The next morning, at dawn, another polar bear tried to break into my kayak, but it ran away when I screamed. In the afternoon, a boat arrived, and the tension of 35 days in the wilderness vanished in an instant. Our odyssey was over.

The Drøneren massif, rising nearly 1,900 meters above the nearby fjord, showing the 1,200-meter line of Odyssea Borealis. A team led by Mike Libecki started up the shadowed face on the left in 2017 but switched to Plan B Tower, off-picture to the left. ***Silvan Schüpbach***

SUMMARY: First ascent of the northwest face of Drøneren (1,867m), near South Skjoldungen Fjord (Inugsuarmiut Fjord) in southeast Greenland, by Odyssea Borealis (1,200m, 35 pitches, 7b R). The ascent was by Matteo Della Bordella (Italy), Alex Gammeter (Switzerland), Silvan Schüpbach (Switzerland), and Symon Welfringer (France). They began work on the route on August 6, 2024. After fixing ten pitches, the team completed the route in two days, summiting August 18, and descended the next day. Their 35 days of wilderness travel included 450 kilometers of kayaking. (*See photos of more peaks and walls in this area at the AAJ website.*)

ABOUT THE AUTHOR: Silvan Schüpbach lives in Thun, Switzerland, and has made expeditions to Nepal, Pakistan, Greenland, and Patagonia. Originally a biotechnology engineer, he now works for the Swiss Alpine Club and as a mountain guide.

DIRTY DANCING

TWO NEW ROUTES IN THE INDIAN HIMALAYA

MANU PELLISSIER

"This **has never been climbed,"** Dhruv tells us. A passionate local climber and a living guidebook, Dhruv Joshi helped put our expedition to India together. He points to a beautiful pyramid just to the south of Nanda Devi East: "About 6,300 meters." Three pairs of skeptical eyes turn toward him. Marko asks, "Are you sure?"

Manu Pellissier leads the tenth pitch of day two on the attempt on Nanda Devi East, a maze of down-sloping rock and rotten ice. ***Marko Prezelj***

Dhruv nods in the distinctive Indian manner, tilting his head from side to side. "Very sure!" The seed is planted. To hell with gradual acclimatization—this mountain is ours. But first, the scene and the players: The idea had emerged almost a decade ago, following a challenging expedition to Cerro Kishtwar with Hayden Kennedy, Urban Novak, and Marko Prezelj. I had told them about Nanda Devi East, an open peak with beautiful ice lines. Then time passed. Hayden was gone. Our lives filled up with other climbs, other obligations. But this mountain stayed in a corner of my mind.

Two years ago, at an Iranian friend's wedding, I met Archil Badriashvili, a young Georgian climber who was in France to receive a Piolet d'Or for his bold ascent of Saraghrar Northwest in Pakistan. He wanted to climb in Chamonix, but autumn monsoons had shut everything down. Instead, I took him to some dry-tooling cliffs in Savoie.

A few months later, following a guided trip in Svaneti, Georgia, we met again in Tbilisi. Over drinks—Georgia's second national sport after alpinism—we talked about mountains and projects, and at some point, Marko's name and Nanda Devi East came up.

Suddenly, everything clicked. A selfie sent to Slovenia, another round of drinks, and the project was born. The three of us, on a big, beautiful mountain.

May 19, 2024. Nine days after leaving Europe, we arrive at base camp at 4,300 meters in the Lawan Valley. With us is Bhagwan, who helped us in 2015 on Cerro Kishtwar, along with Debrash and Mukesh, our two cooks. The team is complete. A few days later, we are joined by Kushal the shepherd, his 300 sheep, and his two dogs, Bachu and Pinkie—expert salami thieves. A small village forms at the foot of the mountain.

Dhruv stays with us for a few days, passionately recounting his ascents and the history of the region's peaks. He delivers details—dates, times, altitudes—with an astonishing level of precision. He works for the Indian Mountaineering Foundation (IMF), which issues climbing permits. Our briefing in Delhi had been surreal. Since satellite phones are banned in India, we asked about the emergency protocol in case of an accident. The IMF director's answer stunned us as much as it amused us: "You make smoke signals!"

After a few days of acclimatization and exploring, we make our final decision: Dhruv's unclimbed peak will be our first objective. The approach requires a long day of hiking. Bhagwan and Debrash help us carry loads. Bhagwan is like the fourth man on our team—he knows us well. He has the spirit of a mountaineer—sharp, critical. His definition of alpine style is blunt and to the point: "Muscle, mind, and money."

THE EAST FACE RISES MORE THAN 1,200 METERS ABOVE US, BUT WE CONVINCE OURSELVES WE CAN PUSH TO THE TOP IN A SINGLE DAY.

We establish a bivy at 5,000 meters. The east face rises more than 1,200 meters above us, but we convince ourselves we can push to the top and start the descent in a single day, bivying at Longstaff Col on our way down. Just in case, though, we've packed for four days. We climb a 300-meter snow couloir, then veer right toward our chosen line. The first technical pitch makes it clear: The rock quality and technical difficulty will stretch this climb beyond a single day.

By 5 p.m., we reach the base of the ice gully we plan to follow to the top. There's no way we'll push through before nightfall. Marko, who has been dragging two-meter-

long bamboo poles for two days, finally reveals his plan.

"We will bivy here," he announces.

Archil and I look at him with a mix of amusement and disbelief. Marko pulls out his magic tarp and fixes the poles to the sides, creating a sort of hammock that we fill with snow. After an hour of shoveling, we have a horizontal platform big enough for our tent.

"I can't believe this works," Archil mutters.

"Welcome to Marko's School of Suffering," I say.

We don't know it yet, but this will become our standard technique for the next month—to Marko's great delight.

Morning comes, and waking up in our ultra-light French-made tent—worth the price of a house in India—is brutal. There's more ice inside than outside.

"This reminds me of my father's stories about Soviet alpinism," Archil mutters, shivering.

The climbing above is harder than expected. Conditions worsen. Water starts running down the rock. The snow slopes we thought would be straightforward feel alarmingly thin.

At 5 p.m., we reach the summit—6,344 meters.

Stepping into the sun, we realize the adventure isn't over. The ridge down to Longstaff Col has unexpected obstacles. Abalakovs, snow mushrooms, pitons, rappels, downclimbing… Seven hours after leaving the summit, we reach the col. But again, things don't go as planned. What Marko had optimistically described as a "ski slope" below the col turns out to be a steep, unstable mix of mud and snow. Four hours of pure focus. Nobody speaks. Even Marko doesn't take out his camera. It takes 12 hours to reach base camp.

TOP: Nanda Shori (6,344m) is on the left; the team ascended the east side, facing the camera, and descended via Longstaff Col in the center. The col was first attained in 1905, in an early attempt to reach the Inner Sanctuary. At right is Nanda Devi East (Sunanda Devi), with the triangular, 1,600-meter central pillar of the southeast face leading up to the south ridge, the route of the first ascent. *Marko Prezelj*

BOTTOM: Preparing the second bivouac site on Nanda Shori. *Marko Prezelj*

Magnificent view of Nanda Devi (left) and Nanda Devi East (Sunanda Devi) from the descent off Nanda Shori toward Longstaff Col. The first ascent of 7,434-meter Nanda Devi East was by the south ridge, facing the camera, in 1939, by Poles Jakub Bujak and Janusz Klarner. *Marko Prezelj*

Archil Badriashvili gets dirty on the southeast face of Nanda Devi East. The freezing level topped 6,000 meters during the climbers' attempt. They reached 5,900 meters. ***Marko Prezelj***

The privilege of opening a new route on an untouched 6,344-meter peak sinks in slowly. We celebrate accordingly. After discussing with Bhagwan, we name the mountain Nanda Shori: "Daughter of Nanda." The route? Dirty Dancing.

On an expedition, time takes on a different rhythm. I appreciate the hyperactivity of a multiday climb just as much as the stillness of so-called rest days. These days are precious—not only for the essential recovery they provide but also for their simple routines: eat, drink, read, talk.

Six days after our ascent of Nanda Shori, we're setting off again. This time for big mama: the southeast face of Nanda Devi East, also known as Sunanda Devi, 7,434 meters.

But first, the ritual: laying out all our gear on a tarp and debating for hours over whether we really need the number 3 Camalot.

Our planned line is the central pillar on the face: 1,600 meters of climbing, linking up with the normal route on the south ridge, first climbed in 1939, at 6,900 meters.

The approach from base camp takes a full day. After balancing along the moraine like highliners, we leave Bhagwan and Debrash behind; they've helped us carry loads, but from here, we're on our own.

The terrain quickly becomes trickier. The glacier is a mess—loose stones covering black ice. The weight of our packs grinds us down. We plan to bivy at 5,200 meters, just below the icefall we're intending to climb. But as we approach, the whole thing collapses before our eyes. In a matter of minutes, the weather shifts violently. Snow starts hammering us as we pitch the tent.

The plan has to change.

We decide to attack via a different gully, farther left. The first pitches set the tone: Marko pulls out all the stops, leading through vertical, unprotected walls. We soon realize we'll have to traverse several gullies and buttresses to link up with our original line. The forecast had called for light snowfall in the afternoon. At 9 a.m., it's snowing like it's Christmas.

By midafternoon, the spindrift is growing heavier. Trying to push through steep, rotten snow, I stop to place protection and hear Marko's irritated voice.

"What are you doing?"

"I'm leading," I snap.

That ends the discussion.

Archil watches in silence as we two old friends argue and then—the privilege of long-standing friendship—make peace a minute later and move on, laughing.

At 6 p.m., after 16 pitches, I find what looks like a potential bivy ledge. I start digging, using our magic tarp to anchor the site. By 8 p.m., we're all crammed into our portable freezer. It's still snowing.

To our great surprise, Archil pulls out half a liter of *chacha*—homemade Georgian alcohol, one step removed from ethanol. I can't help but think about the number 3 Camalot we left at base camp because it was "too heavy"—it would have been really useful today. But a few sips of *chacha* are enough to warm us up and find some dark humor in a day that pushed us to our limits.

Morning brings blue skies but also unseasonably high temperatures. Archil moves into the lead. It takes him two hours to climb the first pitch of steep snow. The next pitch is worse—snow, loose rock, mud. Another two hours.

We reach 5,900 meters. From here, we need to traverse another 200 meters to reach the central buttress. The snow runnels give way to mud, streams, and falling rock.

It's decision time. If we go farther, retreat will become a nightmare, and none of us is confident we can push to the top in these conditions. We take time to listen to everyone's thoughts. The final call is unanimous: We go down.

The biggest reason—besides fear—is the conditions are slowing us so much that we're reaching the limits of the alpine style we love. Style matters.

That day, we learn later, the freezing level rose above 6,000 meters. Delhi hit 51°C. Thousands of kilometers away, in France, dark storm clouds gathered.

Our disappointment seems trivial. We chose to be here. The extreme temperatures we faced will have far greater consequences for people in the world's growing megacities. For us, it's just a few rappels and a long march back to base camp to digest our failure and think about our next attempt. **The heat won't let up,** and our plan to return to Nanda Devi East slips away.

We still have time left, though, and we want to make the most of our trip. Across from base camp, two striking peaks and their north faces are calling: Nanda Kot (6,851m) and Changuch (6,322m). We make our way up the moraine leading to both mountains, and soon it's clear—we'll go for Changuch. The approach to Nanda Kot looks far more complicated.

Changuch was first climbed in 2009, by the northwest ridge, by a British-Indian expedition led by Martin Moran; they approached from the Lawan Valley to the north, same as us. Two years later, Dhruv led an Indian team that repeated the northwest ridge, reaching it from the south. We choose a couloir that cuts through the northeast face—still unclimbed.

THE GLACIER IS A MESS—LOOSE STONES COVERING BLACK ICE. THE WEIGHT OF OUR PACKS GRINDS US DOWN.

This time, better acclimatized, we go light. We leave base camp early, aiming to gain the pillar bordering the couloir and bivy as high as possible. A few hours into the approach, we reach the base of the face.

Then we see them. A herd of bharal, Himalayan blue sheep—30 of them—moving up the pillar. They're much faster than us. Instead of veering off, they keep climbing, heading straight up.

By midafternoon, we have set up camp on a ledge at 5,600 meters, at the base of a rocky tower. Focused on carving out a platform, we barely notice the falling stones. We assume it's the heat. Then the rocks get closer. When we look up, we see the blue sheep, higher up the ridge, scraping at the ledges with their hooves.

Deliberately.

They've climbed all the way to the top of the pillar at 6,200 meters. And now, unable to escape onto the other side,

Pellissier moves up the northwest ridge of Changuch, safe at last from rocks that had been kicked onto the climbers by Himalayan blue sheep on the steep face below. One stone punctured their tent. *Marko Prezelj*

they've decided the best defense is attack. At first, we find it funny. Then it stops being funny. They're 30. We're three. And we're trespassing on their territory.

Night falls. The bombardment slows, but one particularly bold attacker moves closer. He refines his aim. A stone rips through the tent, landing right between Archil's leg and my head. On the upside, the tent now has better ventilation.

The rockfall stops for the night, but we sleep with one eye open, helmets on, backpacks as shields. At sunrise, Marko crosses the couloir quietly. But our neighbors spot him immediately. The barrage resumes. Archil and I wait an hour for a lull before making our move. It takes seven hours to reach the summit ridge. Only when we reach their level do the sheep decide to retreat. They descend the pillar in under a minute, without dislodging a single rock.

The stress lifts, but the final 150 meters to the summit present a nasty mix of black ice, corniced ridges, and whiteout.

There's no summit euphoria. Just the weight of the descent ahead. We'd planned to go light and move fast. Instead, we're slow, exhausted, dehydrated. Eighteen hours after leaving our small tent, and after a long series of nighttime rappels, we stumble back to our bivy.

Marko collapses inside the tent. Archil and I start melting snow. Then I hear it. Voices. At first, faint. But soon, distinct. English. Hindi.

I freeze. "Archil, do you hear that?"

He looks at me—half amused, half uneasy.

I step outside. The voices grow clearer. Conversations. Whispers. It goes on for over an hour. I know what's happening. The exhaustion, stress, dehydration, and altitude—it's creating something between a dream and reality. Eventually, I fall asleep. By morning, the voices are gone. Later, back home, I read *Les Hallucinés* by Thomas Vennin, a book on high-altitude auditory hallucinations. It's reassuring.

This expedition was full of surprises. A wild, intense experience with Marko and Archil, one we feel lucky to have shared. More than ever, unpredictable conditions in the mountains force us to adapt—the essence of alpinism.

Once the sting of failure on Nanda Devi East fades, the idea of returning starts creeping in again.

Next year. Or in ten.

ABOVE LEFT: Badriashvili, Pellissier, and Prezelj (left to right). *Dhruv Joshi*

ABOVE RIGHT: The Blue Sheep Couloir on the northeast face of Changuch (6,322m). The trio continued to the summit by the northwest ridge, first climbed in 2009. *Marko Prezelj*

EPILOGUE

Archil, a few weeks after we got back from India, you went off to guide young Georgian climbers on Shkhelda in your beloved Caucasus. Passing on what you'd learned meant a lot to you—it was part of what you got from your dad, and you really wanted to keep that spirit alive by sharing it with the next generation.

On August 10, 2024, lightning struck blindly and unfairly at the top of that mountain. You fell, and even now I'm still coming to grips with the hole you've left in my life and in the lives of everyone you touched.

We met by chance at a friend's wedding, and after a few drinks, we just clicked. Climbing together was a natural choice. Our expedition to India only deepened that connection. I'll always remember your laughter, your endless *chacha* toasts, and the tears in your eyes when we decided to turn back on Nanda Devi East.

It's painful to write this. I can't help thinking of all the friends we've lost—Hayden, Antoine, Charles, Ben, Attila, and so many others. Despite it all, we'll keep going back out there—imagining impossible lines, hauling heavy packs, slogging through deep snow, and hanging on to holds that are way too small.

Travel light, my friend.

SUMMARY: First ascent of Nanda Shori (6,344m) by the east face (Dirty Dancing, 1,200m, M5 WI5 5a), May 29–June 1, 2024, with descent by the north ridge to Longstaff Col. Attempt on the southeast pillar of Nanda Devi East (7,434m), June 9–10, reaching 5,900 meters in 16 pitches (M5 WI5+). First ascent of the northeast face of Changuch (6,322m) by the Blue Sheep Couloir (1,000m, WI4), continuing to the top on the northwest ridge, June 14–16. All climbs by Archil Badriashvili (Georgia), Manu Pellissier (France), and Marko Prezelj (Slovenia).

ABOUT THE AUTHOR: Manu Pellissier, 50, shares life with his wife and three children, guiding, playing bass in a band, and new-routing around the world—when he has free time and is not injured.

This story was translated from French by Anna Piunova.

CLIMBS + EXPEDITIONS

Climbs & Expeditions reports generally are arranged geographically, from north to south and from west to east, within a specific country or region. Unless noted, the reports cover climbs in 2024. The complete *AAJ* archive, from 1929 to the present, can be searched at *publications.americanalpineclub.org*. Online reports frequently contain additional text, photos, maps, and topos. Look for these symbols indicating additional online resources:

FULL-LENGTH REPORT

ADDITIONAL PHOTOS

MAPS OR TOPOS

VIDEO OR MULTIMEDIA

Aerial view down the eastern arm of Paradise (Akekule) Lake in Xinjiang Province, China. The first rock and alpine routes in this area were climbed in 2024; the peak in back (ca 4,700m) was not climbed. See page 332. *Expedition Photo*

ALASKA | Alaska Range

Looking west-southwest to Mt. Andrew, above the Dall Glacier. The first ascent generally followed the far side of the north ridge, the long ridgeline diagonaling to the summit from right to left. The mountain to the right is Peak 8,900'+ ("Mt. Gannon"), first climbed in 2020. ***Zach Lovell***

MT. ANDREW, FIRST ASCENT AND SKI DESCENT

From April 15 to 21, I led a ski mountaineering trip on the Dall Glacier, south of Mt. Russell, with Marek and Sarah Mrzyglocki. We experienced everything from sunshine powder days to whiteout and breaker crust, and we carefully assessed conditions before focusing on a summit objective: unclimbed Peak 8,205' (62.75572, -151.98751). This mountain is immediately south of Mt. Mason (9,680'), which Joseph Hobby and I climbed for its first ascent in 2022, along with the adjacent Mt. Stansfield (9,200'), both of which we named for our friend Mason Stansfield, who died in a skiing accident on the nearby Eldridge Glacier in 2021.

On April 20, we skied northwest from base camp up the fork of the Dall Glacier south of Mt. Mason and Mt. Stansfield. After skinning and briefly cramponing up a chute to bypass an icefall, we reached our objective's north face and north ridge. We roped up and cautiously climbed a line weaving between the two, avoiding complex seracs and crevasses. We were able to skin the lower portion of our route thanks to ski crampons, but boot crampons and ice tools became necessary as we got higher. The final few hundred feet of névé and blue ice accepted excellent screws.

After a few windless minutes on the summit, we began our ski descent, staying near our ascent line. Ski conditions were variable but edge-able; we made one brief downclimb through the blue ice. All the while, we basked in our dramatic position, surrounded by gorgeous peaks illuminated by soft evening light.

We named the peak Mt. Andrew after a very close friend, Andrew Plagens, who passed away due to cancer in the fall of 2023. He was 31. When they were both alive, Andrew and Mason were inseparable; it felt fitting to have their namesake peaks so close to one another.

Our route, 420 Ridge, included snow and ice up to 65° and 1,700' of roped climbing; we skied 3,800 vertical feet back to camp from the summit, returning after a round trip of 12 hours.

—Zach Lovell

MT. RUSSELL, EAST FACE AND SOUTH RIDGE

At 9:45 a.m. on April 27, Paul Roderick dropped Sam Hennessey and me on the upper Dall Glacier, directly beneath the nearly 6,000'-tall east face of Mt. Russell (11,670')—our objective.

We had in mind a rapid round trip. After quickly setting up a tent to stash food and bivouac gear, we departed half an hour after landing, carrying light packs. We started up the left side of the east face, following the same line that Sam had climbed the previous spring with Courtney Kitchen and Lisa Van Sciver. On that attempt, they carried skis with the hope of descending off the summit. After 3,600' of snow and ice slopes, they reached the south ridge, which they found scoured down to unskiable hard ice. They retreated and skied back down to the Dall Glacier.

The route Sam and I followed on the east face used several rock buttresses as natural protection against hazard from some seracs (that appeared quite benign and inactive). About mid-height on the face, the terrain steepened to 50° and the snow we had been booting up gave way to sustained hard névé and occasional ice—much icier conditions than what Sam and his partners had found. We continued to a flat area at 9,600', near the base of the upper south ridge of the mountain. Until this point, we had climbed unroped for most of the way.

The upper south ridge was the route followed by Mt. Russell's first ascent team in 1962 (*see AAJ 1963*). They accessed it from the west side via an airplane landing on the Chedotlothna Glacier (which is no longer feasible because of glacial recession). This section of ridge was repeated by Freddie Wilkinson and Dana Drummond in 2017 after they climbed a new route up the direct south face and ridge of Russell (5,000', Alaska Grade 4; *see AAJ 2018*).

TOP: Mt. Russell from the southeast, rising above the Dall Glacier. (1) Drummond-Wilkinson (2017). (2) Hennessey-Westman (5,700', 50° ice, 80°+ rime ice, 2024). (3) East face (Auble-Townsend, 1989). (4) Northeast ridge (Brown-Hauck-Jablonowski-Kensler-Osborne, 1972). ***Mark Westman***

BOTTOM: Just beneath the summit of Mt. Russell, Sam Hennessey surmounts a near-vertical wall of rime ice. ***Mark Westman***

From where we intersected the ridge, there were several tricky sections of traversing across 50° ice and tightrope walking on knife-edge ridges. We used the rope for these parts, then continued unroped for several hundred feet up the moderate final ridge, easily avoiding numerous crevasses. Just beneath the summit, we reached a near-vertical wall of rime ice, surrounded by fantastically rimed gargoyle formations that spoke to the ferocious winds that buffet this mountain. We belayed the short bulge of rime and minutes later became only the ninth team to reach the summit, just seven hours after leaving our landing site. There wasn't a breath of wind. I had made storm-plagued attempts on Russell in 1997 and 2019, and there were many other seasons where I had partners and dates lined up but never left Talkeetna due to poor weather. It was truly gratifying to reach the top of this elusive mountain.

Sam and I descended to the landing site in just four hours, making for an 11-hour round trip and the mountain's first one-day ascent. Paul picked us up the following morning.

While all of the terrain we followed had been climbed previously, the east face and south ridge had not been linked as a singular summit route. (The east face was climbed directly to the summit by Dave Auble and Charles Townsend in 1989, following a line farther right on the face, and remains the mountain's most technically challenging route; *see AAJ 1990*.) Having attempted the now very broken northeast ridge in 1997, and having climbed most of the Wilkinson-Drummond route in 2019, I feel confident the Hennessey-Westman (5,700', UIAA Grade V, 50° ice, 80°+ rime ice) is the fastest and most straightforward way to the summit of Mt. Russell. While the technical difficulties are modest, the route is sustained, serious, and committing. Future parties not wishing to single-push the route will find a perfectly flat bivouac site on the south ridge at approximately 9,600', albeit very exposed to the wind.

—Mark Westman

MANTOK I, SMALL TALK COULOIR; MT. CHARLES, FIRST ASCENT, VIA NORTHEAST SIDE

The little-visited Yentna Glacier, west of the Kahiltna Glacier system, is sandwiched between the southwestern buttress of Mt. Foraker and the northeast side of Mt. Russell. The Denali wilderness boundary horizontally transects the Yentna, so planes can't land on its northernmost few miles. Accessing the peaks in this area requires a three-to four-mile approach on skis—hence why it is rarely visited!

In 2023, Fred Caloggero and I blocked out two possible windows to visit the Yentna, but the weather didn't cooperate. We never left Talkeetna.

A year later, Fred and I flew in to the Yentna on April 24. After sledding our kit northeast up the glacier to what seemed like a safe spot, we established base camp. First up, we decided to explore Mantok I. In 2007, Peter Doucette, Ben Gilmore, and Freddie Wilkinson made the first ascent of Mantok I (ca 9,300'), via the All Talk Couloir (3,500', M5) on the east face. We had spotted a potential new line starting up an obvious couloir a bit farther left on the face.

The following morning, around 8 a.m., Fred and I set out on skis to reach the base of our couloir. We began the climb unroped, mostly on snow, but tied in as the angle

ABOVE: Fred Caloggero cresting the summit ridge of Mantok I after climbing a new route up the east face. *Joseph Hobby*

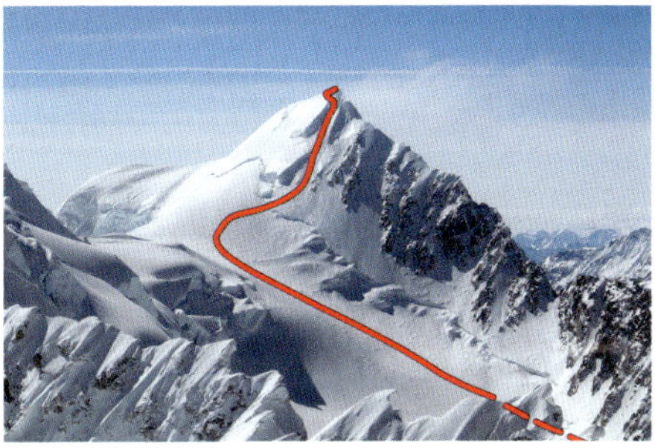

TOP: The east side of Mantok I (ca 9,300′), showing (1) Small Talk Couloir and (2) All Talk Couloir. *Joseph Hobby*

BOTTOM: Spectre (4,000′, 80° snow/ice) on the northeast side of Mt. Charles, the first ascent of the 10,020-foot peak. *Joseph Hobby*

steepened and presented several steps of ice. Relentless winds greeted us on the crest of the southwest ridge; thankfully, a rock cave provided shelter for a short break. After a steep pitch of loose rock that hindered our progress, we found better stone leading to the corniced knife-edge guarding the true summit. We arrived at the top about eight hours after leaving camp. Fred and I descended the climb via several rappels and much downclimbing. We called our route the Small Talk Couloir (3,500', M4 70° snow/ice).

On April 27, we turned our attention to an unclimbed 10,020' peak that overlooks the Yentna from the east. The northwest face, directly above the glacier, is littered with hanging seracs and bordered by a labyrinth of crevasses. In 2010, Joey McBrayer and Chris Wright climbed a 3,000' weakness on the left side of this face, grading it AI4+ M5; weather forced them back before the top.

Fred and I opted for a couloir on the northwest side that looked like it would lead us onto the peak's northeast aspect. After climbing moderate snow and ice up the couloir to reach the northeast side, we transitioned to skis and skinned through a Seussian land of crevasses and serac debris. A couple of hours later, at around 9,300', we basked in our first sunlight of the day. Soon, we had dispatched the final terrain to the summit with simul-climbing and one belayed pitch through steep rime ice. We skied down much of our line of ascent, with a number of rappels mixed in.

We named the peak Mt. Charles as a tribute to my father and Fred's grandfather. We named our route Spectre (4,000', 80° snow/ice), inspired by the Brocken spectre we saw at the top and by the summit cornice, which resembled a large ghost from the glacier below.

—Joseph Hobby

Genya Takenaka descending along the steep, complex east ridge of East Kahiltna Peak, en route to Kahiltna Notch. ***Toranosuke Nagayama***

DENALI, KAHILTNA PEAKS TO CASSIN RIDGE

The Cassin Ridge, the famed south buttress of Denali (Mt. McKinley), rises from Kahiltna Notch to the 20,310' summit. But the geographic feature that forms the complete south ridge of Denali extends from Kahiltna Notch over four miles to the southwest and then west. In between, the ridge crosses two notable summits—East and West Kahiltna peaks—before dropping into the Kahiltna Glacier like a multipronged tentacle.

Denali's full south ridge was tried for the first time by a pair of Japanese climbers, Yuto Inoue and Tatsuro Yamada, two of the Giri-Giri Boys, in 2008. They disappeared near the top of the Cassin. The line was tried again in 2011 by Japanese alpinists Yasuhiro Hanatani and Kei Taniguchi, who had awful conditions and bailed. To this day, the full line connecting the Kahiltna Peaks into the Cassin and up to Denali's summit is believed to be unclimbed. Given the history, it has acquired reverence for Japanese alpinists. With that in mind, Toranosuke Nagayama, Genya Takenaka, and I decided to meet the challenge.

Easier said than done—the start of our expedition was a nightmare. After Genya and I arrived in Anchorage, we went to the apartment we had arranged, dropped our climbing gear near the entrance, and took off for a few hours. When we came back, nearly all the gear was gone—*stolen!* All that was left were our skis and a ski bag with very little equipment. We were in a daze; our expedition seemed to be over before it had even started.

The next day, I reported the theft to the police. At REI in Anchorage, I posted a flyer on the bulletin board, seeking any information about our stolen kit. I woke to a flood of emails—all messages of sympathy and encouragement. One was from Alaska hardman Clint Helander, who drove right over to lend us his gear. Dana Drummond, owner of the Hoarding Marmot shop, became a middleman between us and other Alaskan climbers who made similar offers. Dana even let us stay at his place. The kindness and generosity from the Alaska climbing community was overwhelming.

Re-equipped, the three of us flew onto the Kahiltna Glacier, ready for action. We climbed Denali's West Buttress to acclimatize. Then, on May 25, we left

Camp 1 on the Kahiltna Glacier with everything we needed for ten days.

We started up the West Ridge (Alaska Grade 4, 5.8 75° ice) of West Kahiltna Peak (12,835'), which had been climbed by Italians Diego Giovannini and Fabio Meraldi in 2011 (and possibly by Inoue and Yamada in 2008). It took us about 13 hours to get to the top of West Kahiltna. The next day, we dipped into a col before summiting East Kahiltna Peak (13,440').

From the top, we could see that both sides of the ridge toward Kahiltna Notch were extremely steep, and the cornices were enormous. Aside from a lone rocky section after West Kahiltna Peak, all of the climbing on the traverse was on ice and snow.

On the fourth night, we finally arrived at Kahiltna Notch (11,960'). We had already summited two peaks and covered over 4.2 miles, yet more than 8,000' of climbing rose above us. After climbing straight up the ridge from Kahiltna Notch, then traversing left for four pitches, we reached the entrance to the Japanese Couloir, the standard start of the Cassin Ridge route. By now, we were exhausted. Nevertheless, we started up the Cassin, trying to move carefully, always conscious of the fate of Inoue and Yamada.

On the ninth day after we left the Kahiltna Glacier, the weather took a turn for the worse, and we rested at the 17,700' camp. A bad storm was forecast for the next afternoon. We started to climb before dawn, hoping to reach the summit and get down to high camp on the West Buttress by noon. As we gained altitude, the air became frighteningly cold. Genya was quickly becoming hypothermic. We set up the tent to get Genya warm, rested for about five hours, and then resumed the climb.

Takenaka climbs through the First Rock Band on the Cassin Ridge. The Kahiltna Peaks, which the team traversed for more than four miles to reach the Cassin, are in the center background, with the east fork of the Kahiltna Glacier on the left. ***Toranosuke Nagayama***

Soon we were at Kahiltna Horn, at the top of the Cassin Ridge, only 200 vertical feet below the summit. But we were in the middle of a snowstorm and Genya was in bad shape. We debated whether to set up the tent again and wait out the storm. But Genya chimed in to say he could go no further. I glanced once more toward the top, and we all began descending the West Buttress.

As painful as it was to come so far and not quite achieve our goal, all of us making it back down safely was infinitely more important. I'm proud of our team for making the tough decision.

—Subaru Takeda, *Japan*

BEGGUYA, NORTH BUTTRESS, IN THE SHADOW OF THE WALL

The last 100m had been the wildest alpine climbing I'd ever done: splitter cracks, verglassed offwidths, pumpy roofs, overhanging ice runnels, and big, scary snow mushrooms. A crux sequence had required reaching a full arm's length to my left off an icy chicken wing into a stein-pull, then swinging onto it. I leaned back to feel the sun's warmth on my face, the first comfort of the day on the north buttress of Begguya (Mt. Hunter), where Cody Winckler and I were finally starting to believe our new route might actually go.

We'd spent the last three weeks trying and failing to climb big faces above the Buckskin Glacier. Now we were 400m up an untouched triangular shield of ice-streaked granite on Begguya's north buttress, left of the French Route (Grison-Tedeschi, 1984), which followed a striking ice couloir into a formidable headwall. It seemed we'd finally found good conditions. But was it too late?

In the Shadow of the Wall (1,200m, AI6 M7) on the north buttress of Begguya (Mt. Hunter). The triangular shield of rock that Dane Steadman and Cody Winckler followed for the first 600 meters of the route was previously unclimbed. Above this, they climbed the upper half of the French Route (Grison-Tedeschi, 1984), stopping at the top of the north buttress. *Naoise Ó Muircheartaigh*

During one of the crux "Shroom Tube" pitches that had brought us into the sun, I managed to send a medium-sized mushroom down on Cody, who was hiding beneath our backpacks at the belay. As we looked up at another swollen, evil-looking mushroom blocking our path a couple of pitches higher, we knew we couldn't risk waking that beast. To skirt around it, Cody started up a splitter crack on the right wall of the golden dihedral we had been following. He managed to free the pitch, but as the sun set the crack ended beneath a sea of blank stone. Out left was a narrow ledge that might provide passage around the shroom—but that was a problem for the next day.

Cody found a coffin-sized bivy for one in a horizontal chimney next to the anchor he'd arranged, and as I—still at the lower belay—began to brew up, he fixed the ropes and rappelled down. We ate and drank as snow began to fall, then Cody jugged back up to his coffin and I settled the back half of my butt onto the pitiful ledge I'd managed to excavate from thin ice.

After a mercifully short night, I jugged up to Cody, and from his high point, a pendulum and an exciting traverse left and then back right, above the mushroom, brought us into a perfect ice runnel. Higher, a couple of tenuous mixed pitches led to a dragon's spine of ice and gargoyles of snow that we followed to the top of the triangular shield and the junction with the French Route—still 600m shy of the top of the north buttress, our intended summit. With the weather shutting down, we knew we would go no higher on this attempt. But having climbed 600m of new terrain, we had solved the big question mark of the route. We started down the French couloir as it began to wash with spindrift, desperately hoping we'd get a chance to take the line to the top of the buttress.

After two weeks of marginal weather, and with only five days left before I had to fly home, the sky cleared. The good

Dane Steadman starting up the first of the two crux "Shroom Tube" pitches on the first attempt to climb In the Shadow of the Wall. *Cody Winckler*

weather wasn't forecast to last: A single push it would have to be.

We simuled across the 'schrund at 8 a.m. on May 14 and continued up névé-streaked slabs to the crux rock band. By 1 p.m., Cody had led us through the Shroom Tubes, this time dislodging a snow mushroom on me at the "Friendly Fire" belay, right where I'd hit him two weeks earlier. Now that we knew the way, we were able to eliminate our one point of aid from the previous attempt. At 8 p.m., we stopped at a nice butt ledge in the warmth of the evening sun, a couple of pitches higher than our previous bivy. We ate, drank, and dozed for an hour until the sun set and the cold started to sink in, then we continued climbing.

We reached the top of the lower shield in the long Alaskan twilight, and at 4 a.m., Cody pulled his sleeping bag around his shoulders as I started up ice runnels above the French couloir—finally on previously climbed terrain. Around dawn, we chopped another butt ledge into the ice beneath the headwall; we were exhausted after 24 hours on the go, and it didn't take long to doze off.

When we resumed climbing again an hour later, the singular, icy weakness in the headwall ended after a pitch and a half. The way forward was anything but obvious. I picked my way right, then up, then left, and back right some more, tick-tacking along tiny veins of ice, inching upward toward two widely spaced granite towers that stood at the top of the headwall like goalposts.

At 9 p.m. we crawled into the Cornice Bivy—a narrow crevasse atop the north buttress, historically considered the "summit" of the buttress, though still far from the summit of Begguya. We had completed our new route, In the Shadow of the Wall (1,200m, AI6 M7), with 600m of new terrain and 600m on the French Route. After an hour's rest, with the weather deteriorating again, it was time to go down.

Two hundred meters down the Bibler-Klewin, both of us now in the deepest state of depletion we had ever experienced, we got lost. And then the clouds closed in around us. A long leftward traverse brought us back onto the Bibler-Klewin and we resumed our descent. As I drilled one of dozens of Abalakov threads, I heard a *hummm* ring through the air. A plane—and close! *But Talkeetna Air Taxi never flies at night*, I thought. I stopped working on the anchor for a moment to focus on the sound, but it was gone. As soon as I went back to drilling, it returned. The phantom plane followed me the rest of the way down.

The 28th rappel brought us over the 'schrund, and at 8 a.m. on May 16 we reached our skis, 48 mostly sleepless hours after we'd left them. Back at base camp, we checked in with Gabby, the camp manager, and something came out of Cody's mouth that I never could have foreseen: "Once darkness fell on the way down," he told Gabby, "I started hearing a plane that wasn't there." The phantom plane had been following him, too.

—Dane Steadman

MT. HUNTER, EAST FACE, DIAMOND ARÊTE, ONE WAY OUT

The Diamond Arête on the east face of Mt. Hunter was first climbed in 1985 by Jim Donini and Jack Tackle. Anyone who wants a classic tale of old-school Alaskan adventure climbing would be well recommended to check out their story in the 1986 *AAJ*. They named it after the large rock face—which the lower part of their route follows on the left margin—because it reminded them of the Diamond on Longs Peak in Colorado.

Since the first ascent, there has only been one repeat, in 2005, by Samuel Johnson and Freddie Wilkinson. Jack Tackle had told Michael Gardner about a possible direct start to the Diamond Arête—a big dihedral system up the heart of the intimidating face of the Diamond wall—back in 2018. Ever since, we'd been hoping to try it.

The lack of activity on a line as notable as the Diamond Arête is due to two factors. First, it's a difficult route, even by modern standards. Second, access is only possible via ski aircraft—and pickup is not guaranteed. Because large seracs and avalanche slopes threaten the entire small basin beneath the east face, it would be a dangerous place to wait out a storm. Thus, the three crucial ingredients for the Diamond Arête are a psyched team, a stable forecast, and, most importantly, a pilot bolder than the climbers!

In May 2024, seven seasons after Jack told Michael about the line, the stars finally aligned. On May 14, Paul Roderick of Talkeetna Air Taxi dropped Michael, Rob Smith, and me at the base of the east face so we could attempt the direct line. Paul kept the engines running while we unloaded; he snapped a few photos and quickly took off again. We made our way as hastily as possible to the relative safety of the base of the wall and immediately started climbing.

From the first steps, it was clear we were in for a difficult time, with deep trail-breaking and vertical sn'ice that was alright to climb but difficult to protect. The rock, however, was exceptional, full of beautiful splitters, like something out of Yosemite. A steep, unprotectable pitch after the 'schrund took us to moderate ground and a long, deep traverse to the start of the dihedral.

The initial four pitches of the corner took us around seven hours, with sustained, technical, and sometimes dangerous climbing. Tricky torquing in thin, overhanging cracks on the first pitch, a fragile ice column on the second, and a bold, slabby traverse on the fourth took us to the end of daylight and a small bivy ledge. Two more hard pitches in the morning brought us to the top of the dihedral, where we expected to take a short break before tackling several hundred meters of difficult climbing leading directly to the apex of the wall. However, a glance toward the upper mountain made it quite clear that our expected weather window of three days wasn't likely to last even two. The only sane decision, given our position, was to traverse left and get up and over the

The east face of Mt. Hunter, showing the original Diamond Arête (yellow line, Donini-Tackle, 1985) and One Way Out (red line, Gardner-Hennessey-Smith, 2024). The 2024 climbers intended to continue straight up the rock wall to gain the upper arête, but weather concerns forced them onto the 1985 route to reach the summit. *Michael Gardner*

mountain as soon as possible.

Forgoing the direct line, we made a long traverse back to the left, searching for the fat ice of the original route's exit pitches. Either we wound up in the wrong spot (possible) or things had changed in 40 years (also possible), but a final difficult dry pitch was required to reach the top of the wall.

Simul-climbing on moderate mixed terrain brought us to the namesake arête, where several sideways pitches of calf-burning hard ice led to moderate slopes. After battling deep snow and strong wind, we were thankful to find a large crevasse in which to shelter for the night.

The next day brought more of the same, this time in a whiteout. With the aid of GPS apps on our phones, we were able to find Hunter's 14,573' summit. We descended to the top of the north buttress entirely in a whiteout, which was about as fun as it sounds; nonetheless, we located the familiar rappels down the Bibler-Klewin, and before we knew it we were in base camp.

Our route, One Way Out (2,200m,

WI6 M6+), was more like a variation than the full direct line Jack had envisioned. That awaits a more talented—or luckier—team. Nonetheless, we are proud to have added some hard climbing to an already proud route, and to have reached Hunter's summit, which had eluded the previous two ascents of the Diamond Arête for various reasons. It was a memorable three days, made even more so in retrospect: It was the last big alpine route Rob and I got to share with our friend Michael, who died on Jannu East in October.

—Sam Hennessey

The ridge at the eastern edge of the cirque below Begguya's Southeast Spur. Ben Dewey and Chris Dewey made the first ascent of the 9,957', snow-pyramid-capped summit at the left, which they named the Water Tower; the line of Depth Perception (1,300', IV WI5 M5) is shown. They believe all of the other summits on this ridgeline to be unclimbed. ***Ben Dewey***

TOKOSITNA GLACIER AREA, THE WATER TOWER

"I'm starting to wonder if this is a death mission," Chris called down to me at the belay.

My brother Chris and I (dubbed "the Dewey brothers" in Talkeetna) were 1,000' up the Southeast Spur of Begguya (Mt. Hunter), a route that had lurked in my mind from the moment I saw Bradford Washburn's black-and-white plate a decade ago. So many things had fallen into place to put us here, including a miraculous weather window that began just as we arrived in Talkeetna on April 20 and the fact that Paul Roderick agreed to drop us where no pilot had landed before, corkscrewing his Otter plane down into the cirque right below the route. I was feeling strong after bilateral knee reconstruction. Almost everything had aligned to put us just below the crux of this lifetime dream route. The snow conditions had not.

Chris's comment was the first time either of us had voiced aloud the fears we'd both been suppressing. A few pitches earlier, as he followed me over the top of the approach couloir and onto the ridge, a cornice had collapsed under Chris, flushing down the gully we had just come up. As we continued up the ridge, we encountered endless facets and unsupportive snow. The problem with bottling up your doubts is when you finally give them a tiny crack they come roaring out. Chris was right. I felt an enormous wash of relief as we decided to bail.

We soon found ourselves back on the glacier, a mile-wide basin northeast of the southwest fork of the Tokositna that I had begun

Chris Dewey leading the crux of Depth Perception. The flow on the left would be the most direct line, but it consisted of aerated, unprotectable ice. The first ascent was made up the more mixed flow on the right. *Ben Dewey*

to think of as the "Northeast Southwest Tok." Only a few parties had been up here, and as far as I knew, they all came to climb the Southeast Spur and go over the top of Begguya. I had never heard of anyone spending time in the Northeast Southwest Tok to climb anything else. We looked up at four rugged points along the eastern edge of the cirque. They were all probably unclimbed.

On April 24, we skinned to the base of the northernmost and highest of these points. Capped with a snow pyramid, it rises to 9,957', according to the maps we had with us. Two steep couloirs split the west face. The right-hand one had a single constriction halfway up with what looked like promising ice; we chose that one and crossed the bergschrund.

We simuled 600' of good snow to the base of the constriction, where the couloir forks into two side-by-side ice flows. I put Chris on belay, and he started up the ice on the left, but quickly discovered it was extremely aerated. He backed down and gave the right flow a try. The first half was also aerated, so he traversed over to more mixed and protectable terrain. After almost three hours, I heard a whoop as Chris reached the end of the pitch. When I joined him at the anchor, he told me he had lost one contact lens mid-pitch. We resolved to call the route Depth Perception if we made it to the top.

I led a traversing pitch left to get back to the couloir that would connect to the summit snowfields. A rib of steep snow blocked the way. I chopped and chopped at the snow to try to cut a passage across, but it kept deteriorating. After tentatively reaching a foot around the rib, then my knee, I made up my mind to just hop over. I was on the other side, although I had to lower down to reach the snow in the couloir. Chris followed gracefully and we were back on track.

We belayed two more pitches, then simuled again as the couloir opened into a 60° snow slope. By now, the sun was baking the mountain, and we waded upward through slushy snow. Believing the summit was a large cornice overhanging the east side of the ridge, I climbed up as high as I dared, stopping about 50' shy of the very top. Then we downclimbed off the mountain as fast as we could, chased by visions of wet slides.

Back at camp, sorting the remains of our pitiful rack, we decided to call the mountain the Water Tower in honor of John Waterman's incredible pioneering feat in the cirque. I am quite proud to have put in an honest attempt at the Southeast Spur and to have found our own little first ascent in the area. Depth Perception (1,300', IV WI5 M5) was only one of what appears to be a fair number of exciting objectives in the Northeast Southwest Tokositna.

Thanks to Paul for landing us in the cirque based on an X I drew on the map, and to Talkeetna Air Taxi for giving us a $1,000 grant toward flights, which allowed us to resupply in Talkeetna, fly back to the Tok below Thunder Mountain, climb the forgotten gem Deadbeat (Cordes-DeCapio, 2001), get stuck in a storm, miss our flights home, run out of food, and starve for a few days before our Alaska season came to an end. But that's another story.

—Ben Dewey

ALASKA | Ruth Glacier

MT. DICKEY, SOUTH FACE, THE GREAT WALL

On April 2, Paul Roderick slowed the Otter plane and we landed in a whoosh of snow. Gašper "Pinti" Pintar and I chucked all our stuff onto the Ruth Glacier and Paul, ever cool, flicked the peace sign with his fingers. "Good luck, see you in a month!" he said. The Otter's engine echoed around the mountains, then faded until it was only us and silence.

The bitter cold and short glimpses of sunshine didn't make life easy during the first ten days of our trip. It was like living in a freezer—except one where snow blows in every night. "It's not normally like this—it's usually a lot warmer!" I explained to Pinti

as we stamped our feet one cold morning.

It was hard to know what conditions would be like up on the various faces, as they were plastered white from recent storms. After a few days of scouting, our attention kept returning to Mt. Dickey (9,545'), certainly one of the jewels of the area. Attempting a direct start to Ruth Gorge Grinder on Dickey's east face (5,000', AI6+ M7 A1, Marvell-Rousseau, 2019), I climbed 60m of névé and shouted down to Pinti: "I have no gear or a belay..."

"Well, I'm not soloing," came the reply. I had an ice screw in névé but doubted it would hold a large fall. With no ice in sight, I began downclimbing in that awkward, arse-out, swing-from-the-shoulder way.

TOP: Gašper Pintar leading one of the best pitches on The Great Wall—dry-tooling up a steep crack followed by a finish on blobs of ice—on the second day of the climb. *Tom Livingstone*

BOTTOM: Mt. Dickey from the southeast, showing (1) The Great Wall (2024) and (2) approximate line of the 1991 summer route. A 2002 route, Crime of the Century, climbed the most prominent rock pillar at far left. *Tom Livingstone*

We found Blood from the Stone (5,000', WI6+ X M7+ A1, Easton-Steck, 2002) out of condition, too. From a belay at the start of the business (around pitch five), we looked up and saw only drips of névé plastered to a wall, rather than the gullies of fat ice that Matt Cornell, Sam Hennessey, and Rob Smith found when they repeated the route in 2023.

We also attempted the central groove on the west face of Peak 7,400', to the right of the prow climbed by Optimist (Amano-Masumoto-Nagato, 2010). This was a beautiful line of névé and ice...until it ran out.

During our third week on the glacier, the weather forecast improved and we investigated the south face of Mt. Dickey. Since arriving, we'd continually eyed a big couloir high on the face and wondered if we could reach it via some crazy-looking slabs. Our planned route started just right of an old rock route, climbed in early June 1991 by an Italian team. Above the initial corners, we planned to angle left over the slabs, crossing the Italian route, to reach the big groove system we'd spotted.

On April 14, we spent the day climbing the first few pitches, pleasantly surprised there were cracks for gear and hooking our tools. At the top of a right-facing corner, with the sun casting shadows across the slabs, I pendulumed across to a snowfield and Pinti came over. We fixed three ropes down to the ground. *Maybe, just maybe, this route could work!* I thought as we skinned back to base camp.

Returning the next day, we followed a subtle traversing line through the crazy slabs. Pinti led a memorable steep pitch with hard dry-tooling. I aided through an overlap that boomed every time I moved, then climbed a run-out ramp of crunchy rock—a pitch that was best if you didn't think too much about it.

In the middle of the face, after climbing some ice bulges, we squashed into a little cave to bivy, cradling hot freeze-dried meals and capturing all their energy—every particle of heat and spoon of food.

The next morning, we zigzagged higher as snow fell. Clearly, the forecast had been wrong. We finally got our little slice of Alaskan heaven, though, with a long pitch of real ice, complete with reliable screws for protection. Later that day, we found a plush bivy on a snow arête roughly three-quarters of the way up the face, and Pinti smoked his last cigarette.

The morning brought a short section of overhanging névé, which we climbed between heavy bouts of spindrift, then slogged up to the summit. A proper storm was forecast to arrive that evening, so we spent only a few blustery minutes on top before stomping down the west face.

Our route gained 1,500m, and we settled on The Great Wall for a name—it was meant as a joke. The south face of Mt. Dickey is an impressive and inspiring wall, but our trip involved a lot of time in base camp wishing we had a suitable wall to stop our tents from getting buried.

—Tom Livingstone, *U.K.*

The southeast face of Mt. Bradley, showing the lines of (1) Vitalogy (Allen-Zimmerman, 2010), (2) Sports (Spitulnik-Telstad, 2024), (3) Season of the Sun (Ichimura-Sato-Yamada, 2007), (4) Frieh-Johnson variation (2010), and (5) East Buttress (Jochler-Orgler, 1987). *Eli Spitulnik*

MT. BRADLEY, SOUTHEAST FACE, SPORTS

Michael Telstad, who has become a close friend and go-to partner over the past couple of years, has a knack for finding potential new routes. Before I could make sense of the line he'd envisioned on the southeast face of Mt. Bradley, I found myself entranced as Paul Roderick's plane blasted us with cold early April air and fresh snow as he took off down the great Ruth Gorge. The snow was so deep and our five-week supply of food, fuel, and gear was so heavy that we set up base camp right where we unloaded the small plane, between Bradley and Mt. Dickey.

Over the next week or so, we attempted On the Frozen Roads of Our Incertitudes (Constant-Mercader, 2003) on the west face of London Bridge, but were turned around by aerated, rotten, overhanging ice. The next day, we climbed Prelude Gully to the summit of London Tower, then for several days we shoveled out our tents, Sisyphus-style, through unremitting snowfall and relentless wind. High pressure returned on April 16, and we attempted Shaken, Not Stirred on the Mooses Tooth in a 24-hour push from our base camp, turning around shortly below Englishman's Col.

On April 19, with a promising four-day weather forecast, Michael and I skied to the base of Mt. Bradley's southeast face. In late afternoon, we started up a long, left-trending ramp that was also the start of Mark Allen and Graham Zimmerman's route Vitalogy (4,600', Alaska Grade 5, 5.9 R WI5 M6+ A1), established in 2010. We climbed the first 1,500' of Vitalogy that night, encountering an overhanging snow mushroom and several difficult mixed pitches up to 5.9 R M6. We reached the 2010 team's Prow Bivy on the upper snowfield by morning.

After resting during the warmest part of the day, we took off in late afternoon and traversed steep snow, passing by the gully up which Vitalogy continues and instead aiming for the center of the upper face. [*The 2024 line zigzags up the broad face between Vitalogy, on the left, and Season of the Sun (Ichimura-Sato-Yamada, 2007), on the right.*] A splitter finger and hand crack granted access to the upper face and warranted another switch from boots and crampons to rock shoes—then back again, of course. Night fell again, and we kept climbing. Techy M6 mixed and steep snow brought us to a long, airy pitch of aid. Steep sn'ice, snow traversing, short mixed steps, a rappel, and a long snow and mixed gully dropped us off at a somewhat protected snow ridge in late morning. We chopped our second bivy site with 3,000' of mountain below us.

We rested again during the sunny hours and began our third day of climbing in the afternoon shade. A blur of steep, R-rated névé through rock bands, vertical steps of ice, and long simul-climbing blocks deposited us on the spindrift-plagued upper face. Around 1 a.m., we found a short overhanging rock band and settled in beneath it for our third bivy.

The long, left-trending ramp at the start of Sports terminates in a cave that pinches down to a chimney. Michael Telstad aims for the light on the other side. *Eli Spitulnik*

On April 22, my 25th birthday, we summited Mt. Bradley (9,101') after two more long blocks of simul-climbing. We made quick work of the descent, picking our way down the west ridge, traversing into the Wake-Bradley col, then rappelling and downclimbing to the base of the route, where we had left our skis—only to find they had been hit by an avalanche from the north face of Mt. Wake. After some searching, we hobbled back to base camp with three skis and two skins between the two of us. Three days later, we found the missing ski and skins, hundreds of feet from where we had cached them.

We called our route Sports (4,660', Alaska Grade 5, 5.10 A1 AI4 M6 90° snow): an homage to the song by the Viagra Boys that we listened to a mind-numbing number of times during the trip, and also a nod to the impossibility of describing the spectrum of experience that is alpine climbing.

—Eli Spitulnik

COLD WARS

WINTER NEW ROUTE ON THE SOUTH FACE OF THE MOOSES TOOTH

By Marcin Tomaszewski, *Poland*

When Paweł Hałdaś (Poland) and I set off for Alaska in February, we had no definite plans but two areas on our radar: the Kichatna massif and the Mooses Tooth. We made a final decision without any hand-wringing and simply followed our intuition: The Mooses Tooth it would be, from the south. Our goal was a winter ascent.

Ever since I began climbing in 1990, winter has been my arena. Pushing myself in the coldest months for long stretches of time is a way to discover both my physical and psychological boundaries. My many cold ascents around the world—with Paweł and other great winter climbers, notably Marek Raganowicz—have taught me manifold lessons that I've brought into other areas of my life, from writing to filmmaking. More than anything, though, winter ascents prepare me for ever more winter ascents. [*The author and Hałdaś's ascents include the first winter big-wall routes in Greenland and the Karakoram (see AAJs 2024 and 2022).*]

Searching the web, I could find little information about big-wall routes on the south side of the Mooses Tooth—the best-known existing lines, like Ham and Eggs (Davies-Krakauer-Zinsser, 1975) and Shaken, Not Stirred (Crouch-Donini, 1997), follow icy gully systems—and no information at all about a winter ascent of the 1,000m section of wall I was eyeing. We decided to remain open to whatever the mountain might offer and try to avoid tunnel vision.

On our first morning on the Root Canal Glacier, February 28, we set the alarm clock for 6 a.m. and left the tent briskly at 7—only

ABOVE: Paweł Hałdaś climbing in rough conditions on the Mooses Tooth. ***Marcin Tomaszewski***

Marcin Tomaszewski about 500 meters up the wall on Cold Wars. ***Paweł Hałdaś***

to return even more briskly less than a minute later! It was *really* cold, below -30°C and windy; our fingers immediately went numb. We took refuge in our still-warm sleeping bags. Going forward, we resolved to shift our morning routine an hour later.

When we ventured back out, I spotted a potential line on the steep rock face between The Tooth Obsession (2,900', V 5.10+ WI4 A0, Matusevych-Shirokov-Shuruyev-Vorotnikova, 2005) on the left and Ham and Eggs on the right. I took a series of photos so we could zoom in and study this system of meandering cracks.

During the rest of the day, we focused on getting to the base of the rock, which proved a challenge from the first step out of camp—wading through thigh-high snowdrifts with heavy big-wall bags certainly gets the body temperature up. And the 200m snow apron was no picnic: Ice was only just forming at that time of year, the snow was unconsolidated, and the risk of avalanches was high. We roped up for the 60°–70° slope, weaving between rock outcroppings for protection.

As soon as we reached the rock, we built an anchor, established Camp 1 with our D4 Delta3p portaledge, and fixed ropes back to the glacier. The next day we shuttled up the rest of our equipment: approximately 150kg of gear and enough food and fuel for 20 days. On March 1, we committed to the wall and did not return to our glacier base camp from this point on. The forecast was good: Our inReach showed low temperatures but quite a few sunny days.

From the moment we started up the technical pitches, the battle with winter began. As on my other recent expeditions, I followed the rule that if I lost feeling in my toes or fingers, I would stop where I was and warm up—for as long as it took. I believe this is what has allowed my partners and me to make it through such frigid climbs without the slightest frostbite. We had to make a few more of these time-consuming stops than was advisable, as even during spells of bad weather, Paweł and I couldn't help removing our gloves to take photos and short videos. *We did it again*, I thought to myself each time I weathered another case of the dreaded "screaming barfies."

The battle with the wall was no easier than the cold. There were sand-filled and rock-choked cracks and chimneys, and on most pitches 70 to 80 percent of our protection was beaks and other pitons. But we couldn't believe our luck: The cracks we'd scoped from the glacier never disappeared. The wall always provided passage.

The climbing did demand significant imagination and creativity, though; sometimes the crack was shallow, sometimes the rock was brittle, sometimes there was a thin layer of ice glazing everything. And always there were the unique challenges of winter. Despite warming fuel in our sleeping bags each night, it was still too cold for the stove to burn well in the morning, so we could only melt small amounts of water. Instead of cereal with milk to start our days, we had half a chocolate bar each and lukewarm coffee.

The line of Zimne Wojny ("Cold Wars," 980m, 19 pitches, M5+ A3 70° snow/ice) on the south face of the Mooses Tooth. ***Marcin Tomaszewski***

On March 4, about 270m above our first camp, we established our second bivouac on a convenient snowy ledge and fixed ropes back down to Camp 1. The next day we shuttled all our gear to Camp 2. Our plan was to descend from the top of the mountain by our ascent route.

Snow fell pretty much every two days, which resulted in intense powder avalanches from above, giving us pause every time they crashed around us. But we remained unscathed in our tent. We took turns leading each day, and I don't know which role was preferable, leader or belayer. Leading was mentally taxing, but the belayer, stuck at the anchor, had to avoid falling into the drowsy embrace of winter.

The climbing was not often difficult in the technical sense but was always engaging. On March 8, our tenth day of climbing, we made our final push. After reaching the top of the wall proper, we set off for the west ridge on mixed ground, angling over the upper face. The weather was on our side. Over the course of six full mixed pitches, we used every trick from aid climbing to free climbing. A final stretch of firn and snow brought us to the ridge, at the top of our buttress, and the end of Zimne Wojny ("Cold Wars," 980m, 19 pitches, M5+ A3 70° snow/ice).

The Alaska Range spread out in every direction below us—nearly empty at this time of year!

TWO NEW ROUTES ON THE MOOSES TOOTH ATTEMPTED: *In late spring 2024, British climbers Mark Thomas and Mike "Twid" Turner attempted two new lines on the south face of the Mooses Tooth. The first started up the massive wall left of Shaken, Not Stirred, on a subpeak called the Incisor. (The left side of this big rock buttress was ascended by Gary Bocarde, Michael Clark, Charlie Porter, and John Svenson in June 1974; their Moose Antler route (800m, VI 5.8 WI4) was the second ascent of Mooses Tooth and the first route up the south side.) Thomas and Turner made it a few hundred meters up this wall over the course of three days. They drilled their only bolt placement at their high point to enable safe retreat. "In 38 [years] of climbing big walls we [haven't] seen such bad rock!" they wrote in a report about the trip. The second line they attempted began slightly right of Hałdaś and Tomaszewski's Cold Wars and had rock conditions nearly as dreadful as the first; the June weather also was dangerously warm and wet. After three days of climbing and fixing, Thomas and Turner reached a high point at about the same level as the Poles' Camp 2, about 475m up including the snow apron.*

ALASKA | Wrangell Mountains

Ethan Berkeland on the WI6 M7 crux pitch of Peavine Palace, dubbed the Dangler. ***Elias Antaya***

CHITISTONE VALLEY, PEAVINE PALACE

Jonathan Koenig and I first acquainted ourselves with the Chitistone Valley in March 2022 and quickly realized the immense potential in the area. After repeating the unbelievably classic Star Babies (WI5+, Breitenberger-Comstock-Dial-Tobin, 1987), we attempted a big new route directly above the palatial Peavine Cabins, which are operated by the National Park Service.

The route starts up a snow gully and consists of many steps of steep limestone separated by snow slogs. We surmounted the first few limestone bands via M3 mixed on solid rock. After 1,500' of steep snow, we encountered a beautiful but brief WI5 pillar, followed by another short WI3 step. Above another rock step, we came to the crux of the route—surely one of the most impressive pitches of mixed climbing in Alaska: an ice curtain we dubbed the Dangler. It is visible from the valley floor 3,000' below.

On our first attempt, I reached the Dangler by run-out, difficult mixed climbing, during which I placed one bolt on lead. After finally hooking my tools into the bottom of the Dangler, I looked up to see several ice roofs beyond. I decided to bail rather than get in over my head.

Jonathan and I returned to the Chitistone Valley in 2023 but did not attempt to complete the prior year's route. Instead, we made the first ascent of Hot French Grotto (3,500', IV WI4+) on Chitistone Mountain, with Elias Antaya and Tristan O'Donoghue (*see AAJ 2024*).

In March 2024, we returned to the Chitistone for a third time. After completing nearly a dozen shorter new routes in the area, Jonathan, Elias, and I turned our attention to the Dangler. With perfect névé coating the majority of the snow slope, we quickly gained our previous high point. I then spent nearly two hours leading the beautiful but terrifying crux pitch. It ended in a steep runnel of thin ice protected by beaks in adjacent rock, with overhanging moss climbing to reach a belay cave. It was nearly dark by the time Elias and Jonathan arrived at the belay; spindrift was hammering down the gully. I waited for a lull in the flow and quickly dispatched the final WI5 pitch during twilight.

We rappelled from a V-thread in the highest ice in the gully and continued descending our line by downclimbing and rappelling. The slopes were constantly sliding; mercifully, only five inches of snow had accumulated thus far, making the slides alarming but nonthreatening. The next morning, we awoke to over a foot of wet, heavy new snow outside of the cabin, but inside we were warm, dry, and utterly exhausted from our effort on Peavine Palace (3,000' of vertical gain, 500' of technical climbing, IV WI6 M7).

—Ethan Berkeland

ALASKA | Coast Mountains

DEAN, SOUTHWEST FACE, SPIRIT WALKER

Spirit Walker (500m, V WI3 M5+) on the southwest face of Dean, about 30 miles north of Juneau. The climbers descended to the north after reaching the west ridge. ***Cameron Jardell***

Though long coveted by Juneau locals, the prominent couloir on the southwest face of Dean (5,883') had never, to my knowledge, received a proper attempt. In February 2024, Kelson Rounds-McPherson and I figured we'd take a crack at it. Having been stiffed by flooded muskeg and thick understory before in Davies Valley, the approach route southwest of the peak, we decided that just completing the approach would qualify as a success.

We left the car at 7:30 p.m. on February 7, skis underfoot. The first several miles we knew well from previous water ice missions in the valley. Climbing out of the valley on the looker's left side, we followed a bench through old spruce trees before bootpacking up an avalanche path to the base of Dean's southwest face, where we started climbing at about 4 a.m.

A web of thin ice smears between compact granitic slabs stretched for two pitches. The climbing was moderate, though delicate moves with marginal gear made for achingly slow progress. Our lone Spectre piton proved indispensable in this terrain. The sun finally arrived and, as expected, so did the avalanches; we traversed right to a comfortable ledge to wait for darkness and for the face to firm back up.

About seven hours later, at nightfall, we continued. Half-frozen moss and thin ice brought us to lower-angle snow in the couloir. Mellow ice steps broke up the post-holing as we simul-climbed for several hundred meters. We exited the couloir via a mixed chimney, the technical crux of our route, to reach the west ridge.

Dean has four summits—the true summit is the easternmost of the four, and the couloir is on the westernmost—but we did not tag any of them. Instead, we descended snow on the north side of the west ridge to reach the Dean Glacier, before walking back to our skis, where we stopped for a nap. Fresh snow woke us after a meager two hours of rest on our makeshift ski-and-rope mattresses. After burning the last of our fuel and eating our final bars, we skied back to the car, arriving around 1:30 p.m. on February 9 to cap a 42-hour effort on Spirit Walker (500m, V WI3 M5+).

An alternative start to climber's right of our direct line may provide easier access into the couloir. Additionally, following the couloir proper all the way to the ridge would likely be less difficult than our exit chimney pitch.

—Cameron Jardell

MENDENHALL TOWERS, THE CURTAIN, INSIDE PASSAGE

In August, Sam Cohen, Clay James, and Brandon Kupczyk established a new route on the Curtain, a south-facing wall between the Main and Fourth Mendenhall Towers. Inside Passage (5.10+) follows a crack and corner system for roughly 1,000', to the right of Blake Herrington and Jason Nelson's 2009 routes Iron Curtain and Resisting A Rest (*AAJ 2010*). [*Cohen's first-person account of this climb is at the AAJ website.*]

—Julian Dreiman, *AAJ, with info from Sam Cohen*

ORGANA PIPETTE (PEAK 5,660'), FIRST ASCENT

Loaded up with Costco's finest provisions and two modified plastic sleds, Vincent Lapointe and I helicoptered into Death Valley on the edge of the Juneau Icefield on the morning of July 9. We then traversed deep suncups to reach a band of granite peaks on the east side of the Taku Glacier.

The following day, we climbed seven pitches of immaculate granite on the prominent west face of a peak lodged between the Organ Pipes and Hodgkins Peak, labeled on the maps as Peak 5,660'. We named the mountain Organa Pipette and our route Worth the Jaunt (300m, Alaska Grade 3, 5.10). We descended by the south ridge to join snow ramps leading back to the icefield. [*Following this ascent, the pair skied northeast to Devils Paw, where they attempted Black Roses (Gietl-Schäli, 2015) on the north summit and climbed the north ridge of Michaels Sword (Beckey-King, 1949), then exited north by the Llewellyn Glacier to Atlin Lake. Jardell's full story of this adventurous traverse is at the AAJ website.*]

Worth the Jaunt (300m, Alaska Grade 3, 5.10) on the west face of Organa Pipette (Peak 5,660'). *Cameron Jardell*

—Cameron Jardell

The north face of Castle Peak, showing approximate lines of (1) Ripped Settee (1,200′, 5.12a A0, 2024) and (2) The Drawbridge (IV 5.10+ A1, 2017). The parallel buttress just to the left has two routes: Herrington-Hirst (5.11-, 2008, on the left) and Fred's Hip (5.10+, Glick-Medara-Pennings, 1993). The Harrington-Kearney Route (5.10+, 1987) ascends another buttress on the far left side of the face. The first route up the main north face (5.8, Beckey-Nolting-Tindall, 1979) follows a buttress and ramp to the right of the routes shown here. ***Spencer Gray***

CASTLE PEAK, NORTH FACE, RIPPED SETTEE

On September 8, Sean Reckert and I climbed what we think is a new route on the central buttress of the north face of Castle Peak (8,306') in the Pasayten Wilderness. Our line, Ripped Settee (1,200', 11 pitches, IV 5.12a A0), is east (climber's left) of The Drawbridge, established in 2017 by Jason Schilling and Morgan Zentler at 5.10+ A1.

As reported by other parties, the rock on Castle Peak is high-quality granite, but with cracks occasionally plugged by moss. It reminded us of the Liberty Bell group to the south. By early September, the slabby bedrock at the base of the three main buttresses was ice-free. The unnamed glacier below the face is now limited to a small pocket under Castle's eastern subsummit.

A large, M-shaped roof extends across most of the lower central buttress—the 2017 route surmounted this roof, and, with enough time, more lines might be found through this feature. With only one day to climb, we opted to bypass the roof on its left side by a series of thin, occasionally wet corners (to 5.11a), isolated ledges, and diagonal ramps. This section of rock was very compact, and the movement was beautiful. We then climbed the wide chimney separating the central and left buttresses for one pitch before pulling back onto the left side of the central buttress, which we followed to its apex. (The chimney section might be exposed to rockfall earlier in the season when snow remains.)

The route had a bit of everything: a squeeze chimney; a refrigerator-width pillar (5.11d) that required heel-hooking compression; a crux pitch (5.12a) that started with wide stemming and finished with a tips layback over a bulge; and a fabulous 5.7 panel of knobs near the top. We used one point of aid (A0) for a tension

Sean Reckert leading the fifth pitch of Ripped Settee, chimneying on the left side of the central buttress. The route continued up the clean granite above. ***Spencer Gray***

traverse on the fifth pitch when the 5.10 seam that Sean was leading blanked out and he switched to its neighbor ten feet to the right.

We finished the 11th and final pitch in the dark, scrambled up a fourth-class boulderfield to the summit, and walked off to the east. That evening we arrived back at the pretty campsite where we'd slept the night before, near a copse of alpine larches growing out of a lateral moraine.

The central buttress's upper half has several ledges that can be followed climber's right to moderate terrain, making our choice of line more a matter of fun than necessity. We found carrying a few pitons to be useful. The routes on the north face deserve more traffic.

—Spencer Gray

MT. FURY, WEST PEAK, MONGO RIDGE AND NEW VARIANT ON POLE OF REMOTENESS

In July, Adam "Mo" Moline and Emilio Taiveaho Peláez made the fourth ascent of Mongo Ridge (VI 5.10a, Wallace, 2006), the south ridge on the west peak of Mt. Fury, in the Picket Range. The pair was the second party to complete the Rooster Comb traverse—skipped by the second and third teams up Mongo Ridge—and they added a significant new variation on the Pole of Remoteness gendarme, up the southwest side: Once in a Lifetime (220', 5.9 R). This climb was supported by the AAC's Live Your Dream grant; a detailed report is at the *AAJ* website.

—Information from Emilio Taiveaho Peláez

BOSTON PEAK, FIRST WINTER ASCENT

By 2024, Boston Peak (8,883') was likely the tallest peak in Washington that had never been climbed in winter. Located in North Cascades National Park, it is usually climbed in summer via the fourth-class east face.

I'd photographed all sides of the peak in winter during other climbing trips, and the west face appeared to hold the best prospects for a winter route. The west face was first climbed in September 1956 by Keith Anderson and John Shonle, but, other than the starting point, their exact route is not described in their report.

Cascade River Road, the approach to Boston Peak, is notorious for being blocked by many large fallen trees during the winter. In early February, I chainsawed out trees on the road to prepare for a quick approach. On February 10, Nick Roy and I started shortly after midnight from the Eldorado gate. We strapped skis on our bikes and Nick towed me (on my regular bike) behind his e-bike to snowline, about three miles up.

We skinned six miles to the Quien Sabe Glacier at the base of the west face of Boston Peak, then climbed steep snow to the higher of two gullies (the next gully farther east and above the start of the Anderson-Shonle route). We then climbed five pitches of steep rime ice and snow, using rock protection on the walls

The west face of Boston Peak in winter. The arrow shows the start of the 1956 first ascent of the west face (climbed in summer); the exact route up the face is unknown. The line shows the first winter ascent, completed in February 2024. ***John Scurlock***

of gullies and occasionally hooking rock edges with our tools. Our route crossed to the north end of the face to a rock overhang, then ascended directly up to the north ridge. We followed the exposed—but thankfully uncorniced—snowy ridge to the top. We did 200m of roped climbing.

With a shovel, we dug out the enormous, aluminum-clad summit register that dates to the 1960s and signed in. (It is the oldest register in place on a Bulger List peak—Washington's 100 highest peaks.) For the descent, we decided against the standard south ridge rappel route because of the expected difficulty of excavating anchors buried under the snow. Instead, we downclimbed our ascent route, staying roped up and placing protection. We then skied down the Quien Sabe Glacier and to our bikes, arriving back at the trailhead at sunset.

—Eric Gilbertson

SIX MORE FIRST WINTER ASCENTS: *Boston Peak was one of seven first winter ascents of peaks on the Bulger List that Eric Gilbertson completed with various partners in 2024. The others, all climbed from January to March, were Monument Peak, Blackcap Mountain, Horseshoe Peak, Mt. Rahm, Mt. Custer, and Flora Mountain. As of the end of 2024, Gilbertson had completed 73 of the 100 Bulger peaks in winter.*

CHORAL PEAK, NORTHWEST FACE

Choral Peak (7,972'), in the Entiat Mountains, is one of the 200 highest peaks in Washington, with a popular scramble on its east face. It also has a steep northwest face below a large snow bowl—the perfect combination to form an alpine ice route.

In April 2020, while skiing in the area, I noticed a long ice line on this face and filed it away for the future. After a failed attempt in November 2023 when the ice was too thin, I returned in the spring of 2024. Nick Roy and I left the Cottonwood trailhead at midnight on May 5. We mountain biked up the Entiat River Trail to snowline, then bushwhacked and snowshoed to the face. En route, still in darkness, we had to throw snowballs at a curious mountain lion to scare it away.

The ice was much thicker this time, and we swung leads up three pitches of fun, blue WI3. We first climbed up the right edge of the ten-meter-wide flow, then traversed to the left edge. Steep snow in the upper bowl led to the base of the rocky upper face. Two mixed pitches (up to M3) brought us to the ridge, topping out just left of the summit cornice. A short scramble led to the top (300m, WI3 M3, steep snow). To descend, we walked off the east ridge and back to the base, then snowshoed and biked back out.

—Eric Gilbertson

SLOAN PEAK, WEST FACE, BORROWED TIME

The west face of Sloan Peak (7,835') has been at the forefront of my mind for about as long as I've been winter climbing. Despite numerous attempts, the main face was unclimbed to the summit in winter conditions until 2022, with the completion of Superalpine (IV WI3/4, Legallo-Roy). In 2023, the Merrill-Minton (1,600', IV WI4+) was climbed partway up the center of the face, then rightward to join Superalpine. A previous winter line on Sloan Peak, Full Moon Fever (IV 5.8 AI4 R, Downey-Hinkley-Hogan, 2011), started on the west face, then angled up the northern shoulder.

Directly above the point where the Merrill-Minton cuts right to easier ground, a large hanging dagger is guarded by gently overhanging, compact gneiss. Known as one of the biggest unpicked plums in the North Cascades, the direct line past the dagger was going to get climbed sooner or later—it was just a question of by whom and in what style. When a perfect weather window arrived in the forecast, I convinced Justin Sackett to drive up from Portland for an attempt.

Early on January 19, 2025, we stepped away from the car and into the rainforest. We reached the base of the route at first light. Following the Merrill-Minton for the first three pitches, we encountered climbing up to WI5 R—a far cry from the moderate ice reported on the first ascent. Below the dagger, we took a short break and got ready for an adventure. I'd chosen to leave the bolt kit behind. This route deserved an honest attempt on natural gear before being sieged.

After traversing back and forth a few times, I chose my line to the ice and started up. The rock on this portion of the wall is highly featured but compact and fractured. Just about every seam that might take gear was packed full of frozen moss; finding decent protection was a slow, agonizing process. A steep crux near the end of the pitch held potential for a huge fall, but an improbable no-hands rest allowed me just enough of a reprieve to get good gear.

TOP: The crux mixed pitch of Borrowed Time looms over pitch three. ***Michael Telstad***

BOTTOM: The west face of Sloan Peak and Borrowed Time (1,900', IV WI5 M7). The line starts on the Merrill-Minton (2023) and continues straight up where that route moves right. See the *AAJ* website for all routes on the face. ***John Scurlock***

Justin joined me in the sun, and we continued up a final lead of perfect blue water ice to snow slopes. Rather than finish via the standard scramble route, we opted for an obvious corner system above us. Reminiscent of Shaken, not Stirred on the Mooses Tooth, this narrow slot held steps of water ice broken by sections of steep snow—the ideal finish to an excellent climb.

Arriving on the windless summit around 3:45 p.m., we took a short break and began our descent along the southeast shelf. After what felt like an eternity of steep downclimbing, we post-holed back to the cars, arriving a bit after 8 p.m. Our direct new route is called Borrowed Time (1,900', IV WI5 M7).

—Michael Telstad

Eric Gilbertson with a differential GPS on the summit of Liberty Cap. *Ross Wallette*

WASHINGTON | Cascades

STUART RANGE, JABBERWOCKY TOWER, SONG OF THE SUMMER

Jabberwocky Tower is a unique peak just east of Colchuck Lake in the Enchantments, visible from various spots nearby. Hundreds of people walk by Jabberwocky on a summer weekend without giving it a second look, but the formation was first climbed decades ago, by its short east side. In 2023, while climbing with my wife, Jenn Carter, I took a picture of Jabberwocky without knowing what it was, then did some research back home. In June of 2024, I asked 18-year-old Sam Allen—one of the students-turned-instructors in the Mountaineers' Youth Club—if he was interested in taking a look at the tower's southwest spur with 60-year-old me. He warmly obliged.

By the time we got there in July, another party, Erik Koch and David Wood, had been poking around on the southwest side. We later confirmed they climbed pitches one, four, and seven of our eventual line, but they decided not to share their full route, which wandered more than our line on the crest; they reported a three-pitch alternate start to the southwest spur called Sandpiper Start (5.7+). Sam and I established the first two pitches of our route, a 5.9 and a 5.10b with lovely hand and fist cracks in solid rock.

In early August, Jenn joined the project, and we pushed the climb up three more pitches. On August 16, Jenn, Sam, and I climbed two final pitches (5.10 and 5.10c) to finish. Song of the Summer (7 pitches, III 5.10c) required several 20-plus-hour days of hiking, climbing, clearing loose blocks, and drilling anchors for safer passage. The climb has three protection bolts, and the first two belays are bolted.

—Wayne Wallace

SHRINKING SUMMITS ON RAINIER AND OTHER PEAKS

Between August and October, with the help of climbing partners Saulius Bračiulis, Alden Ryno, Josh Spitzberg, and Ross Wallette, I conducted ground surveys of the current elevations of Mt. Rainier and the other four ice cap peaks in the Lower 48 states: Liberty Cap, Eldorado Peak, Colfax Peak, and East Fury (all in Washington). This work was funded by a Research Grant from the American Alpine Club.

I discovered that Columbia Crest, the historical summit of Mt. Rainier, has melted down 21.8' since the last ground survey in 1998 and is no longer the summit. The new summit is a rock on the southwest rim at 14,399.6'. The melting began in the early 2000s, and the summit likely switched to the southwest rim around 2014. Measurements were conducted in August and September using professional surveying equipment and reviewed by Larry Signani, the geodesist for the 1988, 1998, and 2010 Rainier surveys conducted by the Land Surveyors' Association of Washington.

I discovered that only two of the original five ice cap peaks still have ice cap summits. Eldorado Peak's ice cap has melted down 20', and the mountain now has a rock summit at 8,873.3'. East Fury has melted 30' and also has a rock summit (8,321.5'). Liberty Cap has melted 26.3', but the top is still an ice cap (14,090.7'). As of the survey, Colfax was at 9,439.9' and still had an ice cap summit.

—Eric Gilbertson

CALIFORNIA | Yosemite National Park

MIDDLE CATHEDRAL ROCK, NORTH FACE, GAIA

In the spring of 2023, while walking along the base of Middle Cathedral Rock's north face, Brandon Adams and I stumbled upon an inspiring wavelike corner, just west of the infamous North Buttress (V 5.10a, Harding-Holden-Tarver-Whitmer, 1954). We excitedly climbed the corner and looked up: More corners and features looked to end at a large ledge 1,000' higher. It seemed like a worthy adventure.

Later that summer, we climbed above the wave, linking dirty corners with bold face climbing. From the corners, we could see that the adjacent face and dull arêtes to our right promised fantastic climbing. We did six additional pitches—including an immaculate 5.9 hand crack—up to the big ledge, the site of an amazing bivy we named the Panda Palace.

After fixing ropes down from our high point, we began exploring the wall between the dirty corners—which we believe are part of the North Face Route (V 5.9 A4, Kamps-Pratt-Roper, 1959)—and Morning Lumber (III 5.11c, Wah-Way, 1990s). The line that would become Gaia starts on the wave, then climbs an exquisite white granite face, and finishes on a glorious red dihedral we named the Red Fox Corner in honor of the elusive, beautiful, and endangered Sierra Nevada critter of that name. Pitch four was the hardest, featuring desperate 5.12c slab. We replaced the bolts of Morning Lumber—which protect a steep 5.11+ section—that lead into the Red Fox Corner.

By the end of the summer, in a cumulative two weeks of effort, we'd established the first seven pitches of Gaia. [*This block has become a route unto itself, redpointed by Adams and the author, Lance Colley, in the fall of 2023 at 5.12c.*] We would have to return the next year to take it to the summit of Middle Cathedral.

Gaia (2,200', 18 pitches, VI 5.12c A3+) on the north face of Middle Cathedral Rock. The arrow marks the shared start of Father Time (2012) and Daddy Issues (2024), both of which finish on the steep pillar in upper right. ***Lance Colley***

In late May 2024, we again fixed ropes up to the Panda Palace to establish a comfy base camp. From there, we traversed right and up a pinnacle to the base of a headwall. I led an A2 pitch, at the end of which I found an old anchor and evidence of a climb going left to obvious roofs and corners. We could find no information on this unreported route. In search of an adventure, we looked to the right at much smaller, more elusive features.

We transitioned into the mindset of hard aid to tackle steep, blank granite for three pitches. The A3+ aid crux was protected by thin beaks and ended with a very cool hooking traverse on a golden-orange dike.

The next morning, our friends Miles

Fullman and Sam Stuckey climbed our fixed lines to the Panda Palace to join us. Above our high point, two new pitches of 5.10 free climbing brought us to the Kat Walk traverse ledge, where we bivvied.

In the morning, Miles took the sharp end and free climbed an overhanging arch that he protected with hammered beaks. Sam led the penultimate pitch with a mixture of free and aid. The honor of the last pitch fell to me: A mix of easy free climbing and aid, followed by a long traverse on hooks, took me to a classic, slightly chossy Yosemite top-out. On the summit, we sat in the sun with big, cheesy smiles. Gaia (2,200', 18 pitches, VI 5.12c A3+) is not to be missed.

—Lance Colley

MIDDLE CATHEDRAL ROCK, DADDY ISSUES: *In May, Americans Nik Berry and Will Sharp completed Daddy Issues (5.13+) on Middle Cathedral's north face. The partial new route follows the first ten pitches of Father Time (AAJ 2013) before moving right off a bivy ledge into four new pitches of steep climbing. Daddy Issues links back into Father Time for the Boulder Problem pitch (5.13), then follows six more new pitches to the top. The crux came on pitch 16. After cleaning and working the key pitches top-down, Berry and Sharp completed a two-day ground-up free ascent. Days later, the duo sent the climb in 13.5 hours.*

—Julian Dreiman, *AAJ, with information from published reports*

CALIFORNIA | Eastern Sierra

THE INCREDIBLE HULK, CHOOSE JOY

Over 15 years of exploring and countless days of dreaming led to the discovery of a new route on the tallest section of the Incredible Hulk in the High Sierra. The basis for the route was an array of features I had spied over the years while climbing classics on the peak's roughly 1,200' walls. During the COVID-19 lockdowns and California's smoke apocalypse of 2020, my wife, Monica, and I took extended climbing trips to the area, armed with binoculars and our imaginations. We spent a lot of time gazing from the cliffs surrounding Maltby Lake, which offer a unique perspective from slightly up-canyon of the typical bivy area.

Putting a rough plan in place, I spent the next couple of years roping in various partners for ground-up exploration on different potential lines. We scoured the right side of the west face of the Hulk, trying to link the desired crack systems. After cruising dreamy, well-protected sections, we'd be stymied by closed seams or blank faces that forced us onto existing routes or dangerously loose new terrain. We pioneered some decent pitches that led to nowhere in the area left of what became our final line, and we did a chossy 5.10 that topped out to the left of Red Dihedral, right of our final line.

With our ground-up methods exhausted, we started swinging around to seek out the highest-quality free climbing. The advice I got from other developers was to "make it classic," and we aimed for that. In the end, following the cleanest rock was the key to the line. I spent two summer seasons—2022 and 2023—scrubbing and equipping, primarily alone, rope-soloing Positive Vibrations (5.11a) to access the bottom half of the new line or Red Dihedral (5.10) to access the top.

In the summer of 2024, my wife and I attempted the route and found it harder than expected. We had to redpoint most of the five 5.12s, cleaning and working our way up. The crux third pitch, a beautiful 5.13- splitter, was out of my league due to soaring summer temperatures and my still-developing fitness.

Monica and I worked out a 5.11 variation around the pitch, but the direct route deserved a proper send. Eventually the temperatures dropped, and with refined beta and support from one of the

Sierra's main crushers, Chase Leary, I was able to pull off a no-falls free ascent on August 28. The ascent included a thrilling runout due to skipping the gear placements I had rehearsed for the 5.13- crux—I climbed through the hardest part to a thumb jam, then barely got in a below-knee placement. I also got to witness some amazing onsighting by Chase, and the absolute glory light and stoke we had topping out the 1,200' line.

Choose Joy (12 pitches, IV 5.13a) is a safe, no-grovel endurance route characterized by sustained 5.11 to 5.12- crack and face climbing between nice belay stances. We placed bolts where necessary. This route provided me with a ton of joy, and I hope it will do the same for others.

Other people who made this happen included Josh McClure, Peter Foster, Louie Allen, Brendan Cathcart, Sarah Shaw, Allen Higginbotham, and Joanie Swarthout. The route lies in the Hoover Wilderness: Permits and bear cans are required and waste bags are strongly recommended for the area.

—Abel Jones

Monica Jones on pitch five (named the Green Flame, 5.12b) of the new route Choose Joy on the Incredible Hulk. *Abel Jones*

THE INCREDIBLE HULK, INFINITY GAUNTLET

It's a funny story: My first time hiking in to climb the Incredible Hulk was in 2003 with my friend Allen Currano. He caught wind of a prank I was going to pull, and he found a way to meet me at my own juvenile level. We *both* changed into spandex Spider-Man costumes at the base and did probably the first team Marvel superhero ascent of the peak. Other lighthearted ascents followed as I fell in love

The west face of the Incredible Hulk, showing the new routes (1) Choose Joy and (2) Infinity Gauntlet. Route (3) is the classic Red Dihedral. Many other routes are not shown. ***Jeremy Collins***

with the place, including a stimulating ski-in February ascent of Beeline with Chris McNamara.

In the spring of 2024, when I sent a note to prolific Hulk climber Dave Nettle with an idea for a new line right up the middle of the face, he replied with some advice and gave his blessing: "If you are motivated, why not go explore the possibilities there? Go get it, amigo!" My longtime partner Jarod Sickler also has a Hulk crush, and he was quick to join the effort. Moi Medina, a part-time DJ and full-time history professor in Los Angeles, was headed to Tuolumne at about the same time, but when I told him what we had in mind, he quickly rerouted.

We left the ground with low expectations for rock quality: The line is *the* obvious weakness up the center, so for all we knew there was a great reason it hadn't been climbed. Fortunately, we found the choss manageable and the short sections of crunchy rock cleaned up without too much hassle.

Starting about 100' left of the Red Dihedral (12 pitches, IV 5.10, Bard-Farrell-Locke, 1975) and about 100' right of Tradewinds (9 pitches, IV 5.11+, Davis-Nettle, 2006), we stayed committed to not getting pulled into the "folds" on our right, an accordion series of tight dihedrals that looked like a shattered Devils Tower. In the end, the line was mostly moderate, like its popular neighbor, with short, punchy cruxes and fantastic, airy positions. Notably, pitch four offered a tips layback (5.11c) leading into a bomb-bay chimney, and pitch five had a 5.11d boulder problem (the crux of the route) on a hanging arête. The final pitch (5.10), a flaring hand crack, finished up a spindly, stand-alone blocky tower.

In all, Infinity Gauntlet (12 pitches, IV 5.11d) took us two long weekends to establish. We drilled 17 protection bolts on lead. While our primary goal was to create a quality route, our secondary goal was to create a better descent option for Red Dihedral than the standard scramble-to-single-rappel-to-loose-1,000-foot-gully option. There are 13 rap stations straight to the ground that double as belays on the way up; we added a rappel station halfway up the first 70m pitch to ensure no rap was longer than 35m.

The harder pitches looked to be avoidable via variations to the right (which would need some serious cleaning to be safe). For anyone that is interested in establishing said variations: A) Have at it, and B) learn from us and avoid doing so during high season when other parties are around.

—Jeremy Collins

MT. ABBOT, NORTHWEST FACE, WARNING SHOT

To access the remote northwest face of Mt. Abbot (13,715'), I hiked in from the Mosquito Flat trailhead to the east, past Ruby Lake and Mills Lake, to Abbot's northeast side. The bulletproof ice (AI2) of the Petit Griffon Couloir (leading to the eponymous needlelike spire) brought me to the col between Mt. Abbot and Mt. Mills. I then descended fourth-class terrain to the west for several hundred feet before

Descending off the summit blocks of Golden Trout Spire after the first known ascent of the formation. The mountains in the background (south) are Royce Peak (left) and Feather Peak. Two routes up Royce Peak were climbed on the same day in 2024: the North Ridge Direct, facing the camera, and the East Pinnacle, on the left skyline. *Zach Lovell*

making a very loose fourth-class traverse across the northwest face of Abbot. This traverse crossed several ribs of broken granite. I climbed the farthest right rib via clean finger and hand cracks for about 800' to reach the summit ridge, notching the first ascent of Warning Shot (III 5.5 AI2). I descended by the standard North Couloir route (Brower-Clyde-Voge, 1934).

—Trevor Shumaker

ROYCE LAKES BASIN, ROYCE PEAK, TWO NEW ROUTES

In July 2024, Matt O'Brien and I hiked 11 miles up to Royce Lakes Basin, a beautiful area with three large alpine lakes surrounded by towering peaks. We spent several days there, during which we established two new alpine rock routes.

On our second day in the basin, we set out toward Royce Peak (ca 13,280'), where we established the North Ridge Direct (1,500', 6 pitches, III 5.10). Several pitches of steep 5.10 cracks brought us up to the exposed fourth- and fifth-class north ridge—the end of which is also the finish for the Northeast Face (5.6)—which we took to the summit.

During the walk-off to the south, we decided to hook around the east side of the mountain and go back up an exposed, east-facing ridge of the mostly detached spire that towers over Royce Lake. To our knowledge, there are no other routes on this feature.

While we expected easy ridge scrambling, we were surprised to encounter pitch after pitch of quality rock interspersed with exciting ridge traversing. An exit pitch through a deep chimney deposited us on top of the spire. A bit of easy fifth-class traversing and downclimbing brought us to a final third-class ridge and then the summit of Royce Peak for the second time that day. We called the route East Pinnacle (1,500', 9 pitches, III 5.9).

—Matt Carpenter

Disco Scouts (625′, 6 pitches, 5.11a), the first known route on Moonrise Spire. *Zach Lovell*

PINE CREEK PASS AND GRANITE PARK AREAS, THREE NEW ROUTES

How does one determine whether it's a climbing trip with some fishing, or a fishing trip with some climbing? From August 9 to 16, Mike Hathorn, Dan Wolfskill, and I enjoyed a multisport week, catching several dozen trout and three new climbs in the Pine Creek Pass and Granite Park areas. By the numbers, one might conclude we're becoming better fishermen than climbers, but at least we eat well in the mountains.

On August 9, we hiked in to Honeymoon Lake from the Pine Creek Pass trailhead. The next day, on the northeast face of an unnamed formation (ca 12,050') southeast of Bear Claw Spire (also known as Treasure Peak), we chased crack systems from the toe of the face that led to a crux headwall with a gently overhanging and left-leaning splitter. We continued up the same left-leaning crack on more moderate terrain to the formation's east ridge, which ultimately led us to the summit via a memorable arête pitch. Unable to find any record of a previous ascent, we named the formation Moonrise Spire—after the crescent moon rising in the sky during our descent (made via a plateau to the south and a gully to the east)—and our route Disco Scouts (625', 6 pitches, 5.11a).

On August 12, we focused on a south-southeast-facing wall in French Canyon, on the flanks of Merriam Peak. From camp, we walked over Pine Creek Pass and descended to the first waterfall splitting the wall. We climbed around eight pitches with grades from low fifth class to 5.10, generally sticking to the left side of the waterfall on an arête feature. Meet Your Shower (1,000', 8 pitches, 5.10a) is named for the frequent misting we received from the waterfall and the Perseid meteor shower we watched from camp the previous night.

We reeled in one more climb on August 14, this time in the Granite Park area, on an unnamed spire (ca 12,550') southeast of Granite Park Spire. We hiked up the Italy Pass Trail and followed an easy rib to the spire's east face. We found some of the cleanest granite of the entire week, with three pitches of hand cracks guiding

The arrow marks the start of Dry Flyin' (700′, 5.10b) on the east face of previously unnamed Golden Trout Spire. *Zach Lovell*

us through the main shield of rock. The remainder of the climb rambled up an aesthetic ridge directly to the summit, with optional gendarme boulder problems that could be bypassed to the right. We dubbed our route Dry Flyin' (700', 5.10b) and named the formation Golden Trout Spire. We descended easily via scrambling and scree skiing on the west and south sides.

—Zach Lovell

MERRIAM PEAK, HEART OF DARKNESS

After a successful trip to Royce Lakes Basin earlier in the season (*see report on page 141*), Matt O'Brien and I decided to return in July with our friend Daniel Dunn to try a new route on Merriam Peak. We spied a couple of weaknesses left of the North Buttress (1,000', IV 5.10b, Clevenger-Harrington, 1976) and through the center of the steep wall between this and the northeast ridge. A huge heart-shaped feature in the middle looked like it had two different cracks that might afford passage to the top.

Two long pitches up runnels, corners, and flakes brought us to the base of the heart. We chose the left crack system—a steep stemming corner that led to a series of large roofs. From a stance under the first roof, I was barely able to reach a protruding diving-board ledge. A wild and exposed mantel onto this feature got me past the largest of the roofs—it also made for an excellent and novel belay station.

After another cruxy roof on the next pitch, the steepest part of the wall was behind us. A long, sustained splitter crack led to a feature previously named the Throne Room—a giant, comfortable ledge about 700' up that is shared with Silver Cloud (IV 5.10d A0, Harden-O'Brien, 1994). We followed Silver Cloud for most of a short traversing pitch before branching off again on a previously unclimbed wide crack that brought us to an exposed ledge at the top of the headwall. From here, we witnessed a beautiful sunset followed quickly by nightfall as we rappelled the route.

We returned the next day to connect our route to the top of the mountain via a short, unprotected traverse right. The completed line, Heart of Darkness (1,100', 9 pitches, IV 5.11-), shares terrain with the final pitch of the North Buttress.

Due to grainy rock and the unprotected traverse up high, we would recommend that future parties climb straight up from the fourth-pitch anchor or step left and take easier terrain to gain a ledge system that can be traversed into a better finish on the North Buttress.

—Matt Carpenter

Mt. Goode from the north, showing Tiger Lily (III 5.11-), with the striking thin crack running up the orange and gold panel. The North Buttress, first climbed in 1974, is just to the left. ***Cole Taylor***

MT. GOODE, TIGER LILY

On the north aspect of Mt. Goode (13,085'), a beautiful peak near Bishop Pass, is a narrow gray panel, orange-streaked and mottled yellow, just to the right of the classic North Buttress route. A crack runs up the center of this panel, visible from afar with the naked eye.

On July 30, Crystal Dunbar and I started from the toe of an initial buttress on clean cracks; this pitch could be bypassed via a 4th-class ramp to the left (east). We intersected and then followed the ramp for a second pitch to reach the base of the colored panel.

Many micronuts and occasional cams protected the seam running up the panel until a point where the crack blanks out for a body length or two. Here, one birdbeak was placed for protection and subsequently removed. Above this crux, the crack opens up a bit and the position is excellent. From a large ledge, we climbed left and up to finish on superb golden capstone to complete Tiger Lily (ca 700', 6 pitches, III 5.11-).

—Cole Taylor

CALIFORNIA | Western and Southern Sierra

KINGS RIVER NORTH FORK, THREE DOMES

In 2023 and 2024, Dave Nettle, Brandon Thau, and partners climbed four new routes on three domes along the North Fork of the Kings River, east of Courtright Reservoir: Squatters Right (7 pitches, 5.8), on Cabinland Dome (7,965'); Dry Lube (4 pitches, 5.11) and Jiffy Lube (6 pitches, 5.10) on Dry Lube Dome; and Without a Doubt (4 pitches, 5.10-), on Distant Dome (8,200'). On Cabinland Dome, Thau and Daniel Jeffcoach had put up a line in 2017 called Cabinland (6 pitches, 5.11-). Nettle's report and topos are at the *AAJ* website.

—Information from Dave Nettle

The west ridge of Oyster Peak, dubbed Mother of Pearl Ridge (1,500′ of roped climbing, III 5.7), is along the left skyline. ***Daniel Jeffcoach***

OYSTER PEAK, MOTHER OF PEARL RIDGE

In mid-August, David Stone and I hiked 20-plus miles from the Rancheria trailhead on the east side of Wishon Reservoir to explore Blackcap Basin and the White Divide, an obscure corner of the Sierra in the John Muir Wilderness, just outside the border of Kings Canyon National Park. That first day, we got an up-close view of some formations we'd seen from afar on previous trips. We had a different objective in mind, but when David pointed out the silhouetted west ridge of Oyster Peak (12,323')—right as the sun was setting—it looked too fun to pass up.

The next morning, August 16, we made the short hike from camp to the left end of the lower buttresses and started up. There are many possible starts; we chose what looked to be the most direct. After three mellow 5.7 pitches, we gained the ridge, where another 1,000-plus feet of exposed, fifth-class simul-climbing awaited us. The rock, views, and long ridgeline were all high quality.

Climbing this route turned out to be a great decision, because our other objective swatted us down the next day. After such a heinous approach, we were happy to get Mother of Pearl Ridge (1,500' of roped climbing, III 5.7) as a very fun consolation prize. We didn't see another soul and don't know of any other technical routes on Oyster Peak.

—Daniel Jeffcoach

The Sage (1,060', 10 pitches, 5.10c) follows a series of corners, ramps, and chimneys up the southern aspect of the Fortress. Two prior routes ascend the east face, around the corner to the right. *Sam Fearer*

CASTLE ROCKS AREA: THE FORTRESS, THE SAGE

In early August, under a full summer sun, Dave Meyer and I set out to explore the seldom-visited easternmost formation of the Castle Rocks complex: the Fortress. Neither of us strangers to heavy loads and off-trail travel, we figured the approach would be demanding but still reasonable. We were wrong.

The Fortress was first climbed in 2012, by Daniel Jeffcoach, Vitaliy Musiyenko, and Tom Ruddy, who followed an obvious corner-to-offwidth system up the east face to establish The Siege (1,000', IV 5.10c A0). In 2016, Neal Harder, Chris LaBounty, and Brandon Thau added The Surge (1,000', 5.8), also on the east face.

Much has changed since then. For three months in 2021, the KNP Complex Fire burned along the hillsides of the Kaweah River's middle fork, consuming over 88,000 acres of forest and vegetation. Castle Rocks was not spared. Where pine duff and shade once were present, we found hillsides of loose, ashy, and at times thicket-infested fire soil, with nowhere to hide from the searing sun. We arrived at camp—a spartan, 15° sloping bivy site—much later than anticipated, and were more than a little relieved to hear the comforting tune of trickling water, just a 15-minute bushwhack away.

The next day, we set out on virgin terrain, deviating from the broad east face to explore a series of weaknesses we had noted on the formation's narrower southern aspect; our route corkscrewed around an enormous pillar feature that leans upon the main wall.

The climb begins in a clean left-facing corner on the climber's left side of the pillar and makes its way to the only surviving pine tree in the area, partway up the wall. From here, we climbed through a short, left-angling chimney to a shaded belay below the near-vertical upper half of the wall. A ramp system on featured Sequoia granite and a 200' pitch of jungle-gym climbing through huecos the size of beach balls landed us near the summit of the Fortress's southern turret.

We called our route The Sage (1,060', 10 pitches, IV 5.10c). Though much has changed in the area since the fire, the rock quality remains impeccable and the adventure is still high.

—Sam Fearer

SPRING LAKE WALL, SPRING ROLL

In early August 2024, Jack Schlinkert and I set out from Mineral King to hike in to Spring Lake Wall, intending to climb one of the established routes. As we set up camp, our attention shifted to the leftmost and—as far as we knew—only unclimbed face of the three walls that together make up Spring Lake Wall. (The three walls or buttresses are all part of Peak 11,480', and all with the same northern aspect.) We quickly abandoned our original plan.

Spring Roll (1,000', 5.10) is the first known route up the leftmost of the north-facing Spring Lake Wall buttresses. ***Thomas Sicilian***

The next morning, we started at the toe of the left buttress and found an enjoyable path on clean rock, complete with spacious belay ledges, that led us to a headwall roughly 330' up. We continued up steeper cracks through the headwall until the angle eased, though the climbing remained engaging for two more long pitches (5.9 and 5.6).

The climbing had been amazingly clean, well-protected, and fun. We named our new route Spring Roll (1,000', 6 pitches, III/IV 5.10).

—Thomas Sicilian

HOMERS NOSE, HOME RUN AND MR. BURNS

In late May 2024, Neal Harder, Josef Maier, Brandon Thau, and I established the first free route on the south face of Homers Nose (a.k.a. Homers Brow). This was our second attempt. We started on the first two pitches of Dance of Topo-Usha (5.10 A3), the original route on the formation, climbed by Richard Leversee, Dave Ohst, and John Tuttle in 1980. We freed their second pitch, originally rated A3, at 5.12a, adding a couple of bolts with Richard's blessing.

Dance of Topo-Usha then veers left into the huge gash that splits the south face. We were able to climb cracks straight up, which eventually led to incredible steep climbing on chicken heads. These pitches required some bolts, though a traditionnal rack is still needed. We named our route Home Run (650', 6 pitches, 5.12a).

Although relatively short for the effort involved in reaching it (15 miles and 7,500' of gain, mostly off-trail through dense brush), the continuously steep climbing and remoteness of the area make for a remarkable route. Having gotten to know Richard Leversee before he passed away in 2022, I believe he would have been overjoyed to hear we were able to put up such

Josef Maier, belayed by Neal Harder, enjoys the incredible chicken heads of the 5.11b fourth pitch of Home Run at Homers Nose. ***Brian Prince***

a great free route and that his original vision played a significant role.

On the same trip, we also established a route on the hiker's summit of Homers Nose, across the drainage to the west from the main climbing formation. This route, Mr. Burns (5.11b), connects excellent splitter cracks up the most continuous buttress on the south face for 600', followed by 500' of low fifth class to the summit.

—Brian Prince

Jacket Off (750', 5.10a) on a previously unclimbed formation in the Golden Trout Wilderness that was named Overlook Dome. *Daniel Jeffcoach*

OVERLOOK DOME, JACKET OFF

On November 2, Daniel Jeffcoach, Vitaliy Musiyenko, and I embarked on a nearly 30-mile approach from Monache Meadows to the Kern River region to scout some intriguing formations. We camped at the natural bridge feature near Lava Falls on Golden Trout Creek. The next day, we approached a dome-like formation below Overlook Mountain. This formation is clearly visible from the Needles, 20 air miles away.

We chose the best-looking line on the west face and climbed a direct route to the summit. Jacket Off (750', 5.10a) featured face climbing on textured rock with intermittent cracks and sparse but adequate protection. There is definitely room for more routes, especially if willing to face climb. We called the formation Overlook Dome.

On November 4, we explored Tower Rock, our main objective of the trip and also devoid of routes. Although it is a significant wall, its ledgy and vegetated character deterred us. With a lot of time and work, one could surely find a proud route up it. Instead, we spent the day appreciating this unique corner of the Sierra before the long hike out.

—Brian Prince

CALIFORNIA | Whitney Area

MT. BARNARD, EAST RIB

I had long heard about the classic 1972 East Pillar route on Mt. Barnard's east peak (ca 13,680'): It has a reputation for quality rock and movement, guarded by a big, brushy approach. (Its name also has a convoluted history, having been variously called the East Pillar, the East Face, and the Rowell-Auger, after first ascensionists Galen Rowell and Tim Auger.) Looking at photos of the route and face, I saw potential for a new line up a subtle ridge to the left of both the East Pillar and the 2013 Maiden-Tomczik route (which is itself to the left of the East Pillar). This ridge feature tends to blend into the larger face in pictures. In mid-September, Jake Terry and I hiked in six miles on the abandoned Vacation Pass Trail along George Creek, hoping to climb the classic route and maybe put up our own.

The East Pillar was as good as I had heard, and it gave us a decent vantage point from which to view the unclimbed ridge. The next day we started up this subtle feature. Our first few pitches wandered along the path of least resistance through mediocre rock. Once the ridge feature became more defined, we found typical Sierra ridge climbing, replete with towers and fun trundling. Jake led us up a cool orange face on the second tower. Our eighth pitch was 50m up the last tower on good gray granite. A sharp left here took us to a huge, sandy ledge, where the ridge intersected the larger east face perpendicularly.

We had several options for finishing our new route: Far left was an unappealing gully; center-left looked cool—but also hard. We opted for a weakness on the right. To get there, we climbed a short, shallow, left-facing corner, with thin moves and thin pro right off the sandy ledge. This pitch—a 30m rightward traverse—proved to be the crux of the route. It led us to a crack system that we followed to the top, and a quick hike brought us to the summit. The descent by the northeast slope took us down sand, through a beautiful little meadow, past a remarkably large boulder, and right to our camp. We called our route the East Rib (1,500', 5.10a). [*Editor's Note: The author pointed out that, per High Sierra Climbing, Volume 1, by Vitaliy Musiyenko and Roger Putnam, a route on the right side of Barnard's east face—The Good, The Bad, The Awesome (AAJ 2015), reported by Doug Tomczik—followed some or all of a 1990 route known as the East Dihedral, established by Ken Kanega and Pat Brennan.*]

—Ian McEleney

The East Rib (1,500', 5.10a) on the east peak of Mt. Barnard. The East Pillar route (Auger-Rowell, 1972) climbs almost directly up to the prominent spire. See *AAJ 2015* for other route lines. *Jake Terry*

ARCTIC LAKE WALL, COOLER THAN A POLAR BEAR'S TOENAILS

In August, Daniel Dunn, Rett English, and I visited Arctic Lake Wall and climbed a new route up the center, aiming for the left side of the wall's largest roofs. We took a line to the left of Arctic Beast (700', III 5.11c, Prince-Musiyenko, 2016) on what we believe was entirely new terrain.

We followed continuous cracks and corners from the bottom of the wall up to the roofs, bolting belays along the way. When we reached the stacked roofs, we searched around for a weakness, eventually finding one via a steep layback crack to bypass the first roof, then a traverse under the second roof. Above, we found more vertical to overhanging terrain. The rock quality on Cooler Than a Polar Bear's Toenails (700', 5 pitches, III 5.11-) was excellent, the climbing engaging and sustained, and the exposure exciting.

—Matt Carpenter

KEELHAUL

EXTREME "CALPINISM" ON KEELER NEEDLE

By Andy Puhvel

For five packed seasons, from 2018 to 2022, my main mate, Chase Leary, and I established hard multipitch first ascents on some of the best climbing formations in the High Sierra. In the northern Sierra, we looted the Incredible Hulk, establishing Green Thunder (700', 5 pitches, 5.13b) and Up in Smoke (700', 6 pitches, 5.13a). In the central Sierra, Trapezoid Peak provided a bounty of four great routes, including Shield of Dreams (700', 5 pitches, 5.13b), with the High Sierra's only gear-protected 5.13 pitches (*AAJ 2023*). We were hungry for more, so we turned to the great Whitney Massif in the southern part of the range for more "Calpinism"—the stellar weather and epic granite form of alpinism in California's High Sierra.

At 14,260', Keeler Needle is the proudest spire on the Whitney Massif. Nearly perfectly symmetrical and rising 2,000' from the glacier to the Sierra Crest, Keeler is flanked to the north by Mt. Whitney and to the south by Day Needle, both also over 14,000'. Unlike its blocky neighbors and most Sierra mountains, Keeler is a sheer face capped by an overhanging headwall, a tower that would seem more at home in

Chase Leary leads the immaculate Gemstone crack, the 11th pitch (5.13c) of Keelhaul on the east face of Keeler Needle. ***Cashus Puhvel***

wild Patagonia or Pakistan than in mellow California. Legends such as Warren Harding, Jeff Lowe, and Ammon McNeely have grabbed first ascents up this high-country prize.

In late 2022, I began to study photos and topos of Keeler's east face. I knew about the Harding Route, established in 1960 and freed in 1976 by Galen Rowell, Chris Vandiver, and Gordon Wiltsie, and still considered one of the mega routes of the range. I wanted to learn about the more modern routes.

In the center of the east face is The Crimson Wall (2,000', 16 pitches, 5.12 A3), put up well before its time, in 1991, by Kevin Brown, Mike Carville, and Kevin Steele (with a 5.12 direct finish added by Brown and Carville the following summer). I remember getting an issue of *Climbing* magazine and reading a short but eye-popping paragraph about their ascent. Sport climbing had barely been invented, and there were only a handful of 5.13 climbs in all of California. This was 5.12 at 14,000' in the High Sierra. The Crimson Wall stands as one of the most visionary lines in the entire range.

Most recently, in 2012, the local hardcore duo of Myles Moser and Amy Ness established Blood of the Monkey, a proud and burly free line (2,000', 16 pitches, 5.12a). This hard-fought route has seen only a handful of repeats, with reports attesting to its bold style and engaging climbing.

To me, the most promising route for a new free climb on the Needle came from the legendary aid master Ammon McNeely, a.k.a. the El Cap Pirate. In 1999, Ammon and Kevin Conti spent eight days nailing and hooking up the dead center of the wall, establishing the brilliant line Australopithecus (2,000', 16 pitches, 5.10 A3+). The route takes a thin crack up the middle of the 300' headwall, and Ammon named it "the Gemstone." I was smitten.

The line of Keelhaul on the 2,000-foot east face of Keeler Needle. About half of the route is shared with the 1999 aid line Australopithecus (5.10 A3+, Conti-McNeely). Day Needle is to the left. *Andy Puhvel*

Winter of 2023 arrived, and it was off the charts. The largest-ever recorded snowfall in the Sierra piled up over 700 inches on the East Side. For months I studied Ammon's route in every internet photo and topo I could get my hands on. Almost every morning, coffee mug in hand, I would check out Australopithecus, feeling a strange sense of connection.

February brought a one-week break in the weather. I called Chase, a ski patroller at Mammoth Mountain, and asked if he'd be game to ski up from the desert to scope the route. We planned to go on the following Monday, but on Sunday something terrible happened: Ammon died. He had driven with his partner, Sarah Watson, to watch the sunset from a cliff near his home in Moab, Utah. Walking out onto a rocky point, Ammon lost his balance and fell. Although I had met him only once, and knew him mostly through Valley lore and films, I perceived a powerful omen.

Chase Leary (left) and Andy Puhvel ask Warren "Batso" Harding for his blessing outside the Mill Creek Station museum in Bishop. ***Chip Powell***

Finally, spring arrived, and in April 2023 we got to work. Our strategy was to climb the Harding Route and then traverse the face and rappel our line to see if it would go. This mission proved exciting, with snow, ice, and sketchy anchors. Our morale was boosted when we discovered that the first eight pitches would make for great free climbing up to about 5.12+.

The next mission was to check out the daunting headwall. We slogged up Whitney's Mountaineer's Route and summited Keeler from the back side. We rapped 400' off the top, to Harding Ledge, then lowered into the unknown.

The headwall was mostly a blank panel—steep and airy. The Gemstone crack split the center, much like the Salathé headwall crack, undulating between fingers and hands, with an occasional pod offering a rest. Although a few sections were discontinuous, there were intermittent face holds. We knew we were in for it.

For 18 weeks straight, we made long day trips from Bishop up to the Whitney cirque to clean and buff the line, for beauty and safety. Arriving at the wall after the five-mile, 4,600' approach, we would jumar or Mini Traxion fixed lines to work on different pitches. In the spirit of Captain Ammon, we adopted pirate attitudes and humor, filling our days with seafaring jokes. Ammon's topo included pitches called "The Great White Shield" and "X Marks the Spot," as well as the Gemstone. Half the pitches we established were variations to the aid line, and we added our own monikers: "Release the Kraken" is an ultra-pumpy, overhanging 5.12d flake that tends to drool a slimy black streak after a good rain; "Captain Reach" is a 13a bolted pitch with a painful pinky-lock move that tested even this six-foot-sixer's reach; "Lost at Seams," 5.12a, navigates a tiny off-vertical fissure through a series of intricate laybacks.

As we dialed the other pitches, it became clear the route came down to the Gemstone. At around 5.13c, the pitch was at both of our redpoint limits, and we understood why hard rock climbing at altitude was so much more intense. Climbing 1,500' to rehearse the pitch kicked our asses every time. We adopted new breathing techniques to deal with the thinner air, going into a trance of loud, powerful exhalations for minutes at a time to hyper-oxygenate. Often the belayer would count out the minutes aloud as the climber gasped for air at rests, making sure he stayed long enough to calm his heart.

In late September, we finally took a burn at the one-day send. Reaching the Gemstone without falls, we were both too exhausted even to have a go. The following week we tried again, this time sleeping poorly halfway up the wall in a portaledge. Chase gave it his all on the Gemstone, screaming his way up the final 20' of first-knuckle locks, only to take a spectacular 45-footer onto a tiny purple Metolius TCU. After 21 trips and two failed send burns, our season ended.

In April of 2024 we returned, having trained like fiends all winter. We reacquainted ourselves with the route, and within four quick trips felt ready. On our first redpoint attempt, we arrived at the headwall with fatigue and nerves getting the best of us. We had one more week and one more try before other plans would divert us. As we drove up to Whitney Portal on our 26th mission, deep burnout began to show.

"I'm kinda over it," Chase let slip. I agreed. Both of us knew we couldn't sustain our psych for these trips all season, and if we weren't fit enough now, we doubted we ever would be.

That evening we camped in the talus and strategized. Years of free climbing walls manifested in a barrage of ideas on how to save energy: Don't pull the cam triggers too hard, just gently; never rack the gear on your harness when following, just let it hang on the rope so the belayer pulls it up; relax your hands in every jam; and don't overgrip.

Andy Puhvel high on the first headwall pitch of Keelhaul, dubbed "Captain Reach" (pitch ten, 5.13a). ***Cashus Puhvel***

On June 5, we set sail up the first ten pitches, with me taking the bulk of the leads as a warm breeze blew up from the hot Owens Valley. We arrived at the hanging belay below the Gemstone, pitch 11, as the sun shifted to the west and shade chilled us. Chase bundled up in two down jackets and hunkered down for 45 minutes of rest. I insisted on massaging his forearms to get rid of any lactic acid. We pulled out all the tricks.

This time Chase floated, like nothing mattered, arriving at the belay to screams and tears of sheer mutual elation. I followed the pitch free—we each freed everything on the route, either on lead or seconding—unaware of dark thunderclouds creeping in overhead. As I stuck the final jug, the sky let out a deafening smack of thunder. The timing couldn't have been any crazier; the universe seemed to know we had broken through, and our energy synchronized with that of the mountains. As it began to drizzle, we hustled up the final 5.12a finger crack and onto Harding Ledge, thanking Keeler for her treasure and Captain Ammon for his map.

What about the summit? The next four pitches were only 5.10, but, if it kept raining, they would be unclimbable. Chase always tells me, "If you don't like the weather in the High Sierra, wait half an hour." Sure enough, the skies cleared to California blue, and we climbed to the perfect tabletop summit of Keeler Needle, where we belonged.

The climbers named the route Keelhaul (17 pitches, 5.13c). About half of the route follows the original line of Australopithecus; half of the pitches are new. Twenty-six protection bolts were placed, including some on previously aided pitches to enable safe free climbing.

MT. HITCHCOCK, SHADOW OF A DOUBT

In June, Honz Mikhalek and I approached remote Mt. Hitchcock (13,186') from Whitney Portal, hiking up and over the Sierra Crest to Guitar Lake basin, where we set up camp. We noticed an unclimbed buttress left of Starlight Dihedral on Hitchcock's broad northeast face; this 1,000' buttress has a steep headwall that tops out onto a dramatic 400' ridgeline, which from below appeared to be 3rd or 4th class.

After a 45-minute hike from camp, Honz and I swapped leads up two pitches of fun splitter cracks at 5.9 to low 5.10. Two long pitches of low-angle terrain brought us to the 200' headwall.

Here, delicate stemming (the crux) between flakes that were more secure than they looked led up through a sustained wide hand crack to a ledge 130' above the belay. Right off that belay, a short 5.9 crux protected by a bolt got us to the top of the headwall and around its right side to a low-angle, big-hand-size 5.8 dihedral. Two more pitches of easier climbing gained the top of the buttress.

The ridgeline that had looked like 3rd or 4th class actually consisted of several towers of dangerously stacked blocks. With the sun going down, we opted to rappel the route from there, leaving bolted anchors most of the way. (The next day, we came back with a few more bolts to replace cam anchors we'd left on the lower rappels.) We called our route Shadow of a Doubt (8 pitches, 5.10), after the Alfred Hitchcock thriller of the same name and because, on the final ridgeline, as shadows overtook the sunlight, we questioned the safety of trying to reach the true summit.

—Shaun Reed

SKY BLUE LAKE BASIN, FOUR NEW ROUTES

From July 16 to 24, Japhy Dhungana, Rainbow Weinstock, and I established four new routes in the Sky Blue Lake basin, a.k.a. Miter Basin, south of Mt. Whitney. While none of the climbs are particularly long, they're rich with good stone and great crack systems, with potential for more routes from future parties.

We approached from the Cottonwood Lakes trailhead and set up base camp in the idyllic Penned Up Meadow (36.50518, -118.27652). The following day, we hiked northeast 1.5 miles to the southeastern aspect of a previously unnamed spire (ca 12,300') on the west side of Rock Creek. After three or four pitches of mid-fifth-class climbing, we arrived at the base of a stunning headwall crack that offered two excellent pitches from offwidth to fingers. Our line wrapped to the east side of the formation for one final pitch to the summit. We downclimbed the brief north ridge to the first westerly gully, which needed only one rappel. We named the formation Sky Blue Spire and the route Sapphire Crack (700', 5.11d).

Next we established two routes on what we called the Sky Blue Diamond (ca 12,700'), a formation just north of Sky Blue Spire with a striking diamond-shaped shield on its northeast aspect and stupa-shaped summit blocks.

First, we entered an Altared State (900', 5.12a): one continuous crack system that ranged from strenuous hands to baggy fingers for three or four pitches, a stretch of 5.8–5.10, and a few hundred feet of third-to low-fifth-class soloing to the top.

The following day, we established Stupa Troopers (900', 5.12c), which had multiple pitches of 5.12 before joining the same easier terrain on Altared State. We descended both routes by downclimbing and rappelling the ascent route to a large ledge atop the main shield, from which we found a glorious walk-off to the north.

On the final climbing day, we did a new route on the west-southwest buttress of the Miter, a peak that has been climbed many times. We named our route The Pen Is Miter Than the Sword (600', 5.10), a reference to a series of *Boston Globe* articles written in the early 2000s regarding the Catholic Church. We descended via the north ridge and hiked out on July 24 with full hearts and tired fingers.

—Zach Lovell

ABOVE LEFT: Japhy Dhungana and Rainbow Weinstock hiking into the Sky Blue Lake drainage (a.k.a. Miter Basin). The Miter is the peak on the right. *Zach Lovell*

ABOVE: Dhungana leading one of the headwall pitches of Sapphire Crack (700', 5.11d) on Sky Blue Spire, with Zach Lovell belaying. *Rainbow Weinstock*

MT. LANGLEY, NORTH FACE, FELSIC HIGH ROAD

On August 25, Emma Kluge and I climbed a new route on Mt. Langley (14,026') in the southern Sierra. For a couple of years, I had been eyeballing the ridge to the west of Horizontal Thought Movement, a 5.8 on the north face put up by Ben Cohen and Nate Ricklin in 2009. This summer, the right timing, weather, and partner all aligned.

The independent ridge that we climbed ascends roughly 1,500' and tops out a few hundred yards west of the summit. After the approach from the Tuttle Creek trailhead and some third-class scrambling to the base of the route, we roped up and climbed a vertical crack on crumbly rock for a couple of pitches to gain the ridge proper. We stuck to the ridge and were rewarded with many pitches of awesome, exposed crack and knob climbing. A couple of hundred feet below the summit plateau, we crossed over a small tower and into a shallow notch, from which we climbed two final pitches. We soon reached the summit, elated and exhausted. We descended the Northeast Couloir back to the Tuttle Creek drainage and our camp.

We named the route Felsic High Road (1,500', III 5.8). We left no fixed gear.

—Damien Nicodemi

MONTANA | Lewis Range – Glacier National Park

FLINSCH PEAK, NORTH FACE, LOADED FOR BEAR

It started with a photo taken during an overnight ski trip in March 2021. A friend and I had skinned in to Old Man Lake, and the northeast ridge of Flinsch Peak (9,225') hung over our camp dramatically. I snapped the shot and not long after sent it to Adam Clark.

Loaded for Bear (IV 5.8) on the north face of Flinsch Peak, seen from Old Man Lake. During the October first ascent, autumn snow dotted the face. *NPS / Jacob W. Frank*

Fast-forward to October 2024. Despite talking about it for a few years, Adam and I had never gone up to Flinsch. A great trip to Canada in August proved we had a partnership built for this: both dads (me a new one) with similar risk tolerances, plus a simmering obsession with what that ridge might be like. So we made a plan, met up at 3 a.m. on October 6, and drove over to the Two Medicine area.

Climbing a north face in October means some serious guesswork when selecting gear. We left the car with a double rack of rock gear plus crampons. The pile led Adam to quip, "We're loaded for bear."

The pillars and steep terrain on the northeast ridge of Flinsch looked menacing, so we refocused our attention onto the adjacent north face. We headed for a weakness on the left side, pulling out the rope as the angle kicked up. Three pitches of talus ledges and short steps got us to the main show: the algal reef. (Anyone familiar with climbing in Glacier knows this formation: a limestone band in the mountain landscape that, on many ascents, proves to be the steepest section of the route.) We followed a left-trending weakness through the reef at well-protected 5.8.

From there, we simul-climbed right to reach a large dihedral system. The climbing was engaging, occasionally wet, and required at least one step over Jenga blocks that mercifully stuck together. After four more pitches up to 5.7, I belayed Adam up to the summit cairn, still Loaded for Bear (IV 5.8). We went down on the standard trail on Flinsch's south face.

—David Steele

SINOPAH MOUNTAIN, EAST FACE

Finding quality rock in Glacier National Park is a challenge, yet the plentiful steep faces provide endless potential for adventure climbing. In August, as I drove into the Two Medicine area of the park, a beam of light pierced the clouds, illuminating Sinopah Mountain (8,271') and its multi-gendarmed summit—highlighting a number of crack systems that promised a classic Glacier experience.

I worked my way up to the base of the east face with a light rack and short bail rope, intending to scout a potential line and come back another time. Following the path of least resistance, I reached an auditorium made up of quality red rock near 6,300'. At this point I switched to climbing shoes and decided to attempt a new route to the summit, solo.

Steep stemming and loose jamming, about 5.8, deposited me into the main depression on the left side of the east face. Fourth- and fifth-class climbing on decent rock for 400' brought me to the base of an intimidating headwall. I continued up by a left-facing corner, a hand traverse, and another left-facing corner with great hand and fist jams through two steep bulges, leading to an airy traverse back toward the middle of the headwall (5.9). After a lunch stop at a big ledge about 200' below the top of the headwall, I thrutched up a steep chimney of loose blocks, traversed a wide ledge, and cruised up a final finger crack to reach scrambling terrain and finally the summit.

I could find no evidence of prior ascents of this face—that said, climbing in Glacier has always been shrouded in secrecy. Either way, I believe the line probably climbs through new ground, and the East Face (1,800', IV 5.9) of Sinopah was a great adventure.

—Seth Anderson

IDAHO | Salmon River Mountains

STORM DOME, NORTHEAST FACE, PIKA PARADISE

In September 2023, I returned to Storm Dome, eight miles into the backcountry outside of McCall, Idaho, after having established two long free routes there in 2021 and 2022 (*see AAJ 2023*). Accompanied first by my wife, Erin, and later by several friends (Christina Garcia, Tim Greenwood, Ethan McKay, Duncan Ralph, and Abe Rigeb), I wanted to check out a line right of Heart of Diamond that went through a major roof system high on the wall. We managed to equip and partly clean the route before freezing temperatures shut us down for the season.

Returning in September 2024, Duncan and I fixed lines and got to work cleaning and working out the cruxes. For the first time ever, we were not the only ones out there; friends were simultaneously piecing together their own futuristic (and closed) project between

LEFT: Michal Matyjasik starting up Pika Paradise on Storm Dome. ***Duncan Ralph***

ABOVE: The line of No Rolling Stone on the Redside Wall, Impassable Canyon. ***Matt Ward***

Heart of Diamond and our new line.

Following days of relentless storms at camp and a smoke-induced sinus infection, the weather cleared. A few hours of patchy sunlight dried out our waterlogged gear and clothes. Duncan and I decided to make a push to free the route, starting just after 3 p.m. Right before we began hiking up to the wall, Abe came charging into camp with a pack full of fresh food. Perfect timing!

We freed the route up to the crux fifth pitch, but cold weather, damp rock, and lingering fatigue shut me down there. We left lines fixed to try again the next day. In the morning, Abe and I jugged the lines and I fired the 5.13b crux. I can't recall being more pumped in my life. We easily climbed the last two pitches, and Pika Paradise (200m, 7 pitches, IV 5.13b) was born. The route is a little more than half bolt-protected (39 lead bolts and bolted anchors).

Storm Dome now has three seven-to eight-pitch routes that, in my opinion, are comparable in quality to the best alpine granite climbs in the Lower 48. I think my tenure here has come to a close, but there are still opportunities for awesome new routes.

—Michal Matyjasik

IMPASSABLE CANYON, REDSIDE WALL, NO ROLLING STONE

"Beavers!" Ky Hart yelled over his shoulder.

"No! Bears!" I yelled back.

Actually, it was three bears. Two small black bear cubs were timidly swimming on an eddy line in the Middle Fork of the Salmon River. The large mama bear was waiting for her cubs to follow her across, and she stood up tall when she saw Ky and me about to swim between her and her babies.

"I'm gonna touch one!" Ky yelled out.

My instinct was to do the exact opposite—swim away from them. But the swift current was quickly moving us both directly at the cubs. Fortunately, our appearance shocked them into action. The cubs swam hard for mama, and the current shot us past them. Looking back on the experience later that day, it occurred to me that the fact that Ky's first thought was to swim over and touch a wild bear cub while its mother watched was one of many things that made him the perfect partner for this trip. Unhinged, yes. But our plan to hike 22 miles, swim three and a half miles of whitewater, and climb a new route on a backcountry big wall would require more than a little madness.

Impassable Canyon on the Middle Fork of the Salmon, deep in the heart of Idaho's massive Frank Church Wilderness, is legendary among river runners and all but unknown to climbers. River permits for the Middle Fork can only be won through a lucky pick in the annual lottery. Once a trip has launched, numerous necessary rules regulate the way that boaters can use the wilderness. One of these prohibits any river trip from camping more than one night in Impassable Canyon.

Ky Hart adds some natural flotation to his waterlogged backpack during the three-mile swim down the Middle Fork of the Salmon River. *Matt Ward*

Over three commercial seasons as a raft guide on the Middle Fork, I had become obsessed with what appeared to be the tallest wall in Impassable Canyon. I saw it for the first time as a terrified 15-year-old on a spring kayak trip; since then I've used the wall as a landmark for the famous Redside Rapid. Because of this, I've always called it the Redside Wall.

The Redside Wall is 82 river miles from the Boundary Creek boat ramp. The nearest trail to the wall crosses the river 3.5 miles upstream, but only after a 22-mile hike down Waterfall Creek. Over years of dreaming about trying to climb Redside, that seemed like the best option—except that those 3.5 downstream miles aren't walkable at water level; the river often runs against steep walls, leaving nowhere to hike or scramble. Hitchhiking downstream on river trips would also be illegal, since we wouldn't be listed on the boat's permit.

During one of many conversations with river and forest administrators on how to access the area legally, I finally asked the right question. "I don't need a permit to swim in the river, do I?" The answer was no, I didn't, delivered with a sideways glance and a chuckle.

At that moment, I hatched a plan. Ky and I would hike the Waterfall Creek Trail from the Bighorn Crags trailhead into Middle Fork Canyon, descending over 5,500' in 22 miles. Then we would swim with our backpacks down 3.5 miles of whitewater, including numerous Class III rapids. Then we would spend three days making the first ascent of a dramatically overhanging wall. Then we would join a friend's river trip (for which we were listed on the permit) and paddle out on some of North America's best whitewater.

On August 29, we began the hike. The Waterfall Creek Trail is in prime wildfire terrain, and we could see smoke rising from what had been a small fire in the Big Creek area only the week before. After eight hours on the move, we reached the Middle Fork and made camp near the Big Creek confluence. The charred

Matt Ward leads the first difficult aid pitch (A3) on the upper Redside Wall. Ward had cached climbing gear and a portaledge below the wall during a previous river trip. ***Ky Hart***

hillside across the river was smoking, and trees were still burning. We were awoken repeatedly that night by the sound of trees falling and rockfall.

The next morning, we walked until Cutthroat Cove Rapid, where the bank cliffed out. It was time to swim. We eased into the river wearing our PFDs, gasped at the chill of the water, and began the most ridiculous stage of the plan. The bear sighting happened within the first mile. Soon after, our lips were blue, our teeth chattering. Evidently, we had underdressed. Ky found driftwood logs and lashed them to his backpack. It worked surprisingly well and kept him farther out of the water. I opted for walking on sunlit banks when possible; this paid dividends when I found two beers that had been lost by some river trip. We took this as a good omen.

Despite walking past several rapids, we still swam three miles. After the portage around Wall Creek Rapid, we jumped in for the final swim to the wall. Arriving at the beautiful beach beneath it felt a little surreal. We had been through quite an ordeal—swollen ankles from the marathon hike, the smoke inhalation, the late-night rockfall, the bear encounter—but as we lay in the warm sand, it all brought smiles to our faces. Now, it was time to go up.

That afternoon, we started up the gully leading to the base of the wall and found the wall rack and portaledge I had stashed the week before when guiding a trip down the river. We began climbing beautiful gray granite, smooth as glass in places. The gully pitches had worried us because they'd looked so polished, but we found enough cracks, bushes, and trees to make good, if dirty, progress.

That evening, we were back on the beach, having fixed our ropes on the first three pitches. With seven river-trip launches a day on the Middle Fork, it was inevitable we would see many boats during our time on the beach. So began the endless answering of questions like, *Where's your boat?* And, *You didn't really swim here, right?* And, *Do you need some beers?* I love many things about river people, but especially the ever-present beer supply and the willingness to hand cold ones to suspect characters limping across the beach claiming that they're here to "do a little climbing."

The next morning we packed the haulbag and committed to the wall. I drew the first proper aid pitch. Our progress slowed considerably as the wall reared back and the cracks became seams. Beaks, hooks, and small gear got us to a decent bivy and, just like that, the first A3 pitch was in the bag. Ky went up on the next aid pitch and—long after sunset—was back to his old habit of hooking in the dark. We were, as usual, lost on the wall, but hadn't found any dead ends yet.

Dawn broke hot. The smoke in the air was dense. We decided to pack a day bag, bring all of the rope we had, and see what happened. We cleaned Ky's pitch from the night before and kept climbing. Ky swung 20' away from the wall as he jugged the static line, a reminder of just how steep this thing was.

We were now in the large open book feature that splits the middle of the face, and the angle eased with every rope length. On the 12th pitch, I left the book and headed straight up with hopes of topping out. A mix of hooking and free climbing brought me onto a ledge covered in huge blocks, with a panoramic view of Impassable Canyon. We could see the Waterfall Creek Trail, most of what we'd swum to get here, Redside Rapid, and much of what lay downstream of us. A short scramble and a 5.8 pitch reminiscent of climbs in the Sawtooth Mountains brought us to the top. Not so much a summit as a high point on a ridge, 1,800' above the Middle Fork. We descended to the portaledge by rappelling from natural anchors.

The first lightning strikes happened at twilight but were far enough off to the west not to worry us at first. The Sawtooths and the Salmon River Mountains are both well known for exceptionally violent thunderstorms, and I've been pinned down by them more times than I'd like to remember. As the storm came closer, Ky began shooting photos as the lightning illuminated our exposed portaledge. It may have been an illusion, but it seemed we were above the lighting as it shot through the clouds. I pondered whether our 25 beaks could act as a lightning rod. We fell asleep late that night to a soundtrack of thunder, both silently repeating our trip's mantra: *Unkilled once again, so far.*

The next day, as we lazed in the shade, our friends swung by to pick us up, as planned. Our buddy J.P. and the other 13 people on his river trip loaded us up, fed us, and treated us like royalty. We spent another night on the river and the next day drove out to Salmon, ecstatic and shocked that the logistics had all worked out.

Hart jumaring after the bivouac on the Redside Wall, with the Middle Fork of the Salmon River about 1,500 feet below and wildfire smoke filling the air. *Matt Ward*

Two weeks later in Stanley, Idaho, I married Makayla Hoyt, my best friend and the woman of my dreams, at a beautiful ceremony along the Salmon River. The Redside Wall was my last hurrah as an unmarried man. For the first time in my life, I ain't No Rolling Stone (13 pitches, V 5.10 A3).

—Matt Ward

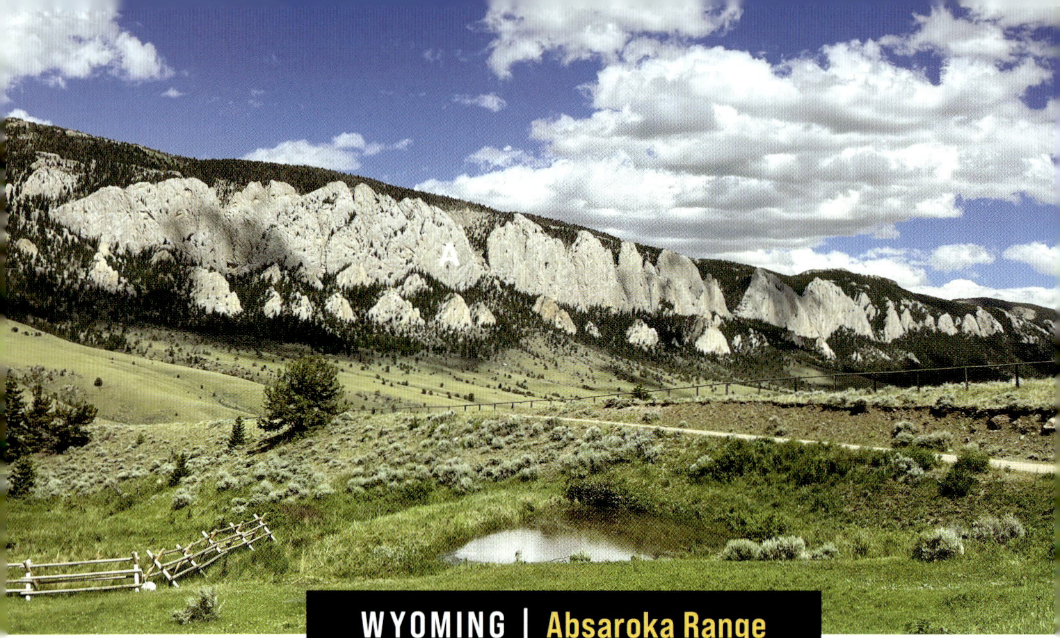

WYOMING | Absaroka Range

(A) marks the formation climbed by Africa Son (900′, 7 pitches, 5.12-), the first full-length route in the Palisades. Lots of good rock up there: See the *AAJ* website for climbing photos. *Zach Lentsch*

CODY, THE PALISADES, AFRICA SON

The Palisades are a row of tall limestone fins on the southwest flank of Rattlesnake Mountain, visible from the Buffalo Bill Reservoir on Highway 14, heading west out of Cody. Many years ago (probably in the late 1990s), Todd Cozzens and the late Bobby Model started a number of lines on the Palisades ground-up, but after hitting multiple dead ends, they abandoned that approach. Todd explored the potential for a rap-bolted line from the top of a Palisade formation he called the Pit Viper and found high-quality rock, but ultimately abandoned the project, having only bolted the anchors.

In 2021, I spent three days bolting a seven-pitch line, top-down, on the Palisade immediately north of Pit Viper, and I enjoyed many solitary days Mini Traxioning or rope-soloing the middle and upper pitches. The climbing was reminiscent of Kalymnos slabs, on hard, blue limestone. By the summer of 2023, I had freed the seven long pitches of the route individually.

Early in the summer of 2024, my good friend and storied South African climber James Mader swung through Cody at the tail end of a U.S. trip. Together, we climbed Africa Son (900’, 7 pitches, 5.12-) in under five hours, completing the line and closing the chapter that Todd and Bobby began to write decades prior. It is the first complete summit route in the Palisades.

The name Africa Son was a gesture of gratitude toward James and also an homage to Bobby, who moved to Kenya in 2004, was critically injured in a nonclimbing accident in Cape Town in 2007, and died two years later. [*More details on the approach and individual pitches of this route are at the AAJ website.*]

—David M. Gauvin

WYOMING | Bighorn Mountains

HALLELUJAH (PEAK 12,594′), YES LAWD

Late in the day on August 29, Chris Hirsch and I began the grueling 13-mile hike from Bighorn Reservoir into the Sawtooth Lakes valley. We arrived in the valley around 1 p.m. on August 30 and

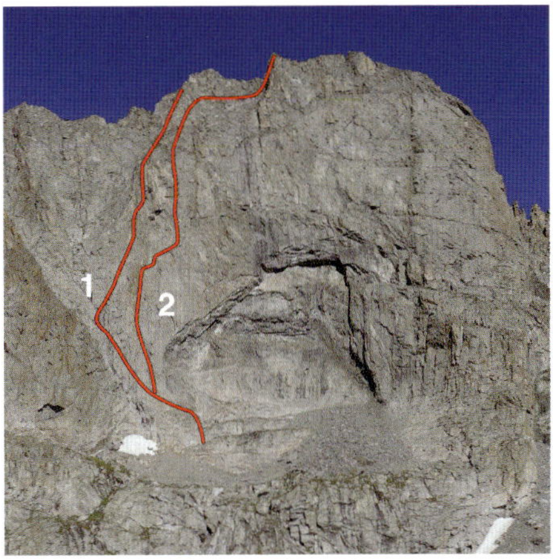

The east face of Hallelujah (Peak 12,594'), showing (1) Grand Delusion (2015) and (2) Yes Lawd (2024). ***Dougald MacDonald***

began to scope objectives, quickly keying in on an obvious line on the broad east face of Hallelujah (Peak 12,594').

Just after sunrise the following morning, we arrived at the base of the wall. Our line started in an obvious right-facing corner and later followed a system of cracks, with a cryptic face section in the middle. [*This line is to the right of the only other known route up the east face: Grand Delusion (Harlin-Jenkins-MacDonald, 2015).*] I took us up the first two pitches—engaging, thoughtful, and enjoyable—and Chris took the reins for pitch three, which brought us out of the corners onto the mysterious face.

The fourth pitch was heads-up and footwork-intensive, culminating in a dynamic move into a strenuous layback. Chris used a bit of aid to place some protection.

I took back the sharp end at pitch five. Despite looking like it would be a dangerously run-out affair, with patience and persistence I was able to free it with reasonable protection. A long, moderate pitch into a low-angle bowl, roughly 200' of simuling, and a last technical squeeze chimney, and we were on the summit.

To descend, we downclimbed the squeeze chimney and made two rappels (30m and 60m) to a major ledge system. Walking and easy downclimbing brought us to the southeast side of Hallelujah, where we slogged down talus to camp.

After a night of food and rest, we returned the next morning and quickly freed the line (Yes Lawd, 1,100', 5.11 R), cleaning and trundling along the way.

Following a long day of approaching and climbing the west face of Innominate in Wilderness Basin and summiting Black Tooth Mountain on the way back to Sawtooth Lakes, we hiked out to the car and returned to life in the Black Hills.

—Matt Scherer

WYOMING | Teton Range

STORM POINT, SOUTH FACE, CHILLY DOGS

On July 4, Chase Krumholz and I established a 1,000' rock climb on the south face of Storm Point. The route lies about 300' east of the popular Guides' Wall and 50' east of Vieux Guide. It adds six pitches above Hot Dogs (5.9), an excellent 140' crack climb established by Paul Gagner and Jim Woodmencey in 1986.

Above Hot Dogs, three moderate pitches led to a fantastic 5.10- we dubbed the "S-Pitch," featuring a finger crack, a blind roof pull, and an unlikely hand traverse. After a penultimate 5.10- hand crack pitch, we scrambled up a rope length of easy fifth and fourth class to the top of a small gendarme on Storm Point's southwest ridge—a logical end point.

In late September, we made the route safer by fixing two pitons on the S-Pitch and a third piton in the belay alcove at its end. We named the route Chilly Dogs (1,000', III 5.10- PG-13). It is likely the first new route in this area since Benja Glatz, Ben Hoiness, and Justin Willis established Attritus (600', 5 pitches, 5.12-) in 2019.

—Brandon Wanthal

THE ENDURO TRAVERSE

SKIING THE TETON SKYLINE FROM BUCK MOUNTAIN TO TEEWINOT

By Adam Fabrikant

Traversing multiple peaks in the Teton Range started in 1932, with Fred Ayres making a solo summertime traverse from the Middle Teton to Nez Perce. Moving across the skyline has been a part of the range's unfolding history ever since. In 1950, the seeds of the hyper-classic Grand Traverse, from Teewinot to Nez Perce, were sown, but it wasn't until August 1963 that John Evans, Richard Long, and Allen Steck completed this traverse, moving from south to north, the opposite of today's usual route. In the 1965 *AAJ*, Steck wrote, "Any route or time of day is acceptable, however, only be sure to finish within 24 hours." For the ski traverse of the Tetons that I envisioned, sub-24 hours was our sole metric, as Steck had laid it out for us.

Skiers got on board early with long Teton traverses, generally crossing through mountain passes and avoiding climbing and skiing the high peaks. This changed in 1993, when Stephen Koch and Mark Newcomb linked the Grand Teton, Middle Teton, and South Teton on a June tour in roughly 17 to 18 hours. It has since been done in under nine hours. The Grand-Middle-South link-up continues to captivate ski mountaineers as a fantastic day of moving through the mountains; I enjoy this tour multiple days every season as a training outing and a proper challenge.

In 2021, Sam Hennessey and I embarked on the "Cathedral on Skis," linking the Grand Teton, Mt. Owen, and Teewinot—a link-up known as the Cathedral Traverse in summer, done in the opposite direction. We took the path of least resistance and avoided most technical challenges. Nonetheless, this felt like the next step in Teton ski traverses and much more challenging than the Grand-Middle-South.

ABOVE: After skiing through the night and watching the sunrise on top of the Grand Teton, Brendan O'Neill strides toward the Koven Couloir (center), the start of the climb up Mt. Owen. ***Michael Gardner***

The Enduro Traverse linked Buck Mountain (far left) and Mt. Wister, continued over the South, Middle, and Grand Tetons (center), then finished over Mt. Owen and Teewinot Mountain (far right). ***Michael Gardner***

In March 2023, Sam, Brendan O'Neill, and I were at it again during a great stint of high pressure. The goal was to ski the Cathedral peaks by some of their most technical routes. After soloing up the Grand by the Ford-Stettner, we pointed our skis down the east face and into the Hossack-MacGowan Couloir on the north face. After crossing the bergschrund, we contoured over to the Koven Couloir and climbed to the summit of Mt. Owen. For our descent, we chose the Northeast Snowfields, one of the range's finest descents on skis. We finished our outing on Teewinot's east face—this was another fine adventure that we labeled the "Skier's Cathedral."

To me it seemed logical to bring all of our experiences together in a much longer traverse—to see how far we could go in under 24 hours. In the Alaska Range, I have enjoyed moving under the midnight sun for 24, 30, hell, even 64 hours—why not see how this would work back home? It gets darker in Wyoming in the spring than in Alaska, but we have headlamps.

In April 2024, Michael Gardner, Brendan, and I embarked on the Enduro Traverse. The idea was to enchain the Teton skyline from Buck Mountain in the south to Teewinot, crossing over Mt. Wister, South Teton, Middle Teton, Grand Teton, and Mt. Owen along the way.

At 6 p.m. on April 22, with the day's heat still in the air, we started skinning up Death Canyon in wet, sloppy snow. Under an endless sunset, we climbed the east ridge of Buck Mountain (11,938') and clicked in on top for our first descent at 9:15 p.m. (A full moon allowed us to complete all the climbs sans headlamps, but we did use the lamps for our descents.) We skied down Buck's hyper-classic east face and used a piece of terrain called the Buckshot to drop into the South Fork of Avalanche Canyon.

The next climb was the South Headwall of Mt. Wister (11,490'), which flows into the upper east ridge. We reached Wister's summit at 10:53 p.m. This was the lowest peak in our traverse, yet it packed a punch. The northeast face offered up some proper steep skiing—it felt engaging via headlamp—and deposited the three of us in the North Fork of Avalanche Canyon.

Our next ascent took us up the South Teton's Amora Vida Couloir (much more fun to descend than ascend), and here we encountered our least efficient travel of the day, with heinous breakable crust and soggy snow engulfing our entire legs. From the top of the South Teton (12,514'), the descent by the Northwest Chute was fast and uneventful.

Now in Garnet Canyon's South Fork, we began our climb up the Middle Teton's Southwest Couloir, where efficient cramponing put us on the summit rather quickly. The descent down the east face into the Middle Teton Glacier route was rather harrowing on the refrozen undulating snow left by skiers who had descended in the warm days before us. But we were not there for the ski quality, rather

Adam Fabrikant on Teewinot Mountain, with the Grand Teton immediately right and the snowy northeast face of Mt. Owen farther right. Far in the distance, (B) marks the top of Buck Mountain, the first summit of the traverse. ***Michael Gardner***

for the continuous movement.

From the North Fork of Garnet Canyon, we made quick work of the Ford-Stettner route, topping out the Grand Teton (13,770') at 6 a.m., 12 hours into our journey. The sun was beginning to rise above the horizon, and it felt great to embrace its warmth again.

With a long block of daylight ahead, the three of us were confident as we descended the Ford-Stettner, with some thoughtful downclimbing in the Chevy Couloir, which is normally rappelled. (To save weight, we did not carry a rope and chose lines that would go without one.) We made our way into the Dike Snowfield and down to Glacier Gulch, where we donned crampons once again and slogged up the Koven Couloir, feeling the heat, as we carried minimal water. We continued up the east ridge and the Koven Chimney to the true summit of Owen (12,928'). After some downclimbing, we were sliding again, down Owen's east ridge and into the Diagonal. From the Owen-Teewinot cirque, we began our final ascent, with rather benign climbing up the Northwest Couloir to the summit of Teewinot Mountain (12,325').

Starting down the upper snowfields, we encountered other mountain travelers for the first time of our outing. We let them cautiously navigate the narrows, the most hazardous and technical challenge of Teewinot's east face, and once they were through we descended to the valley floor, leaving the alpine behind.

We finished at the Taggart Lake trailhead in early afternoon, 20 hours and 12 minutes after starting, well within Steck's 24-hour metric. In all, the Enduro Traverse covered 24 miles and roughly 19,000 to 20,000 feet of vertical gain. (GPS apps often don't agree in the Tetons' steep terrain.) A memorable day of walking across the Tetons' skyline.

This would prove to be my last day in the high peaks with Michael Gardner, as he would lose his life in October 2024 on Jannu East in Nepal. I am grateful he happened to be home to join for the day, as we etched our way across the slopes in the twilight. The Tetons were always Mike's home mountains, and winter and summer he would use his creativity to draw new lines, whether on rock, ice, or snow. His inspiration lives on among the high crags of the range.

GRAND TETON, WISH YOU WERE HERE

On July 24, Michael Gardner and Vic Zeilman completed a new line on the east side of the Grand Teton's Exum Ridge. Zeilman had spotted the crack system several years earlier, but sat on the idea until confirming with Renny Jackson, co-author of *A Climber's Guide to the Teton Range*, that it seemed to be unclimbed. Zeilman named the route Wish You Were Here (III 5.10-), in memory of his father, J Lincoln Zeilman, who passed away in a paragliding accident in 2020.

This was the second route Gardner and Zeilman completed on the Grand Teton together, following Wooden Ships (III 5.10-), on the south face of the Grand, in 2019 (which Jimmy Voorhis also had a hand in). That route was a memorial to Gardner's own late father, George Gardner. Zeilman's report on Wish You Were Here, along with topos for both routes, is at the *AAJ* website.

—Information from Vic Zeilman

TOP: Ryan Evans climbing out of the alcove to start the seventh pitch of Big Chiefin'. *Damien Nicodemi*

BOTTOM: The east-facing Big Chief Buttress in the Washakie Lake Cirque, showing (1) Big Chiefin' (2024) and (2) the approximate line of The Non-Obvious Garden Tour (2016). *Norm Larson*

WYOMING | Wind River Range

WASHAKIE LAKE CIRQUE, BIG CHIEF BUTTRESS, BIG CHIEFIN'

In 1993, Norm and Lorna Larson made a brief attempt on the stunning 900' Big Chief Buttress (42.8136, -109.2382). As far as is known, no one tried it again until 2016, when Norm and Lorna brought Anne Gilbert Chase, Ken Etzel, Kate Rutherford, and Jason Thompson out to the Washakie Lake Cirque to let them have a go. Gilbert Chase and Rutherford established The Non-Obvious Garden Tour (12 pitches, IV 5.11 C1) on the right side of the east face (*see AAJ 2017*). In late June 2024, Damien Nicodemi and I hiked the 13 miles into the cirque to take a look for ourselves, figuring a route straight up the center would make for a good outing.

We started up on June 29. Norm had told us the 2016 team made two attempts at a line in the center of the formation. Sure enough, we found rappel tat at the top of pitch one and a fixed nut at the end of pitch four (roughly halfway up the wall). Beyond this, we found no sign of previous passage.

We climbed quickly up the first three pitches and found ourselves below an exciting-looking rightward traverse toward the prominent crack system in the center of the wall. To our surprise, pitch four climbed at a moderate grade, and a perfect hand crack lay just beyond—we were now established in said crack system.

Damien took off to battle an overhanging offwidth on pitch six, undoubtedly the crux of the route. Neither of us was able to free this 20' burl-fest, but it will certainly go free for the right person. After this, we climbed a 5.11 roof with double cracks, followed by a long pitch to just below the summit. As the splitter crack system petered out into a vegetated seam, we pressed forward quickly to keep fear at bay. By sheer luck, a horizontal crack presented itself below the final large roof; we used this to traverse left into a slot chimney. Before long we were on top.

We left no fixed gear on Big Chiefin' (1,100', 9 pitches, IV 5.11 C1) except for the fixed nut we found on pitch four.

—Ryan Evans

CIRQUE OF THE MOON, TWO ASCENTS

In early September, Mitchell Steinman and I spent about a week in the Cirque of the Moon. After the 12-mile approach and its four river crossings, we made base camp in a meadow nestled within the cirque's vast moonscape.

The following day, aiming to investigate the walk-off descent for many of the routes in the cirque, we connected various features up the right side of the north buttress of Sumac Point, to the right of Bo Mambo (500', 5.9, soloed by Dakota Walz in 2020). This resulted in a short, enjoyable route, despite lichen-covered rock: Martian Moonbase (500', 5.8 PG-13).

The line of Moonrise Kingdom (800', 8 pitches, 5.11- C1), an attempt on the northeast-facing Sunset Wall in the Cirque of the Moon. *Stefanos Apostle*

After waiting out a storm, we attempted the unclimbed northeast face of the Sunset Wall. We hoped to connect two prominent features in the middle of the wall: a leftward-sweeping flake and a vertical splitter above it.

After three pitches up to 5.10-, we reached the flake, which narrowed from offwidth to thin hands over the course of 50' and finished with 20' of easier climbing. Clocking in at 5.11-, this pitch would be a four-star classic anywhere if close to the ground. This was followed by a dirty, flaring finger crack that we aided at C1; if cleaned, it would most likely go free around 5.11+/5.12-.

After three more pitches, we found ourselves under a chossy roof with loose or blank rock in every direction. Without aid gear for the blank sections, we rappelled to the ground. Heading right instead of left on our final (eighth) pitch might have been a way to bypass these obstacles, with perhaps three more pitches to reach easy ground. We called our incomplete route Moonrise Kingdom (800', 8 pitches, 5.11- C1).

—Stefanos Apostle

COLORADO | Indian Peaks Wilderness

LONE EAGLE CIRQUE, LIMBO, EAST DIHEDRALS

The east face of Limbo with (1) East Dihedrals (2024) and (2) East Face Right (2020). *Luc Aurand Collection*

The Lone Eagle Cirque, on the west side of the Continental Divide in the Indian Peaks Wilderness, is known for breathtaking views, beautiful alpine lakes, and the classic north face of Lone Eagle Peak (11,946'), climbed by brothers Joe and Paul Stettner in 1933. The area has abundant rock, but with a minimum seven-mile approach, much of this stone is rarely climbed or still untouched.

In 2024, I began looking over maps, photos, and social media posts, trying to get a feel for the walls around Triangle Lake, at the head of the basin south and east of Lone Eagle. In mid-August, Will Beach and I headed up there. During the first part of our trip, we were often tentbound, as monsoon rainstorms left the area soaked. When the weather improved, we hiked Lone Eagle's Solo Flight route (4th class) to get a look at the east face of the informally named "Limbo," rising between Lone Eagle and the larger Iroquois Peak (12,799') to the south.

We began climbing Limbo's east face on ledgy steps that quickly turned to vertical cracks. For our second pitch, we chose the central of several intimidating corner systems. After aiding the corner crack to suss the protection, Will led it free at 5.10d. After our fourth pitch, we descended by a ramp, as the afternoon forecast wasn't great.

On August 16, we reclimbed the ramp and started up what we later learned was pitch five of a 2020 route called East Face Right (5.10), but instead of traversing to the wide crack out right, as the earlier party had, we continued directly up the dihedral, which pinched down to a seam, with a committing stem corner followed by a difficult mantel. A pitch of scrambling followed by a steep crack led to the narrow summit, and East Dihedrals (750', 5.10d) was in the bag.

—Luc Aurand

PRIOR CLIMBS ABOVE TRIANGLE LAKE: *On August 30, 2020, according to their post at Mountain Project, Clint Brooks and Dylan Oliver climbed East Face Right (600', III 5.10) on Limbo—erroneously placing it on the neighboring Iroquois Peak—ascending cracks and corners on the wall's right side. The 2020 and 2024 routes may share some ground on the first pitch and definitely share about 25' of the fifth pitch. The large east face of Lone Eagle Peak, half a mile to the north, has been climbed by at least two routes.*

COLORADO | Rocky Mountain National Park

PTARMIGAN MOUNTAIN, TOWERS 1 AND 5, EAST FACES

In August 2024, friends and I established two routes on Ptarmigan Mountain (12,324') on the west side of Rocky Mountain National Park (RMNP). I first came across the Ptarmigan Towers while flipping through Richard Rossiter's RMNP guidebook; I hiked out to see them for myself and was amazed at the size and beauty of these monoliths—roughly 700' to 800' tall—way deep in the park. The five prominent southeast-facing spires are mostly vertical or overhanging and above treeline. Only Tower 2 and Tower 4 have documented routes in the guidebook, though a short 5.9, Between the Blinds, was established on the south side of Tower 5 in 2022 (*AAJ 2023*).

The Ptarmigan Towers in western Rocky Mountain National Park, showing the approximate lines of (1) Fifth Element on Tower 5 and (2) Rain Dancer on Tower 1. Only two other routes have been recorded on the main faces of these towers. *Michael LaDue*

Tower 5 features many crack systems on its impressive east face. Sam Beane, Lyle Harte, and I picked a plumb line up the middle, aiming for a massive left-facing dihedral about halfway up. The rock was good overall, although protection was sparse in places. Every belay was at a good ledge, and the route featured nice cracks and face climbing on solid rock. The final two pitches are steeper but easier, following slightly lower-quality cracks to the summit. The route can get quite hot in the sun in midsummer. Fifth Element (700', 5 pitches, 5.11- R) was climbed ground-up and onsight by all three climbers on August 3.

Tower 1—the first tower you see from the trail during the approach, rising 1,000' over Lake Nanita—is the narrowest and most imposing of the group. It is about 750' high and has a summit that—as Mike Lane and I would learn—requires a rappel or an exposed fifth-class downclimb to escape.

Mike and I established Rain Dancer (750', 7 pitches, 5.12- PG-13) ground-up in late August, taking a somewhat meandering path toward an obvious left-facing dihedral about two-thirds of the way up. The rock quality varied from loose to bulletproof, with some memorable sections, including the beautiful 5.10+ corner on pitch five that's easily visible from the ground. The sixth pitch included a fun 5.12- crux: an overhanging number 0.3–0.5 crack on nice white rock with no footholds, climbed clean after several attempts. The route then skirts the massive, loose roofs at the top of the tower by going around to the right (north) side and ascending a dirty but moderate gully.

On our first attempt, on August 23, we got rain on pitch four and had to rappel; we fixed the last rap line to our temporary pitch two anchor. On August 24, we top-roped up to pitch two via a direct line and then continued to the summit. On the crux pitch, a heavy rain squall came in for about 30 minutes, but it was blowing from the west, so the rock stayed mostly dry—hence the Rain Dancer name. We encountered an old, rusty piton about 15' up pitch one but saw no further evidence of previous attempts.

—Michael LaDue

Michael LaDue ascends the clean corner of the fifth pitch of Rain Dancer in the Ptarmigan Towers. *Mike Lane*

Sean McLane leading pitch eight (the second of three M9 pitches) on The Penitent Path, a week after redpointing the 12-pitch route. *Jon Jugenheimer*

The Penitent Path (350m, 12 pitches, IV M9) in Provo Canyon; some of the pitches are connected by big ledges. The Stairway to Heaven ice climb can be seen to the right. *Sean McLane*

UTAH | Wasatch Range

PROVO CANYON, CASCADE MOUNTAIN, THE PENITENT PATH

After about 20 days of work over two months, Jon Jugenheimer and I completed what could be the longest fully bolt-protected dry-tooling route anywhere. There are dry-tooling and mixed routes of similar or greater length in the United States—for example, some of the newer routes on the Dark Side Wall, near Ouray, Colorado—and abroad, but these aren't all bolted, nor as sustained. The Penitent Path climbs high-quality rock on all natural holds to the left of Stairway to Heaven (9 pitches, WI5) and runs the full 350m height of the buttress. The 12-pitch route turned out harder and more sustained than we expected, with three pitches of M9 and most of the rest M7 or harder.

Just before Christmas 2023, Jon invited me to try to redpoint a pitch he'd bolted a couple of years prior—and which would become pitch three of The Penitent Path. The crux involves finding a hidden, natural pocket in a slab over a bulge and using your knees to stabilize yourself. I tore a good hole in my knee while figuring out the beta and proceeded to reopen it with more alpine knees later in the route-development process. Something clicked as I finally figured out the genuflection beta: I remembered the first challenge that Indiana Jones must face to reach the Holy Grail in *Indiana Jones and the Last Crusade.* Before he, too, figures out he must kneel to avoid spinning blades that have decapitated untold numbers of suitors, Indy continually mutters to himself, "Only the penitent man will pass." Even though it wasn't done yet, our route had a name.

We equipped and freed the rest of the pitches in various styles over the next two months. I bolted pitch four ground-up and first climbed pitches five, six, and seven ground-up, rope-solo. Everything else was cleaned and bolted top-down.

On March 4, 2024, after a couple of days of cleaning loose rock and rehearsing the movement, I felt ready to go for the redpoint. The day started inauspiciously, with blowing snow and a fall on the M4 first pitch after a hold broke. We almost called it then and there, but decided to just see how far we could get. I pulled the rope and re-led the pitch clean. Jon led the second pitch, as he had never sent that one, and did it on the first try. Jon also led the easy fourth pitch.

As the sun began to set, we reached the last pitch. I had led every crux pitch first go—Jon, having switched to support mode by this point, had jugged a couple of the harder pitches. When I got to the second bolt on the final pitch, an M8+, my biceps cramped so hard I had trouble straightening my arms. I found a stance and waited for the cramps to subside while darkness crept in. At the ninth bolt, my feet skated off a sloping rail and I miraculously caught myself on one arm. Regaining composure, I worked up the final roofs and let out a whoop at the belay.

The Penitent Path (IV M9) is climbable year-round, which was one of our goals, since Utah's ice season is only getting more inconsistent.

—Sean McLane

UTAH | Zion National Park

ANGELS LANDING, NORTH FACE, CIVIL DISOBEDIENCE

In late May, I completed a new route on the north face of Angels Landing. Civil Disobedience (1,250', 10 pitches, V 5.9 A3) takes a direct, independent, and rather sheer path immediately right of the historic Lowe Route (1,200', 12 pitches, V 5.10 C3, Bryan-Lowe, 1970; FFA: V 5.13a R, Anderson, 2004).

The north face of Angels Landing with (1) Lowe Route (Bryan-Lowe, 1970), the first route up the face, and (2) Civil Disobedience, climbed in 2024. Other routes not shown. ***Nathan Brown***

I climbed and equipped the route mostly solo. Pitches seven and eight were equipped during an incomplete ascent—we ducked left and finished on the Lowe Route—with Sam Macke and Jackson Marvell. Jackson took a good whipper on that trip. During the complete first ascent from May 24 to 27, I climbed solo, establishing new ground on the last couple of pitches.

The route is independent but for 20' of pitch six that overlaps with the Lowe Route, and the final pitch, which it shares with Lucifer's Ladder (1,200', 8 pitches, VI 5.8 A3+, Shock-Trump, 1998). The last pitch is no joke: In my contemporaneous notes from the ascent, I described this A2+ affair as "scary desert-alpine shit." Most of the rock on the route is really good, with hard, thin nailing typical on many of the pitches. I believe solo aid to be the safest method for leading the big roof on pitch eight. I drilled about 20 lead bolts and about 20 anchor bolts, all stainless steel.

—Nathan Brown

Canada

YUKON TERRITORY | St. Elias Mountains

The line of Wizard's Ridge (800m, Alaska Grade 4), the south ridge of Queen Peak (5,380m). The climbers descended toward AINA Peak, to the right, then down to their skis below the ridge. ***Ryan Driscoll***

QUEEN PEAK, SOUTH RIDGE

On May 26, Nick Aiello-Popeo and I enjoyed a scenic flight with Icefields Discovery from Silver City, Yukon, passing by Mt. Logan before landing on the Quintino Sella Glacier at 2,743m. Our plan was to ski about eight miles up the King Trench route (MacCarthy et al., 1925) toward Mt. Logan and establish a high camp below the unclimbed north face of King Peak (5,172m). Five days later, after shuttling loads and taking our time to acclimatize, we were comfortable in our camp at just above 4,000m. Feeling ready, we packed our bags for an attempt on King.

We trudged up 300m of snow, taking a roundabout way to avoid triggering a large slab. We'd chosen this part of the wall to avoid serac hazard, but finding a spot to cross the bergschrund proved difficult. The area of wall we could reach had unsupportive sn'ice and rock mostly devoid of gear. As Nick tried to aid through some steep rock, I began to dig a bivy ledge while still belaying. Then Nick ripped a Tricam out and came flying off. Shovel in one hand and brake strand in the other, I caught him. I guess the Grigri was worth the weight.

Bivy ledge half completed, we sat looking across the valley at the unclimbed south ridge of Queen Peak (5,380m). Joe Josephson, a veteran of Yukon climbing, had suggested it as a consolation prize, in case our plans for King Peak didn't work out. Shining in the evening sun, the south ridge looked magnificent and less frightening than what we were currently trying. We descended and found ourselves back in camp four hours later.

After a day of rest, we packed our bags with the bare minimum: three ice screws, six nuts, and a 50m twin rope. Our emergency kit was a belay jacket and a pair of mittens each. We left camp at 7:45 a.m. and skied northeast for a little over a mile to the base of the route at 4,580m, stuck our skis in the snow, and put on crampons. The skies were totally clear, and we were confident in the forecast.

Once on the south ridge, we tried to avoid chossy rock and hard, calf-burning low-angle ice by linking sections of thin, sugary snow. The wind was whipping at us a lot harder than we'd anticipated, and the sky was looking increasingly cloudy.

Nonetheless, we continued to the summit, never once using the rope or protection. As we pulled through the final couloir, we could hear the wind roaring like a freight train above.

On the summit, visibility dropped to less than 50'. It was unclear if we were in a storm or just a low cloud; either way, a whiteout at high altitude on a rarely climbed peak was less than ideal. We tied in and both took coils, ready to navigate the ridge eastward to the saddle between Queen Peak and AINA Peak (5,630m).

Hours of slow progress finally brought us to the saddle. We descended the slope to the south and walked southwest by feel for hours back to our skis. Multiple crevasse falls and a few sketchy rappels later, we were back on skis. It only took about ten minutes for us to realize we would almost certainly fall to our deaths in a crevasse if we continued in this style. Skis back on packs, we roped up and fumbled our way through the whiteout. Fifteen hours after leaving camp, we crawled back into our relatively sheltered home and made some dinner.

We named the route Wizard's Ridge (800m, Alaska Grade 4) in honor of our friend and mentor Rick Wilcox (nicknamed "The Wizard") from New Hampshire. Rick spent months on Mt. Logan in the 1960s doing altitude studies for the U.S. military, and his images and advice were crucial to our success. [*The first ascent of Queen Peak was by the southeast ridge, starting from King Col, in 1966. The climbers, Ed Nester and Pete and Tom Hall, were members of an American expedition that also traversed King Peak from west to east en route to the summit of Mt. Logan; see AAJ 1967.*]

—Ryan Driscoll, *USA*

Ryan Driscoll on the snowfield leading to the upper gullies on the south ridge of Queen Peak. In back is the unclimbed north face of King Peak (5,172m). *Nick Aiello-Popeo*

BRITISH COLUMBIA | Coast Mountains

TSINI TSINI PEAK, FIRST ASCENT, VIA NORTHEAST RIDGE

On August 6, Katie Beringer and I made the first ascent of a previously unnamed peak adjacent to Mt. Nyland (2,816m) and the Horn (2,907m) in the Tsini Tsini Valley, near Bella Coola. We've decided to call it Tsini Tsini Peak (2,646m, 52.30776, -126.19538), as all other summits in the area lack indigenous names.

With friends helicopter-sightseeing in the area, we were able to get dropped off at the eastern saddle of the northeast ridge of the peak. After a short scramble, we roped up and began the

Tsini Tsini Peak (2,646m) in winter conditions, with the steep northeast ridge in profile on the left side. The climbers were dropped off by helicopter at the sharp saddle in the center and picked up on the summit after the climb. The steep ridge in back is on Mt. Lobachevsky, climbed in 1973 from the south. *Tyler Ravelle*

first of 12 pitches up the ridge. Our route more or less wandered up the right side of the ridge until near the top, where vertical, lichenous climbing forced us to deviate onto harder but cleaner rock to the left, which brought us to a shoulder just below the summit. A final pitch of 5.7/5.8 climbing took us to the top, where our friends were able to pluck us off in the heli and give us cold beers and a short flight to the valley bottom.

We called our route Twirly Birds. We placed seven bolts (all as anchors) and found multiple pitches of great climbing on solid rock. The crux was a short 5.10 section on the tenth pitch.

—Andrew Councell, *Canada*

PANTHEON RANGE, SEDNA PEAK, CULBERT CRAG, TRIDENT TOWER

The Pantheon Range, located just 20km north of Mt. Waddington, sees very little activity from climbers despite the beautiful and rugged terrain. The first two mountaineers to explore the range were Dick Culbert and Glenn Woodsworth, on a trip in 1964 (*see CAJ 1965*). They were foiled by bad weather for much of the trip, but noted in their report that the range "will continue to supply worthwhile exploration and first ascents for many years to come."

Inspired by their stories and driven by a desire to climb in a relatively untouched corner of the Coast Mountains, Francis Bailey and I drove up to Tatla Lake and flew by helicopter with White Saddle into the less explored southwestern end of the Pantheons in August 2024. Our principal objective was a summit that Glenn had told us about, which he had named Culbert Crag to honor his late friend and longtime climbing partner. The two of them never had the chance to return to the range, so this section of mountains towering above Frontier Creek remained unclimbed.

The helicopter dropped us at a col (51.52059, -125.37742) at the south end of a broad cirque between two summits believed to be unclimbed, and we made camp there. On August 4, we hiked up the southwest ridgeline of the peak to the west-northwest of our camp, summiting a mountain that apparently had only ever been climbed by mountain goats. We propose the name Sedna Peak (2,480m), following in the god-themed names in this range (Zeus, Juno, the Furies, Vishnu, etc.) and honoring the Inuit goddess of the ocean.

On the following day, we did a reconnaissance around the north side of Culbert Crag (2,567m), hoping to find a

Trident Tower (the square-topped peak left of center) from the southwest. The ascent route was near the left shoulder of the peak but is not visible from here. Diana Mountain is on the far left. ***Francis Bailey***

line on its north face going up from the glacier. Our mission proved fruitless, though, as the north face was too steep and loose for our liking, and the nearby gullies were filled with broken chunks of the dwindling glacier.

Opting instead to attempt Culbert Crag by its south side, on August 5 we hiked back over Sedna Peak, then lost some elevation to skip the ridge crest, which looked to be blocked by several unclimbable gendarmes. After several hours of traversing, we reached a south buttress that would connect us upward toward Culbert Crag. Four pitches of no more than 5.7 took us to the first of three false summits, where we made one rappel, followed by three more pitches to the true summit.

This involved journey had taken us nearly 15 hours, so we bivouacked directly below the summit block, nestled into a small rock shelter out of the wind. Thankfully, there was a patch of snow just below us for water. By the time we had tea and our small dinners going, the sun had already set. We did our best to sleep through a very, very cold night, having opted to sacrifice camping gear to increase our speed.

After basking in the morning sun and enjoying the incredible views for a while, we descended by a loose gully between the second and third false summits. It took until afternoon to traverse back to camp, and when we arrived we were happy to crawl into our sleeping bags. The following day, we took a full rest day, relaxing by a small waterfall of fresh snowmelt.

With a few more days before our planned helicopter pickup, on August 9 we scrambled the west side of Diana Mountain (2,639m), making its second ascent, and scouted another unclimbed peak, along the curving ridgeline between Diana and our camp at the col. It looked like a route on the north side would be the most feasible, so we set out the next day to see what we could find.

We dropped southeast down into the valley for a ways, then climbed straight up the bowl below the north side of the peak. After a chossy scrambling approach, the technical climbing involved three excellent pitches of no more than 5.8. This turned out to be the most fun day trip we did during our time in the Pantheons. We propose the name Trident Tower (2,679m).

—Andrea Tate, *Canada*

Combatant Mountain with the line of The Smoke Show on the 600-meter Incisor pillar. The 2024 team's Smoke and Mirrors free variation is in yellow. Their finish via Kshatrya (1982) on the upper mountain is shown. *Drew Brayshaw*

COMBATANT MOUNTAIN, SOUTH BUTTRESS, FREE ASCENT OF THE INCISOR

A helicopter is a sort of magic portal. On August 7, after a long afternoon of waiting to see if pilot Mike King would be called away to fight wildfires, Tim Emmett, Matt Maddaloni, and I took off in his heli from White Saddle Ranch, and it felt as if we were transported immediately to the heavily crevassed landscape of the Tiedemann Glacier, with Mt. Waddington (4,019m) towering to the left and Combatant Mountain (3,762m) towering to the right.

We worked well into the night to get the essentials across the glacier and up a pitch of 5.10 to reach a large, protected platform at the start of our planned route on the south side of Combatant. Loud couloirs constantly dumped snow to our left and right. We dubbed it Madd Camp.

Sitting on a rock was a faded bottle of Jim Beam whiskey left by Matt, Paul Bride, and John Furneaux almost exactly 20 years prior. It seemed wrong not to take a swig of the ancient bottom-shelf booze that had sat through snowstorms, sunshine, and wind for two solid decades.

In an incredible 11.5-hour push in 2004 (after previous work on the lower pitches), without placing any bolts, Matt and John had established a route they named The Smoke Show (1,371m, ED2 5.12d A0). Their route started on the south side of the Incisor, a 2,000' pillar, then continued up the Jawbone, a knife-edge that connects to the steeper upper south face of Combatant Mountain. Their ascent stood on the shoulders of Greg Child, Greg Collum, and Steve Mascioli's route Belligerence, accomplished in an eight-day push in 1994; this was the first team to climb the Incisor, farther left and more on the west side than Smoke Show, and they also pioneered the Jawbone and upper south face. [*Another route up the Incisor, also to the left of The Smoke Show, was climbed by Joshua Lavigne and Craig McGee in 2009 and called Defiance.*]

We were here to free the feature in its entirety. Matt and John had come achingly close to accomplishing this when I had just finished high school. During their summit push, Matt took just one fall on the crux fourth pitch. Matt had returned with us this year, enthusiastic to revisit the place of one of his greatest adventures and gather some stills and drone footage of our efforts.

The next day, we ferried the rest of our gear up to Madd Camp and set to work on freeing the pitch that had eluded Matt all those years ago. After deeming it very difficult and snapping off a couple of critical crimps, I looked for other options. Swinging around, I found a series of holds to the right, then tagged up the power drill and we fired in a series of bolts. Sacrilegious in these mountains? Perhaps. But we had found an amazing 5.12+ pitch, which we called Smoke and Mirrors, that allowed the dots to connect.

The next pitch, called the Incision, was one of those pitches that belong in dreamscapes—an endless wide hand and fist crack (5.12) of the finest, fine-grained

granite, culminating in a heart-pounding roof encounter, set in a place more akin to the Himalaya than British Columbia. It was followed by the Wobble Flake, which is basically unprotectable as it shifts as one climbs it. (Though disconcerting, it didn't appear to me that it was at risk of disconnecting from the rock entirely.) Furneaux, in a lead for the ages, had linked these two pitches in 2004.

With the crux pitches more or less figured out, and Matt on drone duty, Tim and I set the alarm for a predawn start. Our strategy was "team free," with only one of us freeing the cruxes.

After simul-climbing a handful of pitches, Tim handily dispatched the bolted pitch. I managed to repeat John's link of the Incision and the Wobble Flake and hollered at the top of my lungs. We were now off to the races, following the line of least resistance. After a couple of variations to what Matt and John had done, we were atop the Incisor, staring down the Jawbone ridge.

This loose, stegosaurus-like crest of choss is a committing feature. Retreat from either side would almost surely result in disaster. Maddaloni, climbing like a bat out of hell, had pulled a block during their 2004 ascent and injured his arm. We took it slowly, dekeing from one side of the crest to the other in search of less unstable terrain. By nightfall we were feeling dangerously tired, and we opted to open-bivy without sleeping bags, almost at the end of the Jawbone. With a stove on hand, we passed a hot-water bottle back and forth through the hours. The sunrise came with a cloak of clouds over the peaks. Just beautiful.

Will Stanhope leading the Incision pitch during the ascent of Smoke and Mirrors (1,371m, ED2 5.12+) on the Incisor, south side of Combatant Mountain. ***Matt Maddaloni***

At the end of the Jawbone, a huge ramp offered a possible escape, but we wanted to summit Combatant. We followed the south-facing route called Kshatrya (Down-Cairns, 1982), and the rock went from awful to sublime. A handful of hours of simul-climbing later, we gained the top of Combatant. The vista was incredible. We could make out Bute Inlet and the ocean, which filled me with a sense of comfort, though we were a long way from home.

By the time we reached the Waddington-Combatant col, it was nightfall. I convinced Tim to march another hour back to an open bivy in a bergschrund. Sitting on our packs, we took turns rubbing each other's feet. At one point, with my approach shoes soaked, I donned my TC Pros and stuffed them in my chalk bag. We shivered until a merciful hint of dawn had us staggering to our feet and down the frightening descent from the col, rappelling into and climbing out of gigantic slots. Looming seracs were kissed by the morning sun, but luckily nothing toppled onto us. It was one of the most hazardous places I'd ever traveled through.

Arriving back at Madd Camp, I felt shattered. Matt was busily deconstructing our tents, planning for our pickup, and Tim and I had a brief nap. I awoke, still exhausted, and started lowering packs onto the glacier. I coiled and fixed a line for Tim, and in my deeply fatigued state, I only fixed a portion of the amount of rope needed to get to the glacier. There was no knot in the end. Tim jumped on his Grigri and headed down. "Oh fuck!" he shouted, when he realized he was about to rap off the end to a horrible, perhaps fatal, fall. At the very last second, he halted his descent.

Back home in Squamish, my big toe would remain numb for two months. The weight of the experience felt heavy after Tim's near miss at the end of a long and at times risky climb. If I've learned anything, it's this: When mentally tired, allow oneself time to rest and make sound decisions. We got lucky.

—Will Stanhope, *Canada*

Columbia Mountains

SELKIRK MOUNTAINS, MT. SIR SANDFORD, SOUTH COULOIR SKI DESCENT

On February 14, 2024, Canadians Christina Lustenberger, Mark Herbison, and Joshua Lavigne skied the south couloir of Mt. Sir Sandford (3,519m), the highest peak of the Selkirk Mountains. After flying to a base camp at the foot of the mountain, the trio climbed to the top and skied down the 1,100m, 45°–50° couloir, with one 30m rappel at a choke. The narrow couloir is on the far left side of the south face; the main south face was skied in February 2012 by Troy Jungen, Rob Martin, and Doug Sproul. [*In March 2023, on their second attempt, Lustenberger and Andrew McNab made the first known descent of the southwest couloir of Mt. Niflheim (2,871m) in British Columbia's Monashee Mountains.*]

—Dougald MacDonald, *AAJ*

BUGABOOS, NORTH HOWSER TOWER, RAT RACE

On September 2, Ryan LaRocque and I tied in below the west face of North Howser Tower (3,411m). We had rappelled into the cirque below the face intent on exploring the left side of the headwall, which has a laminar aspect to its geology: plaques of immaculate granite stacked in such a perfect planar nature that each layer's edge seems to allow passage for incredible corner climbing. After some research, it appeared there was a corner system that hadn't been explored, seemingly because the Bugaboos guidebook had described this feature as the line of Spicy Red Beans and Rice (Greene-Tague, 1997); this was rectified in the second edition, revealing that the relatively obvious plumb line was, in fact, unclimbed.

After a late summer storm, the lower apron of the magnificent face was gushing with water, and we opted to climb the first

six pitches of Spicy Red Beans and Rice to reach a decent bivy ledge that separates the lower-angle apron from the steep upper headwall. At sunrise, we started up one more pitch of Spicy Red Beans off the bivy ledge before deviating to the right halfway up the pitch to reach our dihedral.

Our route then stayed roughly 20m to 30m to the right of Spicy Red Beans all the way. The cracks, although mossy in places and still seeping a touch from recent snowfall, gave incredible, punchy free climbing between good stances, along with bouts of cleaning cracks with a nut tool. The textured Bugaboo granite never let us down, and where the corner slammed shut, sharp face holds and snaking fissures would arc across the face and back into the dihedral, allowing us to continue our quest skyward.

The stone cleaned up the higher we ascended, and the second-to-last pitch proved truly extraordinary, making it hard to believe that no one had laid hands to this stellar igneous architecture. A mirror copy of the final dihedral on Young Warrior (Harkness-Russel, 2006), the perfect open-book corner was split by a laser-cut finger-to-hands crack for a full rope length. Jackpot.

We climbed ten independent pitches before reaching the lower-angle north ridge of North Howser, where we intersected with past lines and continued to the summit. Snowpatch and Bugaboo spires basked in burning amber hues as a red sun dipped west past this stunning part of the Purcell Mountains.

We named our route—or variation—Rat Race (800m, 5.11+ A1) after the rodents that chewed into our lead line, helmets, packs, and cams at every bivy cave and ledge between the car park and the top of the mountain, proving they are the true locals of this alpine climbing paradise, and that we are just fleeting visitors.

—Sebastian Pelletti, *IFMGA guide, Canada*

TOP: Ryan LaRocque leading pitch 11 of Rat Race (800m, 5.11+ A1) on the west face of North Howser Tower. *Sebastian Pelletti*

BOTTOM: The yellow line shows the first six pitches of Spicy Red Beans and Rice (Greene-Tague, 1997). Above the bivy ledge is Rat Race (red line, LaRocque-Pelletti, 2024). *Alex Buisse*

The line of Attachment Theory (16 pitches to the summit ridge, 5.11+). The first nine pitches are all 5.10 or 5.11. ***Jon Walsh***

SNOWPATCH SPIRE, EAST FACE, ATTACHMENT THEORY

This is a story of perseverance, creativity, and joy that began in 2017 and finished seven years later. The east face of Snowpatch Spire in the Bugaboos has inspired me and many other avid climbers who stay at the Applebee Campground and are fascinated by its enchanting, flawless granitic features. A clean, banana-shaped crack halfway up the east face, directly under the south summit, had caught my eye and heart. Scouring the face, I started linking the features to the bottom of the wall.

Pre-childbearing, Carla Demyen, a mountain guide from Golden, was the first brave soul to join me in exploring this route in 2017. We began about 30m to the left of the Beckey-Mather (1959); the eventual route we climbed is now the farthest left on the face before you get to the peak's namesake snowpatch. The first 60m can be done in two or three pitches and has one short crux of 5.11+ on the second pitch, which we dubbed "the Microdose." This pitch seems slow to dry, and we managed to climb it in very wet conditions—it's amazing what motivated climbers can do!

The next couple of attempts were made with Timothy McAllister, a mountain guide from Invermere, in 2017 and 2018. We climbed up to the banana crack, which we named "Anxious Attachment," pitch six on the wall. We were excited by the quality of the climbing and the minimal cleaning required, and we couldn't wait to unlock the line through the looming roofs above.

Tim had been enthusiastic about finishing the route with me, but after a couple of summers of waiting, I started inviting others to help me. In 2022, Katy Holm, a powerhouse climber and entrepreneur from Squamish, said yes. Katy and I quickly made it up past pitch six, after a couple of days of setting fixed lines on the lower pitches. Pitch seven, "Avoidant Attachment," required a lot of cleaning. We started to get impatient with the process and intimidated by what appeared to be a lack of protection in a seam below big, gaping roof cracks. Katy encouraged me to pendulum off the line and try another crack system to the left. We continued up beside the spire's huge snowpatch for a few pitches until the rock quality deteriorated, then bailed across the steep snow and down the Snowpatch Route, systematically donating our rack in the retreat.

My full schedule as a nursing student did not allow me to return to the Bugaboos that summer or fall, and I didn't want to leave our fixed ropes in place for the winter. In August, I contacted the talented Stephen Senecal, a ski guide from Nelson, to ask if he would help me retrieve the fixed lines and to see if he wanted to help me finish the route. He excitedly agreed and, partnered with Stefan Sander-Green, established the final nine pitches to the top of the mountain. Luckily for me, they didn't climb it all clean, so I still had the opportunity to participate in the first free ascent.

In 2023, Stephen and I established bolted rappel anchors for the first nine pitches to the roof. Then, in 2024, after Stephen had completed his ACMG apprentice alpine exam, we set aside a few days to attempt the free ascent.

Before dawn on September 7, we creatively established a T-slot anchor using wooden CMH heli-ski stakes and lowered out across the wide moat at the base of the wall. I led the first crux and Stephen the next two—we were cheering each other on. We both had to dig deep to free climb the intimidating roof of pitch nine (I seconded clean). We called this pitch "Ghosted" (5.11+), as we did not send it on earlier visits. I was surprised by my success and incredibly grateful that all my hard work had come to fruition.

Stephen Senecal on the 5.11c pitch seven of Attachment Theory (900m, 5.11+) on the east face of Snowpatch Spire. *Jennifer Olson*

We continued upward on easier terrain to where we could step left and join the Honeymooners variation on the Snowpatch Route for the last two pitches to the summit. I am grateful to Stephen's supportive wife, Kristen, and to everyone else who supported this ascent. [*A pitch-by-pitch description of the route and more photos are at the AAJ website.*]

—Jennifer Olson, *Canada*

NUNAVUT | Baffin Island

SIRMILIK NATIONAL PARK, WEST-TO-EAST TRAVERSE AND FIRST ASCENTS

From May 3 to 29, 2023, our team of four (Philippe Gauthier and son Simon Gauthier, and Charles Gauvin and son Marc Gauvin) made the first west-to-east ski mountaineering traverse of Sirmilik National Park on northern Baffin Island.

We skied 350km, starting at Arctic Bay, one of the northernmost permanently inhabited communities in Canada. The first part of our route crossed the rugged and geologically intriguing Borden Peninsula to reach the shore of Navy Board Inlet. A crossing of sea ice allowed us to reach Bylot Island and the Byam Martin Mountains for the second part, finishing at Pond Inlet. We skied in full autonomy, with no caches or resupply.

While the mountainous Bylot Island had been traversed by skis a few times (*see AAJ 2005*), a key challenge for our Sirmilik traverse was to select and navigate a route across the deceptive Borden Peninsula. The northern Borden is a complex ramble of incised ravines, small glaciers, and rocky peaks—not your typical terrain for winter sled travel.

After moving up valleys of the Strathcona River drainage, we explored a series of exciting canyons—namely Upper Fox Canyon and Termites Bench—until we reached the western edge of Sirmilik National Park on day four. Once past the Gates, an intricate and

LEFT: On the summit ridge of Peak 1,438m during the first ascent. *Philippe Gauthier*

ABOVE: Descending the lower part of Kilutea Canyon toward Navy Board Inlet. *Simon Gauthier*

obligatory passage at the base of Military Survey Mountain, the snow got more plentiful, the landscape bigger, and the overall route more gripping.

On day seven, whiteout conditions led us to change our planned exit to Navy Board Inlet, opting for an uncharted descent into the upper reaches of the Kilutea Canyon. This was absorbing and perhaps the crux of the route, descending broken glaciated slopes and ravines to reach the main canyon.

Eight days and 150km after departure, we found ourselves at sea level again, camping near the shore of Navy Board Inlet. On day nine, we crossed the 20km of solid sea ice separating us from Bylot Island, keeping a sharp eye out in this prime travel corridor for polar bears.

On Bylot Island, the 25km long Savik Glacier was our highway into the interior. From a high camp on day 14, we took the opportunity of a brilliant day to make a few ski ascents and descents of unclimbed peaks, on terrain up to 45°. [*The names and coordinates of peaks climbed and skied are at the AAJ website.*] Another break from our daily routine of "grand touring" gave us the opportunity to scale Angilaaq (1,944m) and Nukaq (1,798m) mountains.

However, we were quickly brought back down to earth. A four-day Arctic storm brought gale-force winds and deposited 30cm of snow. After a day in the tent, we started skiing again, navigating mainly with GPS in whiteout conditions. We reached the top of the Sermilik Glacier a couple of days later and began the long, gradual descent to sea level.

On the morning of the last day, after navigating crevasses at the toe of the glacier, we started skiing on sea ice. Soon we heard the engine of our Inuit friends' snowmobile. After 25 days of skiing and camping out as a group of four, meeting these folks was truly heartwarming.

—Philippe Gauthier and Charles Gauvin, *Canada*

AUYUITTUQ NATIONAL PARK, MT. NORTHUMBRIA, TWO NEW ROUTES

Having both turned 50, Owen Lunz and I felt like we could no longer procrastinate, so we committed to a long-discussed trip to Baffin Island to climb Mt. Asgard (2,015m) and whatever else we could. In April, our outfitter, Peter Kilabuk, snowmobiled 157,300 carefully packed calories from Pangnirtung into the Weasel

Valley, along with a substantial chunk of our climbing and camping gear, and stashed it under a boulder below Mt. Northumbria (1,633m).

We flew into Pangnirtung on July 3 only to find the head of Pangnirtung Fjord still covered in ice and the mountains draped in snow. A fortunate warm, windy day followed, and 48 hours after arriving, we were dropped near the head of the now iceless fjord. Upon reaching our cache, we found the river still frozen over, the glaciers covered in an isothermal snowpack that delivered the post-holing nightmares of legend, and the mountains showing lots of snow and limited dry rock. Therefore, during the next two weeks, we focused on lower, less committing objectives and were fortunate to establish two excellent routes.

Below Northumbria, the west side of the valley is formed by a long, brown slab, about a 40-minute walk upstream of the Thor Emergency Shelter. An obvious line of attractive splitters and corners leads up the tallest part of the slab. We climbed this route on July 13 during a brief weather break and found generally excellent, moderate climbing over ten pitches; we named it Pang Ten (424m climbing distance, 5.10).

Looking down pitch eight of Pang Ten (424m, 5.10) with the 1,250-meter west face of Mt. Thor prominent in the background. *Darin Berdinka*

From the route's top, we scrambled west across slabs and talus for about an hour to reach the base of the east buttress of the east tower of Northumbria. This was another obvious and attractive feature, with long crack and corner systems.

Having scoped the line, we returned to Northumbria on July 15 by hiking up the walk-off descent from Pang Ten. We climbed the east buttress in nine long pitches of consistent 5.8/5.9 difficulty. It was one of those rare climbs where a majority of the pitches would be classic and popular single-pitch routes. We descended the route in eight clean rappels off solid anchors: Say Hello to Heaven (394m, 5.9).

Later in the trip, after climbing Asgard and other peaks, we returned to Pang Ten to add rappel anchors. Weather prevented us from linking these two routes in a day, but this would make an obvious and attractive objective.

—Darin Berdinka, *USA*

Greenland

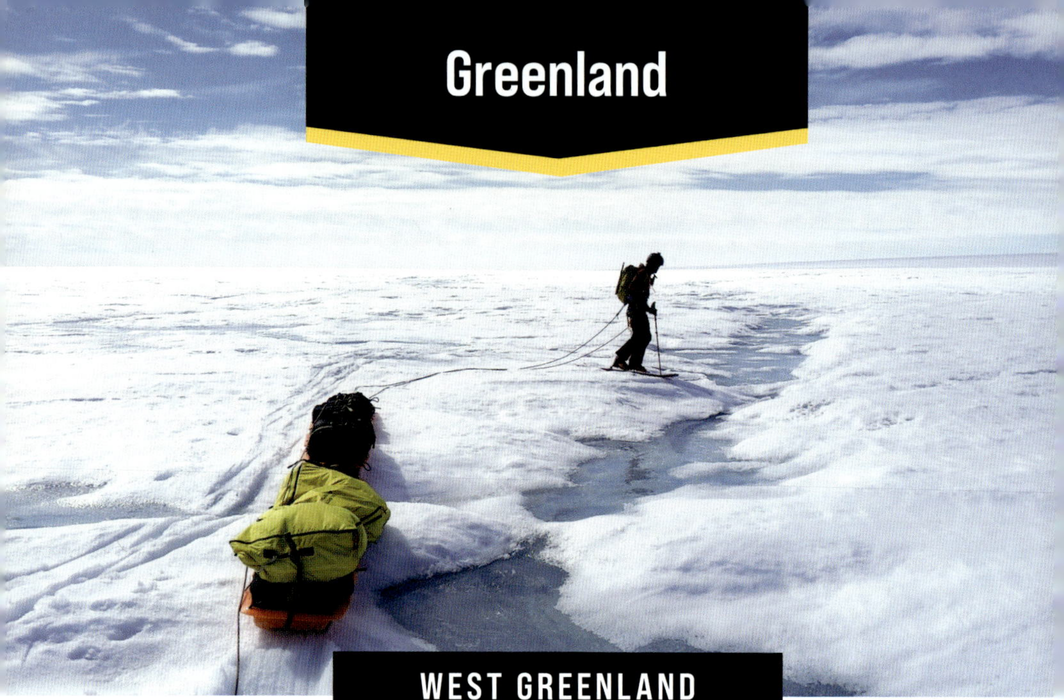

WEST GREENLAND

Navigating a "slush swamp" while ascending the ice cap toward kiteable terrain. Each skier pulled about 400 pounds. Near this area, a rainstorm trapped the pair in the tent for three days. *Eric Gilbertson*

FOUR FIRST ASCENTS DURING SOUTHEAST–NORTHWEST CROSSING

The Umiammakku Nunaat region of western Greenland contains many remote unclimbed peaks in a rugged strip of land between coast and ice cap. We learned about these mountains from historical *AAJ* reports by teams that approached by boat and climbed near the coast. [*AAJ 1968 reported the first ascent of three coastal peaks in Umiammakku Nunaat by an Italian team; other reports are vague or describe ascents on nearby peninsulas or islands.*] We were interested in climbing less-accessible peaks farther inland as part of a 1,539-mile southeast-to-northwest, coast-to-coast traverse of Greenland.

According to Greenland experts, including polar guide Lars Ebbesen, such a traverse had not been done before, though there have been various crossings by other routes from east to west. Of the two of us, Branden was an experienced kiter, having previously kited across northern Scandinavia, but I was just learning. Neither of us had been to Greenland.

We flew to Kulusuk, in southeast Greenland, in mid-June. After 16 days of waiting for favorable sea ice and weather, we reached Isortoq village on June 27. From there, a local hunter took us by boat to a point on the coast near the ice cap. The katabatic winds on the west coast of Greenland, blowing reliably from the southeast, made it sensible for us to begin here.

Over the next week, we each manhauled 400 pounds of gear, distributed in four sleds apiece, up to safe kiting terrain (flat and snowy, with no crevasses or filled-in slots) above 4,000'. This section involved traveling 35 miles up icy and at times heavily crevassed, steep terrain. Sometimes we only made five to ten miles per day.

Once on the ice cap, we kite-skied west for 10 days, roughly along the Nansen Route. (This is the route of Fridtjof Nansen and five companions, who in 1888 spent six weeks making the first crossing of Greenland's interior, east to west, via skis and sledges.) We each towed sleds in two-by-two grids, with around 100 pounds in each sled.

We encountered one set of polar bear tracks 15 miles from the coast, and we slept with guns close at hand. The terrain felt flat, but in fact gradually rose to a pass at around 8,000'. We encountered some sections of difficult sastrugi, which at times got us briefly airborne as we hit the icy ridges at 20+ mph.

Near the west coast, we hit the predicted favorable winds and kited for five days, covering up to 200 miles per day, to reach Umiammakku Nunaat, a peninsula of rugged peaks sandwiched between the Umiammakku Sermiat and Kangilliup Sermia glaciers. When the terrain got too complex and crevassed for kiting, we established camp atop a 6,000' snow dome, surrounded on three sides by rugged peaks, with the huge, flat ice cap extending to the east.

On July 18, we descended north, crossed an unnamed glacier, then scrambled up bare rock on the southeast face of Peak 1,857m to the ice-capped summit, at coordinates 71.885, -51.914.

We rested the next day to untangle kites, then manhauled two sleds each farther into the mountains and camped atop the rounded, snowcapped Peak 2,152m (71.804, -51.97), having left our remaining sleds and gear cached in a snow cairn.

On July 21, we skied west and climbed Peak 2,171m (71.751, -52.094). First, we attempted an eastern aspect in the sun, but slushy snow bridges collapsed when we touched them. We then diverted to the steeper, shady north aspect, which required frontpointing and weaving through seracs to a gentle summit ridge, from which we got our first views of the ocean since June. From there, we skied northwest and scrambled the rocky south ridge of Peak 2,063m (71.772, -52.12). Icebergs floated in the distant sea, with no boats or other signs of civilization. We felt very remote, in an area perhaps no other people had visited. Our journey was now just halfway complete.

We returned to camp on Peak 2,152m, then spent a few days manhauling back to kiteable terrain on the ice cap. Before we could resume kiting, we had to wait out a two-day blizzard.

When the weather cleared, we continued north in favorable winds, covering up to 218 miles per day, to reach the edge of the ice cap near Qaanaaq, on the northwest coast. It took three days to triple-carry our gear five miles from the ice cap down to the sea, with packs up to 115 pounds. We then got a boat ride with a local hunter to town. After waiting 17 days in Qaanaaq for a flight, we returned home to Seattle on August 22.

—Eric Gilbertson and Branden Joy, *USA*

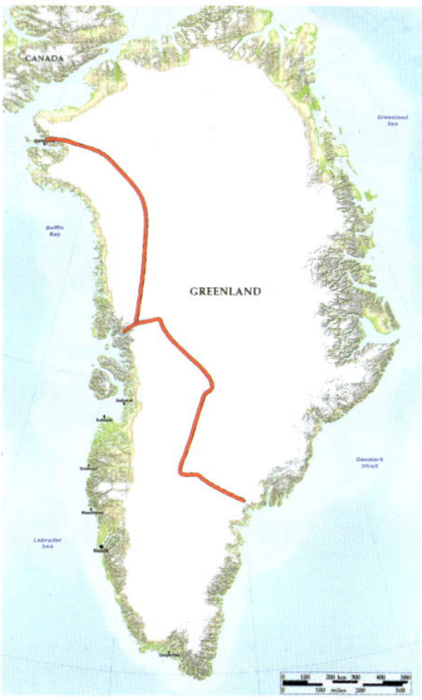

TOP: Branden Joy descending Peak 2,171m after the first ascent. On this day, the climbers had their first view of the sea in three weeks. *Eric Gilbertson*

BOTTOM: General route of Gilbertson and Joy's southeast-to-northwest crossing, starting near Isortoq in the east and ending at Qaanaaq. They covered more than 1,500 miles on foot and kite-skis. The midroute jog to the left marks the detour to Umiammakku Nunaat, where four first ascents were completed. *Blue Green Atlas, licensed under CC BY 4.0*

ABOVE: The west face of Innaarsuit, showing the five routes completed in 2024: (1) Encore (E4 6a), (2) Twist of Fate (417m climbing distance, E5 6a), (3) Gas Mark Five (E5 6b), (4) Uliaq (E3 5c), and (5) Loweswater Gold (E4 6a). ***Ben Kent***

LEFT: Ben Kent simul-climbing during the first ascent of Encore. ***Chris Moore***

KEKERTARMIUT ISLAND, INNAARSUIT, VARIOUS NEW ROUTES

In June and July, the British team of Indie Fallowfield, Ben Kent, and Chris Moore established a flurry of new climbs on and around a previously unclimbed 400m formation named Innaarsuit (approx. 65°33'49.7"N, 53°10'57.0"W) on Kekertarmiut Island. The nine routes ranged in length from 27m to 417m, and from E1 5b to E5 6b, with the two standouts being the west-face climbs Twist of Fate (417m climbing distance, E5 6a)—their first up the formation—and the neighboring Gas Mark Five (404m, E5 6b).

The trio had intended to visit the Upernavik archipelago, about 800km farther north, having sailed to Greenland's west coast from the U.K. in a 49' sailboat. However, unusually heavy sea ice and wintery conditions on land prompted them to hop off in the fishing village of Maniitsoq. (They'd heard about the climbing potential nearby from British captain Bob Shepton, who led a sail-and-climb expedition that explored this area in 2015; *see AAJ 2016*.) On July 3, having learned about the Innaarsuit cliff from a local friend, Jørgen, who had seen the wall near his fishing grounds, the climbers and 100kg of food and equipment were dropped off on Kekertarmiut Island, where they headed 500m inland to establish base camp below the wall.

For their first route, Twist of Fate, they selected a central line up faint cracks and grooves, starting the climb the same day as their drop-off. All went well until they hit a blank section guarding a midheight ledge on day three; eventually they placed removable bolts to supplement hooks on the technical E5 6a/b face, taking a "British ethics" approach of minimal fixed gear. After a storm forced retreat, the trio returned to finish the upper six pitches in a single push on July 11–12, including completing the route's money pitch, "a 50m questing E4 from Chris [Moore]."

The trio returned on July 15 to free Twist of Fate in a day, swinging leads over 14 hours. With more than a week remaining and the weather holding, they established eight more climbs—four on Innaarsuit proper—all done ground-up (*see photo above*). On July 23, a boat picked them up for the return to Maniitsoq.

—Matt Samet, *AAJ, with information from Ben Kent/ UKClimbing.com and Chris Moore, U.K.*

SOUTH GREENLAND | Torsukattak Fjord

Crossing Torsukattak Fjord en route to Maujit Qaqarssuasia. The 1,350-meter wall directly behind the paddler, known as the Thumbnail, is often called the highest seacliff in the world. ***Callum Johnson***

MAUJIT QAQARSSUASIA MASSIF, TWO NEW ROUTES, AND OTHER CLIMBS

In August 2024, Miška Izakovičová (Slovakia), Callum Johnson, Simon Smith, and I (all from Scotland) explored the area around Torsukattak Fjord in southern Greenland. We established multiple new rock routes, including a partial new route on our primary objective, the 1,350m east face of Maujit Qaqarssuasia, a.k.a. the Thumbnail, contender for the world's tallest seacliff. We also made the first ascent of the southern headwall of Maujit Qaqarssuasia East and established many shorter climbs on other cliffs.

The Thumbnail was first climbed in 2000, by a 31-pitch all-free route, by a U.K. team. In the years since, four more routes or major variations were climbed, including one to the right of the original route, completed in 2016 by the French-Belgian team of Lionel Daudet, Enzo Oddo, and Siebe Vanhee. Our eyes were likewise set on the right side of this formation.

On August 1, a boat dropped us at our base camp on the west shore of Pamiagdluk Island, across Torsukattak Fjord from the Thumbnail. We were treated to wall-to-wall blue skies, and this, along with the horrendous blackflies, prompted us to head straight for the wall. We paddled both of our packrafts two kilometers across a beautifully flat turquoise sea. Miška led the first pitch onto the wall, well to the right of the 2000 and 2016 routes, and hauled the enormous bags out of our boats. Then Simon and I paddled round to the descent gully, about 1,500m to climber's left of our line, to stash one raft, then returned to the base of our line. That evening, we set up the two portaledges and slept 40m above the sea.

We had 70 liters of water, sleeping and cooking kit for four people, and many ropes. This also meant we had exceptionally heavy haulbags. We were keen to use natural anchors, which sometimes meant using up to 12 points of gear. The next day, we climbed good rock up a series of moderate corners and soon realized the climbing was going to be the least of our worries: Ledges, long traverse pitches, chimneys, and grooves all made hauling a mammoth challenge—someone had to be with the bags constantly. We kept climbing until late in the evenings, as our horizons grew and distant pointy peaks came into view from our portaledges. After 800m of climbing and four days on the wall, we reached the halfway ledge.

ABOVE: Traversing the midway ledge on Maujit Qaqarssuasia under heavy loads. Base camp was across the fjord by the cove in back right. ***Tim Miller***

LEFT: Tim Miller on the headwall of Mussels for Tea, Packrafts in the Sea. ***Miška Izakovičová***

We woke to gray clouds amassing on the horizon and decided to head back to base camp until the storm passed, then return to our high point. We stashed ropes, gear, portaledges, stove, and food on the ledge and then started the long traverse to the descent gully, moving slowly with our unwieldy haulbags on the steep, loose, vegetated slopes over a gaping drop straight to the sea.

Eventually we reached the snowy gully, which was much steeper than anticipated and fraught with crevasses. None of us had crampons or axes, so we each carried a spiky rock for self-arrest and abseiled over the crevasses. We finally reached the sea late in the day and under darkening skies. Miška and I set off to retrieve the stashed raft, battling choppy seas and a fierce headwind. Back at the gully, we faced a dilemma: either head out across the whitecapped fjord in the dark or sit in the miserable gully, with no food, until the storm cleared.

We took the former option, paddling ferociously in the gloom, our frayed nerves set even more ajangle when a humpback whale breached just meters away from the boats. It was a relief to be back at base camp, even if that night a storm would flood our group tent; the next day the wind ripped the big tent from our hands as we relocated it, shredding one side against some rocks, and also flattened Miška's tent, snapping a pole.

The following day, Simon went down to the sea to fish, passing the boulder where we'd stashed the packrafts—only to find that an unexpectedly high tide and storm waves had washed the expensive rafts out to sea. It seemed we wouldn't be able to finish our project. Worse, we looked like total idiots—though, on the upside, Simon caught a fish.

That evening, as we sat under our tarp miserably trying to turn our fish into something edible, a small boat approached our camp. It was a local fisherman. Miles down the fjord in the murky mist, he'd found one of our rafts. What a miracle: The show could go on!

After a week, the sun re-emerged. This allowed us to shuttle kit across the fjord in our single raft and then retrace our steps back up the gully and across the ledge to our previous high point. After the complexities of hauling the lower half of the wall, we had opted to attempt the top of our route in light alpine style, in a single push.

Early the next morning, we set off in two teams, climbing parallel lines. Simon and I climbed an immaculate corner up one side of a pillar, while on the other side, Callum and Miška climbed cracks and

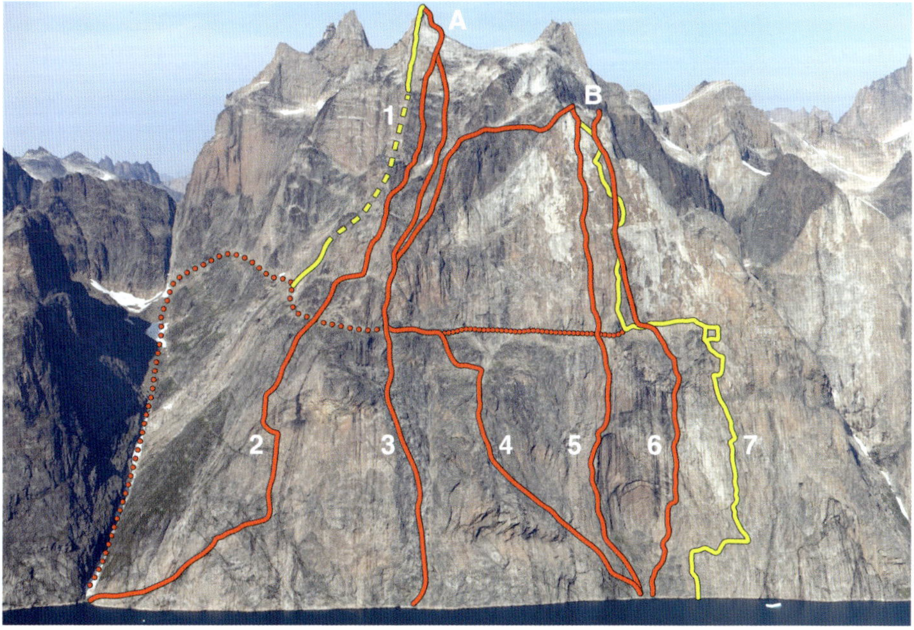

corners. We regrouped at the top of the pillar. Above, at the steepest part of the wall, Miška set off up a difficult crack in an airy position with the whole fjord far below. Callum followed with a brilliantly sustained pitch above. Meanwhile, to the right, I climbed up to a steep chimney, which Simon exited via a precarious move to reach easier climbing. These four pitches proved to be the route's crux, ranging from British E4 to E6 (5.11b to 5.12b). We all managed to onsight and second these pitches free, bar one fall by Miška on the hardest pitch.

As we learned later, some of our headwall pitches likely shared ground with the French-Belgian route from 2016. (We found what I believe is their tat high on the face, at the time erroneously assuming it was from a failed, undocumented attempt.) But since our team climbed two different lines on much of the headwall, we undoubtedly climbed a lot of independent terrain.

The climbing above remained exposed and on quality rock right until we pulled onto the summit, late in the evening of August 15. We called our line Mussels for Tea, Packrafts in the Sea (1,350m, 33 pitches, E6 6b or 5.12b). After sharing hugs, we started down ledges behind the Thumbnail, heading generally south, until it became so steep we had to abseil. A blood-red moon emerged over the horizon; time slowed as we worked to rig abseils, pull ropes, and find the next abseil station. Soon the northern lights made a faint appearance, and a constant flow of shooting stars escorted us back along the ledge to our bivy.

We spent a lazy morning listening to music and recovering. The forecast showed continuing top weather, and we had plenty of enthusiasm, so we relocated our camp to beneath the spectacular

The east faces of (A) Maujit Qaqarssuasia East and (B) the Thumbnail, with approximate lines of (1) Texture Like Sun (2024), on the southern face of the peak's headwall—see the *AAJ* website for a straight-on photo; (2) Golden Lunacy (2007); (3) Hidrofilia (2003); (4) The Cruise Line (2003); (5) British Route (Bransby-Dickinson-Parnell-Parry, 2000); (6) French-Belgian Route (Daudet-Oddo-Vanhee, 2016); and (7) Mussels for Tea, Packrafts in the Sea (2024). The two teams on Mussels for Tea climbed different variations, some of which likely overlapped with the French-Belgian Route in places. The dotted lines show the traverse ledge on the Thumbnail and the descent gully. *Tim Miller*

TOP: During the all-day approach to Spire of the Northern Fire, the orange wall in back. See the *AAJ* website for the three new routes. *Miška Izakovičová*

BOTTOM: Dream Corner on Orange Wall, viewed from the top of Mark. *Callum Johnson*

southern headwall of Maujit Qaqarssuasia East, which we had set our eyes upon while walking beneath it on the ledge system. During the awkward load-carry, Simon tweaked his back, meaning he'd have to miss the climbing the next day.

On the morning of August 17, Miška, Callum, and I made quick progress up easy slabs until we stood beneath the main difficulties. We alternated leads, moving efficiently up corners and cracks we'd seen through binoculars. The climbing was constantly engaging, never desperate but sustained. We each had huge smiles after every pitch, and we could see Simon sunbathing on the ledge below.

I led a spectacular hanging corner as the sun left the wall. Then Miška climbed a final pitch up a tower, which—surprise!—led directly to the summit. Having completed the first ascent of the southern headwall of Maujit Qaqarssuasia East via Texture Like Sun (800m, E3 5c or 5.10d), we watched the sun sink behind a rugged horizon of rocky spires bathed in a deep orange glow. It was a special moment, and we would have stayed longer if not for a bitterly cold wind.

—Tim Miller, *U.K.*

PAMIAGDLUK ISLAND CLIMBS: *After their ascents on Maujit Qaqarssuasia, these four climbers accessed various cliffs on foot from their base camp on Pamiagdluk Island.*

Two climbs were done on the west face of Mark, located in the same valley as the Baroness: Warmonger (Johnson-Smith, 400m, E4/5 6a or French 6c+) and Slow off the Mark (Izakovičová-Miller, 400m, E4 5c or 6b+). Warmonger may share some ground with an earlier attempt dubbed Arms Trader (300m, Mehigan-Roberts, 2002); Slow off the Mark is just left of a 2016 route and likely shares some terrain in the upper part. Johnson and Smith also climbed the east face of Mark by a six-pitch route they called Inversions (280m, E4 6a or 6c). All climbs descended to the north.

After an all-day, semi-technical approach into the mountains east of base camp, Izakovičová and Miller bivouacked for several nights and climbed three routes up the southwest face of a superb tower they called the Spire of the Northern Fire after a northern lights display above the tower. The three routes take parallel crack systems, up to five pitches long and French 7b. Descents were by rappel.

On the last day before their boat pickup, Izakovičová and Miller climbed what's likely the first route up a formation they called Orange Wall, across the valley from Mark. Their route up the southeast face, Dream Corner (600m, E3 5c or French 6b+), involved 300m up moderate slabs followed by a steep six-pitch corner system. Descent was by a ridge to the northeast, then down a break to the southeast (two rappels), followed by a ramp to the northeast.

Topos and many photos from these climbs and one other are at the AAJ website.

—Dougald MacDonald, *AAJ*

EAST GREENLAND | Schweizerland

The three-day Trident VI Orobica traverse went west to east (left to right) over (A) Baby Molar, (B) Molar, and (C) Incisor. (D) is Cavity Ridge, showing the incomplete line of No Me Moleste Mosquito. ***Thomas Triboli***

FOX JAW CIRQUE: THREE-PEAK TRAVERSE; CAVITY RIDGE, NO ME MOLESTE MOSQUITO

In 20 years, we'll be more disappointed by the things we didn't do than by the ones we did. With this philosophy in mind, Daniele Bonzi, Francesco Fumagalli, and I—friends from the province of Bergamo and fellow members of Italy's Corpo Nazionale Soccorso Alpino e Speleologico rescue team—embarked on an adventure in Greenland. Our goal: to explore the imposing gneissic walls of Fox Jaw Cirque.

The first climbers to visit Fox Jaw, accessed from the head of Tasiilaq Fjord, were Americans Dave Briggs and Mike Libecki, who named the area and climbed the Molar in 1998 (*see AAJ 1999*). Since then, many routes have been established on the cirque's toothlike spires (search "Fox Jaw Cirque" at the *AAJ* website).

We set off on August 4 from Tasiilaq, where we'd been hosted by Robert Peroni, an explorer from South Tyrol, at his Red House hostel. After 70km by boat and three exhausting overland trips to transport 200kg of gear and supplies, we established base camp at 66°08'40.9"N, 37°01'42.0"W, 12km from our landing point.

With favorable weather, we spent August 7–9 establishing Trident VI Orobica (1,000m of climbing, UIAA V+), a link-up of three peaks—Baby Molar (a.k.a. Milk Tooth Spire, 1,132m), Molar Spire (1,270m), and Incisor (1,360m)—moving west to east along the ridge. On day one, we climbed Baby Molar in 14 pitches, bivouacking on the summit with a breathtaking view. It's possible our climb shared some terrain with Matteo Della Bordella and Riky Felderer's 2009 route, Qui, nell'Universo (480m, UIAA VI), but it's hard to know for sure; our route stayed right of the upper ridge but without coming onto the south face. On day two, after five rappels off Baby Molar, we followed unclimbed terrain up the west side of Molar for six moderate pitches and then four pitches on Incisor. We spent the second night on top of Incisor. On the third day, we descended via Tears in Paradise on Incisor, completing the link-up.

After a few days of rest and fishing, we set out for Cavity Ridge and its 700m south face. [*The broad Cavity Ridge formation has had one known ascent, in 2000, by a Swiss party that climbed a pillar on the right side in 16 pitches (6a); see AAJ 2010. The left side of the face, attempted in 2024, has no known summit routes.*] We set out on August 12 at 3:15 a.m., facing tough conditions: snow, rain, and slippery rock. Despite this, we covered 600 vertical meters in 12 pitches up cracks, slabs, and corners, coming within a few pitches of the summit before exhaustion forced a retreat. The descent lasted until 5:30 a.m., and we named the route to our high point No Me Moleste Mosquito (600m, 12 pitches, VII/VI+ obl.), after the area's annoying mosquitoes and inspired by lyrics in the Doors song "The Mosquito." On August 17, a boat came to take us back to Tasiilaq.

—Thomas Triboli, *Italy*

Mexico

Baja California

CAÑÓN DEL TAJO, EL GRAN TRONO BLANCO, ESTRELLA FUGAZ

On October 26 and 27, Iván Acosta, Sergio Acosta, Jesús Avalos, Phany Cano, Israel López, Carlos Sanchez, and I climbed Estrella Fugaz (420m, 5.10b A2) on El Gran Trono Blanco's southwest face. Our route is now the first you encounter near the bottom of the descent gully that leads to the south face. It is to the left of The Millennium (Anderson-Smallwood, 1999).

The goal of this trip was to show my friends how to open a traditional multipitch route. In April, I climbed the first six pitches, but we abandoned our attempt and rappelled the route due to lack of time. I returned in October with the team of six friends.

This time I managed to open all nine pitches, following a crack system with a mixture of free climbing and aid. The rest of the team jugged behind. We spent a night bivouacking on a ledge on pitch four and the next day reached the summit around 9:30 a.m. It was a challenging descent as the walk back south was difficult to find. [*This route was free climbed in late November at 5.10+. It has some protection bolts, and most anchors are bolted.*]

—**Luis Carlos García Ayala, *Mexico***

Estrella Fugaz ascends nine pitches up the southwest face of El Gran Trono Blanco. It was free climbed at 5.10+ in late November 2024. ***Luis Carlos García Ayala***

Nuevo León

SAN ISIDRO CANYON, HARD VERY CACTUS

El Salto is known primarily for sport climbing. However, on December 15, 2023, Matt Reeser (USA) and I established Hard Very Cactus (5.11 R or E5 5c), a 400m traditional route on limestone in nearby San Isidro Canyon. The ascent was completed without bolts or pegs, relying entirely on traditional gear. With seven pitches following an initial 100m scramble, this is the first multipitch climb in the canyon.

Our climb followed a natural weakness on the east side of the canyon, linking crack systems, arêtes, and exposed traverses with sections of appalling rock. Cacti were present throughout, making protection and movement more difficult. After pitch five, a cactus spine got lodged into my eye, and Matt led the remaining two pitches to the canyon rim.

The descent along a steep spur proved to be as challenging as the climb itself, involving several hours of difficult bushwhacking through dense vegetation. Reeser, an experienced route developer at the Black Canyon in Colorado, described it as the worst bushwhacking he had encountered. Both of us spent the next two days removing countless cactus spines from our bodies and faces.

—**Patrick Hill, *U.K.***

Colombia

Sierra Nevada de Santa Marta

The north sides of (A) Pico Cristóbal Colón (5,713m), (B) Pico Simón Bolívar (5,720m), and (C) Pico Simmonds (5,594m). The arrow marks the start of the 2023 route on Pico Colón. ***Google Earth***

PICO CRISTÓBAL COLÓN AND PICO SIMMONDS, NEW ROUTES FROM THE NORTH

The Sierra Nevada de Santa Marta is a range near Colombia's Caribbean coast, with around 17 peaks. During an expedition from January 13 to 27, 2023, Daniel Anzola, Sergio Garcia Gomez, and I climbed two new routes there, one on Pico Cristóbal Colón and another on Pico Simmonds.

From Santa Marta, we took a 4WD truck to the Arhuaco indigenous community of Yerba Buena. The next morning, we traveled 18km with horses and camped at a lake at 3,600m. We then trekked four days to reach Carcuina Lake at 4,600m and established base camp. The next day, we crossed a 4,900m pass to an advanced camp at the toe of the Colón Glacier. Our first objective was Pico Colón (10°50'21.3"N, 73°41'10.7"W), whose north face rises 600m from the bergschrund to the summit at 5,713m. [*Pico Cristóbal Colón was surveyed in 1939 at 5,775m, but substantial melting of the summit ice cap and a recent survey now put the elevation at 5,713m; see report on page 197.*]

The line we'd planned to climb was blocked by the bergschrund, so starting at 8 a.m. on January 21 we climbed an obvious gully on the right side of the northeast face. The route consisted of nine 50m pitches with an average angle of 65°–70°, with vertical steps; we felt it was rated D+. The ice took screws, and the granite offered solid protection with cams and nuts. From the top of the gully, we moved onto the easier northwest face and followed this to the summit, which we reached at 3:30 p.m. We descended the northwest face and Colón Glacier to return to camp. As far as we could determine, there were no prior routes up Colón's steep north side.

The next day, we decided to attempt the north ridge of Pico Simmonds (5,594m, 10°50'27"N, 73°42'20"W) and camped below the ridge in the high pass we had crossed earlier to reach Pico Colón. At 4 a.m. on January 23, Sergio and I started up the glacier; Daniel stayed back because of knee pain. Upon reaching the ridge, we pitched out the climb, taking care because of loose rock in the ice. The difficulty was AD, and we reached the summit around 9 a.m. We believe this was the first ascent of the ridge.

We hiked down the mountain via the snowy west ridge. On this same day, we met with the Arhuaco team at the Carcuina Lake base camp to celebrate and organize our return to Santa Marta.

The Colombian government officially has closed these mountains to the public, but rangers don't visit the area because the mountains' real owners are the indigenous communities. A special thank-you to the Arhuaco, Kogi, Wiwa, and Kankuamo communities—the real authorities of this land. [*In recent years, thanks to cooperative arrangements between guiding companies, the Arhuaco, and other indigenous communities, some expeditions have been granted access to these mountains, employing local people as support staff. See the reports below.*]

—Alex Torres, *Colombia*

Steep rock on AYU, the first route up the south face of Pico Simón Bolívar. *Rubio Collection*

Looking toward Pico Bolívar from Pico Colón. The new routes up Bolívar climbed the rocky south face (left) to the east ridge. *Ricardo Rubio*

PICO SIMÓN BOLÍVAR, SOUTH FACE, AYU

The Sierra Nevada de Santa Marta is considered the Heart of the World in indigenous cosmogony and is among the highest coastal ranges in the world. On December 11, 2024, Alexander Chávez, Brian Kalet, Salomón Torres, and I embarked on an adventure to reach Pico Simón Bolívar (5,720m), Colombia's highest mountain, which would take us through all types of ecosystems, finally reaching tropical glaciers. We were accompanied by a team of 12 porters from the Arhuaco community, including the indigenous leader's son.

We established base camp at approximately 4,850m, and on December 18 began our ascent from the north, climbing the Colón Glacier to the col between Pico Cristóbal Colón and Pico Bolívar. We navigated a crevasse field and stretches of snow and ice up to 65° to reach the col and summited Pico Colón around 6 a.m. During our final ascent, we spotted a striking potential route up Pico Bolívar. We returned to the col around 7:30 a.m. and moved onto the south face of Bolívar.

I led four 50m pitches of mixed climbing (approximately M5), and by 11 a.m. we had overcome the rock face and were at 5,300m. We proceeded along the beautiful east ridge toward the summit of Bolívar, which we reached at noon. We returned to base camp at 4 p.m., highly satisfied with opening a new route—named AYU—and completing the ascent of Colombia's two highest mountains in just 18 hours. Salomón Torres's ascent marks the first time an Arhuaco climber had reached these summits.

—Ricardo Rubio, *Colombia*

PICO SIMÓN BOLÍVAR, SOUTH FACE VARIATION AND ELEVATION MEASUREMENTS

Until now, Colombia's highest mountain was thought to be Pico Cristóbal Colón, surveyed in 1939 at 5,775m. A neighboring peak, Pico Simón Bolívar, 650m to the west, was surveyed at 5,773m and was considered the second-tallest peak in the country.

Since the late 1990s, accessing this area has been difficult, as local communities have largely prohibited climbing the peaks for religious reasons. In 2021, however, the Arhuaco community started granting permission to select groups to climb Colón and Bolívar, and I was fortunate to join an expedition there in December 2024.

My goal was to reach Colombia's high point, but I suspected it might no longer be Pico Colón. In Washington state, I'd recently discovered that Mt. Rainier has melted down seven meters since it was last measured (*see report on page 136*), and I suspected something similar or even more extensive might be occurring in Colombia.

On the east ridge of Pico Simón Bolívar, looking back at Pico Cristóbal Colón. Both peaks have summit ice caps, but probably not for long. The two peaks each lost more than 50 meters of elevation in the last 85 years because of melting summit ice. *Eric Gilbertson*

On December 15, the team left from Santa Marta and met five local Arhuaco members who'd help porter gear. We hiked for six days over several 4,000m passes, reaching base camp on December 21. On December 22, Ginge Fullen, Jonathan Suarez, and I ascended the Colón Glacier and climbed a WI2 and steep snow pitch (50°–60°) to the Colón-Bolívar col. We then downclimbed the south side of the col, following a route climbed by Ricardo Rubio and his party four days earlier (*see report above*). We climbed low-fifth-class rock and snow, following ledges and traversing across the south face for three pitches, until arriving directly below the upper of two rock steps on the east ridge.

From here, Rubio's route continued traversing snowy ledges, but we took a direct rock line straight to the top of the upper step, then followed the east ridge to the summit. We propose a grade of 5.6 M2 for our line from the col. In descent, we downclimbed and rappelled the route, reaching base camp after a 21-hour push.

While on Bolívar's summit, I took a 45-minute, highly precise dGPS reading as well as measurements with an Abney level from the summit of Bolívar to the summit of Colón. All five of the independent measurements showed that Bolívar is taller than Colón—it is Colombia's new high point. Bolívar now measures 5,720.42m, with rocks visible two meters below the summit, and Colón measures 5,712.79m, with rock three meters below the summit—meaning Colón has melted down 62m and Bolívar 53m since 1939. If this rapid melting continues, the summits soon will be rock-covered—and Bolívar will remain Colombia's high point.

—Eric Gilbertson, *USA*

Venezuela

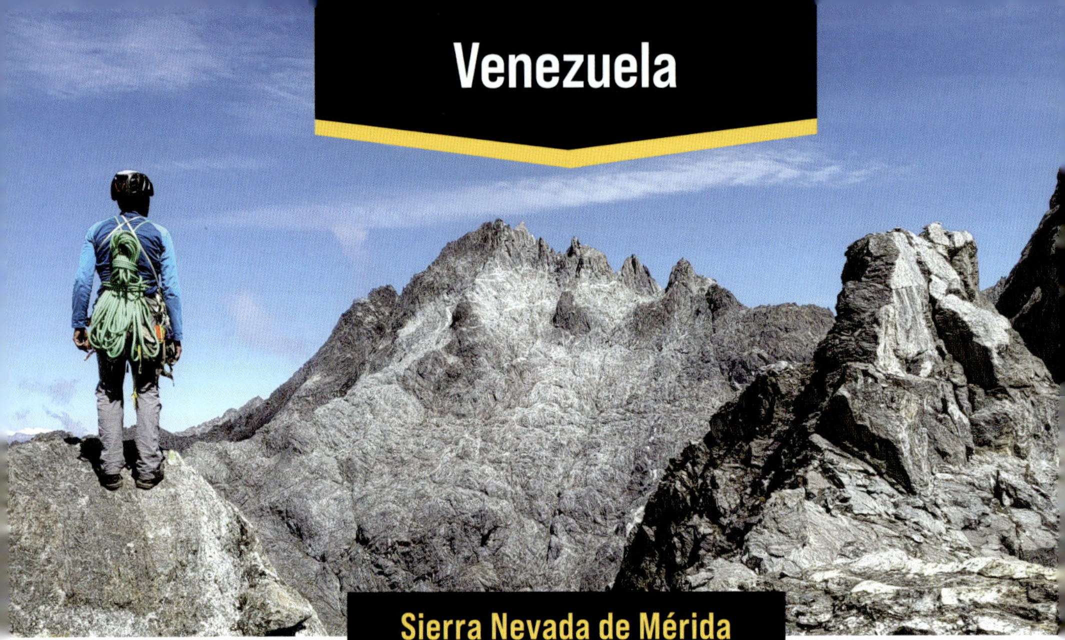

Sierra Nevada de Mérida

Lenin Zerpa surveys the west-northwest face of Pico Bolívar (4,978m), the highest mountain in Venezuela. Forty years ago, the top half or more of this face was glaciated. ***Cheo Garcia***

MUKUMBARÍ INTEGRAL LINK-UP

Situated southeast of Mérida in far western Venezuela, the Sierra Nevada holds the country's highest peaks, culminating in Pico Bolívar (named after Simón Bolívar, the Venezuelan military officer who liberated many South American countries from Spanish rule). Historically, the altitude of Pico Bolívar was recorded at just over 5,000m, but more recent calculations have decreased the heights of most peaks in the range, and Bolívar now stands at 4,978m (8°32'28.15"N, 71°2'47.51"W).

The range is also notable for having the highest cable car in the world. Known as the Mukumbari, it rises from the city of Mérida (1,600m) to Pico Espejo (4,765m) through the complete spectrum of Andean vegetation.

The Sierra Nevada has been dramatically impacted by climate change. Even in the 1980s, melting had reduced the range's glaciation to only two glaciers on Bolívar and two on Pico Humboldt (4,919m), the second-highest peak and most easterly major summit in the range. By 2009, only a Humboldt glacier—La Corona—remained, and by 2024 it had shrunk so much it was downgraded to an "icefield," making Venezuela the first Andean country to lose all its glaciers. Ostensibly to protect Humboldt's vanishing ice mass, the government forbids climbing on both it and close neighbor Pico Bonpland (4,863m).

In January 2025, Venezuelan climbers Cheo Garcia and Lenin Zerpa aimed to reach all the legal high points along the range's main ridge, beginning with Pico El León (4,731m) in the southwest and ending at the Agujas Bifidas (beyond which a long, scrambly ridge leads east to the restricted Humboldt and Bonpland).

The two started at around 6:40 a.m. on January 10 for the classic León–Toro traverse, a seven-kilometer ridge, often sharp and airy, with excellent granite. They soon realized the weight of their packs was too much to downclimb exposed steps and they resorted to rappelling. Because of this, they took longer than expected, and having completed the ridge and descended to the Alto de la Cruz pass, they did not reach their planned bivouac site until 8 p.m.

Thereafter, they adopted a different strategy for their traverse: They would first carry to their next camp, then backtrack and traverse the day's section with only climbing gear.

On the 11th, they traversed several summits to bivouac at the Pico Espejo cable car station. On the 12th, in windy weather, they headed east on the most interesting part of the ridge, negotiating vertical spires and exposed steps, the sight of which, Garcia said, "would either captivate or intimidate you."

They eventually reached the west face of El Vertigo, an impressive spire shortly before Bolívar. Here, they climbed a new three-pitch line at 5.9. (The first ascent of Vertigo was made in 1962 by Kangchenjunga first ascensionist George Band from the U.K., who was based in the country while working for Shell.) The two continued over the next point, La Salle, by a modern route, Projecting the Dimension (55m, 5.10), then continued over Bolívar and Pico Jahn before descending to the Garganta Bourgoin couloir, where they left the ridge and returned to Pico Espejo for the night.

The two spent the 13th moving camp farther east. On the 14th, they climbed the steep Abanico via five pitches up to 5.9. After descending, they moved carefully through the very loose terrain of Valley of the Mica to reach Aguja Joma West, which they climbed via another new route, the three-pitch Moscovita (5.10). Continuing over three more sharp summits, they descended back to their camp.

TOP: Looking approximately east in early January 2025 to (A) Agujas Joma, (B) Aguja Franco Anzil, (C) Aguja Sin Nombre, (D) Pico Humboldt, and (E) Pico Bonpland. ***Cheo Garcia***

ABOVE: Picos Humboldt and Bonpland covered with glaciers in late December 1985. ***Lindsay Griffin***

The 15th was their final day, and they traversed the remaining ridge over La Concha, La Garza, and the Agujas Bifidas, with no rope needed—this section gave spectacular views of the ground they had covered. They named the adventure Mukumbarí Integral. Mukumbarí, a name bestowed on the range by former indigenous people, translates as "the place where the sun sleeps." [*See the AAJ website for a list of all the summits reached.*]

—Lindsay Griffin, *AAJ, with information from Cheo Garcia, Venezuela*

(A) Taulliraju (5,830m), (B) GMHM Buttress, and (C) Taulliraju Sur. (1) Fowler-Watts (1982). Other routes on this face not shown. (2) Voie des Guides (1978), finishing up southeast ridge. (3) ANZAC variation (2016). (4) GMHM Route (1988). (5) Middle Earth (2001). (6) West Ridge (2023). (7) South Ridge (2016). ***Alex Buisse***

TAULLIRAJU SUR, WEST RIDGE, AND LA TRAVESÍA DE LOS BURROS

From July 10 to 12, 2023, Tucker Merrill (USA) and I climbed a new line on Taulliraju Sur (ca 5,400m), the highest summit on the lower southeast ridge of the Taulliraju massif. We then traversed to the southeast ridge of Taulliraju itself and climbed to its 5,830m summit.

On July 10, we woke at our high camp and started up Taulliraju Sur in a shallow right-facing corner (M5) on the west face. Once past this, we transitioned to simul-climbing on névé. After reaching a false summit we traversed the west ridge, ascending and descending past loose granite blocks, cornices, and crumbling "kitty litter." A series of mixed pitches got us to better névé and finally the summit of Taulliraju Sur. [*Taulliraju Sur may first have been climbed in 2001 via an ice/mixed route on its northwest flank called Middle Earth (Donahue-Gribble); the report covering their climb mistakenly called the peak Tuctubamba. The south ridge of Taulliraju Sur was climbed in 2016 by a trio from New Zealand (Fortune-Pearson-McDowell).*]

We descended the ridge to the north toward Taulliraju. As the sun intensified, progress required inching across precarious snow. Beyond the low point in the ridge lay a sheltered depression in the snow, perfect for pitching our single-wall tent.

The following night, we left by midnight with light packs on easy glaciated terrain, only to be slowed by knee- to waist-deep snow. We methodically trenched a path, marking crevasses for the return. We bypassed the top of the GMHM Buttress, then started up moderate snow and ice on the lower southeast ridge of Taulliraju proper.

Tucker tackled the first pitch, a mixed gully (M4) leading to a ramp littered with granite blocks. The final 40m of his pitch involved swimming up a halfpipe of unconsolidated snow. On the next pitch, my tools were racked as I plunged my hands deep into the snow, using them like paddles.

The short but steep section that followed was AI5. After a couple of strenuous body lengths, I reached an overhanging section. I began excavating through the mushroom-like feature, revealing thin veils and threads of ice beneath the snow. It looked like Swiss cheese. Hooking my heels and legs through the holes, I excavated upward.

On the next pitch, we found a weakness in the wall to the right and Tucker shimmied across a thin foot rail of ice and snow with his tools placed in the sn'ice above. He got to a thinner part of the cornice and broke some off before fiddling upward. It was a short but very committing pitch.

We were atop a large flat section, with no anchor in the faceted snow. A stone's throw away was a steep, faceted ramp leading to the summit. The snow was so translucent you could see through it. Spurred on by my feverish four-year dream of climbing Taulliraju, I gingerly led upward. Twenty minutes later, I edged above the crest and onto the summit.

Tucker Merrill near the top of Taulliraju Sur (ca 5,400m). From this summit, the pair traversed toward Taulliraju and bivvied on the snow beyond the saddle visible to the left of Merrill. The next day, they continued up the southeast face and ridge of Taulliraju. *Jonathan Sage*

I downclimbed back to Tucker, who remained at the belay below the summit. Near the end of the ramp, where it met the flat section, the snow collapsed and I took a small fall—a sobering reminder of the mountain's fragility.

We painstakingly downclimbed the upper ridge until we reached some ice and from there made V-threads to abseil back to our trench and the easier ground leading back to our bivy. Early the next morning, we decided to try our luck rappelling the steep face to the west instead of traversing over Taulliraju Sur. Using double ropes, pitons, nuts, and threads, we abseiled to the glacier and soon reached our high camp.

As thanks to the burros that brought our gear to base camp, we named our route La Travesía de Los Burros (ED1 AI5 M5 100°).

—Jonathan Sage, *Canada*

NEVADO COPA, SOUTH FACE, A LA SOMBRA DE LA DUDA

In May, I was part of a team of young climbers of the French National Alpinism Excellence Group (GEAN) that climbed in Peru. Following an ascent of the south face of Ocshapalca (5,888m), we were acclimatized and had time for another objective. After hours

Nevado Copa (6,188m) from the south, showing (1) Puro Floro (2024, continuing to the summit), (2) Mostro Africano to the southwest ridge (2007), and (3) A la Sombra de la Duda (2024). ***Martin Germann***

of examining the guidebooks and photos at the Casa de Guías in Huaraz and on the internet, a possibility resurfaced in my memory—the unclimbed direct south face of Nevado Copa (6,188m). In a photo at the Casa de Guías, the south face looked steep, rocky, and glaciated. It seemed hard and technical—maybe too much so. Doubt set in, but the face inspired us.

We headed toward Laguna Paccharuri (a.k.a. Laguna Rocutuyoc) in Quebrada Honda to try to see the route, which is visible from the last bend before the lake. Clouds hung over the peak, but as we arrived, the mountain revealed its southern slopes to us. The face was completely white compared with the photo at the Casa de Guías.

But what was this snow like? Hard or powdery? Would it be an asset or a hindrance? Would we be able to find protection? Could we retreat? We had many questions, but the face had ignited something in us and we had a good feeling.

There would be four of us on the attempt: Stéphane Benoist (our GEAN coach), Manuel Bréchignac, Victor Garcin, and myself (Martin de Truchis). We returned to Huaraz after the initial recon, then Stéphane and I headed back up to observe conditions. We set up a camp around 5,100m on a ridge at the top of the valley, and Victor and Manu joined us the next day. We spent two days observing the mountain.

The serac above part of the southeast face, overlooking our objective, was fascinating and terrifying. Farther left, the tops of the chutes caught the sun, and falling stalactites exploded on the rock slabs in the shade below. However, our line appeared calm and peaceful. It did not see the sun, and no blocks of rock or ice seemed to have rolled down the slope. In the middle of the face we saw a dark spot that looked like a cave and might offer a good bivouac site, but how could we be sure?

We left camp on May 22. Three hours of approach separated us from the bergschrund. The glacier wasn't as terrifying as the huge serac looming above. We wound across the cracked glacier with doubts lingering in our heads: Would the snow on the face be firm enough to climb?

At 6 a.m. we crossed the bergschrund. The first blow of the ice axe was solid, and a feeling of euphoria overcame me. We climbed six or seven steep pitches in snow and ice. Overall, the pitches were similar, some a little steeper than others. It was difficult to find good protection, with very little rock. We reached the tantalizing dark spot in the middle of the face, and I let out a cry of joy, because the bivy was better than a cave—it was a palace! There was room for

The French climbers rappelled out of their cave bivy to start day two on the south face of Nevado Copa. Puro Floro, also climbed in 2024, breached the left side of the rock wall in back. ***Martin de Truchis***

two or three tents. Manu and Victor fixed two pitches above the bivouac, one of which was very steep (WI5+).

The next day, we left the cave via a short rappel, then ascended the fixed ropes and continued climbing. The following pitches were less steep, but we felt the altitude. By digging through the snow, we managed to find black ice for protection. After a traverse to the right, we were now beneath a huge serac that sits to the right of the summit cornice. I felt like I was in a great mountaineering film as I climbed very steep ice flutes with a wall of ice above me. The four of us met at the foot of the serac, which was so massive that our carefully chosen climbing line—intended to avoid serac fall—had obviously provided only an illusion of security. All we could do was laugh.

We had to choose between exiting to the ridge on the right and going up and left, more directly toward the summit. Manu took over the lead, and I insisted that he go left. A good fight with a pitch of inconsistent snow (85°) and a final passage of M6 that Manu negotiated wonderfully brought us to the summit ridge.

From the top, we descended via the normal route, down the west face. We crossed a flat crevassed area at 5,200m, and a pass to the south led to the Laguna Lejiacocha base camp and our cached gear.

After the doubts we had to overcome, opening a line on an unclimbed face in a much-explored massif, accompanied by people I appreciate and admire, created a memory that will remain engraved in my mind. We called our route A la Sombra de la Duda (800m, ED WI5+ M6 85° snow). [*Other members of the French expedition—Annabelle Bouchardon, Mathieu Détrie, Amaury Fouillade, and Clovis Paulin—repeated the difficult 1982 Fowler-Watts route on the southwest face of Taulliraju (5,830m).*]

—Martin de Truchis, *France*

NEVADO COPA, SOUTHEAST FACE, PURO FLORO

From July 3 to 6, Basque brothers Iker Pou and Eneko Pou, alongside Micher Quito from Peru, completed a difficult new route up the southeast face of Nevado Copa (6,188m). Named Puro Floro, the 1,000m climb featured mixed climbing difficulties up to M7 95° snow, with some A2.

On July 4, the team approached the wall in darkness from a high camp at 5,000m, then climbed for 12 hours to reach a small, exposed bivy ledge about halfway up the face (5,640m). They reported it was their only option, as "the wall was so vertical that we hadn't seen another spot like it the entire way." They slept tied in and, with light sleeping bags, endured a miserable night, "moving our fingers and toes to avoid freezing."

On the 5th, the climbers woke at 8 a.m. and soon began climbing, hoping to summit and then descend that day. The terrain remained very steep, but near the top of the wall they encountered more ice and began to move quicker. The trio reached the summit ridge at 5 p.m., after climbing 19 pitches over two days, still facing a long slog to the summit. Tired and cold, they decided to stop and bivouac at around 6,030m. Without tents, they dug a shallow cave and huddled for warmth, sharing their last packet of soup. While trying to shelter their stove from the wind, Iker Pou burned part of his sleeping bag.

They began the next day at 5 a.m. and summited at 8:15 a.m., then descended the normal route on the opposite side of the mountain, reaching the base at 5 p.m.

The team wrote, "Each of us had lost four kilograms.... But all the suffering was worth it, because we completed our best route in mountaineering to date.... We've previously climbed significant routes in this range, but the number of difficult pitches, the two bivouacs during the ascent, and the altitude of this mountain made this climb very special."

—Pete Takeda, *AAJ, with info from the Pou brothers and published reports*

TORRE TAUAR, FIRST ASCENT; OCSHAPALCA, NEW ROUTE

Torre Tauar, the slender formation in back, was climbed in nine pitches at 7a+ (5.12a). The summit is at about 4,600 meters. *Marek Radovský*

On May 30, Slovak climbers Marek Radovský and Juraj Švingál climbed a tower they named Tauar (ca 4,600m, approx. 8°55'52.36"S, 77°33'09.56"W), southeast of Taulliraju. The tower sits above the popular Santa Cruz trek, east of Punta Union.

The pair climbed the west face in nine pitches, calling their route Guardian of Tuctubamba Valley (340m climbing distance, 7a+/5.12a). They drilled ten bolts: seven for belays and three as lead protection. Radovský wrote to the *AAJ*, "There is a lot of really nice rock in the area to discover. Much of it will be hard to protect, with a lot of grass and mud, but the climbing will be great." [*In 2023, near here, the Slovak pair made the first ascent of The Line Under the Sky (1,100m climbing distance, 6b M6+) on Tuctubamba West (AAJ 2024).*]

With less than a week left in their trip, they decided to attempt a new line on the south face of Ocshapalca in the Llaca Valley. On June 9, they climbed a difficult mixed route to reach the ridgeline just west of the western summit of Ocshapalca. The route alternated steep ice with several difficult mixed pitches, "one more beautiful than the other," according to Radovský. Roughly the top third of their climb overlapped with Cotations (500m, TD+ 80°–90°, Roux-Sicart-Vigne, 1995), which started up a gully farther left on the face.

Radovský and Švingál reached the ridgeline in darkness and whiteout, at approximately 5,650m, at the same point as Cotations. As with the 1995 team, they did not traverse to the western summit (ca 5,750m, possibly still unclimbed). The main summit (5,888m) is over 500m to the east. The Slovaks rappelled back to the start of the route and returned to their tent 16 hours after leaving. They named their line Orgasmo Multiple (500m, WI5 M7 90°).

—Pete Takeda, *AAJ, with information from Marek Radovský*

CASHAN OESTE, NORTHEAST FACE, LA SUERTE VIENE LA SUERTE SE VA

Our original plan was to attempt the unclimbed southeast face of Huantsán (6,395m). However, Mike Bowyer and I realized that abnormally warm temperatures, combined with a very lean snowpack, made that face quite dangerous, so we decided to look for other objectives.

After some high-altitude sport climbing and acclimatization on Vallunaraju (5,700m), Mike and I decided to check out the northeast face of Hualcán (6,122m). There was a beautiful unclimbed line in the middle of the face, the rock quality was amazing, and the temperature tropical—but frequent rockfall drove us off the face after one bivy.

Back in Huaraz, after a few days of our "cruising-around-town-looking-for-the-best-fried-chicken" recovery routine, we made plans for an appealing unclimbed line in the middle of the northeast face of Cashan Oeste (5,732m). This face had a few lines on the right side, reaching the northern foresummit, and the original line on the left that climbed the glacier to the main top. In the middle was a big gap, and a line of weakness seemed to lead straight to the true summit.

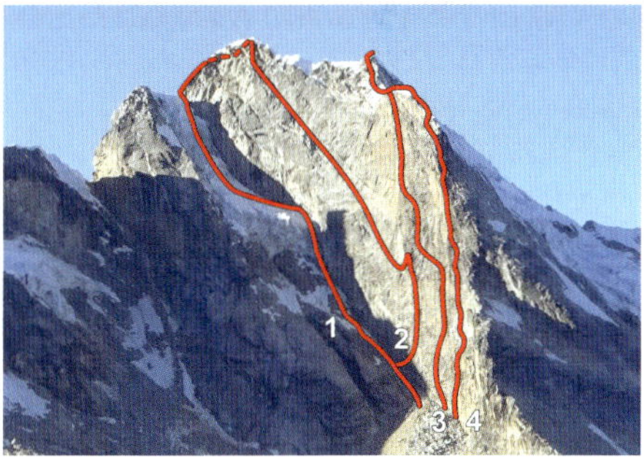

TOP: Tom Schindfessel on the first crux of La Suerte Viene La Suerte Se Va. The new route had long sections of high-quality rock and was the first new line to reach the true summit of Cashan Oeste since 1993. *Mike Bowyer*

BOTTOM: The northeast face of Cashan Oeste and (1) Richey-Rugo (1993), (2) La Suerte Viene La Suerte Se Va (2024), (3) Andean Kingdom (2019), and (4) El Pájaro y el Potrillo (2019). *Sebastian Pelletti*

A couple of days later, Mike and I were standing at the base of the wall. The face was steep, and the rock quality was outstanding. After building a bivy platform in the boulderfield at the base, we stared at the wall, mentally connecting lines. Most of the crack systems seemed to peter out after a rope length. Tired of speculating, we made food while enjoying the beautiful sunset and went to bed.

We woke at 4:30 a.m. on July 12 and started climbing as the sun hit the face. A 60m traversing pitch brought us to the base of a promising corner system. The next five pitches followed thin, vertical corners. The rock was steep, sustained, and technical, with several pitches of 6b. The rock quality seemed amazing on this part of the wall.

As I stemmed in the corner to place a cam, a melon-sized block snapped under my weight and sent me flying for a few meters—not so solid after all! As the rope caught me softly, I heard Mike moaning in pain. The block had hit him in the shoulder. After a few minutes, Mike regained his psych and we kept weaving our way up.

A pendulum connected us with a ramp traversing the middle

of the face, aiming toward the top of the mountain. On this section, the angle eased off, and we alternated between belaying and simul-climbing until we got near the summit. After a last pitch of loose, steep, and icy climbing, we stood on top of the pointy, snowcapped mountain, just in time for sunset. We rappelled through the night with minimal hurdles, grateful to find three bolted rappel stations put in by the Pou brothers a few years earlier. A final 60m free-hanging rappel in complete darkness dropped us 100m away from our tent—what a luxury!

We called our route La Suerte Viene La Suerte Se Va (600m, TD+ 6b C1). Our trip was made possible through a grant from the John Lauchlan Memorial Award.

—Tom Schindfessel, *Canada*

John Ebers following pitch 11 (5.11+), above the crux of Big Fighter. While potential for big new free lines in the area is plentiful, Josh Wharton says, "Just come prepared to place lots of bolts or do lots of gardening." *Josh Wharton*

CHAUPI HUANCA, BIG FIGHTER, FREE ASCENT

On July 8 and 9, John Ebers and I made the first free ascent of Big Fighter (750m, VI 5.13b) on Chaupi Huanca (4,850m) in Quebrada Rurec. Big Fighter was first climbed in 2021 by Spanish climbers Álex González and Jaume Peiró, who spent four days establishing a 19-pitch route at 6c/5.11 A2. [*The route had been attempted twice before; it takes a line to the left of Qui Io Vado Ancora (Palma-Pavan-Pedeferri, 2006). Big Fighter was the first climb to reach Chaupi Huanca's south summit.*]

Our ascent clocked in at 5.13b and is pretty sustained in the 5.11 to 5.12-range. It is relatively high quality through the first 11 pitches, but the quality diminishes and vegetation increases on the final pitches. There is a fantastic forest bivy at the end of pitch eight. [*The Americans climbed Big Fighter in 16 pitches versus the Spaniards' 19.*]

There are only two "hard" pitches: pitch seven (5.12+) nearing the big bivy ledge and pitch ten (the crux) above the ledge. The crux pitch is an exceptional 8a, long and involved, with multiple cruxes. It climbs out a steep roof off the belay and into a pumpy layback section. A bit of easier climbing then leads to technical and powerful face climbing. After that comes a tricky corner with gear-protected stemming.

Generally speaking, the best rock and crack systems in the Blanca seem to be quite vegetated, which isn't conducive to free climbing. The Rurec Valley does seem to have lots of potential, especially for people willing to invest the time and energy necessary to develop face routes away from major crack systems. Given its proximity to Huaraz, I think it's probably the best place to put up a free climbing "king line" in the Blanca (especially if you're hoping it will be repeated). There is obvious potential up the center of Chaupi Huanca and on the impressive headwall on the formation to the east. The Pou brothers' route Zerain (860m, 7a+ A1), just right of Chaupi Huanca, is also in need of a free ascent.

—Josh Wharton, *USA*

Descending from Cerro Amparay (ca 5,427m) after the first known ascent. The climbers ascended the right arm of the forked glacier to reach the summit. ***Lukas Steffen***

CORDILLERA VILCABAMBA: CERRO AMPARAY, NORTH FACE

I have been working as a surgeon at the mission hospital in Curahuasi, Peru, and from the hospital I can see several beautiful peaks of the Vilcabamba Range. In 2021, friends and I climbed Cerro Chaupiloma (*AAJ 2022*). The neighboring peak to the northeast, Cerro Amparay, has been on the to-do list since then. I tried an ascent from the southeast during the rainy season, in January 2024, but had to abort about 50m below the summit because of bad weather and rockfall danger. After that, using satellite images, I planned a new route from the north.

On June 7, Matthias Rehder (Germany) and I left Curahuasi and drove for ten hours to the Chalán Valley, northwest of the mountain. We left our car at 2 p.m. at 3,500m (13°22'09.5"S, 72°40'12.0"W). Thanks to a local horse herder, we found a trail through the thick woods and made it to a campsite at 4,500m before nightfall.

We left camp at 2 a.m. and hiked south toward the glacier, reaching the ice at 5,000m around 4 a.m. The lower part of the glacier was heavily crevassed; some sections were steep and required ice screws. The upper part was easier, with 30°–40° firn. The last 50m to the summit had some loose rock.

We summited (13°24'12"S, 72°40'4.65"W) under blue skies at around 8 a.m. My altimeter showed 5,427m and my cell phone 5,418m. There were no traces of past climbers on the summit. We built a small stone tower on top, where we had beautiful views of the neighboring peaks: Chaupiloma (5,339m), Soray (5,428m), Salcantay (6,279m), and Padreyoc (5,771m).

We descended the glacier more on the eastern side to avoid crevasses and found it much easier than our ascent route. We reached camp around noon and went down to the car the same day.

—Lukas Steffen, *Switzerland*

EASTERN VILCANOTA: RARELY CLIMBED PEAKS

In November, Nathan Heald, an American guide based in Cusco, and some friends climbed several peaks in the 5,000m to 5,550m range in rarely visited areas of the eastern Cordillera Vilcanota, including Yanaruna II and "Humanalipani Grande." Some of these may not have been visited by climbers since the 1970s. Read Heald's full report at the *AAJ* website.

—Info from Nathan Heald, *USA/Peru*

Bolivia

Juan Gabriel Estellano after exiting the roof traverse on Triple 000, along the northeast ridge of Jati Khollu. *Alexander von Ungern*

Cordillera Real

JATI KHOLLU MASSIF, TRIPLE 000

On July 31, Juan Gabriel Estellano (Bolivia) and Alexander von Ungern (Switzerland) climbed a new route near the northeast ridge of Jati Khollu (5,421m). The pair climbed the right-hand of two granite towers on the west side of the ridge; Estellano, von Ungern, and Lilen Sosa had climbed the left tower in 2015. (The report in *AAJ 2016* includes details on the lengthy approach route.) After a bivouac near the base, the two climbed the 2024 route in five pitches (150m, 6b+ A1), naming it Triple 000 for the tiny cams used to aid a thin roof traverse on pitch four. Von Ungern's full report is at the *AAJ* website.

—Julian Dreiman, *AAJ*

Cordillera Occidental

NEVADO SAJAMA, NORTHWEST RIDGE, COMPLETE SKI DESCENT

On April 17, Erik Olerud and I skied virtually the entire northwest ridge of Nevado Sajama (6,542m), Bolivia's tallest peak. We descended approximately 1,000m on skis from the summit to about 5,450m (250m below our high camp). We had to remove skis for a short traverse across a narrow ridge at about 6,000m but managed to ski a steep couloir (at least 50°) in the headwall below this section. Aside from some hard snow and variable conditions just below the summit, we enjoyed soft corn snow for the entire route.

The previous day, we had started from the *queñua* forest at 4,350m and hiked to the high camp (5,700m) with two porters. At 5 a.m., we left camp and climbed the northwest ridge, using crampons and relying on ice axes and a rope to navigate the steep headwall. We put on skis for only the last few hundred feet, after crossing a massive crevasse near the summit. We arrived on top around 12 p.m., allowing the sun to soften the snow on most of the route.

After conferring with Bolivian IFMGA guides, we believe our ski descent of the northwest ridge is the most complete to date. Previous descents have covered the 450m directly off the summit.

—Josh Fischel, *USA*

The northwest ridge of Nevado Sajama is the left skyline; high camp is in the lower of two notches. The headwall couloir is between the last two rocky sections before the snow dome. *Erik Olerud*

Willian Lacerda on the fourth pitch of the new route O Trem da Minha Vida (830m, 7a) on the granite dome of Pedra da Lajinha. *Ed Padilha*

PEDRA DA LAJINHA AND PEDRA DO CABRITO, NEW ROUTES

In September 2023, Willian Lacerda, Valdesir Machado, and I spent five days opening an incredible line on the southwest face of Pedra da Lajinha (20°00'21.7"S, 41°05'53.4"W), north of the city of Afonso Cláudio. Called O Trem da Minha Vida ("The Train of My Life"), our route has 830m of climbing and went completely free, with difficulties up to 7a. We protected around 80 percent of the route with bolts. There were big holes in the middle of the wall that were sheltered from the rain and could be used for bivouacs.

Pedra da Lajinha is a beautiful mountain, with well-preserved natural surroundings and a pristine farm at its base, where we stayed. This region has great potential for new routes: Ours was only the second line on this mountain, after O Tempo e o Vento (1,100m, 6c A1), climbed in June 2015 by Oswaldo Baldin, Fábio Guerra, Zudivan Peterli, Robson Silveira, and Sandro Souza.

In September 2024, Valdesir, Willan, Daniel Amorim, Javier Franco, and I returned to Espírito Santo, 1,500km from our homes in Paraná state, to attempt the first route up the southeast face of Pedra do Cabrito (20°37'08.2"S, 41°19'16.5"W), near the city of Castelo, a couple of hours south of Pedra da Lajinha.

We had already been here on two other occasions, opening incredible routes on the mountain just south of Cabrito, called Pedra do Fio. The first was in 2015, when Valdesir, Elcio Muliki, and I opened No Fio da Navalha (700m, 7a+ A1) on the southeast face in four days. In 2021, Valdesir and I returned with Willan and Tomás Kampf to open Um Brinde à Vida (900m, 7b+ A1), to the right of our previous line. Um Brinde à Vida follows a slab for the first 500m before following a dihedral nearly to the top of the rock. It took us seven days to complete this

Pedra do Fio (left) and Pedra do Cabrito, showing (1) the 1972 route, (2) No Fio da Navalha (2015), (3) Um Brinde à Vida (2021), and (4) Carpinteiro do Universo (2024), the route described in this report. These routes are 700 to 900 meters long. ***Naoki Arima***

line. (Prior to our efforts, Pedra do Fio had only one route, completed in 1972 by a team led by Jean Pierre von der Weid; it angled right up slabs and into a chimney on the left side of the face, at 6c+ A1.)

During our 2024 trip, we stayed in a refuge that welcomes BASE jumpers from all over the world; many believe this is the best place in Brazil to practice the sport. On our first day, we opened a trail to the base of Pedra do Cabrito that took us 20 minutes to walk. That same day, we opened the start of our route, a beautiful slab.

For another three days, we climbed a beautiful, well-marked dihedral that had good cracks, though sections were covered in dirt and weeds. On the third day, we managed to overcome two large roofs with offwidth cracks. Then we went back to the refuge and spent a night there to take a shower and rest. As it was September and we were in the middle of a heat wave, the temperatures exceeded 35°C each day, leaving us very worn out. Beers and pizzas recharged our energy.

We then returned to the wall with portaledges and water for four nights. We set up an advanced camp about 500m up, on a slightly inclined plateau, and continued upward. Very quickly the wall became steeper and very smooth, without the possibility of free climbing. Here we drilled holes to aid for approximately 70m.

Past this, we encountered another good dihedral that took us to a final ramp. After eight total days of climbing, we reached the top of the wall, completing our route Carpinteiro do Universo (910m, 7a+ A2). We protected roughly half of the route using traditional gear and bolted the other half.

This mountain was incredible and demanding, and the surroundings were beautiful, with many birds, including toucans, and flowers in the forest at the top of the mountain. We rappelled the entire route the same day we topped out. That night, we took a well-earned shower in the refuge and had a cold beer to celebrate the achievement.

—Ed Padilha, *Brazil*

Paraná

PICO PARANÁ, SUBMUNDO DAS SOMBRAS

Discussing the possibilities for new adventures close to home, one day the south face of Pico Paraná (1,877m), the

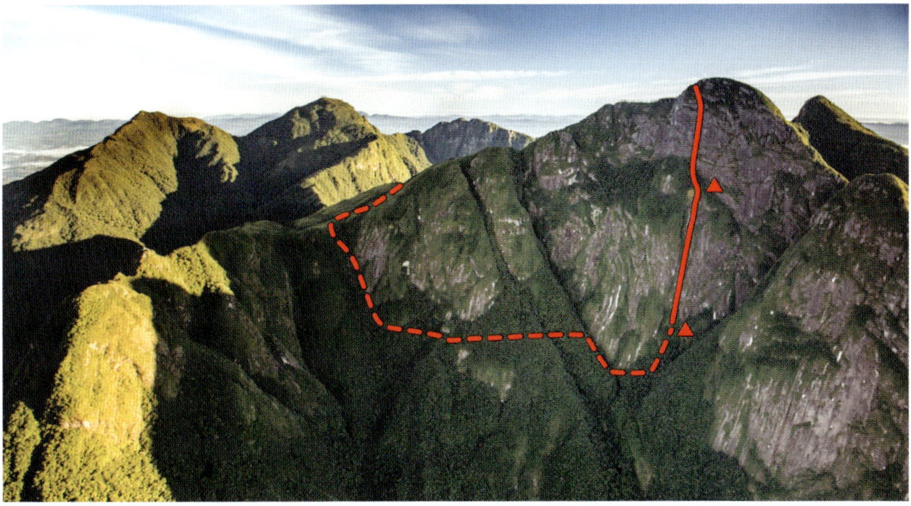

Submundo das Sombras (655m of climbing, 7a A2), the first route up the south face of Pico Paraná (1,877m), climbed in July 2022. The approach over the ridge to the west took eight hours. ***Lucas Pontes***

highest mountain in the state of Paraná, came up in conversation. In southern Brazil, where I live, the mountains are always green and show few bands of rock. Paraná's northeastern subsummit, Ibitirati (1,846m), had established rock routes (*see AAJ 2009*), but not the main peak's big south face. This face would be difficult to access with a load and is always in the shade in the Southern Hemisphere's winter, the climbing season in our region—which probably explains the lack of routes.

On July 23, 2022, Daniel Covatti, Willian Lacerda, Valdesir Machado, and I headed northeast from Curitiba, the state capital, toward Pico Paraná. We spent eight hours trekking to the base of the wall, with 25kg backpacks loaded with enough equipment and supplies for at least four days. Part of the approach went along a well-marked path, but after crossing over Pico Paraná's west ridge, we dropped into a very steep valley with dense vegetation.

We found the base of the face to be seeping water. For a bivouac site, you could choose between sleeping on rocks or in the mud. During the first two days, we fixed ropes up the first half of the wall. It presented significant technical difficulties (up to 7a free climbing) and also contained a lot of dirt and few cracks, which made progress slow.

On the third day, we worked hard to move our camp up to a large, bush-covered plateau in the middle of the wall. The final two pitches (90m) leading to the ledge were climbed entirely through vegetation. Unfortunately, we found the plateau to be very wet, with no places to sleep comfortably. In addition, the water we had collected from a puddle at the base of the wall must have been bad, and our entire party had vomiting and diarrhea. Luckily, it seemed to strike us in waves, so when one was ill, the others continued climbing.

Above the plateau, there were still many wet sections, which was a shame, as there were sections that we could have climbed free, but we had to aid because of the dampness. Not once did the sunlight touch us during the ascent. At the end of the fourth intense day of climbing, we arrived at the top of Pico Paraná, very tired but happy to have the sunlight touching our skin again! Our new route, which is mostly protected by bolts, is called Submundo das Sombras ("Underworld of Shadows," 655m of climbing, 7a A2).

—Ed Padilha, *Brazil*

Argentina & Chile

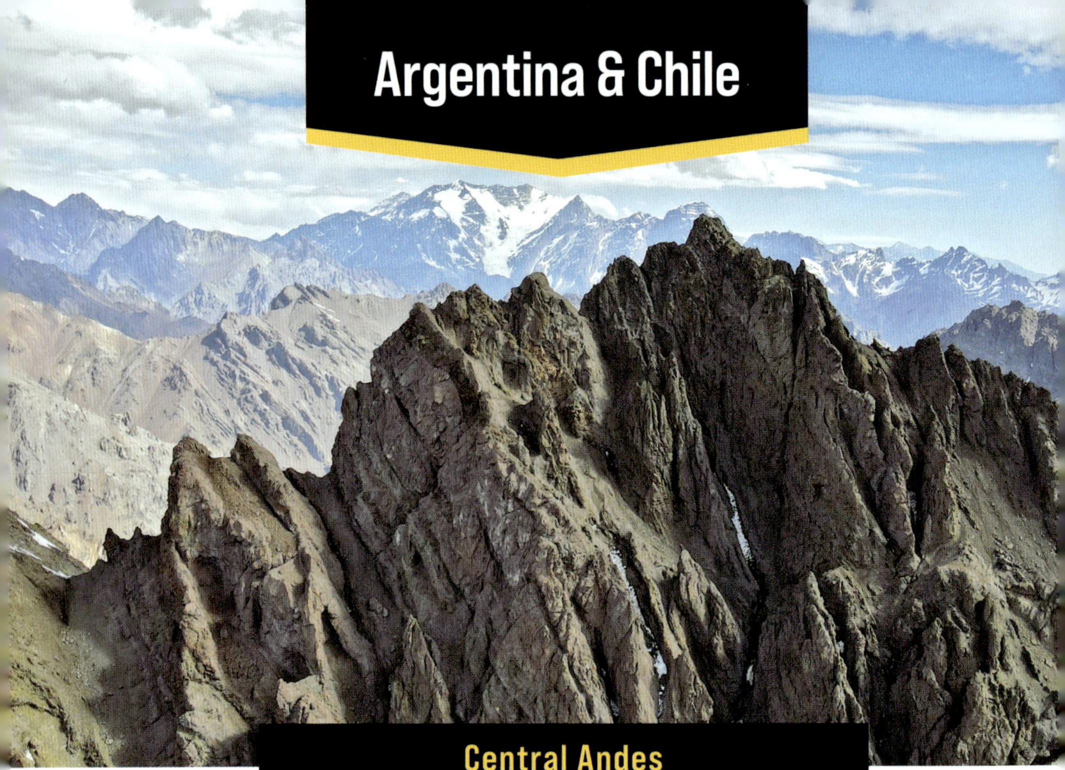

Central Andes

Cerro De la Iglesia from the north. Via Cruxis follows the east ridge on the left. In the background is Nevado Juncal (5,966m). *Álvaro Zerené*

CERRO DE LA IGLESIA, EAST RIDGE

In March 2024, Federico Caballero, representing the Club Andino Universitario, and I (from the Club Andino Leones de Montaña) opened a new route up the east ridge of Cerro De la Iglesia (4,297m, -32.80097, -70.09844), on the border between Chile and Argentina. The peak was first summited in 2015 by Lito Sanchez (Argentina) and Julian Quinteros (Colombia) via the north face.

After two failed attempts, in 2021 and 2022, on March 15 Federico and I followed the Juncalillo River into the southern cirque, past two glaciers and through a chute to a col on the east ridge at 4,159m, where we bivouacked. The next morning, we started up the ridge, and the first three pitches (5.8–5.9) went smoothly. The fourth pitch proved to be the crux, as we had to climb an unprotectable solid-mud wall. The fifth pitch brought us to the summit. To descend, we made five rappels back to the col and followed our approach path down.

As the route was climbed near Easter, we named it Via Cruxis (5.9) in reference to Via Crucis, the Way of the Cross, and to our joy in overcoming the crux pitch, which had shut us down twice before.

—Álvaro Zerené, *Chile*

CERRO MONO NEGRO, SOUTH RIDGE

In March 2020, Nicole Siña, Paolo Alarcón, Sergio Aspe, and I, all with the Club Andino Leones de Montaña, made the first ascent of Cerro Mono Negro (4,826m, -32.96514, -70.04194) in Chile's Parque Andino Juncal, about 35km south of Aconcagua. I had made an unsuccessful attempt in 2018 with Edison Sanhueza and returned two years later, more experienced and motivated.

We approached from the north to the end of the Navarro Valley and bivouacked at 3,700m. The following morning, we gained

Cerro Mono Negro from the north. After climbing to the saddle on the left, the first ascent team followed the south ridge (hidden) to the top. *Álvaro Vivanco*

the saddle east of the peak, then climbed the south ridge to the top. Our route, Glaciar de Roca, involved scrambling plus three pitches of roped climbing. I led all three pitches (5.7, 5.8, 5.6), and my partners followed on a fixed rope. From the summit, we made three rappels and returned to the road by our approach route, reaching the cars in nine hours.

—Álvaro Zerené, *Chile*

CERRO TRONCO, SOUTH FACE

In October, Chileans Cristóbal Cament, Nicolás Gutiérrez, and Alexis Rojas climbed the huge, steep south face of Cerro Tronco (5,567m, -33.1796, -70.0652). The peak was first climbed in 1960 (*see AAJ 1961*) by Wilfred Siegel and Walter Stehr—both of Chile—who followed the long glacial slopes between Cerro Tronco and Cerro Risopatrón to the north. They promptly made the second ascent the following morning to retrieve a forgotten camera.

The 2024 ascensionists had begun eyeing Cerro Tronco's south face a couple of years earlier. When a weather window opened in late October, they arranged a ride in a helicopter to a base camp at 4,000m, high above the Olivares River valley. Using a drone, the team studied the face and laid plans to attempt the main ice line breaching the lower face, which is topped by an imposing serac.

On October 29, Cament, Gutiérrez, and Rojas left their camp at 2 a.m., approached the face, and tackled three pitches of poor rock before reaching the icefall. Three more pitches of very steep and physical ice climbing led the group to their first bivouac, at 4,800m, where they were able to set up their tent in an ice cave.

On the second day, the group zigzagged up four more pitches of vertical and bulging ice. After a total of 500m of steep climbing, they finished the lower wall and started angling to the right on a 55° névé slope, soon reaching the level of the large serac, which days before had released ice over their route. At around 5,100m, they established their second camp.

The tired climbers started late on

The south face of Cerro Tronco (5,567m). The climbers bivouacked twice during the ascent and once on the way down. They descended by the steep gully on the right side. *Gonzalo Robert*

their third day, October 31, and ascended several mixed pitches up to 65° and M4 before following a névé ridge to the summit. Hugs and tears were shared on top before the team began rappelling along the ridgeline bordering the right side of the face. They set up their third camp at 5,200m.

On the fourth day, using rock and ice anchors, they continued rappelling down the prominent gully on the right side of

Nicolás Gutiérrez leads mixed terrain low on the south face of Cerro Tronco. Three pitches of rock were climbed to reach the main ice flow. See a photo of steep ice on the route on page 5. ***Gonzalo Robert***

the main face and finally returned to base camp, where photographer Gonzalo Robert greeted them with Odissea beers, inspiring their route name: Odissea (WI6 M6 A3+). The ascent had gained 1,575m from their base camp and about 1,250m from the foot of the face. The helicopter returned to pick them up on November 2.

—Marcelo Scanu, *Argentina*

CERRO EVELIO, SOUTH FACE AND SOUTHWEST RIDGE

In 2020, while attempting Cerro Aparejo, a friend and I noticed an attractive summit visible from the road through the Aparejo Valley in Chile's Cajón del Maipo, two hours from Santiago. We saw possible routes on the peak's south face but found no information about prior ascents after talking with many people.

In 2023, late rains kept the valley snow-covered until November. It was my opportunity to solve this old project. Our team consisted of Fernando Quilodran, Rafael Reinoso, Emil Stefani, Victor Zavala, and myself. On November 4, we drove to the entrance of the Aparejo Valley (2,600m), where the snow started, and made a short approach on skis and snowshoes to a bivouac at 3,100m, at the base of the south face.

The next morning, we started up the face at roughly 5 a.m. The 800m snowfield (up to 55°) required only ice axes and crampons—we climbed it unroped. We reached the southwest ridge between two cornices, and the last 100m to the summit was easy scrambling on rock and snow. We reached the summit (4,225m, -33°33'14.3", -70°0'24.3") after 11 a.m., and we looked for evidence of previous climbs but found nothing. We retraced our ascent route for the descent.

The peak was unnamed, and we decided to call it Cerro Evelio in memory of Evelio Echevarría, the Chilean-born mountaineer who dedicated much of his

Cerro Evelio, named for Chilean mountaineering historian Evelio Echevarría. The climbers ascended the obvious steep snow up the south face to the southwest ridge, then up the ridge to the summit. ***Rafael Reinoso***

life to writing about Andean climbing history and archaeology and contributed countless reports to the *AAJ*. [*Echevarría immigrated to the United States in 1953 and taught literature at Colorado State University for three decades. He died in 2020; see AAJ 2021.*] Echevarría loved to visit this valley; in fact, the cover of one of his last books, *The Andes*, is a photo of the Yeso River valley's upper basin, less than ten kilometers east of Cerro Evelio. [*Although skiers have been active in this area, this was the first recorded ascent of the peak.*]

—Agustín Ferrer, *Chile*

CHILE | Northern Patagonia – Cochamó Valley

CERRO TRINIDAD CENTRAL, NORTHWEST FACE, NUNCA SAY NUNCA

Angelo Contessi on pitch 13, the "Changing Corners" of Nunca Say Nunca (1,000m of climbing, 5.12+ A1) on the northwest face of Cerro Trinidad Central. This pitch and one other required a bit of aid during the first ascent, but the climbers believe both pitches will go free. *Leo Gheza*

After a reconnaissance in February 2023, Diego Diaz Aguilera (Chile), Angelo Contessi (Italy), and I returned to Cochamó in 2024 to begin a project in the heart of the valley. Our plan was to establish a new route up the northwest face of Cerro Trinidad Central, an 800m monolith.

With about 200kg of food and gear, we loaded horses and set off. By February 7, we were at the wall, but then we encountered a big problem: The line we wanted to open had already been opened! [*It's not clear what climb the author observed; local expert Daniel Seeliger said there had been an attempt in this area in the early 2000s but was not aware of a completed route.*] Fortunately, I had a Plan B: a potential line to the left of El Cóndor Pasa (710m, 5.13d), which I'd spotted during a paraglider flight a few days before. This new line was a little more exposed to rockfall than our original goal, but we decided it was a manageable risk.

We immediately used a good three-day window, from February 12 to 14, to open the first 500m, winding between technical slabs, cracks, and some artificial steps (probably freeable, but very hard). The rock was consistently solid. The lower slabs ranged between 5.11 and 5.12, but after a big roof above pitch five, the difficulty lessened to 5.9 and 5.10. This middle section led into an 80m gully on pitch nine, where Diego took a 20m fall. Fortunately, nothing was broken, but he was too bruised and cut up to continue. We helped him out as some bad weather descended.

Returning on February 24, Angelo and I jugged up our fixed lines and opened the second half of the route, another 450m, following an obvious system of sustained, vertical 5.12 cracks, with a couple of easier slabs near the top. This upper portion was exceptionally beautiful.

We reached the top around 9:30 p.m. on the 24th, with a full moon and clear sky overhead, and bivouacked 100m below the true summit, knowing that Diego was with us in spirit. The following morning, I "raised anchors" with my paraglider under perfect wind, and in 15 minutes I was at the bottom of the valley, landing directly inside our campsite. Angelo, meanwhile, took four hours to descend on foot. Perhaps I owe him a few beers.

We dubbed our 19-pitch line Nunca Say Nunca (1,000m of climbing, 5.12+ A1). The route went free save for aid on the third and 13th pitches. (The latter we dubbed the Changing Corners of Trinidad Central, due to the similarities with the infamous pitch on the Nose of El Capitan.) I believe it's possible to free the whole route.

—Leo Gheza, *Italy*

ARGENTINA | Northern Patagonia

Todo lo que se Comparte (5.11 A0) on Pirita Central. The upper wall is about 500 meters high. Prior routes are not shown. *Flavie Cardinal*

TURBIO IV VALLEY, PIRITA CENTRAL, TODO LO QUE SE COMPARTE

My interest in Argentina's Turbio Valley was piqued in January 2024 when Jasper Pankratz sent me a video of the valley. I half jokingly, half seriously responded, "We're going!" A year later, she and I began hiking into that wild valley with the goal of climbing a new route.

We departed from Bariloche on January 8, 2025, after receiving invaluable help from local climber Sebastian de la Cruz. With the assistance of gauchos, we covered 60km to reach the Don Ropo hut, where Osvaldo, the caretaker, welcomed us with a warm meal—an indication of the kindness we'd find throughout our journey. Another three days took us to the Don Chule refugio in the Mariposa Valley, where we established base camp.

Our goal was a new route on the north side of Pirita Central, part of a tri-spiked massif. The Piritas have quite a few routes but are still rarely visited by climbers—the last recorded ascent was in 2016 by Tess Ferguson and Alan Goldbetter (*see AAJ 2016*). We ended up climbing our new route to the right of their line on Pirita Central.

In mid-January, we launched our first attempt. Approaching the climb was brutal—an eight-hour bushwhack with multiple waist-deep river crossings, dense bamboo, and bags that weighed half our body weight. Three pitches up to 5.11 brought us to the huge slabs leading toward the 500m headwall on Pirita Central. After a bivouac partway up the slabs, we reached the headwall and started up, but poor cracks halted us after about 300m. We retreated all the way back to the hut.

A few days later, another window approached, and on January 24 we started up the slabs again, climbing through light rain that was forecasted to stop in the afternoon. By 2 p.m. we reached the base of the headwall, and as we started up, rain and hail forced us to retreat and bivy again. We got soaked and huddled for warmth, praying for better weather.

Miraculously, by dawn, the sky had cleared and our morale soared. We had opted for a new line to the left of our previous attempt, and the rock quality was better, with a continuous crack system that made for excellent climbing. Over 14 pitches, the only aid was a tension traverse into an adjacent crack. We reached the summit by late afternoon, just as another storm approached. We quickly started down, building anchors with nuts, pitons, and slings (we did not carry a drill or bolts) and soon intersecting the rappel route we had established during our earlier attempt. We reached the base just as the storm hit.

We named our route Todo lo que se Comparte (5.11 A0) as a tribute to the generosity we had encountered throughout our journey. For the last leg, we packrafted down the Río Turbio to Lago Puelo, reflecting on this valley's wild, rugged nature. Far from civilization and surrounded by endless peaks practically begging to be climbed, we felt incredibly lucky to have experienced its raw, untamed beauty. [*This expedition was supported by a Jen Higgins Grant from the Alpine Club of Canada, and both it and the trip reported below were supported by Grit & Rock Awards. Both grants support adventurous women's climbing.*]

—Flavie Cardinal, *Canada*

Apollo 13 on the previously unclimbed El Cohete formation. The climb gained about 600 meters. *Julia Cassou*

TURBIO IV VALLEY, EL COHETE, APOLLO 13

Wanting to go on an expedition with friends and colleagues, I organized a team of five women including Julia Cassou, Fay Manners, Belén Prados, Rocio Rodriguez Guiñazu, and myself to explore the Turbio IV Valley. We are all driven by a deep love for climbing and exploration, and after hearing the stories of first ascensionists like Leo Viamonte, Sebastian de la Cruz, and other locals, we were excited to explore this part of Argentina.

Our expedition began in late January with two days of hiking and horseback riding bringing us to the nexus of the Turbio II, III, and IV valleys, a place called La Horqueta (The Fork). We entered the Turbio IV Valley at the Don Ropo hut, then ferried loads on small trails through dense forest and over two zip lines to the Don Chule hut. After exploring various walls and climbing some pitches to get a feel for the granite, we established a camp near Lago Mariposa and decided to open a route up the southeast face of El Cohete (The Rocket, 42°21'39"S, 72°7'3"W), an unclimbed formation.

On January 29, we started work on the

Fay Manners leads the tight groove of pitch nine (6c+/7a) on Apollo 13, a tricky pitch with everything from crimps to chicken wings. ***Julia Cassou***

climb and fixed a couple of pitches, but days with heavy rain forced us back to the hut. Fortunately, the periods of rain during our visit never lasted more than two days, and we usually had a couple of good days at a time to make progress. In all, we spent 15 days on the wall cleaning, placing protection, climbing, and removing all our gear at the end.

Our objective was to open a route that would be nice for people to repeat. This involved a lot of cleaning, because the cracks were full of plants with deep roots and the slabs were covered by lichen. While two of us pushed the line, the other three cleaned and protected the lower pitches.

Opening the route involved some aid, but the cleaned pitches offered amazing, varied, and sustained free climbing up to 7b+ on solid granite. We only placed bolts when necessary (approximately 40 10mm protection bolts in all); each belay station is equipped to rappel. We climbed 600m over 13 pitches to reach the top of the rock pillar, then continued up to a ridge and eventually the first snow peak above the wall. We called our route Apollo 13 (7b+).

After carrying everything back down to the valley, we concluded our monthlong adventure by packrafting the Río Turbio to Lago Puelo and a boat ride back to civilization.

—Caro North, *Switzerland*

TURBIO IV VALLEY, CERRO TRES NEGROS, SOUTH FACE, AND OTHER ASCENTS: *In January 2023, an international team visited the Turbio IV Valley and made several ascents. John Collis, Mike Coyle, and Gareth Leah climbed most of a south-facing wall beneath Cerro Tres Negros, finding many flared and mostly unprotectable cracks. Out of time, they stopped about 100' below the top, calling their incomplete route Soft Hammer (1,000', 9 pitches, 5.11d A1). Meanwhile, Vianney Lhoumeau and Belén Prados put up a shorter route on the left side of the same formation, Devorame Otra Vez (150m, 7b+), and Jose Luis Hartman and various teammates added two pitches to an area classic, El Palito (580m, 6c+) on the north-facing Pared de La Oreja, which Hartman and friends had put up in 2008.*

—Information from Gareth Leah and PeakPatagonia.com

MONTE SAN LORENZO, NORTHWEST SPUR OF WESTERN SUBPEAK

Over six days from May 13 to 18, 2024, during a cold window of high pressure in Patagonia, Martin Arteaga, Pablo Miranda, and I, all from Chile, climbed a western subsummit (3,134m) of Monte San Lorenzo (3,706m), the second-highest mountain in Patagonia.

We accessed the mountain on skis from the southern edge of Lake Calluqueo, following the glacier of the same name that guards the peak's western flanks. We spent four days crossing this glacier and making our way to the base of the face. This approach, more than the route, was complex and dangerous, as we had to cross a large glacier in autumn, with many open crevasses and very little snow cover.

On May 17, we began the ascent from our high camp. Over 900m of climbing, we first found mixed pitches up to M4 in high-quality fissured granite, then connected to the upper mountain, where we climbed three high-quality pitches in blue ice tubes that took us to the western top (3,134m). [*This is the westernmost of two small subsummits to the northwest of San Lorenzo's south summit.*] These were by far the best pitches of the route, pristine and consistent. After basking in incredible views of all the surrounding Patagonian mountains, we descended from the summit via nine rappels, mostly off pitons but also a few Abalakovs.

—Raimundo De Andraca, *Chile*

TOP: The western subpeak of Monte San Lorenzo, seen from the Calluqueo Glacier to the north. The right skyline is the top of the northwest spur, climbed in May 2024. *Raimundo De Andraca*

BOTTOM: Rime and ice pillars near the top of the route on San Lorenzo. *De Andraca Collection*

CHILE | Southern Patagonian Icefield

Thor Retzlaff launches into a pitch of deep powder between two serac bands on the exposed southeast ramp of Cerro Ambrosio Oeste. The climbers completed the first ascent of the peak, then skied down their ascent route. ***Matthew Tufts***

THREE ICEFIELD PEAKS: FIRST ASCENTS AND FIRST SKI DESCENTS

The Southern Patagonian Icefield—the world's second-largest nonpolar icefield—is frequently visited by climbers on its margins, but the icefield's notoriously volatile weather makes extended expeditions quite rare. Between November 2023 and November 2024, I ventured onto the icefield three times with two different partners for first ski descents.

In November 2023, Thor Retzlaff (USA) and I approached the icefield from the Eléctrico Valley near El Chaltén. In a region known for fast and light alpine style on peaks closer to town, the ice demands a heavy and steady approach—or "back to the future" style, as an elder Chaltén local called it. We carried an abundance of culinary luxuries and a minimal amount of technical gear: one 30m Petzl Rad Line and a pair of ice screws. We're skiers, not climbers, after all.

Pushing through days with up to 120 kph headwinds and zero visibility, we traveled north roughly 80km along the ice to the cirque below the twin Cerro Ambrosio peaks (-48.78791, -73.24561). Cerro Ambrosio Oeste is a brilliant glacier-clad behemoth that was most likely unclimbed, and Cerro Ambrosio Este, which boasts an intimidating alpine rock and ice headwall, was climbed a year later (*see story below*).

We started up Cerro Ambrosio Oeste on the eighth day of our expedition, but deteriorating weather forced us to bail after attempting to climb a 45m glacial ice headwall that guards the southeast ramp.

On day 14, we approached our line in less windy but low-visibility conditions. Thor led a run-out 30m pitch of vertical ice above the bergschrund on our 6mm line with just two ice screws, and another 15m of less vertical ice delivered us to the ramp, where we found incredible stable powder. We simuled through steep snow, ice bulges, and crevasses to reach the summit arête (greater than 50°), which provided incredible climbing on névé coated in chicken-feather sastrugi.

We topped out at just under 2,600m in a complete whiteout, wary of the steep

drop-offs shown on the map in three directions. After transitioning to skis, we descended along our track, which was rapidly being wiped away by wind. We skied the steep, icy arête crux with ice axes in hand, then linked turns in perfect snow on the serac-lined ramp to the top of the ice headwall. We rappelled three times on naked V-threads and descended the glacier to our camp after a 12-hour day. We jokingly called this new descent Mate de los Dioses (600m, 45m rappel, 50°)—an ode to the name Ambrosio.

I returned to the ice cap for a 20-day trip in October 2024, hoping to ski Cordón Ilse Von Rentzell. The precise location of the peak given the name Cerro Ilse Von Rentzell is unclear. The northern summit is the highest point and was first climbed in 2021 by Natalia Martínez and Camilo Rada (*AAJ 2022*), and was first skied by Cedric Babec, Andres Bosch, Bernabe Lopez, and Mike Dahlquist in 2022 (*AAJ 2023*). However, it's fairly likely the Cordón's aesthetic southern summit, with its striking fin-like protrusion, was actually the one with the original Ilse Von Rentzell name, because it would have been more visible to the team that named it in 1959. The southern peak was still unclimbed, and this became the objective for me and Fer Ferrandez (Spain).

Again approaching from the Eléctrico Valley, we eventually established a camp in the glacial cirque below the southern fin, about 25km northwest of Refugio O'Higgins.

From camp we could see that the lower portion of our dream line—descending to the south from a col on a 300m face with a sustained pitch greater than 60°, a line we first glimpsed years ago from a great distance on a peak close to El Chaltén—was full

TOP: Fer Ferrandez traverses the east ridge of Cordón Ilse Von Rentzell's south peak, en route to the first ascent and a ski descent. *Matthew Tufts*

BOTTOM: Thor Retzlaff carves perfect chalk on the immense headwall of Volcán Lautaro's north face, with Cerro Mimosa and Cerro Pangrec below. The relief of the north face above the Southern Patagonian Icefield is more than 2,200 meters. *Matthew Tufts*

Cerro Ambrosio Oeste (left) was climbed and skied via a route that gained the saddle and then continued up the southeast ramp, on or below the right skyline ridge. Cerro Ambrosio Este (right) was climbed by the southeast ridge (near the right skyline), approached by the glacial slopes to the right. ***Matthew Tufts***

of glacial ice and significantly steeper than expected.

Adjusting our plans, we bootpacked an icy but skiable 300m, 45°–50° couloir on the climber's far right of the south face to the east ridge, where we encountered double cornices and unprotected climbing. We descended the north face slightly, wrapping under the ridge to a spot on the north side of our original target col. Fer led a 45m pitch of M4 to the base of the final ridge. We easily booted up to the pyramidal peak in crusty névé snow and topped out at 2,171m.

I descended the arête on skis, then we rappelled the mixed pitch, reversed our tracks back to the ridgetop, and skied the couloir we had ascended, in variable conditions. The ascent of the south couloir and east ridge was roughly 1,000m from base camp, with 600m of technical terrain (VI 50° M4) above the glacier.

Less than a few weeks later, I returned to the icefield with Thor Retzlaff and the goal of the first ski descent of the north face of Volcán Lautaro. At roughly 3,600m, Lautaro is the tallest peak on the ice cap and was first climbed by Peter Skvarca and Luciano Pera in 1964 (*AAJ 1964*). From Ilse Von Rentzell several weeks prior, I had an unobstructed view of Lautaro's unknown north face: a large planar upper pitch and 2,200m of vertical relief to the icefield below.

From a refugio at the edge of the ice cap, we made a 30km crossing to establish a camp below Lautaro's standard route up the southeast ridge. Starting at 11 p.m. on our sixth day out, we climbed this route, ascending roughly 2,000m from the east to the ridge, which connects over multiple subsummits to the top, generally in moderate terrain with a few sections above 50°. We passed massive D3+ avalanche debris and used ski crampons until the rime ice became too firm, necessitating boot crampons. We navigated the southeast ridge's infamous "angel feather" sastrugi, crevasses, and a few steep snow pitches to reach the summit (3,580m) at 8 a.m.

To start the descent, we booted down approximately 30m of rime-encrusted mushrooms and dropped into the north face in top-down onsight style. One hundred meters of chicken-feather sastrugi gave way to perfect chalk conditions on the upper pitch (about 700m). We then passed the crux—a 55° icy slope that ran between large cliffs and crevasses—and continued down. After a total of 2,200m of descent onto the icefield, we circumnavigated the east side of the massif past Cerro Pangrec and Cerro Mimosa to return to camp. We arrived at 4 p.m. to finish a 17-hour, 33km, and 2,400m push.

We capped this 11-day trip by circumnavigating the Chaltén and Torre massifs via the popular Vuelta al Hielo, allowing us to walk straight into town—a complete "Vueltón del Lautaro," so to speak.

—Matthew Tufts, *USA*

CERRO AMBROSIO ESTE, SOUTHEAST RIDGE

On September 3, 2024, Emil Stefani, Martín Hurtado, and I—all members of the Club Andino Universitario (CAU) mountaineering group—crossed Lago O'Higgins to Punta Nahuelcar, adjacent to the Southern Patagonian Icefield. Once on the glacier, we ferried equipment to the DGA hut (managed by Chile's water authority) and waited one week for a good weather window.

We then crossed to the southern base of the Ambrosio group in the O'Higgins massif, navigating around crevasses to the west. (Ambrosio O'Higgins was the father of Bernardo O'Higgins, a leader of the Chilean independence movement in the early 19th century.) On September 18, we skied to the plateau north of Cerro Hipólito (2,364m), again navigating crevasses. We left our skis there and continued with crampons along the southeast ridge (50°–60°) of Cerro Ambrosio Este, protecting crevasse crossings with stakes. To reach the summit (2,640m, 48°47'31.0"S, 73°13'54.0"W), we climbed a snow mushroom a couple of meters high. We were rewarded with views as far as Cerro Chaltén (Fitz Roy) and Cerro Torre.

We descended the same route, skiing down from about 2,100m. Afterward, we waited another week for good weather before crossing back to Villa O'Higgins. In total, we were away 25 days.

Our climb was the first known ascent of this peak, but nearby Cerro Hipólito and Cerro Ambrosio Oeste were climbed in 2022 and 2023, respectively. Hipólito was summited by Pablo Besser, Elvis Acevedo, and Tomás Torres, and Ambrosio Oeste was climbed by Thor Retzlaff and Matthew Tufts (*see report above*).

—Agustín Ferrer, *Chile*

Seán Villanueva O'Driscoll redpointing the crux overhang on The Approach Team Line (450m, 8a). ***Florian Delcoigne***

ARGENTINA | Chaltén Massif

EL MOCHO, THE APPROACH TEAM LINE, FIRST FREE ASCENT

The long, sustained splitters on the north face of El Mocho provide some of the best free climbing in the Chaltén massif. If this were in the Sierra or Chamonix, it would be a major destination, but in the shadow of giants, the face is often an afterthought. Seán Villanueva O'Driscoll has been doing his best to change this perception.

In 2021, Seán put up two stunning free climbs: Chaltén sin Clecas (450m, 7b) and Chaltén sin Chapas (7a+; see *AAJ 2021*), and later he free climbed Grey Yellow Arrow (7a+).

After an early attempt at Sin Clecas with Mecha Rocamora, they rappelled the lower pitches of The Approach Team Line, first climbed in early 2016 by Martin Marovski and Viktor Varoshkin, at 6c A2+. Noting the quality, they could not help but try some of the pitches, giving them an idea of what might be in store.

A year later, Seán was back with Pete

Whittaker and Julia Cassou, but the crux pitch resisted their redpoint efforts. They continued to the top to check out the rest of the climb, and a couple of weeks later, Seán returned with Pol Domenech. They worked the three crux pitches, then a storm plastered everything.

In February 2025, he returned with Florian Delcoigne. On February 15, they started climbing at 6 a.m. Seán sent the crux third pitch (8a/5.13b) on his third go: a physical boulder problem through a roof, protected with previously placed bolts. Flo was unable to send that pitch but managed to flash the following one, at 7c, a long technical dihedral with pods, tricky to protect and with a crimpy, run-out five-meter slab to the anchor. Seán was also able to send that pitch first go.

The second 7c pitch awaited. A tricky short pitch, it has two stacked boulder problems: a mantel onto a slab, followed by a powerful undercling move with feet on smears. It was soaking wet, so they sacrificed their toilet paper and Flo's socks, drying it just enough for Flo to flash it and Seán to redpoint it. They used two Peckers to protect the mantel.

With the hardest sections behind them, their climb turned into pure fun on splitters, including a stunning 60m offwidth to hand crack. At the top of the face, they put on crampons and reached the summit of El Mocho at 1 a.m. They quickly rappelled the route and reached camp at 4:30 a.m., 23 hours after departing.

Seán described the climb as being "really good quality, not too committing, but technically very hard." He pointed out that a number of things had to align for the ascent: "a good window and conditions, being rested, and having good bouldering strength—on a multipitch route like that, you only get so many tries before your power levels go down."

This is the hardest free climb of the massif to date. Patience, persistence, a fresh pair of socks, and spare toilet paper often pay off.

—Rolando Garibotti

Aguja Pollone with (1) La Granja (6c, 1997) and (2) Joviejo (350m, 7a). The former, with its direct start (shown), is said to be one of the great rock climbs of the range. The latter was established in 1998 and was free climbed in early 2025. ***Rolando Garibotti***

CHALTÉN MASSIF SEASON SUMMARY

Similar to the previous season, the weather in the summer of 2024–25 was statistically "average," with mean temperature and levels of precipitation, which meant there were few favorable windows and mostly difficult conditions. After quite a few anomalously dry and warm seasons, some climbers appear to have forgotten that weather in Patagonia is challenging.

There were no fatalities in the mountains this season; however, tragically, there was a fatal accident in the front country, on one of the multipitch rock climbs at the base of Cerro Eléctrico, when a climber rappelled off the end of his ropes. Seven serious rockfall accidents occurred in the mountains. These resulted in broken bones and, in one case, a severe concussion. Three of the accidents required external rescues.

The most dramatic incident occurred when a team that spent three days climbing the Supercanaleta reached the summit of Cerro Chaltén (Fitz Roy) utterly exhausted. Apparently unfamiliar with the area's limitations, they requested a helicopter rescue. As they started down the Franco-Argentine Route, they lost a rope at the first steep rappel and made a critical route-finding error by descending south instead of southeast. It took them three days to descend to La Silla, where rescuers met them and assisted them to the glacier. Their inReach device ran out of battery because it was set to tracking mode to share their live location on social media. One of the climbers suffered severe frostbite.

In addition to the routes described elsewhere in this section, Tasio Martin and Ibon Mendia (Spain) established Dardara (450m, 7a A0) on the east face of Aguja Mermoz, just left of Pilar Rojo. Meanwhile, Alessandro Baù, Matteo Della Bordella, and Mirco Grasso (Italy) opened ¿Quién sigue? (350m, 7a A1) on the east face of Aguja Val Biois, immediately right of La Torcida.

Pedro Navarro and Tomás and Pedro Odell (Argentina) completed Efecto Mariposa, an 11-pitch new route on the lower east pillar of Aguja Standhardt. They encountered difficulties up to 6c and A1. After crossing the snow ramps at mid-height, they continued to the summit via Exocet.

In December, Mati Korten (Argentina) and Ignacio Mulero (Spain) established Eternal Flauta (220m, 7a+) on the east face of El Mochito, and in January, on the second of two visits, Korten free climbed Joviejo (350m, 7a) on Aguja Pollone.

—Rolando Garibotti

CERRO PIER GIORGIO, VIA GRINGOS LOCOS

The northwest face of this peak is a stunning, steep 800m granite wall with few obvious features—what the prolific Swiss first ascensionist Michel Piola described as "the perfect wall."

In 1995, Maurizio Giordani and Gianluca Maspes from Italy attempted the central line on this face. Using fixed ropes, they climbed 21 pitches (600m) to a point 200m below the ridge. The climbing required 60 hook moves to link discontinuous features. Planning to return, they left all their fixed ropes in place. However, when they came back a year later, the ropes were frayed and unusable, forcing them to abandon the attempt. They named their attempted line Gringos Locos, a nickname given to them by the caretaker of the Piedra del Fraile campsite.

Maspes returned in 2006 with Elia Andreola, Kurt Astner, Hervé Barmasse, and Yuri Parimbelli. They re-climbed 11

The northwest face of Cerro Pier Giorgio, with the west face on the right. (1) Via Gringos Locos, completed in 2025. (2) Via del Hermano (2008). Other routes not shown. ***Rolando Garibotti***

pitches before retreating when Maspes was struck by rockfall. There had been no further attempts before 2025.

In February 2025, Matteo Della Bordella, Dario Eynard, and Mirco Grasso (all from Italy) spent three days fixing ropes on the lower 500m. During their final push, they jumared the fixed lines and continued climbing, spending a windy night on a G7 ledge. The next day, they reached the 1995 high point, climbed two new pitches to join the Via del Hermano (Barmasse-Brenna, 2008), then continued for five more pitches on that route to reach a small saddle along the long summit ridge at 3 a.m. Anticipating a storm, they descended immediately, removing their fixed ropes.

Although nearly two-thirds of the pitches required aid, the route offers incredible free climbing, up to 7b (5.12b)—often run-out and interspersed with aid moves, frequently involving hooks. The style of climbing is unique for the area, with much face climbing and only occasional flakes and cracks.

Out of respect for Giordani and Maspes's original approach, the team minimized the use of bolts: In total, there are only five bolts and nine pitons between belays. Della Bordella described their ascent as "a hell of an adventure" and suggested the line might be free climbable. They kept the original name: Via Gringos Locos (7b A3).

The ascent occurred as part of a young alpinists' expedition organized by the Club Alpino Italiano, with Eynard participating as one of the program's members.

—Rolando Garibotti

CHILE | Torres Del Paine

El Escudo from the north with (1) Las Aventuras de Don Quijote (1992) and a 1993 variation immediately right, (2) Millacahuin (2025) to the start of the long summit ridge, and (3) Bukowski (1999). In back left is the chain of Torres; La Fortaleza rises above El Escudo's summit. *Francisco Bedeschi*

TORRES DEL PAINE SEASON SUMMARY

In addition to the climbs described below, there were several notable ascents in Torres del Paine National Park.

In February, Nicolás Gutiérrez and Aron Roca (Chile) completed a route called Espolón Chykillan on the north spur of Paine Chico Oeste. It climbs 24 pitches (650m, 5.12c), which took them 11 days over four outings, during which they fixed 15 pitches. The crux, pitch seven, is fully bolted, as are several other pitches and all the belays—they used a power drill. The name Chykillan pays tribute to the original inhabitants of the region in central Chile where both Nico and Aron are from. In 2003, Tomaž Jakofčič and Grega Lacen (Slovenia) had attempted this line, encountering "less than perfect rock" and retreating after 300m, when they came to a blank section that required bolts.

Elsewhere in Paine, Maximiliano Arias, Ulises González, and Vicente Urzúa (Chile) completed the first recorded ascent of Cuerno Chico, which they did via a nine-pitch line on the east and south faces (5.11-). Earlier in the season, Urzúa and Felipe Marín Moreno climbed a 14-pitch route called Millacahuin on the north face of El Escudo that joined Las Aventuras de Don Quijote (Gore-Perkins,

1992). They retreated upon reaching the start of the long summit ridge.

On the east face of Cuerno Norte, Nicolás Navarrete, Sebastian Pelletti, and Hernán Rodríguez established Kundalini (500m, 5.11+). The route weaves up the face like a snake—hence the name—connecting slabs, a prominent dike, a vertical section of questionable rock, a traverse, and a finish on high-quality golden granite on the upper pitches. For a repeat, they recommend bringing doubles to number 3, a 4 and 5, TCUs, and nuts.

—**Rolando Garibotti**

LA MASCARA, WEST FACE, ALBORADA

Hernán Rodríguez and I dumped our packs and enjoyed the mid-day sun, watching as hundreds of toudrists scurried like ants between the foot of the valley and the famed Británico lookout. Deep in the French Valley, I was happy to finally be off the busy trail and to quietly savor this magnificent cirque of big walls and glaciated behemoths. A dry riverbed led us to the foot of the west face of La Mascara (a.k.a. the Mummer, 50°59'48"S, 73°1'10"W), and a giant detached flake of golden granite created the perfect lean-to for a bivy.

With binoculars, we scanned the face. Light and shadow played tricks as the sun arched over the valley. Still not completely convinced the features on our envisioned line would connect, we agreed to leave the bivy at 4 a.m. and to study it from closer at sunrise.

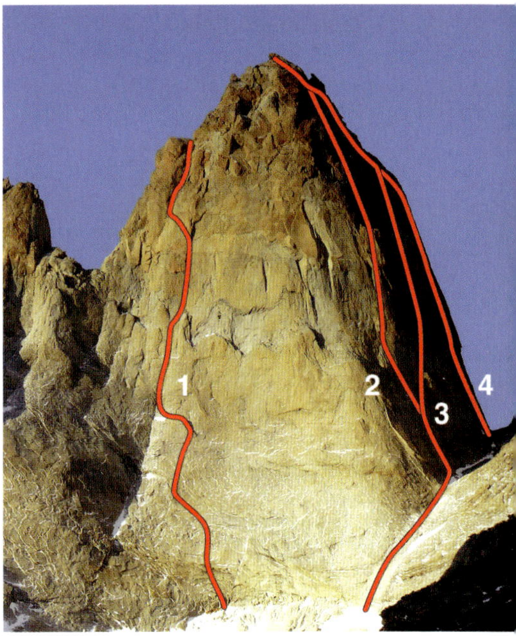

TOP: Sebastian Pelletti leading pitch six of Alborada. *Hernán Rodríguez*

BOTTOM: La Mascara from the southwest. (1) Zanetti attempt. (2) Alborada. (3) South African Route. (4) Duncan's Dihedral. *Galen Herz*

As the early morning coffee finally took effect below La Mascara, a clear blue on the horizon began to dilute the inky night sky. The first light was flat and honest, revealing a system of fissures that breathed possibility into panels of what had seemed like blank stone.

Carrying three liters of water, a few bars, and our belay jackets, we committed to our line and I began a block of run-out but gentle face climbing. Once in the main crack system, the wall steepened, yet mercifully lent itself to amazing free climbing, sculpted with face holds to appease sections where the crack slammed shut. The west faces of the French Valley seem to be so beaten by centuries of gale-force winds that grains of granite have carved incredible texture into the golden giants that encircle the valley.

My second block began at pitch seven. A strenuous hands-to-fists crack led into an overhanging, flaring offwidth, and my helmet stopped upward progress. After placing our widest piece overhead, I committed to laybacking the sharp wave of stone, pasting my feet against a pattering of small dishes on the opposing face.

At 2 p.m., I weaved the rope up and around a series of poised flakes to reach the top. Hernán soon joined me, belayed off a couple of pitons that had been bashed into the summit many moons ago. A carpet of black lichen covered the summit block, inviting us to enjoy a siesta in the sun and rehydrate while taking in the view. Two more of Paine's proudest big walls, La Hoja and La Espada, rose sharp and thin to the north, while the park's tallest mountain, Paine Grande, relinquished tons of ancient glacial ice to gravity's incessant pull, causing the entire valley to tremor in awe.

We rappelled the South African Route (500m, 5.10 A3, Cheesmond-Dawson, 1976), arriving at our bivy in the evening before escaping to the park rangers' hut at Campamento Italiano as dark clouds and rain began to engulf the valley at midnight.

We named our route Alborada ("The Light at Dawn," 600m climbing distance, 5.11+). I highly recommend it to parties looking for a steep single-day objective. We climbed 50m of the Cheesmond-Dawson line before branching left and climbing new terrain all the way to the summit shoulder. We left the route entirely clean. The trip up and down the face took 13 hours.

La Mascara's west face holds potential for more high-quality free routes. The only other route on this aspect is an Italian line (Zanetti-Zanetti, 2020) on the far left side; this did not reach the summit and employed dozens of expansion bolts.

—Sebastian Pelletti, *Chile*

The line of Ultima Ronda (700m, AI3 M4) on the south face of Cerro Trono Blanco, climbed in December 2024. *Sebastian Pelletti*

CERRO TRONO BLANCO, SOUTH FACE, ULTIMA RONDA

Hernán Rodríguez and I awoke above a sea of clouds in Torres del Paine's French Valley. Freezing levels were low, and raging spring winds had buffed most of the snow and ice from our main objective, forcing us to descend. We gazed deep into the French Valley, searching for a consolation prize on the south faces that guard the head of the cirque.

Cerro Trono Blanco's rugged south face was unclimbed and crisscrossed with couloirs and ramps. On December 6, we pulled over the bergschrund at sunrise and began to simul-climb the sn'ice ramps that made up the majority of our route. Short mixed and ice sections separated simul blocks, with a variety of "choose your own adventure" options to keep things technical and engaging when we wanted.

We arrived at the ridge 50m to the east of the summit (2,197m) and continued up

easy ground to the top. Sharp, frigid winds warned that our weather streak had ended, and we were lucky to have had a chance to climb anything at all. We downclimbed the south face, making three rappels, to descend our route before mid-day. We named the route Ultima Ronda ("Last Round," 700m, AI3 M4).

—Sebastian Pelletti, *Chile*

TORRE NORTE DEL PAINE, ERRESISTENTZIARA KONDENATUAK

Opening a new route was not in our plans when Ibon Mendia and I left Puerto Natales in Chilean Patagonia and walked in for a six-day stay beneath the famed Torres del Paine. The first four days brought horrible weather. We barely managed to climb a variant of La Via dell'Agordino on Peineta and to summit Torre Norte del Paine by the Monzino.

On our fifth day, December 27, 2024, the weather began to clear, but it was still cold and windy, and we did not leave the tent until 11 a.m. The window was too small for our initial objective, so we shifted gears and started up unclimbed terrain 50m to the right of Taller del Sol on the west face of Torre Norte del Paine.

Our new route, Erresistentziara Kondenatuak (420m, 10 pitches, 7a), takes a direct line up the face, following obvious crack systems up very good rock. After reaching the ridge, we descended Monzino, forgoing the summit of Torre Norte, which we had reached just a few days prior. We would recommend future parties bring three sets of cams to number 2 and two number 3s.

—Tasio Martin Elorrieta, *Basque Country*

TOP: Tasio Martin following the fourth pitch on the new route up Torre Norte. *Ibon Mendia*

BOTTOM: The line of Erresistentziara Kondenatuak (10 pitches, 7a) on the west face of double-topped Torre Norte del Paine. Earlier routes are not shown. *Ibon Mendia*

Antarctica

The south face of the Bergführerspitz (2,325m) in the midnight sun. The mountain was climbed by two routes, on the west and east sides of the main wall, finishing on the back side. ***Christoph Höbenreich***

GRUBER MOUNTAINS, SEVEN FIRST ASCENTS

In November 2024, I made my eighth expedition to Queen Maud Land, this time with fellow IFMGA guides Robert Miller and Tom Rabl and medic Katrin Oertel. We explored the rarely visited Gruber Mountains of the Eastern Wohlthat Mountains and climbed nine peaks, seven of which were first ascents.

The most prominent peaks of this group are Ritschergipfel, Bastei, Mentzelberg, and Zuckerhut. These and other notable geographical features, such as the frozen Untersee and Obersee lakes and the Schirmacher Oasis, were discovered and named in 1939 by the Deutsche Antarktische Expedition on reconnaissance flights using Dornier Wal flying boats, catapulted from the ship *Schwabenland*. Our expedition climbed and named several previously unnamed peaks and also has proposed a new name for the stunning peak of Mentzelberg.

During a break in a raging katabatic storm on November 4, we ascended the little Däumling (Tom Thumb, 2,193m, 71.403°S, 13.452°E) to get a better overview of the surrounding mountains. On November 6, exactly one year after my second ascent of Ritschergipfel (2,791m, 71.406°S, 13.348°E) with New Zealand mountain guide Mike Roberts (*see AAJ 2024*), we made a new route up the mountain following an ice couloir (max. 55°) on the eastern side to reach the unclimbed east peak (Ritscher-Ostgipfel, ca 2,700m, 71.407°S, 13.358°E). (*See the AAJ website for more history on Ritschergipfel.*)

On November 8, we did the second ascent of the north (snow) peak of Zuckerhut (Sugarhat, 2,468m, 71.422°S, 13.453°E) up its 60° northern ridge, following the Finnish route. The south (rock) peak and main summit of Zuckerhut (2,525m) was first climbed by Patrick Degerman and Pekka Holma from Finland on December 4, 2013. The mountain was named by the 1939 expedition due to its beautiful shape and color, which reminded the discoverers of a white sugar cone; in a descriptive play on words, we called the brown rock peak Kandisturm (Rock Candy Tower); however, we did not climb it.

Two days later, we climbed the highest peak in the massif between Zuckerhut and Bastei over 45° firn, scree, and a rock step of UIAA Grade III, naming it Breitwand (Broad Wall, 2,362m, 71.386°S, 13.466°E).

On November 11, Miller and Rabl climbed a distinctive tower southeast of the Bastei massif via the southwest couloir. Later, on November 17, Rabl and I climbed the east glacier up to the saddle and joined the upper section of the southwest route. Both routes involved 60° ice and an exposed UIAA Grade III climb to the narrow, rocky summit needle. As the peak was climbed by three Austrian IFMGA mountain guides, we called it the Bergführerspitz (Mountain Guide Peak, 2,325m, 71.381°S, 13.548°E), in tribute to the many achievements of all mountain guides in the exploration of Antarctic mountains and their contributions to the research programs.

On November 12, all four of us climbed beautiful Mentzelberg (2,330m, 71.370°S, 13.657°E) via a crevassed icefall and the 50° west face, with Rabl breaking the trail as usual. On the pointy summit, there was neither space to stand nor build a cairn. Instead of commemorating a former Nazi official, a member of the SS who backed the 1939 German expedition, I would propose renaming the peak Friedensgipfel (Peace Peak), recognizing a quality needed today more than ever, even in Antarctica, the continent of peace and international cooperation.

On November 14, all four of us ascended Bastei (2,460m, 71.372°S, 13.542°E) despite stormy weather and bad visibility. We went up the easiest route via the saddle of Windeck (Windy Corner), followed by a 45° firn slope and crevasse-free plateau glacier to the summit, where we built a cairn to mark the highest point. On the evening of November 17, Miller and Rabl climbed Bastei a second time via a 55° diagonal couloir through the southwest side, while Oertel and I repeated the first ascent route, enjoying the low polar sun, marvelous light, and fantastic views down to Untersee 2,000m below.

TOP: Tom Rabl, Katrin Oertel, and Robert Miller below the 800-meter-high east face of Ritscher-Ostgipfel (ca 2,700m), which was climbed by the obvious couloir. ***Christoph Höbenreich***

BOTTOM: Beautiful Zuckerhut (Sugarhat) was first climbed by a Finnish pair in 2013. The 2024 team made the second ascent of the lower north peak. ***Christoph Höbenreich***

Earlier that same day, while Rabl and I climbed the new route from the east on Bergführerspitz, mentioned above, Miller and Oertel walked about seven kilometers from camp and climbed an easy unnamed peak above the Azimut Glacier, which was named Azimutgipfel (Azimuth Peak, ca 2,130m, 71.396°S, 13.727°E).

As Germany and the USA plan to "protect" (practically close) almost the whole mountain range as an Antarctic Specially Protected Area (ASPA), our team might be the first as well as the last private expedition to climb these majestic peaks. I would like to raise awareness about amending the ASPA boundaries to keep these high mountains accessible for private expeditions in the future.

—Christoph Höbenreich, *Austria*

Africa

MAURITANIA | Adrar

The granite dome of Ben Amira has climbing routes up to 500 meters long. ***Les3corbiers | Wikimedia***

BEN AMIRA AND OTHER DOMES, NEW ROUTES

I founded the nonprofit organization Médecine et Montagnes du Monde (MMM) in 1995, with the aim of practicing medicine and developing climbing in regions with limited tourism, in order to provide work opportunities for the local populations. We have worked in many countries in Asia and Africa, focused on opening and equipping routes, training local guides, and donating equipment, all to encourage visiting climbers.

I have known for a long time about the existence of three huge granite domes in northern Mauritania, including Ben Amira (a.k.a. Ben Amera), one of the largest monoliths in the world. Since Mauritania is one of the safest countries in West Africa, I decided in 2020 to explore the possibility of climbing on the three monoliths: Ben Amira (ca 560m), Aïcha (ca 400m), and Haddad (ca 343m).

Our sponsor, the charter company Le Point Afrique, offered us four plane tickets to Atar airport, located four hours by 4WD from Ben Amira, and put us in contact with Kadi, the manager of the local agency Mauritanie Voyages. In February 2020, four of us arrived at the base of Ben Amira (21°13'56.0"N, 13°39'46.2"W). Our group consisted of Jean Kanapa, Maxime Groppo, Anne de Belinay, my wife, and me, all from France. We didn't even know if climbing would be possible.

To our surprise, everything exceeded our expectations. The granite was of excellent quality, and the huge slabs in varied inclinations allowed for the possibility of opening routes at all levels of difficulty. Why had no routes been opened until now? A mystery! In truth this was surely due to the place's isolation.

Ben Amira is located in the middle of the desert, 650km east of the country's capital, Nouakchott, and roughly 10km south of the border with the disputed territory of Western Sahara. The airport of Atar is only served by chartered flights during the coolest season, from December to April. We also assume tourists may have associated Mauritania with the terrorism risks of its neighbors (such as Mali), even though it is actually very safe.

On our first stay in 2020, we opened three routes: Point Afrique Ouvre la Voie (400m, 6a) and Mauritanie Voyages (500m, 5a) on Ben Amira, in tribute to our sponsor and outfitter, and Même les Chameaux Meurent de Soif ("Even Camels Die of Thirst," 350m, 6a) on Aïcha, in memory of a very long day of climbing where we ran out of water!

After ten trips to the region, MMM has opened more than 30 routes on Ben Amira, Aïcha (21°17'39.1"N, 13°41'47.4"W), and Haddad (21°16'03.4"N,

13°36'40.8"W), from quite easy to 7b (5.12b); they are equipped with bolts, though there often are long runouts. We have also trained three local guides and provided climbing and rescue equipment. We created a website (escalademauritanie.com) that provides extensive information on climbing in the region, including descriptions and topos for the established routes; contact MMM via our site for help finding plane tickets, climbing permits, transport, and lodging.

—**Jean Louis Lauféron, *France***

Climbers on a 65-meter tower in the Ennedi Massif. The formation was climbed in two pitches at 5.9 PG. *Cedar Christensen*

CHAD | Ennedi Massif

MANY FIRST ASCENTS OF TOWERS AND ARCHES

Mid-November of 2024 found me and four friends in two Land Cruisers, hurtling at breakneck speed through the Sahara Desert along dirt roads, rutted-out sand tracks, and sometimes no trail at all. Our destination was the Ennedi Massif, an expansive region in northeastern Chad consisting of more than 10,000 square miles of rugged terrain. The swaths we visited were rife with sandstone towers, buttes, and arches, reminiscent of Utah's Arches National Park, but we were only able to access a minuscule portion of the massif and cannot attest to what awaits elsewhere.

After landing in Chad's capital, N'Djamena, and uniting with our outfitter, Adolfo Guasti of Eyte Voyages, we crammed the two vehicles full of gear, food, and a meager ration of 36 bottles of wine, and embarked on the four-day, 600-mile journey toward our destination. Our self-inflated perceptions of grand adventure were tempered by the reminder that, up to this point, we were simply tourists on a safari, but that didn't quell our enthusiasm. It wasn't until the fourth day of driving that we finally laid eyes on rocks of any size, and we watched with anticipation as they grew into a Martian landscape of epic proportions. It truly was a climbers' paradise.

Our team consisted of myself (Cedar Christensen), Natalie Afonina, Sam Stuckey, and Dakota Walz, all from the United States, and Bosco Bonilla from Spain. Adolfo's team was completed by an indispensable Chadian translator, driver, and all-around badass named Andjami Ali, as well as a local chef, Djamila Kodndebe. Together, we spent the next two weeks moving camp almost daily, exploring the territory by Land Cruiser and on foot, and pausing to climb the wild formations that most captured our imagination. [*Visits to the Ennedi by European climbers began in 2000, and an American team climbed in the area in 2010 (see AAJ 2011).*]

The Ennedi Massif, like much of rural Chad, is divided into cantons, each of which is ruled by a tribal chief. Arrival to a canton necessitated a visit with the chief to negotiate the terms of our visit, pay a small fee, and secure permission to climb. Oftentimes, the chief would appoint a "guide" to keep eyes on us as we visited the area, and in one case the chief himself accompanied us for two days. Our exploration took us through four different cantons.

Cedar Christensen spans a chimney on a 45-meter tower, climbed at 5.10. ***Natalie Afonina***

In total, not including free solo scrambles, we climbed 23 unique lines on 20 different unclimbed arches and towers. The difficulties for our routes ranged from fun 5.6 to 5.10 X and splitter 5.11. The tallest formation we climbed was a 140m tower, but the majority of the features were shorter than 80m.

Grading routes presented a challenge, as often we found ourselves avoiding alluring holds in fear of the sandstone exploding in our hands. I regularly expended 5.12 effort to climb routes that may have been graded 5.9 elsewhere, contorting my body to avoid treacherous-looking features, and gripped with fear that a jug might crumble into refined sugar.

Our goal was to leave features as pristine as we found them, preserved for future teams to have their own exploratory climbing adventures. In this spirit, we placed zero protection bolts, and on 18 out of 20 formations we were able to descend by simul-rappelling off either side of the summits, leaving no trace of our ascents. We exclusively climbed ground-up, and only one line required any aid.

All told, the Ennedi ranks as one of the most memorable landscapes I have ever laid eyes upon, and we all left full of gratitude for the opportunity to visit such a magical corner of our planet. [*Following the expedition, Dakota Walz researched and prepared a climbing guide to the Ennedi, replete with historical, cultural, and environmental information on the area, along with logistical info and dozens of photos, maps, and topos. Find a link to Walz's website in the online version of this report to download this remarkable 100-page PDF.*]

—Cedar Christensen, *USA*

ANGOLA | Cuanza Sul

CONDA AREA, NEW ROUTES AND FIRST ASCENTS OF DOMES

During July 2024, our team of five Spaniards—Miguel A. Díaz, Alex Gonzalez, Indi Gutierrez, Jaume Peiró, and I, Manu Ponce—traveled to Angola in search of new big walls in the Conda region of Cuanza Sul province, around eight hours south of Luanda, the capital. Once in Conda, we headed about ten kilometers south to the village of Cumbira Segundo (11°12'29.0"S, 14°20'17.8"E).

We knew from past reports that we would find walls, but the reality far exceeded what we imagined. Amid the lush jungles surrounding the small village of Cumbira Segundo were granite domes between 200m and 400m tall. Some of these had been climbed, but many had not.

In this type of adventure, the easiest aspect is often the climbing itself, and this was true here, as the dense vegetation, full of snakes and arachnids—many of them poisonous—required us to open paths to the walls with extreme care. Taking turns, we chopped through the jungle with machetes meter by meter until we reached our starting points. Once on the wall, we were in our element, though temperatures were scorching: between 20°C and 25°C, with almost 100 percent humidity. We tried to choose walls in the shade, although this wasn't always possible.

We climbed everything ground-up, using bolts as sparingly as possible, though some of the walls had very little opportunity for removable protection. Most of our routes involved technical slab climbing, with few cracks, poor handholds, and friction-dependent footwork. At the end of the day, you would end up mentally fried.

We had several wild moments during the expedition: falls of more than ten meters with a drill included, scorpions as big as your hand defending their nest as you climbed, and running into black mambas on the nightly return to camp. Despite this, if asked if we would return, we would all answer without hesitation: *Sim, claro!*

The impressive Umbi (a.k.a. Hande) formation. Bon Día Boa Noite (10 pitches, 7a) angles left to right across the face in front. ***Manu Ponce***

In total, we opened seven routes on six peaks, two of which had never been summited. This totaled around 2,000m of climbing, all of which made us sweat meter by meter. [*Topos of these routes, coordinates of the formations, and notes on other climbs in the Conda area are at the AAJ website.*]

We received much valuable help from Nathan Cahill of Climb Angola, as well as Lucho Birkner and Javiera Ayala from the nonprofit Climbing for a Reason. The humble local community helped us from the moment we got up each day until we returned in the evening. Due to the incredible climbing and potential for route development, we are sure this place soon will be visited by people from all over the world. Climbing for a Reason is helping teach the inhabitants what can be done in their "garden."

—Manu Ponce, *Spain*

Nordic Countries

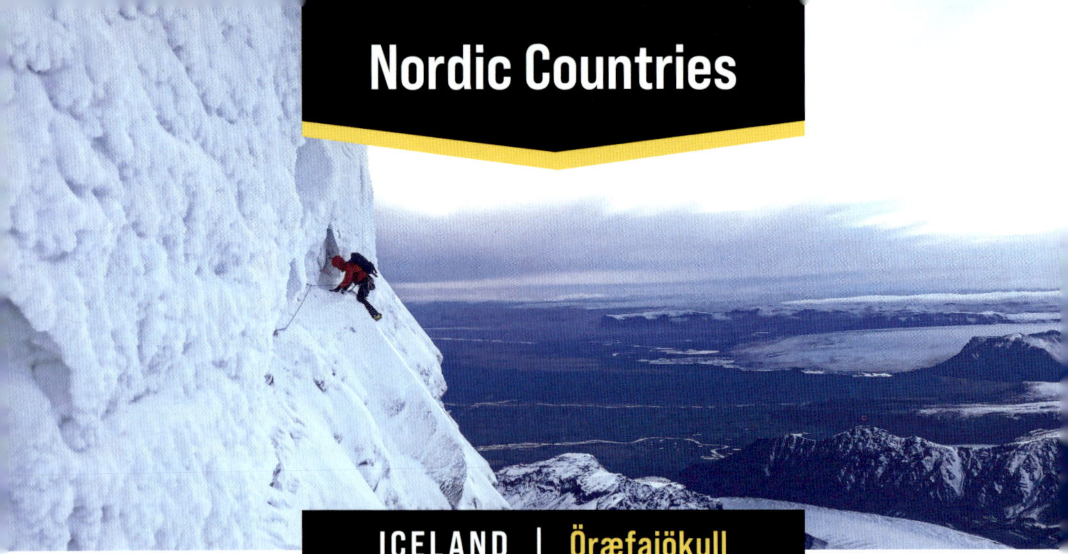

ICELAND | Öræfajökull

Andrea Fiocca traversing toward the exit from under the serac on Hvannadalshnúkur. The approaches to this remote peak in southeast Iceland average about seven hours. ***Matteo Meucci***

HVANNADALSHNÚKUR, PÓKER ÁSANNA

Located along the rim of the Öræfajökull crater, Hvannadalshnúkur (2,110m) is Iceland's highest peak. The northwest face was first climbed in 1986, solo, by Helgi Benediktsson. Various routes have been added over the years, including four lines I've climbed in the past decade, most recently in October 2024.

The approach to the face is very long, limiting its popularity. Over the years, we have tried four different ways, but it always takes about seven hours. The window for ascents is very slim, sometimes opening for only a couple of days in the fall, before winter storms plaster the wall with rime.

I had already bailed on the new line three times, for three different reasons, when Andrea Fiocca and I finally succeeded. On October 22, we made the long approach from the south, which requires crossing the crater and descending the north side to the start of the climbs. Our line is now the leftmost on the wall, climbing to the huge serac atop the face, then escaping to the right. We called it Póker ásanna (480m, WI4), meaning "four aces," referring to the four new routes I've climbed here.

High wind made the return trip challenging, but at 11 p.m. we were back at the car, 19 hours after starting. [*Editor's Note: In late October 2023, Bergur Sigurðarson and Kaspar Sólveigarson completed another new line here: Katabatic (WI3+). See the website for details and more about climbing on Hvannadalshnúkur.*]

—Matteo Meucci, *Iceland*

NORWAY | Lofoten

STJERNTINDEN, NORTHEAST FACE

Despite spending a lot of time winter climbing in Lofoten, Stian Bruvoll and I had never bivouacked on a route there. In March, we decided we should test an ultra-light ice hammock before a planned expedition to the Himalaya. We figured we'd probably learn something from spending a night crammed into a bivy, though neither of us could have said exactly what.

With a thousand objectives on the to-do list, we settled on one that looked better that season than it had in the past: the northeast face of Stjerntinden (938m) on Flakstadøya. It looked reasonable to get up with a heavy pack, and because the face did not normally appear climbable at all, it had not been climbed in any season.

The line up the northeast face of Stjerntinden. The descent was to the south and east. ***Chris Wright***

The third pitch of Magic Hole (330m, WI5+, 2021) at Nieras. A line farther right on the same icefall, called Nattsudd, was done in 2022. ***Rafa Vadillo***

We set off on the morning of March 9, and as usual the day began with a scenic walk that transitioned into absurdly good climbing on the classic Lofoten mix of thinly iced slabs, turf, and frozen corners. In keeping with tradition, the climbing was steeper than it looked and of the highest quality. Eventually we neared one of the horizontal tiers that we thought might offer a suitable bivy, but after a long lead I was bitterly disappointed to find a cave that not only did not require a hammock but also would be nearly impossible to jump out of. When Stian arrived, we agreed it would provide a glorious bivy but did not suit our present need for a bad one.

We continued upward, and as the sky grew dark we accepted our fate: The mountain was offering only comfortable ledges broad enough to pitch a tent. We unroped on one and settled in for a night with a remarkable aurora light show. In the morning, we traversed toward the summit headwall, where we discovered an absolutely brilliant series of perfectly iced corners. These brought us to the summit ridge, where we followed a mixed version of the summer route to the top, concluding the first ascent of the northeast face (650m, AI4+ M5).

We tested the hammock later that season at the base of Stian's new mixed crag behind the petrol station at Osan. I have yet to use it anywhere else.

—Chris Wright, *USA*

STETIND UPDATES: *In September, Dave MacLeod and Calum Muskett (Scotland) opened a probable new route called Line Dancing (E5 6b) on the left side of Stetind's southwest face. The two continued up the classic west ridge to the summit (800m total).*

In AAJ 2024, a report described a new route on Stetind called the Southwest Face (790m, N7 A0, Dolmans-Widlund, 2023). In August 2011, Joakim Olofsson and John Williams climbed a significant part of this line as a direct finish to Guldfisken (1981). Based on photos, Olofsson estimates they climbed the upper two-thirds of the 2023 route.

SWEDEN | Stora Sjöfallet

NIERAS AND KUNGSFALLEN, HISTORICAL ICE CLIMBS

In *AAJ 2022*, a story reported several big ice climbs on the northeast and southeast faces of Nieras, a massif in Stora Sjöfallet National Park in Swedish Lapland. Two of these were quite similar to routes completed earlier by Spanish and Italian climbers, in 2019 and 2021. See the *AAJ* website for details and many photos. These climbers also opened ten routes (averaging 100m) on the remote Kungsfallen cliffs.

A link to download an extensive guide to Swedish ice climbs is included in this report at the *AAJ* website.

—Info from Rafa Vadillo, *Spain*

The Alps

ALPINE HIGHLIGHTS, 2023–2024

This report covers *climbing exploration, innovation, and performance in the Alps during 2023 and 2024, through a small but representative selection of significant ascents.*

The west face of the Aiguille de Blaitière with approximate lines of (1) Brown-Whillans (1954), (2) Northwest Face (Livingstone-Smith, 2023), and (3) Blast (2021). ***Lindsay Griffin***

Exploration

High above Chamonix, France, over three days in January 2021, Thomas Auvaro, Léo Billon, Jordi Noguere, and Sébastien Ratel climbed the hard mixed route Blast (700m, M7+ AI4+) on the northwest face of the Aiguille de Blaitière. The route begins in the prominent deep gully immediately to the right of the West Pillar (Galbraith-McKeith, 1966, VI A2). After four pitches in the couloir, Blast strikes up the flank of the large rock buttress on the right to reach its apex, then weaves through complex terrain above to finish at the north summit, Pointe de Chamonix (3,507m). Later the same year, the first four pitches were equipped with rappel anchors, forming the increasingly popular Mini Blast (AI4+ in a steep, narrow corner on pitch three).

Starting on January 27, 2023, Tom Livingstone and Rob Smith climbed Mini Blast and then continued above in a narrow, icy couloir before eventually exiting onto the Fausses Vires Fontaine, the lowest of the ledge systems that cut across the upper west face of the Blaitière. The next day they continued to the north summit, climbing similar terrain to the upper part of the old Allain-Fix route (1947). Livingstone and Smith called their ca 700m route simply the Northwest Face and rated the technical difficulties M6+ AI4+.

On July 17, 2024, Léo Billon and Enzo Oddo made only the fourth ascent of a route on the north face of the Petit Dru that was put up nearly 40 years ago. In August 1986, Patrick Gabarrou and Alexis Long climbed the steep walls left of the Lesueur Route, eventually cutting through this and the Voie des Guides to finish directly on the summit. The route was largely free and was named Direttissima Jean-Claude Bertrand after Gabarrou's best friend, who was killed by rockfall in 1975. Billon and Oddo climbed the route free in just seven hours, with three pitches of 6c and 7a, the rest easier. The rock was surprisingly good and looked equally so out to the left, where, between the Direttissima and the 1979 Czechoslovak Route, lies the steepest and most compact area of this austere wall.

They returned on July 24. After scoping a possible line with binoculars, they set off at 1 p.m. and quickly dispatched the initial pitches, finding the rock sound and very abrasive. Billon then started up pitch five, and after placing a bolt and leaving the drill, ran it out. The terrain proved much harder than expected, and at one point he was unable to move up or down, but completed the pitch with mandatory 7c climbing. The two bivouacked and the next day quickly arrived at the technical crux (8a). After Oddo had fallen twice, Billon got it second try. After another bivouac, the two reached the top in late morning of the 26th, having created Les Bâtards (800m, around 24 pitches, 8a with obligatory 7c climbing). [*The online report describes the remarkable history of the Lesueur Route, first climbed in 1952.*]

Also on the Petit Dru, Baptiste Obino joined Philippe Bruley and Amaury Fouillade on a seven-day ascent of a new route, Petit Pont (1,000m, 6a A3 M5), on the west face. They reached the summit on New Year's Day of 2025. The new line lies on the left side of the giant rock scar, roughly parallel and a little to the right of the 2021 French route BASE, joining it toward the top. Though often in the firing line from a party repeating the somewhat looser BASE at the same time, the three alpinists found reasonably solid if extremely steep, compact rock and felt it could all go free.

The north face of Les Drus. (D) is the northeast couloir (a.k.a. Dru Couloir). (1) 1979 Czechoslovak Route and (2) Les Bâtards, both to the summit of the Petit Dru. (3) Lesueur Route to the Grand Dru. The Direttissima Jean-Claude Bertrand is between routes 2 and 3, finishing to the right of 2. *Alex Buisse*

Patrick Gabarrou, mentioned above, might be the most prolific exploratory climber in the history of the Western Alps. In August 2024, he returned to the west side of Mont Blanc and over two days climbed a new line, Marie, Porte du Ciel (700m, TD 6a) on the Pointe Louis-Amédée (4,460m), with Clément Dumont and Clément Parisse. This plugged the gap between Gabarrou's own 1989 line, Himalamiage, and the 2018 route Perfect Storm. Gabarrou was 73 at the time and has suggested this will be his last new route on the great mountain.

The most notable new line completed in the Écrins Massif of France during 2023 was arguably that by Julien Cruvellier de Luze, Nicolas Jean, and Benjamin Védrines, who ascended the last major unclimbed couloir on the south face of the Barre des Écrins (4,101m). De l'Or en Barre ascends La Gorge, the stone-swept, 1,000m-high canyon that lies between the classic South Pillar (TD V+, 1944) and Arête Rouge (D+ IV+, 1926, one of the first major new routes climbed guideless by a French party). A direct ascent of La Gorge had never been tried.

Rather than follow the standard summer approach up the Glacier Noir from Pré de Madame Carle, the team elected to skin up to the Col des Avalanches from the southwest, where they left skis and descended the couloir on the far side to the base of the route. That day, January 28, they climbed to a comfortable snow cave bivouac, and the following day finished on the summit at 7 p.m. The three climbed the route in around 24 pitches, some of them wild, with difficulties rated as 6a+ A1 M7 WI5+. For the last

200m, they followed the direct finish to the Arête Rouge, climbed in July 1976 by Jean-Michel Cambon, Bernard Francou, and Catherine Martin-Cambon (TD- V+). It only remained for them to downclimb to the Col des Avalanches, regain their skis, and descend by moonlight to the valley.

One year later, Baptiste Obino made the first ascent of possibly the last logical unclimbed line on the south face of La Meije (3,983m), rope-soloing, with three bivouacs, the couloir dropping from the Brèche Zsigmondy (3,925m). It was too dry in the upper part, which had loose granite

Herbstwanderung on the previously unclimbed 1,050-meter southwest face of the Rottalhorn in the Bernese Oberland. ***Silvan Schüpbach***

and significant rockfall, so he finished up the right-hand face, though in hindsight a direct and more aesthetic finish out left to the summit looked possible. Pantouflage et Sabotage was 750m (11 pitches) with difficulties of 6c A2 WI5+ M7. Obino spent a rough night—February 18—at the top of the couloir, buffeted by high wind that prevented a traverse to the normal route the next day. Instead, he rappelled his ascent route.

A big unclimbed face in the Alps, let alone in Switzerland's Bernese Oberland, is something of a rarity, but the southwest face of the Rottalhorn (3,971m), immediately south of the Jungfrau, had been noted by Matteo Della Bordella and Silvan Schüpbach, who made the first attempt on this untouched 1,050m rock wall during the summer of 2011. The face was not visited again until October 12, 2023, when Schüpbach returned with Peter von Känel and Rolf Zurbrügg.

The three climbed the lower face (III and IV with two pitches of 6a) and at dawn reached a steep barrier where the rock changes from gneiss to limestone. Here they found two demanding pitches of 6b, leading to an upper pillar of gneiss where they opted to climb the better rock rather than the easiest line. Reaching the summit in early afternoon, rather quicker than expected, they traversed the glacier to the tourist-thronged Jungfraujoch station, a complete contrast to the solitude of the morning, and took the train down to the valley. The route was named Herbstwanderung and was climbed on natural gear throughout.

One of the most notable summer ascents in the Eastern Alps during 2023 was the new route Madre Roccia on the south face of the Queen of the Dolomites, the Marmolada.

In 1988, the accomplished Maurizio Giordani and his wife, Rosanna Manfrini (the first woman to summit Cerro Torre), climbed a steep and compact, barrel-like buttress on the lower half of the south face of Marmolada di Ombretta (3,343m), then continued more easily above the halfway ledge to the summit. Their route, Specchio di Sara (800m, 7b+/7a obl.) was a masterpiece of bold slab climbing and featured very spaced, hand-drilled bolts. A little later Stefano Righetti tried a futuristic line on the far right of the buttress but ground to a halt when faced with "blank" rock. Since then, around eight routes have been added to this excellent buttress, including Steps across the Border by Luggi "Darshano" Rieser and Ingo Knapp, who eventually freed their route in 1995—possibly the first big route in the Dolomites of grade 8a to be climbed without bolts.

Madre Roccia completes Righetti's project, and the team that did it—Iris Bielli, Matteo Della Bordella, Massimo Faletti, and Giordani—spanned four "generations" of Italian climbing, from the rising star Bielli to the elder Giordani. Beginning work on the line in 2023, they eventually split into two teams to complete the free ascent. On September 28–29, 2024, Bielli and Della Bordella climbed the ten-pitch lower wall at 8b (7c obl.), while the other two completed the ten-pitch line on the upper wall, left of Specchio di Sara, at 6b maximum. With only 18 bolts placed, there are often long runouts over difficult terrain, and a continuous ascent remains.

Immediately to the right of the Specchio di Sara wall stands the Elephant Pillar, a steep, rounded buttress falling from the midway terrace. Giordani climbed its compact slabs and walls in 1983, creating Ali Baba. In 2024, Faletti and Berni Rivadossi started up Ali Baba and then continued direct to the top in a total of ten pitches, forcing the compact wall between Ali Baba and Enola Gay to give Ego Land. On August 28, Rivadossi and Luca Bana made the first (team) free ascent at a grade of 8c/8c+ (7c+ obl.), making this one of the most difficult multipitch routes in the Dolomites.

Innovation

In January 2023, Marcel Schenk (with Simone Porta) made a rare winter ascent of the Isherwood-Kosterlitz Route (600m, originally VI A1/A2, climbed free at VIII and in winter at M8) on the east-northeast face of the Piz Badile in Switzerland. Realizing that conditions were excellent, with not too much winter snow on the ground, Schenk enticed David Hefti with a proposal to try the first winter ascent of the seldom-climbed Battaglia-Corti Route just to the left. [*See the AAJ website for the history of this 1953 ascent, which ended in tragedy, and of the Isherwood-Kosterlitz Route.*]

Hefti and Schenk left the Sciora Hut on February 14 and made quick progress up the first three pitches, which are shared by the Battaglia-Corti and Isherwood-Kosterlitz routes. However, the leftward traverse onto the 1953 route was difficult, with good axe placements but little for the feet, and, characteristically for

TOP: David Hefti following run-out climbing on the Battaglia-Corti Route during the first winter ascent. ***Marcel Schenk***

BOTTOM: The left side of the northeast face of the Piz Badile in winter with the Battaglia-Corti Route rising out of the northwest couloir of the Colle del Cengalo. ***David Hefti***

The Lavaredo Group from the northwest, with Cima Grande and Cima Ovest in the center. The 2024 traverse crossed all nine summits from west to east (right to left). ***Micha Rinn***

the Badile in winter, run-out climbing. Two pitches higher up on the face were considered among the best the pair had ever climbed.

Thirteen hours after leaving the hut, they exited onto the east ridge about 50 vertical meters below the summit. With only two hours of daylight remaining, they decided to go down from this point, descending the ridge to the Colle del Cengalo, then down the northwest couloir to regain their skis. During their ascent, they found only six pitons, most of these originating from the first ascent. They climbed the entire route in ten pitches, sometimes up to 70m, with difficulties of M7 AI4+ R, all on natural gear.

The north side of the Cime di Lavaredo is perhaps the most recognizable view in the Dolomites. A west-to-east traverse from Cima Ovest to the Cima Piccolissima, crossing the famed Tre Cime, has been completed a number of times in both summer and winter. However, before 2024 no one appears to have traversed the *entire* skyline of the nine Lavaredo summits, adding four summits on the west end. In preparation for their traverse, Germans Christian Bickel and Micha Rinn equipped a rappel descent from the summit of Torre Comici into the gap before Cima Ovest, re-equipped the rappel anchors from Punta Frida toward the Piccolissima, and cached water before the Ovest.

Starting from the Forcella Col di Mezzo (2,315m) in the west at 4 a.m. on July 23, they completed the skyline traverse to the Forcella Lavaredo (2,454m) with one bivouac near the summit of Cima Ovest. The climbers used approach shoes throughout and climbed much of the route unroped, which required intense concentration on exposed, brittle limestone. The total ascent was 2,030m; the most difficult climbing was 6a on the Torre Lavaredo; and the technical highlight was a pendulum across the couloir between Frida and the Piccolissima.

Performance

On February 15, 2023, Léo Billon and Benjamin Védrines left Chamonix at 1:30 a.m., walked up to Montenvers, and continued up the Mer de Glace to the foot of the Grandes Jorasses, which they reached at around 7 a.m. In just 9 hours, 15 minutes, they scorched up the Serge Gousseault Route, named for the climber who died on the first attempt, on the left flank of the Walker Spur (Bertone-Claret-

Desmaison, 1973, 1,200m, 30+ pitches, ED3 and free at around 6b M6). From the summit, they took a further four hours to descend to the Val Ferret, completing a valley-to-valley odyssey in 19 hours.

The two upped the ante almost one year later with a project barely imaginable until relatively recently. Over three days, January 28–30, 2024, they linked the Voie des Guides (850m, M8+) on the north face of the Drus, the 1,000m Šimon-Slavík (M7+, often referred to as the Rhem-Vimal after the winter ascensionists) on the north face of Les Droites, and No Siesta (1,100m, M8 WI6) on the north face of the Grandes Jorasses. Each route—ED3 or above—was completed in 12 hours or less.

A similar achievement, this time in July 2024, was a round-trip ascent from Courmayeur of the historic rock route Divine Providence on the Grand Pilier d'Angle in just 23 hours and 45 minutes. Having trained all spring with this project in mind, François Cazzanelli and Giuseppe Vidoni approached at night via the path toward the Brenva Bivouac, crossed the Brenva Glacier, and then climbed the 18-pitch route in ten hours. They continued for four hours to the summit of Mont Blanc via the Peuterey Ridge, then down the normal Italian Route via the Gonella Hut, for a total of 28km and 3,900m of vertical gain.

Peter von Känel during the tricky cross-country flight from the Valsorey Hut on the Grand Combin, where he and Christian Maurer climbed three summits that same morning, to reach the Torino Hut. A few days later, they traversed the peaks of the Grandes Jorasses group (at right in the photo), took flight from the top of Pointe Walker, and were back at the Torino Hut in 12 minutes. *Christian Maurer*

In June and July 2024, Swiss mountain guide Peter von Känel and professional paraglider Christian "Chrigel" Maurer climbed all 82 of the Alps' 4,000m peaks in just 51 days, linking the summits by non-mechanized means. This took nine days off the record established in 2008 by Franco Nicolini and Diego Giovannini, who used only foot, bike, and skis. The two Swiss used skis as well, but also made extensive use of paragliders to transfer between peaks.

But there was an even more impressive performance to come. In just 19 days, finishing on August 31, Kilian Jornet completed all 82 peaks by foot and bike, including more than 160 different routes (up to 5c) climbed up or down. On many days he pushed his body to the limit, for instance when he left the Monte Rosa hut after three hours' rest and traversed 18 4,000m peaks that same day. He was accompanied to 34 of the summits by friends, and at times by a small film crew, who also helped with the complex logistics. [*See page 76 for more on Jornet's feat.*] As a purely sporting achievement, combining endurance with speed over medium-grade terrain, there has been nothing quite like this in the Alps.

—Lindsay Griffin, *AAJ, with assistance from Rodolphe Popier and the climbers*

Greece

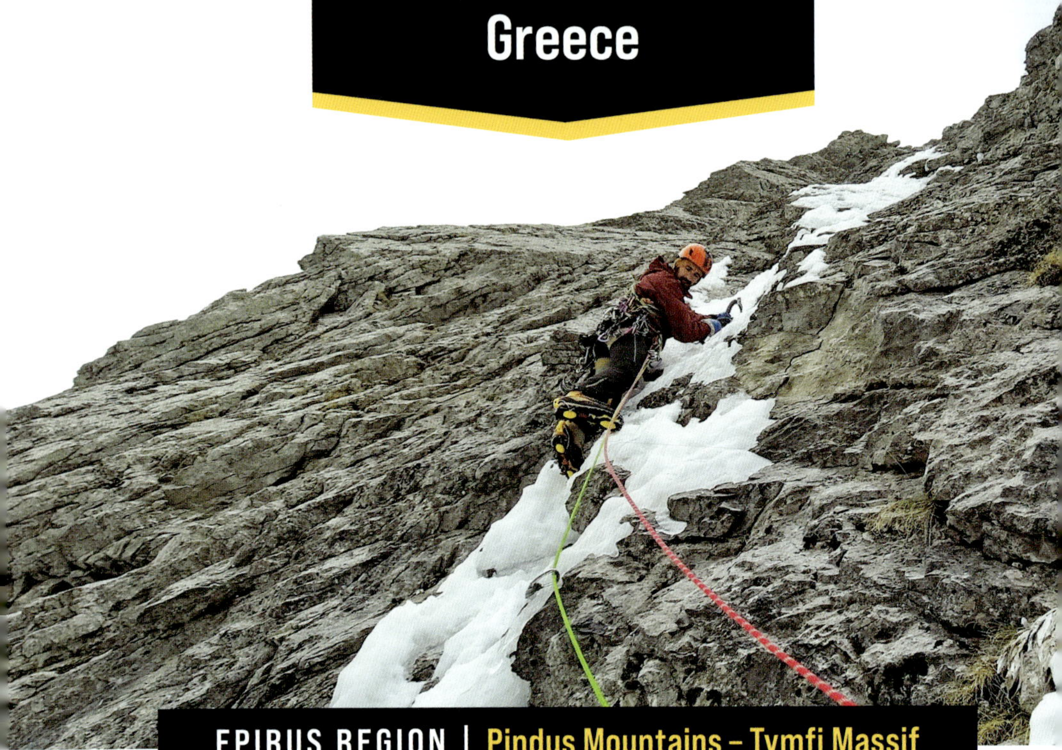

EPIRUS REGION | Pindus Mountains – Tymfi Massif

Christos Tsoutsias leading the fourth pitch of Scream of the Butterfly on Tsouka Rossa, tackling mediocre, poorly protected ice warmed by a south wind. ***Dimitris Daskalakis***

TSOUKA ROSSA, SCREAM OF THE BUTTERFLY, WINTER ASCENT

February 10, 2024, 6 p.m. After 12 hours of demanding climbing, nightfall and a killer wind caught us on the northeast spur of Tsouka Rossa (2,377m) in the Pindus Mountains while we searched for the easiest way through a labyrinth of mixed terrain. In the end, Dimitris Daskalakis, Christos Tsoutsias, and I would need six more hours to reach the summit and complete one of the "most wanted" alpine ascents in Greece: the first winter ascent (FWA) of the summer rock route Ourliahto tis petaloudas (Scream of the Butterfly, VII-/5.10, 300m in summer, 500m in winter with the northeast spur, Kallos-Rokas, 1993).

The Pindus are the backbone of Greece, running about 140 miles through the western part of the mainland, stretching from the Korytsa Plateau (southeast Albania) to the north side of the Peloponnesian peninsula. Tsouka Rossa is among the most imposing features in the range. Located in the Tymfi Massif, Tsouka Rossa's limestone north walls stand 500m tall. This impressive formation is isolated, with approaches from three to five hours and tough descents, away from huts or lifts and any possibility of rapid rescue.

Greece is a warm, maritime country, and the typically unfavorable winter conditions have taught us to deal with whatever the season brings for alpine climbing. Yet, the tradition of winter alpinism dates back to the 1960s. According to G. Voutyropoulos, C. Belogiannis, and A. Asimakopoulos's guidebook *Alpine Climbing in Greece* (2022), winter alpine climbing solidified in the '70s, thanks mainly to leading climbers D. Korres and D. Boudolas, who made a push for the FWAs of summer rock routes on the big headwalls of the Greek massifs, following the most obvious lines; their "alpine" style involved using ice tools for snow-covered terrain but boots and bare hands for dry rock. Starting in the late 1990s, Greek alpinists began exploring thin ice runnels and modern mixed faces on many of the Pindus massifs. [*See the online version of this report for extensive notes on the history of winter ascents in northern Greece.*]

The Tymfi Massif remained less explored in winter, with its isolation, stout routes, mediocre rock, and sparse protection, especially in winter. In 2003, P. Athanasiadis and G. Voutyropoulos established the first true winter climb in the massif, on the north face (500m, TD) of Goura. Every few years, another coveted FWA would be completed, including in 2013, when A. Karapetakos, G. Karnakis, and K. Karnakis climbed the summer route Tsekouri (400m, III AI4 M4) on the north face of Gamila. In 2018, T. Moutafis, Y. Torelli, and G. Voutyropoulos carried out another cutting-edge winter ascent: North Tsouka Rossa, on the eponymous formation's north face (400m, AI5 M5).

Meanwhile, almost every winter, dead center on the north wall of Tsouka Rossa, Scream of the Butterfly froze into a thin ice runnel. This route—its poetic name taken from the Doors song "When the Music's Over"—had captivated our alpine climbing community for the last 20 years. It had seen many failed attempts, due to bad luck and poor conditions, leading to near-mythical status as Greece's most demanding alpine climb. Now, standing on our predecessors' shoulders, we began to dream of our own attempt.

In February 2024, a photo of Tsouka Rossa showed it plastered with snow and ice. This was enough to lure me, along with Dimitris and Christos—two of the most talented climbers I know—for an attempt. Two days after seeing the photo, we were in the car to Tymfi. The plan was to make the three-hour approach, bivouac below the route, and, at first light, try our luck.

Dimitris undertook the first three pitches, which ended up being the driest and most difficult, with challenging dry-tooling, mediocre protection, and a wet, slick, narrow chimney on the third pitch

Scream of the Butterfly ascends the runnel on the right. The summit is hidden far above the ice line. ***Spyros Kyriakou***

that surely wasn't meant to be climbed in winter. The terrain was very steep, making for slow going. For the next three pitches, up mediocre alpine ice, Christos took over, leading the heady terrain with true courage. It was now 6 p.m. and night had fallen. Even though we had completed the route's steepest, most difficult section, we still had to climb up through the maze of Tsouka Rossa's northeast spur.

Climbing by headlamp through strong winds, sometimes pitching out the terrain and sometimes simul-climbing, we reached the summit at midnight. After two rappels down the south face, we hugged with emotion, having completed a route that will be etched in our memories forever. Some five hours later—and after 23 hours on the go—we were back at the car, having completed the FWA of Scream of the Butterfly (500m, III AI5 M6+).

Winter climbing in Greece, even though it sounds improbable, really does exist—and right now it is enjoying some of its best days.

—Spyros Kyriakou, *Greece*

Tajikistan

PAMIR ALAI | Fann Mountains

View to the southwest showing (A) Sakharnaya Golova, (B) Moscow Peak, (C) Skal'naya Stena, (D) Energia Peak (5,120m) with the 2024 ski route down the northeast face, and (E) Chimtarga. ***Daniel Birdwell***

ENERGIA PEAK, NORTHEAST FACE, SKI DESCENT

Admittedly, all I knew about Tajikistan was that it's the most mountainous country on Earth, with 90 percent of its landmass over 3,000m in elevation. None of this turned out to be exactly true, but it convinced Robin Hill and me to go. Robin has a kid, my wedding was six months away, and neither of us wanted to be gone for long. Eyeing a 19-day trip, we chose an objective in the eastern Fann Mountains, about 50 miles northwest of Dushanbe, Tajikistan's capital, on the recommendation of Daniel Birdwell at the Archa Foundation, our in-country fixer.

Energia Peak (5,120m) sits in an elevation band where Robin and I have found frequent success on this sort of timeline, and the northeast face, first climbed in 1979, looked like a good target for a ski and snowboard descent. (The mountain's first ascent was from the north in 1936.) The AAC Library helped our research immensely in a range where the peaks have innumerable spellings and some information is found only in the Cyrillic alphabet. Library staff also lent us some of the area's (outdated) Russian maps.

In late April, Robin and I were dropped at the end of a rough 4WD road and we started carrying a load uphill. By the time we returned to gather our remaining gear, a few rural Tajiks had appeared for a mountain barbecue. They were already vodka drunk and invited us to kill their evening's meal: an erratic pigeon trapped in a very small cage. As a lifelong vegetarian who doesn't drink, I suggested to Robin that we quickly gather the rest of our gear and leave before things got any weirder. With 80-liter frontpacks and 120-liter backpacks, we hiked uphill until we could each hide one pack amid sparse trees to await our return.

ABOVE LEFT: Robin Hill making the only rappel during the descent of Energia's northeast face. In back is Chimtarga (5,489m). ABOVE: Climbing Energia Peak. ***Brody Leven (both photos)***

We built an advanced base camp at 3,510m, just above Mutnye Lake (various spellings), below the shoulder of the Fann Mountains' high point, Chimtarga (5,489m), just north of Energia. We then had a week of bad weather and some misfortune, as a poorly mounted binding tore out of my ski during an acclimatization day. Following an emotional breakdown, 1,500 vertical meters of single-leg skiing, defeat, re-emergence, a lot of hiking, and heavy reliance on our local fixer, my binding was remounted, albeit eight centimeters in front of the other.

The apparent line on the northeast face of Energia was a slightly disconnected couloir and face combination featuring a skier's left traverse over a 450m cliff. Acclimatized to nearly 4,500m, we planned to gain the summit of Energia by climbing the northeast face up to the final 350m of the north ridge, then on to the top.

However, having shot most of our time and motivation during the binding debacle, we decided to leave at a casual 8 a.m. on May 1, intending only to retrieve our gear cache from 4,500m, then bail to return home. Then, when we reached our cache under clear skies, we decided to continue. The lower couloir harbored considerable avalanche hazard, the bottom of the northeast face was faceted, the smooth north ridge was windblown, and the final 150m had low-angle, calf-burning ice. Nevertheless, we found ourselves at 3 p.m. standing atop Energia's darkly shaded northeast face, which was quickly forming a crust. The summit was large enough for us to stand shoulder to shoulder, or for one of us on skis, but not both.

The first turns were the steepest and featured exposure of more than 850m to the snowfields below. Only a dozen turns into the couloir, we made our only rappel, over rocks and very shallow snow. At the end of our 40m ropes, I measured the remaining slope at 52°. We descended the lower, slightly left-trending face and fall-line couloir.

At the bottom, we were rewarded with 900 vertical meters of the worst breakable crust imaginable to reach our tent. Robin, a snowboarder, couldn't understand why I was making half-kilometer-wide traverses across the low-angle glacier before almost falling while executing a jump turn on nearly flat ground.

The following day, a disconcertingly drunk Tajik man in an SUV arrived to pick us up in the meadow at the end of the road. Noticing the man's intoxication as he loaded our gear, Robin told me that, no matter what, we were not getting in that car. Completely conflict-averse, I was prepared to ride with that man as he drove the SUV directly into the rapids of the dark gorge's raging river if it meant avoiding any awkwardness. Robin, a real adult—and also taller than my 170cm—handled the situation perfectly, and another man drove us the six bumpy hours back to Dushanbe.

We didn't see that much ski potential in this area, though there certainly are additional descents available on nearby 5,000m peaks for the creative steep skier. Huw Kingston (Australia) and David Cowell (U.K.) were generous with beta following their 2018 ski traverse of this part of the Fann, and Daniel Birdwell at the Archa Foundation was extremely helpful.

—Brody Leven, *USA*

PAMIR ALAI | Gissar Range

APHRODITE AND ZEUS, FIRST ASCENTS

I had Tajikistan on my list for 2024, and I'd started to look into various ranges for possible first ascents when I came across Eric Gilbertson's report about his trip to the Gissar Range (a.k.a. Hissar Range; *see AAJ 2024*). The place looked amazing, and Andreas Parparinos and I, both from Cyprus, started planning a trip.

After six days of travel and a big logistical exercise to find gas for our stove, we arrived at Sarytag village on September 26. It took us two days to carry our food and equipment southwest along the Dikondara River to a base camp at 3,050m.

On the 30th, we got up very early and ran up the northwest ridge (300m, 5.7) of the unnamed peak east of base camp, marked 3,627m on the old Soviet map. We named it Aphrodite (38'58'14"N, 68'14'6"E); our GPS showed 3,630m.

Foreshortened view of the craggy west face of Zeus (4,200m), with the general line of the first ascent, which gave around 600 meters of climbing up to 5.11b. In the foreground is part of the northwest ridge of Aphrodite (3,630m), also climbed in 2024. *Constantinos Andreou*

From the top, we had a good look at the west face of the prominent peak above us, marked 4,207m on the map. The next day, we carried our climbing equipment up the dry glacier at the base of the wall to around 3,600m. Our proposed route would go more or less up the middle of the west face.

After a rest day, we started from our tent at 3 a.m. and arrived at our gear cache just before sunrise. The first two pitches were in a gully with poor rock and difficulties around 5.9. After the second pitch I traversed to the left to very good rock, then went straight up a thin crack system (60m, 5.11b) that ended up being the crux of the route.

We continued up with mostly 60m pitches in the low to mid-5.10 range. (*See the AAJ website for details.*) After 11 pitches in all, we arrived at the summit as the sun was setting. After a quick photo, we downclimbed around 200m on the south ridge, then did five 60m rappels in the dark to reach the bottom of the wall and start walking back to our tent, which we reached by 1 a.m.

In all we climbed around 605m. We called the peak Zeus (4,200m GPS, 38°58'3"N, 68°14'34"E).

—Constantinos Andreou, *Cyprus*

Kyrgyzstan

PAMIR ALAI | Turkestan Range

ASHAT VALLEY, 7 O'CLOCK SHARP

The British quartet of Theo Elmer, Sam Harvie, Oliver Hill, and Patrick Hill trekked to the Ashat Valley from the Ak-su Valley after climbing several routes there, including the famed Perestroika Crack (800m, 5.12-) on Slesova Peak. After a five-day walk to the west, crossing over four passes, they established a base camp in the Ashat Valley on August 16.

Poor weather then covered the high peaks with snow, preventing alpine climbing, so instead the team explored what they described as "incredible" bouldering on granite blocks, and Oliver Hill and Patrick Hill established a traditionally protected route on a limestone wall about two kilometers below base camp, on the east side of the valley: 7 O'Clock Sharp (9 pitches plus scrambling, E3 5c). They reported significant potential for new limestone routes, comparing the walls in quality and size (up to 800m) to the Taghia Gorge in Morocco. Bolts would be required for protection on most routes. A full report is at the *AAJ* website.

—Information from Patrick Hill, *U.K.*

KARA-SU VALLEY, PEAK 4,810, SAMURAI WAY

In July 2024, Anton Kashevnik and Ivan Temerev (both from Russia) completed a new route on the northwest face of Peak 4,810m. Graded Russian 6B (approx. ED+), the climb spans 1,300m of sustained technical difficulty, threading between the Sakharov and Kritsuk routes on one of the Kara-su Valley's most challenging walls.

The expedition began with unusual challenges for the Karavshin in summer: Frequent storms of rain and snow soaked their gear and delayed progress. After establishing an advanced base camp below the face, Temerev and Kashevnik began ferrying loads and examining the line, which presented blank slabs, thin crack systems, and overhanging corners.

Ivan Temerev works up technical terrain on pitch ten of the northwest face of Peak 4,810m. *Anton Kashevnik*

The initial pitches combined free and aid climbing, using skyhooks, cams, and nuts. Bolts were used sparingly, limited to anchors and sections without other viable protection. (The pair placed 30 bolts in 25 pitches.) Sections of thin, poorly bonded ice required careful movement. Higher up, the climbing became more technical, with overhanging cracks giving way to shallow corners, while blank sections of granite necessitated significant aid climbing, including many hook placements, both natural and drilled.

Progress was interrupted many days by bad weather, forcing the climbers to retreat to their portaledge until conditions improved. After 11 days on the wall, Temerev and Kashevnik reached the summit on July 27 at 5:10 p.m. They descended their line in 34 rappels and returned to base camp late on the 28th.

They named the climb Samurai Way (ca 1,300m, Russian 6B VI A3e; the "e" refers to drilled placements). [*See the AAJ website for the route line. The first four pitches followed a line climbed in 2002 by a Czech expedition that completed three new routes on the northwest face of Peak 4,810m. One team from this expedition—Marek Holeček, Pavel Jonak, and Vazek Satava—climbed a line to the right of the Sakharov Route, joining that route after 15 pitches; this is the route the Russians started up in 2024.*]

—Anna Piunova, *AAJ*, with information from Ivan Temerev, Russia

AK-SU VALLEY, PEAK 3,850, MESSY DREAMERS

Camilla Reggio and I met on the Eagle Team of the Italian Alpine Club (CAI) and immediately became friends, connected by our huge passion for the mountains. We decided to plan our first expedition together and ended up in Kyrgyzstan, with the intent of climbing the incredible granite of the Ak-su Valley and hopefully opening a new route.

Walking up and down the valley in search of possible lines, we were impressed by the 500m south face of Peak 3,850m (a.k.a. the south buttress of Slesova Peak). The following morning, August 12, we brought all our gear up to the wall, carrying incredibly heavy haulbags for hours. We found a five-star bivy spot—a small cave for two people lying close together—and got to work.

The line of Messy Dreamers on Peak 3,850m. Two prior routes up the face are not shown. In back is Slesova Peak. *Expedition Photo*

We opened the first pitches, placing cams and pitons and one bolt for each anchor, then returned to base camp, as excited as little kids. We returned the following day with food and sleeping gear. The route that followed was amazing, but harder then expected. We mostly opened it traditionally, bolting only when strictly necessary (ten lead bolts in 15 pitches).

In all, we spent about a week on the route, with four bivvies in the cave, including one night with a terrible storm, trapped in the dripping cave and wondering if we would drown. The very next day, we managed to climb all the wet pitches and open the last ones, reaching the foresummit of Peak 3,850m (about five or six pitches of easy climbing from the true summit) in the dark, screaming with joy after 15 pitches of struggles.

When we finished the rappels, we had a final night in our luxury hotel and went back to base camp the following morning, with backs destroyed by the heavy sacks but hearts full of happiness and satisfaction. We called our route Messy Dreamers (500m, 7b). [*The two women freed all but two pitches of Messy Dreamers during the first ascent; Elias Annila (Finland) and Misha Mishin (Russia) repeated the route soon after and freed the eighth and 12th pitches at 7b and 7a, respectively. The route lies between Una Stella per Ulughbek (1996), to the left, and Un Train pour l'Espace (2019) on the right, briefly intersecting the latter.*]

—Alessandra Prato, *Italy*

AK-SU VALLEY, PAMIR PYRAMID, NEW ROUTE

Alex Manoliu and Ionuț Papa from Romania reached the Ak-su Valley in early July, hoping to repeat the famed Perestroika Crack on Slesova Peak and possibly to establish a new line of their own. When poor weather kept them off Perestroika Crack for more than a week, they decided to attempt a route on the west face of Pamir Pyramid (ca 3,700m), which was closer to base camp.

Using a portaledge, the two pushed the route up about nine pitches amid frequent rain showers. With only two days left in the valley, they saw a one-day weather window opening. After hiking up alongside the cliff, they rappelled and traversed to reach their high point and then added several more pitches, then continued to the top of Pamir Pyramid.

The new route, Pamir Rainy Avenue, diagonals across the left side of the west face, crossing Russendisko (2006) midway. The pair encountered a few old bolts in this area and placed numerous bolts of their own on the line, which involved mainly difficult slab climbing. The route had about 700m of climbing, with 11 new pitches; the Romanians freed most of the route, with some aid on hooks, trad gear, and bolts in a few places. They estimated those pitches could be freed at 7b to 7c+.

—Dougald MacDonald, *AAJ, with information from Ionuț Papa, Romania*

TIEN SHAN | Ala-Archa

AK-SAI HORSESHOE IN WINTER

Seen from Korona Peak, across the Ak-sai Glacier: the north face of Svobodnaya Korea (4,778m), with Ak-too Peak on the right and a shoulder of Simagina on the left. *Archil Badriashvili*

A traverse of the Ak-sai Horseshoe, an arc of 15 peaks encircling the Ak-sai Glacier, has long been considered one of Central Asia's most elusive alpine objectives. With many difficult summits and ridgelines known for their sharp exposure and technical difficulty, the traverse had defied numerous attempts over decades. Though teams had tried in both summer and winter, no one had managed to link all the peaks in a continuous effort.

In February 2023, a three-member Russian team—Egor Matveenko, Roman Abildaev, and I—set out to change that.

Egor Matveenko leads below the main tower of Dvurogaya Peak (4,814m) during the Ak-sai Horseshoe traverse. ***Roman Abildaev***

We planned to attempt the traverse in winter, knowing the cold would stabilize the snowpack but also add extreme temperatures and high wind to the already daunting task.

Starting on February 17, we climbed the Mikhaylov Route (5B) on the north face of Box Peak (4,293m). Carrying loads that exceeded 30kg, we worked through deep snow and overhanging mixed terrain. The technical face took two and a half days to ascend. Reaching the ridgeline was a relief, but it was only the beginning of our effort.

The traverse stretched approximately 27km, with a total elevation gain of nearly 5,000m across peaks such as Teke-Tor (4,441m), Ak-Too (4,612m), Svobodnaya Korea (4,778m), and Korona (4,860m). On the exposed ridge, severe weather was a constant companion, with temperatures routinely dropping to -25°C and wind gusts reaching 100 kph. Storms frequently obscured visibility, forcing careful navigation.

On February 22, we summited Svobodnaya Korea, where the seldom-traveled eastern descent presented a critical technical challenge. The following days brought us to the six towers of Korona Peak, which were particularly grueling, with icy, unstable rock and minimal opportunities for protection. Temperatures hit -39°C on February 25, our coldest night. By this point, more than a week into the expedition, exhaustion was a constant companion.

The final push began with the ascent of Semenova-Tyan-Shanskogo Peak (4,895m), the highest summit in the area, on February 26. The heavily corniced summit ridge required careful climbing. The descent was slow, involving multiple rappels and cautious route-finding down icy slopes. At 11:45 p.m., after ten days on the ridge and 93 hours of climbing, we reached the Ratsek Hut, completing the first winter traverse of the Ak-sai Horseshoe (Russian 6B)—a symbol of all that alpine climbing in Kyrgyzstan represents: beauty, danger, and always the possibility of failure.

—Tikhon von Stackelberg, *Russia*

Western Kokshaal-Too

OBZORNY PEAK, SKI DESCENT; VERNIY PEAK, ATTEMPT

On July 1, Evgenii Murin (Russia), Maxim Popov (Kazakhstan), and I, along with photographer Denis Lukyanchuk, rode from Bishkek in vehicles provided by Kokshaal-Too Adventures to reach a base camp by the outflow from the Kyzyl Asker glaciers. We traveled the last 20km in a tracked all-terrain vehicle. I had been to this area in 2022 as part of an expedition that completed two new routes (*see reports below*).

After some acclimatization, we moved to a camp at the foot of Obzorny Peak (4,857m), approaching it from the West Kyzyl Asker Glacier. Our goal was to get a close view of the 1,500m northwest face of Kyzyl Asker (5,842m), which has had only one prior ascent, in 1985, by a large Kazakh team led by Kazbek Valiev; they climbed the face over eight days and continued to the summit for the first ascent of Kyzyl Asker. Evgenii was unwell, but Maxim made a solo ascent of Obzorny by the right couloir of the west face (AD+) and completed a first descent on skis down the west slope. Meanwhile, I crossed the glacier to study

The six-kilometer-wide northwest wall of Kyzyl Asker North (left) and Kyzyl Asker (summits not visible). The approximate line of the 1985 Kazakh route is shown; the team continued to Kyzyl Asker's summit for the first ascent of the peak. ***Grigoriy Chshukin***

Kyzyl Asker's face through binoculars and identified several potential routes.

Back at base camp, we rested for three days before heading to the East Kyzyl Asker Glacier, aiming for the west face of Verniy Peak (5,250m), where we hoped to climb a new route along an ice runnel on the right side—an 800m route with about 500m of steep water ice. Early on July 9, we started climbing. Initially, conditions were suitable, but soon we encountered heavy snowfall and strong spindrift. After eight 50m pitches, we were forced to turn back. We estimated we were only two rope lengths from reaching an easier couloir that leads to the summit.

Regrettably, the forecast predicted 30cm to 40cm of snowfall in the coming days. We would not have time to wait out the storm and allow the avalanche-prone slopes on the upper northwest face of Kyzyl Asker to stabilize for an attempt, so we left the area on July 12.

—Grigoriy Chshukin, *Kazakhstan*

VERNIY PEAK, NORTHWEST FACE, NEW ROUTE

In July 2022, seven members of a Kazakh expedition—Zakirzhan Abduraimov, Leonid Krupa, Stanislav Lainopulo, Roman Shesternin, Maxim Ten (leader), and national team coaches Artem Skopin and Vyacheslav Titov—climbed a very difficult new route up the northwest face of Verniy Peak (5,250m).

The team reached the area in early July and established advanced base camp (4,200m) on the East Kyzyl Asker Glacier on July 8. Snowshoes were needed on the glacier. Their target was the left wall of the enormous corner that runs up Verniy's northwest face. Two routes had been completed some distance to the left and right of the corner: No Shachlik (700m, 6c A3 M6, Christie-Gal-Gal-Gottofrey, 2010), on the left, and a route on the right climbed in 2009 by Nikolai Bandalet, Dmitry Golovchenko, Alexander Malakhovski, Sergey Mikhailov, and Sergey Nilov (700m, 6B). Several other teams had attempted new routes, but a direct route up the corner walls had never been done.

The ascent began on July 15, with the climbers working in teams, one to push the route and the other to carry and haul loads. After a steep initial snow and ice slope and two pitches on rock, they established their first camp. Above this, they climbed capsule style, with a total of four portaledge camps (six nights in all). The steep wall required extensive aid. On July 21, the climbers finished the last two pitches of the rock wall and continued up a snow and ice ridge to the summit, carrying packs weighing more than 30kg. They

reached the top at 8:20 p.m. and dug in for a final bivouac on the summit.

Early the next morning, they headed down to the col between Verniy and Unknown Soldier Peak, followed by six long rappels to the east toward the glacier below Unknown Soldier, then down the glacier and icefall to base camp. Their route was graded Russian 6B (970m, with 1,670m of climbing distance). All of the climbers lost eight to ten kilograms during the adventure, and Ten, the leader, "even developed six-pack abs that he hadn't had before," according to the team report. [*The full report with many photos is at the AAJ website.*]

—Dougald MacDonald, *AAJ*

The line of the 2022 route up the northwest face of Verniy Peak. The rock wall is about 700 meters high and was climbed capsule style with six nights in four portaledge camps. *Expedition Photo*

GRONKY PEAK, CHSHUKIN ROUTE: *During the same 2022 Kazakh national team expedition, Grigoriy Chshukin (leader), Leonid Krupa, and Roman Shesternin climbed a new route up the rocky west face of Gronky Peak (5,050m), above the East Kyzyl Asker Glacier. The trio made the ascent on July 26, 2022, completing the 18-pitch rock wall in about 12.5 hours, with a mix of free climbing and aid. They continued up a moderate alpine ridge to the summit, then descended to the north to the col with Yurnos Peak, then down to the glacier, returning to their camp by 10:30 p.m. A full report is at the AAJ website.*

TIEN SHAN | Ak-Shyyrak Range

KARA-SAI VALLEY, VARIOUS ASCENTS

In July 2024, Jing-jie Cheng, Martha Gutteridge, Isabel Jones, Charlotte Krishek, Caitlin McHale, and I (all U.K.) traveled to the Kara-sai Valley on the southwest side of the Ak-Shyyrak Range. This range, a part of the larger Terskey Ala-Too, has been visited a number of times over the last two decades, mostly for ski mountaineering.

After acclimatizing at a base camp (3,790m) in the upper Kara-sai Valley and making an unsuccessful attempt on the nearest peak, due to soft snow, Jones, McHale, and I returned much earlier in the day to reach Peak 4,660m (41.710065N, 78.227877E). The route ascended the northeast glacier before climbing a steeper section onto a col east of the summit, then the short and nontechnical south ridge to the top (PD+).

After attempts on other mountains impeded by bad weather and poor rock, Jones, McHale, and I moved east to an advanced base and reached the summit of Peak 4,749m (41.719439N, 78.249644E) on July 21 via its northeastern glacier and a snowy shoulder (F+).

Caitlin McHale and Isabel Jones descending from the top of Peak 4,749m in the Ak-Shyyrak Range, on the south side of the south fork of the Kara-sai Glacier, after the first ascent. The team attempted Peak 4,825m, at far left, reaching a point about 200 meters below the top in very warm snow. *Expedition Photo*

The Ak-Shyyrak continues to offer potential for first ascents, especially on the eastern side of the range, which is still relatively unexplored. However, we recommend traveling earlier in the season to avoid the warm weather and poor snow that thwarted many of our attempts. [*A detailed trip report is available at the AAJ website.*]

—Elizabeth Porter, *U.K.*

TIEN SHAN | Central Kokshaal-Too

DJANGART RANGE, LINE PEAK

In September, Małgorzata Ilkiewicz and I traveled to the Djangart area in the Central Kokshaal-Too. To our surprise, the road over Djangart Pass was in good condition, allowing us to cross into the valley on the far side in a UAZ truck.

We focused our activity on the western of the two long arms of the Djangartynbashi Glacier. We followed the main glacier south and, upon reaching the base of Howard-Bury Peak (4,766m), turned west to take the far right branch of the glacier. We had found no report suggesting this westernmost glacier branch had ever been visited. [*The eastern branch of the western Djangartynbashi has been explored extensively by climbers, starting in 2010.*] Reaching the upper glacier, we found a beautiful cirque. We spotted an appealing ice face, and a few days later, after a storm, returned to climb it.

On September 20, we climbed this steep northwest-facing slope. The new snow had created a pleasant firn layer, while black ice beneath ensured great protection with ice screws. After a few hundred meters of steep snow and ice, we climbed onto a ridge, then reached a top at 41°37'09.3"N, 78°50'59.5"E. Our altimeter showed 4,730m. [*This top is on a ridge that extends south to a higher peak (at least 4,900m) that is likely unclimbed.*]

We called our summit Line Peak, in memory of Dutch alpinist Line van den Berg, and named the route White on Black (D- 70°). We abseiled the line using V-threads.

—Maciej Nieścioruk, *Poland*

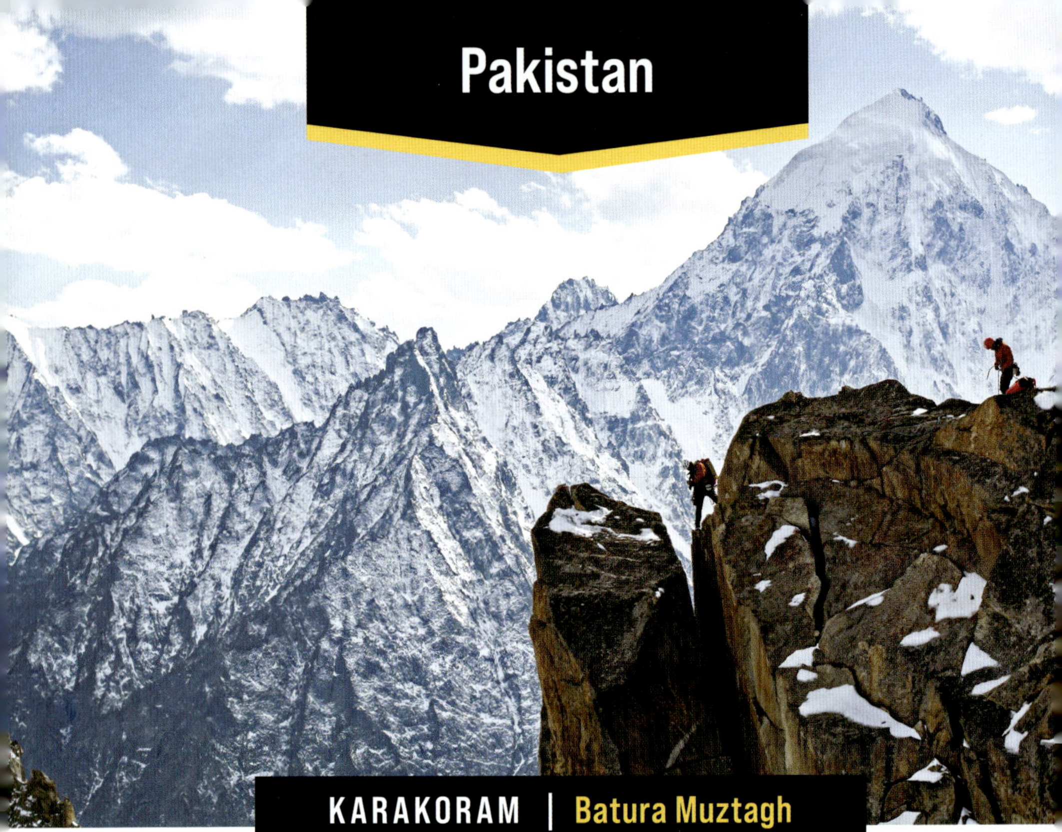

Pakistan

KARAKORAM | Batura Muztagh

Looking for a route on the west ridge of Sachban Sar in the Karambar Valley, with unnamed peaks of the Hindu Raj behind. ***Takemi Suzuki***

KOZ SAR GROUP: SACHBAN SAR, WEST RIDGE, ATTEMPT

At the end of the summer, Ryo Masumoto, Takaaki Nagato, Takemi Suzuki (photographer and filmmaker), Katsutaka "Jumbo" Yokoyama, and I drove via Ishkoman to the Karambar Valley, an area little frequented by mountaineers. We had a permit and met with the authority in charge of the area, who said, "You are the first foreigners here since I have held this position. I hope you guys enjoy the climbing."

One hour's drive farther along, we were turned back by a military check post. We returned to Gilgit and negotiated with the army for three full days until a commanding officer arrived from Skardu and gave us permission to proceed.

Ryo and Takaaki sought a steep big wall they would climb with portaledges but were unable to find a good objective quickly. They did no climbing but eventually discovered a good objective and will return for it in 2025.

Jumbo and I opted for an alpine-style ascent of a rock peak west of Koz Sar and immediately above the Karambar Valley. Locals refer to it as Bokh Parit, while the Jerzy Wala map of the area designates it Sachban Sar (5,398m).

On September 29, Jumbo and I established a 3,500m advanced base at the start of the west ridge. On our first day of climbing, we scrambled and climbed loose rock over an initial top, then continued up solid rock to just below the first tower on the ridge. We struggled to find a bivouac spot but eventually found a passable site at 4,500m and put up the tent at 9 p.m.

On day two, we climbed a steep section on aid—it was too cold to free climb. After four pitches on a sharp arête, we had to make a couple of rappels, losing

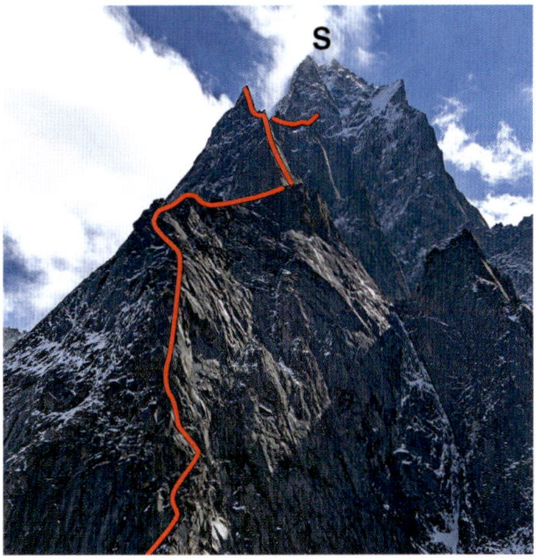

ABOVE LEFT: The 1,900m west face of (S) Sachban Sar (a.k.a. Bokh Parit, 5,398m) and the line of the 2024 attempt, which reached 5,000 meters. ***Takemi Suzuki***

ABOVE: Spanish climbers approaching the Tisar falls near Hushe village. The lower tier was climbed in February 2024. ***Rafa Vadillo Collection***

100m of altitude. This led to a perfect bivouac at 4,800m, just below the second tower. The next morning, it was snowing heavily. The rock above was sound, and the climbing wasn't difficult, but it was wet and icy, and our progress was slow. Eventually, we traversed onto the north flank, where a snow slope allowed us to cut a tent site.

At first, on the following day, the steep ridge above looked unclimbable, but Jumbo found a way through via a tiny crack (number 0.1/0.2–sized cams). We then simul-climbed until we met at a belay and discussed how loose it had all become, with dangerous, unstable, refrigerator-sized blocks that we couldn't avoid.

A little farther on, we hit the final headwall, which towered above with no obvious crack system. My altimeter said 5,000m. We soon decided to retreat. Putting on our hiking boots and thin gloves, we made 20 rappels down the north face, constantly in the path of spindrift avalanches, to reach the glacier below.

—Genki Narumi, *Japan*

WATER ICE CLIMBING IN GILGIT-BALTISTAN

In December 2018, Giovanni Trambaiolo (Italy) teamed up with Pakistani climbers Javed Ali and Naveed Iqbal and completed various ice routes in the Hunza District. The routes were in the Nagar Valley, southwest of Karimabad, and near Attabad Lake. The biggest of these routes, Happy New Year Falls, near Phakker village, was climbed in 12 pitches (up to WI4+) by Ali and Trambaiolo.

In early February 2024, Spanish climbers Jesus Almarza, David Graells, Pere Montasell, Joan Picola, Juampi Sabbione, Javi Sánchez, Rafa Vadillo, and Jordi Vigatà traveled to Pakistan at the invitation of the Discover Karakoram agency. In the valley north of Hushe village, they completed four new climbs from 75m to 420m in length. With support from CAMP in Italy, they also did some training with local guides and donated ice tools and crampons for their use. [*A mini-guide to the 2018 climbs and Vadillo's full report from 2024 are at the AAJ website.*]

—Information provided by Giovanni Trambaiolo and Rafa Vadillo

On the 1.5-kilometer, high-altitude traverse to Muchu Chhish. The top, reached by a 150-meter headwall, is in the center. Behind and right is Passu Sar (7,478m). ***Jaroslav Bánský***

MUCHU CHHISH, FIRST ASCENT

I had planned to visit Afghanistan's Hindu Kush, but when this didn't work out, Radoslav "Radar" Groh suggested we try Muchu Chhish (7,453m, 36°30'10"N, 74°32'49"E). The mountain had been a long-standing goal of our countryman Pavel Kořínek, who first took a team there in 2020, when he reached 6,300m (*AAJ 2021*). Kořínek also was part of two later Czech expeditions to Muchu Chhish: in 2021 when he reached 6,500m, and in 2023, when two of his team, Groh and Tomáš Petreček, reached around 7,200m (*AAJ 2024*). After a phone call to Pavel, the decision was made: Radar, Jaroslav "Banana" Bánský, and I would leave for Pakistan on June 6.

We planned to acclimatize around Bublimotin (a.k.a. Lady's Finger, 6,000m), but I was ill, so we ended up moving to the Muchuhar Glacier, where we established base camp at around 4,000m. We would have to acclimatize there.

The line attempted by previous parties from this glacier followed the 1983 Polish-German route along the south spur of Batura V (7,531m) as far as the Batura main ridge. From there, the plan was to traverse to the east to reach Muchu Chhish. For acclimatization, we decided to climb the first part of this route and sleep at 4,600m, 5,400m, and 6,100m. We left base camp on June 25 and completed our goal, returning to base camp after three nights out. It wasn't ideal acclimatization, but we didn't have more time and the forecast promised that good weather would hold for the coming week.

On July 1, we again hiked up the rocky couloir leading to the glacier at 4,800m and followed it to 5,350m, where we spent the night. We had ascended around 1,400m from base camp, and it was only 10:30 a.m. when we stopped, but already unbearably hot.

The next day, we started climbing. The first pitches were rock and mixed to M4, and above it was ice—endless ice. We slanted up the west flank of the ridge to make Camp 2 at 6,300m, below a prominent serac. On the 3rd, we continued over more snow and ice. It was physically demanding, with a maximum angle of around 70°. In parts the snow was so deep that we used special snowshoes made by Auftriib that fit between the crampon and boot—often called ascent plates in North America and used by ski mountaineers—and without them we wouldn't have been able to move higher.

It was a hard-earned 450m to our Camp 3 at 6,750m, from where a further 500m of elevation would take us to the main Batura ridge. The next day, using the ascent plates again and carefully finding a route around

crevasses, Banana blazed trail throughout the day and brought us to 7,250m, just below the ridge, where we made Camp 4. The summit of Muchu Chhish was more than 1.5km to the east.

The following day, we gained the ridge and followed it over a few bumps to a large rock tower below a headwall and about 150m below the summit. Banana led, and at 10:20 a.m. on July 5 we reached the top, where we left a snow stake inscribed with our signatures.

Our descent was hampered by decreasing visibility and wind-filled tracks. Often we had to climb back uphill with the little strength we had left. Luckily, we located the little rock corner that would lead down to the tent. We continued on autopilot, as we couldn't find our steps. Fortunately, whenever I am climbing through this sort of terrain, I often look back to try and memorize the terrain below, and this helped me navigate through the crevassed area. Below 7,000m, the visibility improved and we continued easily to our 6,750m camp.

Leaving early the next morning, we descended 1,500m to the glacier, rappelling only 100m. It was mid-day and terribly hot. Avalanches were coming off the mountain, and even the glacier didn't look safe. We awoke at base camp to a gloomy morning and began our descent to the Hunza Valley, accompanied by raindrops.

—Zdeněk Hák, *Czech Republic*

TOP: Downclimbing the south spur of Batura V below Camp 3 (6,750m) in the early morning of July 6, following the ascent of Muchu Chhish. *Jaroslav Bánský*

BOTTOM: Radoslav Groh mixed climbing above Camp 1 on the south spur of Batura V. *Jaroslav Bánský*

EDITOR'S NOTE: *There has been debate over the status of Muchu Chhish, which was sometimes quoted as the highest unclimbed mountain in the world for which it was possible to get a permit. Some suggest Muchu Chhish's very low prominence and dominance make it barely a mountain and more a subpeak of the Batura chain. Regardless, until 2024, it was the highest named and unclimbed summit in Pakistan.*

KARAKORAM | Ghujerab Mountains

YAWASH SAR I

FIRST ASCENT VIA THE WEST-NORTHWEST FACE

By Mick Fowler, *U.K.*

In September, Victor Saunders and I made the first ascent of Yawash Sar I (6,258m), a shapely peak at the head of the Koksil (a.k.a. Shop Dur) Glacier, located in the Khunjerab Group of the Ghujerab Mountains, very near the frontier with China. [*In 2022, a British team made three attempts on the south face and southern ridges of Yawash Sar I, on the opposite side of the mountain, starting from a spur of the Northwest Ghidims Glacier. (See AAJ 2023.) No prior attempt on Yawash Sar I from the Koksil Glacier, which drains to the northwest, has been reported.*]

Victor and I met in Islamabad on August 26, flew to Gilgit, spent a night in Karimabad, and arrived at Koksil (ca 4,000m), 12km west of Khunjerab Pass on the Karakoram Highway, on the 28th. Bad weather delayed us for a day, but on the 30th, after one day of walking, we established a base camp at around 4,600m on the highest grassy meadows below the Koksil Glacier.

The weather was unstable over the period from August 31 to September 9. However, we were able to explore the approach to Yawash Sar and get good views of its north and northwest flanks. During this period, to aid acclimatization and get more views of Yawash Sar, we ascended Peak 5,636m, first climbed by a Polish-Italian team in 2011 (*see AAJ 2012*).

On September 10, we left base camp to attempt our main objective. That day we walked up the main Koksil Glacier to camp at a point below the 5,426m West Yawash Col. On the 11th we climbed through an icefall to gain the previously unvisited glacier basin between Yawash Sar I and Peak 6,072m.

The west-northwest face of Yawash Sar I has three groove/couloir lines. We

climbed the central one. On September 12, we crossed the bergschrund and were pleased to find excellent conditions. Once established on the line, we climbed thin ice runnels to a bivouac at about 5,750m. There was a notable dearth of good bivouac sites, and we had to traverse about 35m out of the couloir to a point where we were able to fashion a ledge on a sharp rock crest. On the 13th, we climbed more thin ice streaks and mixed ground to meet the southwest ridge at about 6,050m. Here, we endured a very uncomfortable and windy sitting bivouac.

On the 14th the weather deteriorated, and it began to snow. We traversed left across a rock wall (where we'd been concerned we might be stopped) and gained the summit slopes, which we followed to the top, arriving at around 11 a.m. We stayed about five minutes and then rappelled all the way to the bottom of the face, reaching the glacier at about midnight on the same day. On the 15th and 16th, we returned to base camp.

The upper reaches of the Koksil Glacier had only been visited by one previous party, the Polish-Italian team noted above, and numerous possibilities for climbers remain. On Yawash Sar I, the northwest ridge looks like it might provide an excellent climb. Peak 6,072m, now the only unclimbed 6,000m peak in this area, is a fine objective and could be climbed safely from this side. All the peaks on the southwest side of the upper Koksil (the highest being 5,916m) remain unclimbed. [*Of note is the climbers' ages: Fowler, 68, and Saunders, 74. The two British climbers completed their first major route in the Karakoram together—the Golden Pillar (northwest pillar) of Spantik (7,027m)—37 years earlier, in 1987.*]

TOP: Victor Saunders negotiates the thin ice runnels on Yawash Sar I's west-northwest face.

ABOVE: Victor Saunders (left) and Mick Fowler—more than a century of climbing experience between them.

OPPOSITE PAGE: Yawash Sar I (6,258m, left) and Peak 6,072m from the route to Peak 5,636m, climbed during acclimatization. The first ascent of Yawash Sar I followed a couloir and groove system hidden just behind the prominent rocky ridgeline dropping from the top to the right. (The route line is at the AAJ website.) Peak 6,072m is unclimbed. *Mick Fowler (all photos)*

Mashallah Sar (Peak 132, 6,060m GPS) and the route of ascent, as seen from the top of Shams Sar. The prominent summit on the right is Peak 117 (5,987m on Wala map). ***Masha Gordon***

MASHALLAH SAR, SHAMS SAR, AND POZEVE SAR, FIRST ASCENTS

In July, inspired by lines on a Jerzy Wala map, together with ample opportunities for first ascents in a less explored area of the Karakoram, Oswaldo Freire, Joshua Jarrin, Jacques Sturm, and I traveled to the Karun Koh group of the Ghujerab Mountains. We came with the mindset of exploratory climbing, looking to visit the area north of the Malungutti Glacier, where there was also a possibility of trying the unclimbed southeast ridge of Karun Koh (6,977m).

Having more or less no photos of the approach to the Southeast Karun Glacier, we traced a route on Google Earth, hoping to access base camp via a steep but seemingly passable valley north of the bridge next to Shams Sar Shrine at Ziarat (Shimshal Valley). Once we were on the ground, the physical valley bore little resemblance to its digital twin. It was a steep and narrow, scree-covered canyon, cut by raging river flows.

After a few days of drone research and hiking, we managed to find a difficult but plausible access route via a wider canyon east of the Southeast Karun Valley, starting opposite the Malungutti Glacier; this is the West Kuk Dur Valley on the Wala map. The route involved Houdini-like vertical rock passages next to two 20m waterfalls, and trekking over a previously uncrossed 5,000m pass, reached via 1,200m of steep scree. Though we celebrated our success, the next crux was to convince a small army of Shimshali porters to venture into the unknown with some 600kg of gear. On July 10, a week after leaving Europe, we finally were able to set up base camp at 4,250m, around eight kilometers from the southeast ridge of Karun Koh.

We spent the next few weeks acclimatizing by hauling gear up the Southeast Karun Glacier to the base of the ridge at 5,450m. This involved passing through a broken 250m icefall. In temperamental weather, we did not get a good view of the route during this period, but eventually we saw a heavily corniced, three-kilometer-long ridge bejewelled with seracs. This, combined with the warm temperatures and short weather windows, made us rule out any attempt.

We decided to try some lower unclimbed peaks. On July 21, we climbed rocky Peak 144 on the Wala map (5,750m, 36°35'58.34"N, 75°6'14.33"E, near the foot of Karun Koh's southeast ridge). We climbed snow ramps on the northwest flank (F, 40°) and named it Pozeve Sar due to its heart shape.

The following day we climbed nearby Peak 143 (5,859m GPS, 5,792m Wala map, 36°36'8.38"N, 75°6'58.27"E) via the southwest face (500m, D+). Starting at sunrise, we simul-climbed steep snow slopes to a rock band where pitches of M4 led to the

On the southwest face of Shams Sar (Peak 143, 5,859m GPS) during the first ascent of the mountain. *Jacques Sturm*

rocky summit. We named the peak Shams Sar after the local saint. The same day, we descended the icefall and back to base camp.

After a few days of rest and reconnaissance of the Hidden Glacier, northeast of camp, we decided to attempt the attractive Peak 132 (6,043m on the Wala map, 36°34'47.40"N, 75°10'33.14"E, attempted by Polish climbers the previous winter; see note below); we had spotted this mountain from the summit of Peak 143.

On the 26th, after spending a night at 4,900m on the Hidden Glacier, we left at 3 a.m. to climb the west face. After a steep snow ramp of 700m with sections of 70°, a few pitches of WI3-4, and then four pitches of steep mixed climbing (M4), we reached a corniced summit, which we recorded as 6,060m.

With the freezing isotherm at 7,000m, the rapidly warming temperatures made for a harrowing descent. Snow stakes would not hold, and we had to dig almost a meter into the snow to find rotten ice we could use for Abalakovs. Late that evening, we were safely back in base camp. We called the peak Mashallah Sar—Mashallah means "God has willed it"—to express gratitude for ending our expedition with a beautiful peak in a remote yet hospitable part of the world. We rated the ascent TD (1,000m, WI4 M4).

—Masha Gordon, *U.K.*

PEAK 132, WEST RIDGE, WINTER ATTEMPT: *In January 2024, starting from Ziarat in the Shimshal Valley, Grzegorz Bielejec, Robert Cholewa, and Piotr Tomala made their way up the narrows of the Southeast Karun Valley to a base camp at the terminal moraine of the Hidden Glacier. They then attempted to climb the west ridge of Peak 132 (6,043m). Details and photos are at the AAJ website.*

—Information from Robert Cholewa, *Poland*

ABOVE LEFT: Murilo Lessa nearing the top of the west face of Yazpurs Sar (6,030m GPS), with unclimbed Dih Sar behind.

TOP RIGHT: Dih Sar (reported to be at least 6,200m) seen from the northwest.

BOTTOM RIGHT: Unclimbed Shalghagin Sar (6,080m) from Avduzhi to the northeast. ***Lee Harrison (all photos)***

YAZPURS SAR, FIRST ASCENT, VIA WEST FACE

Murilo Lessa and I visited the Ghujerab Valley, north of Shimshal, in September, with a view to attempting peaks around Dih Sar from their north side. After a three-day trek via Boesam Pass (5,000m), a base camp was made at the herder settlement of Avduzhi (4,060m, 36°38'40"N, 75°20'42"E), where several hundred goats and sheep became our neighbors. From there, the Yazpurs, Shalghagin, and Zangaish valleys were all accessible, albeit with moderately long approaches and height gains.

With a fine weather outlook, we immediately made an attempt on the 6,000m peak at the head of the Yazpurs Glacier: Peak 41 (6,175m) on the Wala map; 36°34'52"N, 75°19'01"E. [*This peak was attempted unsuccessfully by the east ridge in 2017; see AAJ 2018.*]

We spent the first night midway up the glacier at 5,040m on the eastern lateral moraine and made a second bivouac at 5,400m on the western moraine, beneath a rocky buttress and its neighboring scree gully. That night, rocks cartwheeled past the tent as close as 25m away. A pit between the gully and our tent swallowed any rocks that deviated in our direction, but there was always the fear that one might breach the defenses.

On the 9th, we left the bivouac at 3:30 a.m. and gained the Yazpurs Col (5,650m) at the head of the valley. This involved one pitch of 55° snow below the cornice and some brief exposure to large seracs. From the col, we followed the left edge of the west face (40°–50°). The face was firm névé and often icy, requiring pitching and/or simul-climbing with ice screw protection.

We reached the top at 12 p.m. (6,030m GPS), stopping just below the highest point due to a cornice of unknown magnitude. After discussion with local porters, Yazpurs Sar seemed the logical name for the peak. The route difficulties felt around AD+.

The descent proved to be a slow affair: We had underestimated the difficulties and brought only one 60m half rope. Murilo abseiled first, placing a few screws as he went, then I downclimbed. Both of us fell through crevasses up to the thigh. We reached the bivouac site at around 5 p.m. and moved the tent away from the rockfall zone and onto the glacier. The next day, we descended to base camp.

On the 16th, we attempted a 6,050m peak (36°36'22"N, 75°18'20"E) from a bivouac at 5,040m on the neighboring Shalghagin Glacier. Initially, the climb involved 380m of scree ascent to reach the snowline, which was much higher than the previous season (*see AAJ 2024*). We soloed the snow face as high as 5,730m before abandoning the attempt due to lack of energy.

I then reconnoitered the Zangaish Glacier, and we decided to attempt the 6,030m peak at the head of the western branch (36°36'57"N, 75°15'21"E). We made two attempts to reach the base of the mountain, but both were aborted due to a similar lack of energy.

—Lee Harrison, *Norway*

The north end of the Sim Gang Glacier with Peak 6,433m on the left and Virjerab Sar (6,616m GPS) at right, separated by Virjerab Pass. Virjerab Sar's first ascent, in 2024, was by the opposite (north-northwest) side of the mountain. *Murilo Lessa*

KARAKORAM | Virjerab Muztagh

VIRJERAB SAR, FIRST ASCENT, VIA WEST FLANK AND NORTH-NORTHWEST RIDGE

A small, multinational team left Shimshal on July 17 with the intention of ascending the Virjerab Glacier to its head, reaching Virjerab Pass, and from there making the first ascent of the large snow peak Virjerab Sar (6,601m on Russian and Japanese maps, 6,601m/6,635m and Peak 122 on the Wala map, 36°4'16.08"N, 75°43'31.12"E).

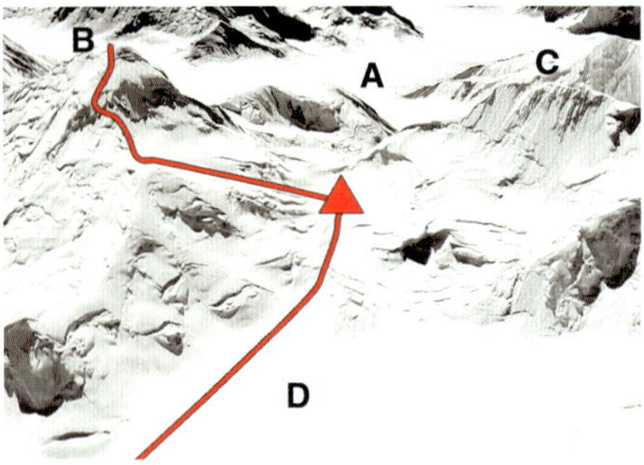

The head of the east branch of the Virjerab Glacier, seen from the northwest. (A) Sim Gang Glacier. (B) Virjerab Sar. (C) Unnamed Peak 6,433m. (D) East Virjerab Glacier. The 2024 high camp at 5,894m is marked. ***Google Earth***

In 2022, Phil de-Beger (U.K.) and Murilo Lessa (Brazil) had tried this peak from the south, coming up the Braldu and Sim Gang glaciers. Unfortunately, their porters turned around 30km from the peak. When the climbers eventually reached the base of the mountain, they were thwarted by large crevasses (*see AAJ 2023*).

This time, de-Beger, Lorenzo Heis (Switzerland), and Aleksi Mujirishvili (Georgia) planned to approach by the Hispar Glacier and Snow Lake to reach the Sim Gang Glacier, crossing Virjerab Pass and descending the Virjerab Glacier to Shimshal after the climb. However, on arrival, they were told this would require high-altitude porters, and their budget wouldn't cover that expense. On the advice of their Shimshal agent, they opted to approach and descend via the Virjerab Glacier.

The team made seven camps on the approach, the last being their base camp at 5,353m on the upper east branch of the Virjerab Glacier. On July 26, they climbed to Virjerab Pass (around 6,000m) to look at route options, then dropped back down to a camp at 5,894m (36°6'7.09"N, 75°43'10.53"E). The next day, they decided to head across the northwest side of the mountain to reach the north-northwest ridge, which they climbed to around 6,400m, avoiding a difficult section via the east flank. Close to the summit, strong sunlight made the snow conditions poor, and the trio decided to descend.

After a rest at base camp and some bad weather, they started up the mountain again on August 7, camping that night at the 5,894m site. They rested the next day, then, on the 9th, followed the same route to the north-northwest ridge and up to the summit. The GPS altitude was 6,616m.

Leaving the mountains, the three descended the Virjerab Glacier, carrying loads up to 45kg each, until they reached the site of their fourth approach camp at 4,333m. Here, they were met by six porters and a guide. On August 16, they all arrived back in Shimshal. The team's Mount Everest Foundation (MEF) trip report is available at the *AAJ* website.

—Lindsay Griffin, *from MEF report*

Hispar Muztagh

The route to Naseer Baig II (right) and continuation to Naseer Baig I (ca 6,100m). High camp was in the saddle between the two summits. ***Louis Rousseau***

NASEER BAIG I AND II, FIRST ASCENTS

Adam Bielecki (Poland) and I were inspired to investigate the potential of the Gharesa Valley, which rises northeast from the village of Nagar and has been traveled in the past by expeditions attempting the Lupghar peaks and Momhil Sar. From an advanced base at around 5,000m on

the lower South Lupghar Glacier, we climbed two peaks.

On September 29, we spent five and a half hours ascending a large couloir (60°) on the east face of a summit of around 5,800m (36°16'59"N, 74°57'16"E, Peak 9 on the Jerzy Wala map, south of the previously climbed 6,453m Borondo Sar). After reaching the south ridge, we followed the corniced arête to the top. Believing the peak to be unnamed, we called it Alu Sar ("Potato Peak" in Balti). The 1,030m ascent was D.

TOP: Louis Rousseau on the summit (south) ridge of Naseer Baig II. In the distance are high peaks of the Spantik-Sosbun Mountains. ***Adam Bielecki***

BOTTOM: Rousseau at the last bivouac during an attempt on an unnamed peak above the South Lupghar Glacier. Rousseau and Adam Bielecki were stuck for three hours in these conditions before a lull enabled them to descend. ***Adam Bielecki***

We descended the ridge to a col at 5,700m and bivouacked. Next morning, after a comfortable but cold night, we continued along the ridge to the southwest, overcoming complex terrain to reach a higher summit of around 6,100m (36°16'32"N, 74°57'02"E, Peak 8 and 6,134m on the Jerzy Wala map). We graded this ascent D+ and named the summit Zang Sar ("Rusty Peak").

A subsequent attempt to climb a more difficult, higher peak was thwarted on October 11 due to the cold and increasing avalanche hazard. We endured a bad bivouac with serious spindrift until a lull enabled us to descend. Once on the glacier, we witnessed a medium-sized avalanche sweep our descent route.

On our return to Nagar, we showed villagers pictures of the two mountains we'd climbed. They told us the higher peak was called Naseer Baig I and the smaller one Naseer Baig II. The name Naseer Baig refers to the campsite at the foot of the higher peak.

—Louis Rousseau, *Canada*

KARAKORAM | Spantik-Sosbun Range

Ekaitz Maiz on pitch 13 (6b) of the southeast pillar of Sosbun Spire III (a.k.a. Mun Brakk II), with spires IV and V behind. ***Markel De La Fuente***

SOSBUN SPIRE III (MUN BRAKK II), SOUTHEAST PILLAR

Markel De La Fuente, Oier De La Fuente, Josu Linaza, and I planned an expedition to the Sosbun Valley similar to my 2023 trip to Ladakh (*AAJ 2024*), where we had a base camp close to a variety of rock walls. We opted to visit the South Sosbun Glacier after seeing photos from a past expedition sent by our friend Asghar from Skardu.

The weather was not ideal: There were rain showers and light (occasionally not so light) snowfall on each day. We reconnoitered the area and dismissed Sosbun Brakk (6,413m) and Sokha Brakk (5,956m), as they seemed full of objective danger. Instead, we selected one of the Sosbun Spires, which looked "safe," with little evidence of rockfall, and had good-looking rock with a multitude of cracks and corners.

Soft snow, crevasses, and difficult moraine meant it took us 4.5 hours to reach the foot of the wall. We ferried gear to this point and established a camp (4,600m). It appeared there would be a good ledge for a second camp about 400m above. We would fix ropes to that point, then try to complete the route in one day. However, we had to wait through more than a week of bad weather before we received a favorable forecast.

Back at the spire, we all climbed, fixed ropes, and hauled the necessary gear to the proposed camp at the top of pitch seven. The rock was quite good, and although the cracks were sometimes blind, there was no vegetation. While climbing the first two pitches, we spotted three ancient bolts about 50m to our left, but then nothing more.

On what we hoped would be our final push, all four of us spent the night on the ledge and set off the following morning. At 8 a.m., while we were trying to place a bolted belay, the drill stopped working. The rock on our route had not always offered good natural protection, so we thought the most sensible thing was to descend and return with our backup drill. [*In addition to bolts at anchors, more than 25 protection bolts were placed on the route.*]

Two days later, Markel and I completed the approach up the glacier and by 1 p.m. had climbed the ropes to our camp. (Josu and Oier had opted to attempt a peak from the North Sosbun Glacier but were eventually unsuccessful.) The day was still young and the weather was good, so Markel and I decided to push on to a higher camp. This would have to be our final

Looking up the South Sosbun Glacier at the Sosbun Spires; the arrow marks Sosbun Spire III (Mun Brakk II). The high, snowy peak at the head of the glacier is Sokha Brakk (5,956m), while the ridge to the right divides the South and North Sosbun glaciers. *Ekaitz Maiz*

The southeast pillar of Sosbun Spire III (Mun Brakk II), showing the 20-pitch new route. The three X's to the left mark ancient bolts of unknown origin (likely rappel anchors), spotted during the 2024 ascent. *Ekaitz Maiz*

attempt, as the porters were due to arrive the next day.

We awoke early at our upper camp, on a ledge at the top of pitch 12, at 4 a.m., and soon began climbing. The rock quality was worse than the previous day, and we had to climb through difficult and sparsely protected slabs, wet from melting snow above. After a mixed section, we reached a small shoulder below the final wall. We'd hoped to climb a corner on the southwest face, but it was obviously too wet, so we were forced to climb to the right. There, the excellent granite was interrupted by two overhanging schist bands. On the second band, a small edge broke under my foot and I almost fell. This penultimate pitch proved to be the crux of our route. Pitch 20, a poorly protected thin slab finishing with a nice crack, then took us to the sharp summit.

With continuous rockfall in the couloirs on either side of the pillar, reversing our route was the most sensible option. We needed to make many diagonal rappels, but by 8 p.m. we were back at our top camp.

We named our route Izar Gorri, Mamuon Betiko Argi (800m, 1,140m of climbing in 20 pitches, 7b M4). These central spires of the Sosbun group have been known as Sosbun IV, III, and II, and we climbed Sosbun III. However, the porters referred to our spire as the central of three Mun Brakks ("cut peaks"), and we adopted that name: Mun Brakk II (5,430m, 35°55'7.68"N, 75°30'40.73"E). [*The online version of this report includes notes on the climbing history of the Sosbun peaks.*]

—Ekaitz Maiz, *Basque Country*

Mnich in the Sosbun Valley, seen from the south. Very Lucky Ladies (2011) climbed just inside the right-hand skyline. ***Danuta Piotrowska***

MNICH AND OTHER ASCENTS

On September 4, 2011, an all-women team of Polish mountaineers—Paulina Janczar, Anna Kładzińska, Irena Kładzińska-Wituska, Joanna Nowosadzka, Danuta Przybylska, Bernadeta Szczepańska, Danuta Wach, and photographer Danuta Piotrowska—established base camp at 4,000m at the entrance to the South Sosbun Glacier.

On the 6th, as part of their acclimatization, Janczar, Nowosadzka, Przybylska, and Szczepańska left to climb three tops of around 5,000m at the southern end of the long ridge that divides the South Sosbun and North Sosbun glaciers. They were successful and returned to base camp on the 8th.

Two days later, Janczar and Nowosadzka climbed a previously unvisited rock peak a little to the northwest of base camp at approximately 35°52'7.51"N, 75°33'2.67"E. The pair climbed the southeast face in six hours and rappelled their route in another six hours. They named the summit Mnich ("Monk," also a famous tower in the Polish Tatra) and the route Very Lucky Ladies. The lower half was generally loose or crumbly but moderate in difficulty, while the headwall was solid and steeper, giving difficulties to VI A1. [*The online report includes many photos showing peaks and spires of the Sosbun Glacier.*]

—Janusz Majer, *Poland, based on an account by Danuta Wach*

Shimshak Mountains

TANPA LUNGMA AND KURU LUNGMA, EXPLORATION AND ASCENTS

The little-known Shimshak Mountains, southeast of Shigar, are described in a booklet published in 2021 by Janusz Majer and Jerzy Wala. From this information, it appeared that only two valleys—Ghoro and Kiris—had been visited by trekkers and mountaineers. We decided to investigate the other two: the Tanpa Lungma and Kuru Lungma.

From July 19 to 27, Stanisław Pisarek, Voytek Walas, Mateusz Winkler, and I visited the Tanpa Lungma valley. Starting from the village of Narh (2,400m), reached by road from Skardu, we walked for two days to a base camp at 4,447m (approx. 35°22'47.91"N, 75°56'38.15"E). At this time of year, only the gullies and cirques of the higher peaks were snow-covered. The highest peak on the valley rim is Thalle (5,851m).

Mateusz climbed Peak 5,206m (dubbed Mateo Peak, 27.1 on the Wala map) and Peak 5,273m (33 on the map), finding no technical difficulties. All four of us climbed Peak 4,802m, south of base camp and near to Peak 41. Voytek and I tried Meraq (43.2) from the northeast, retreating from high on the mountain (UIAA III). We also reached a 5,197m pass between Peaks 30 and 32.1 on the watershed ridge south-southeast of Thalle Peak. We hoped this might provide a connection between the Tanpa Lungma and Thalle valleys, but on the far side of the pass there was a big drop over a cliff.

From July 30 to August 4, we operated in

the Kuru Lungma valley, farther to the southeast. The road to Kuru village at the entrance to the valley crosses a rope bridge over the turbulent Shyok River.

On the first day, we walked through the deep, rocky gorge of the lower Kuru River, camping at 3,450m, then walked another five hours the next day to a vast pasture called Gamba Chokeel (4,450m, 35°15'29.63"N, 76°3'42.37"E), where we established base camp.

From here, Stanisław climbed three nontechnical summits: Peak 5,187m (Wala map 107.3), north-northwest of base camp; Peak Shingpiou Gab (5,154m, 139.2), east northeast of camp; and Shingpiou II (5,146m, 140). Mateusz climbed Abadan (5,011m, 123), southwest of base camp, and Voytek and I reached the Kheel Pass (a.k.a. Kuru La, 5,150m, UIAA III) at the head of the valley.

The day after our ascent to the pass, local men Ghulam Mehdi Kurovi, Muhammad Khan, and Muhammad Saleem Bargoli also reached the pass and then descended the far side to the Thalle Valley, the first people to do so. Ghulam Mehdi wants to popularize the valley as a trekking destination.

According to locals, we were the first foreigners to visit the two valleys, and we were able to learn local names for around 15 peaks. However, it was difficult to determine definitively which peaks and passes had previously been visited; we found cairns on some of them. The peaks that require difficult technical climbing, such as Thalle and Shimshak (5,609m), remain unclimbed. [*Editor's Note: An Italian team visited the Ghoro Valley, south of the Tanpa Lungma, in 2018 and reached a couple of peaks, including the first ascent of Kiris Peak (5,428m) by a difficult wall. See AAJ 2019.*]

—Grzegorz Chwola and Voytek Walas, *Poland*

TOP: Looking at the northeastern head of the Tanpa Lungma. The highest summit in the center is Foo Rey Peak. The distant triangular summit on the left is Peak 36 (5,445m) on the ridge at the head of the valley behind Foo Rey. *Mateusz Winkler*

BOTTOM: Unclimbed Snpo Brakk (ca 5,500m) from the south, at the head of one arm of the Tanpa Lungma. The small rock summit at far right is Mateo Peak, climbed by Mateusz Winkler in 2024. *Stanisław Pisarek*

KARAKORAM | Baltoro Muztagh

ABOVE: Climbing above high camp on Great Trango Tower. At right are Paiyu Peak and Uli Biaho Tower. ***Drew Smith | The North Face***

RIGHT: The descent on Great Trango, with Trango Tower on the left. ***Erich Roepke | The North Face***

GREAT TRANGO TOWER, FIRST SKI DESCENT

On May 9, on their second attempt in two years, Christina Lustenberger (Canada) and Jim Morrison (USA), along with Chantel Astorga (USA), skied down from the main summit of Great Trango Tower (6,286m). The trio climbed and skied the normal route on the north-northwest face, first climbed over four days in 1984 by Americans Andy Selters and Scott Woolums.

The climbers acclimatized and dealt with illness at base camp for three and a half weeks before their final push. Starting from a high camp at 5,000m, they completed the ascent and ski descent in one long day.

From the summit, their route descended a hanging glacier atop the face and then continued along the narrow, snow- and ice-covered north ridge to reach the top of the broad couloir that descends southwest to the Trango Glacier from the foot of Trango Tower. Lustenberger and Morrison made two short rappels during the descent, and Astorga made a third rappel. The total vertical drop from the summit to base camp is more than 2,000m.

Lustenberger, Morrison, and Nick McNutt attempted to climb and ski the same route in the spring of 2023, reaching a point about 500m below the summit.

—Dougald MacDonald, *AAJ, with information from Christina Lustenberger, Canada*

Tagas Mountains

SCKEM BRAKK, NORTHWEST FACE, AZZARDO ESTREMO

Each of us has a dream drawer. Mine is overflowing with images of walls, all over the world. From time to time, I take one of these images and hang it on the wall, starting a journey that will transform a dream into reality.

Chiara Gusmeroli and I arrived in Pakistan in early August and a few days later set up base camp in the Nangma Valley, south-southeast of Amin Brakk and directly opposite Peak 19 on the Jerzy Wala sketch map. To reach here, we had crossed gravel and moraine, and then as if by magic we emerged onto a lush plateau with grazing cows and their herders. The latter said nothing but were obviously happy to see our amazement at their beautiful surroundings.

After a week spent with altitude headaches and classic intestinal problems, and studying nearby walls through binoculars, we realized a lifetime wouldn't be long enough to climb all the peaks within a three-hour walk from camp. However, almost immediately we were forced to cross off some potential projects due to huge amounts of rockfall. Scared, we decided to look at the northwest face of Peak 19 (5,259m GPS, 35°21'56.82"N, 76°29'27.24"E), which appeared to be the most compact wall in the valley. It had no name, so we christened it Sckem Brakk (*see note below about a prior attempt on this peak*).

We climbed as fast as possible, convinced we could be up and down in two days. Cracks were all the same width, meaning we had to use our cams carefully, and we often found ourselves 20m above protection. Higher, the cracks became superficial and choked with grass. I tried to clean with a hammer, but it made progress far too slow, and we returned to base camp dejected.

On August 21, we made a second attempt, carrying provisions for five days and a small ice axe for cleaning the cracks. We were slower this time due to heavier packs and much colder temperatures. After two days of climbing, we were forced to take a rest day on the large ledge below the headwall (top of pitch nine) due to bad weather.

We continued up on days four and five, using aid where we couldn't garden the cracks. After three complex crux pitches, we arrived, late in the evening, at a small bivouac spot on top of pitch 19. We spent the night in almost sitting positions and the next day left for the top amid a small snowstorm. Seven pitches later, we reached the summit at 9 a.m., in weather that was now almost perfect.

High above the Nangma Valley, Chiara Gusmeroli looks southeast at (A) Sckem Brakk, attempted in 2021 and climbed in 2024, (B) Takub Tower, (C) unclimbed Hasho Peak, and (D) Roungkhanchan III (a.k.a. Logmun Tower). ***Matteo De Zaiacomo***

We started down our route to the big ledge where we had left the tent. On arrival, we found it completely destroyed: A large rockfall had swept the area. Thinking about how lucky we had been, we accelerated our pace toward base camp, with a feeling this paradise could easily turn into hell. Only in base camp with a Coca-Cola in hand did we understand we had made it. We named the route Azzardo Estremo (900m, 26 pitches, 7a A3). [*In August 2021, Pete Fasoldt and Jonathan Schaffer (both USA) climbed a line in the lower half of the face that appears to be quite close to that followed by the Italians. They then moved well to the left and climbed to a point very close to the summit, where they were shut down by the blank final slab. The AAJ 2022 report gives the altitude of the peak as 5,007m, but it is considerably higher—the 5,259m figure is more accurate.*]

—Matteo De Zaiacomo, *Italy*

India

JAMMU & KASHMIR | Kashmir Himalaya

UMBRELLA PEAK, EAST FACE, MAVIN'S ROUTE

Umbrella Peak, east of Thajiwas (4,854m; *see AAJ 2024*), was climbed in 1944 by British military personnel stationed in Sonamarg. Royal Air Force (RAF) instructors Wilfrid Noyce and A. Jones climbed Umbrella Peak (4,798m) from Glacier 3; the exact line is unknown, though they appear to have gained the north ridge shortly above a formation known as Glacier Crag. The mountain was climbed again at least twice in 1945, but no other ascents are known to have taken place since.

In June 2024, Inayat Ullah Bhat from India, having observed the complex and crevassed slope of Glacier 3 from nearby summits in 2020, arrived at Sonamarg with Waseem Raja and Shariq Rasheed. On the 22nd, they trekked to a base camp at 3,300m below Glacier 3. The following day, they navigated around the foot of Glacier Crag (which now has rock climbs from British VD to HVS) and ascended the glacier to 3,900m, setting up tents for the night.

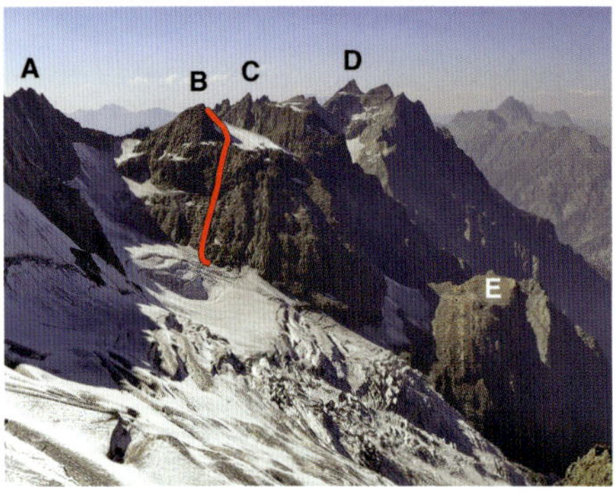

Looking west across Glacier 3 in 2020 at (A) the western end of Kazim Pahalin Bal, (B) Umbrella Peak with Mavin's Route (2024), (C) Cefn Carnedd, (D) Thajiwas (4,854m), and (E) Glacier Crag. *Inayat Ullah Bhat*

On the morning of June 24, the three climbed icy ground to reach a couloir in the rocky face below and a little to the north of Umbrella's summit. They ascended this steep, snowy couloir (about 300m) to an upper glacier, and from there reached the top section of Umbrella's northwest ridge and followed it to the summit. There they found a collapsed cairn and, in the rubble, an old empty food can, which could not have been left less than 79 years before. Their new line, named Mavin's Route, is most likely the first route climbed from Glacier 3 since the days of RAF exploration.

Inayat Ullah Bhat notes that access to the Thajiwas Valley is now quite good and that the area is safe for foreign climbers to visit.

—Lindsay Griffin, *with information from Inayat Ullah Bhat, India*

HARMUKH, WEST COULOIR

In August 2023, the Indian team of Vinod Chandra Joshi, Karn Kowshik, and Zeeshan Mushtaq climbed the 5,080m central summit of Harmukh, in alpine style, by a new route up the west couloir and upper northwest ridge.

Around 35km almost due north of Srinagar, Harmukh (a.k.a. Haramukh, 34°24'13.49"N, 74°54'6.54"E) is a somewhat isolated massif with five summits. The northwest summit (Station Peak, 4,698m) was first climbed in 1856 by Thomas Montgomerie and the Great Trigonometric Survey of India. It was from here that Montgomerie first identified a very high peak far to the northeast that would become known as K2. The first recorded ascent of the east summit (main peak, 5,142m) took place in 1899.

From Kudar, on August 20, the climbers trekked to a base camp at approximately 3,500m, west of the mountain and close to Sarbal Lake. The next day, they camped a little below 4,100m. From here, the standard ascent from the west goes north via a glacier to reach Station Peak, then back southeast along a ridge to the west summit.

On August 22, the team shortcut the normal route by climbing a broad open couloir on the west face to arrive on the west ridge at around 4,800m. Finding hard blue ice in the couloir, the climbers traversed to the rock rib on the right side and climbed this (estimated at F6a) and the 60° slopes above. From the exit, they traversed over the west summit to the central summit, which they reached at 3 p.m.

—Lindsay Griffin, *AAJ*

BRAMMAH I, SOUTH FACE

A team of 12 mountaineers from Kolkata, India, led by Rudra Prasad Halder, and six Sherpas led by Phursemba, made a probable new route on Brammah I (6,416m, 33°30'23"N, 76°03'04"E), climbing a couloir on the right side of the south face to reach the upper southeast ridge.

After a strong attempt in 1972 by a British party, which reached a point around 100m below the top on the southeast ridge, this elegant pyramidal peak was first climbed the following year by Chris Bonington and Nick Estcourt, via the same ridge. They ascended the Kibar Glacier, then through an icefall to the col at the base of the 1,050m ridge, and then followed the

Camp 2 on the south face of Brammah I, looking southeast at (A) Brammah II, (B) Flat Top, (C) Peak ca 6,130m (confusingly, this peak is known locally as Brammah and thought to be unclimbed), and (D) unnamed, unclimbed peak. *Indian Brammah Expedition*

Base camp below the south face of Brammah I (6,416m). The foreshortened view of the mountain shows the couloir climbed in 2024, slanting left from directly above the tents. ***Indian Brammah Expedition***

crest throughout, overcoming pitches of crumbly granite up to UIAA V.

The southeast ridge was repeated in 1978 by another British team, approaching the col from the other side; tragically, two members of this team were killed. In 1980, a French team almost climbed the north-northeast ridge. It appears there has been no ascent of this mountain for many years, partially due to access being very tricky after the late 1980s because of Kashmir's political turbulence.

The Indian expedition arrived at their 4,150m base camp in the Kibar Nullah (valley) on June 6. On June 9, some team members left base camp to open the route to Camp 1 (4,950m). Thereafter, with the Sherpa climbers in the lead, the expedition fixed 4,000m of rope up a couloir toward the right side of the south face, negotiating sometimes steep and interesting climbing, including a difficult rock wall in the gully below Camp 1. They exited the face above the difficulties on the southeast ridge, making their new line possibly an easier proposition than the first ascent route.

A summit attempt on the 16th stopped less than 150m below the top due to an accident involving one of the Sherpas. A second attempt shortly after was successful, with 14 members, including the leader and five Sherpas, reaching the top.

—Lindsay Griffin, *AAJ*

View to the southeast from the top of Laknak Kangri (6,496m; see photos of the climbing route at the *AAJ* website). In the distance at far left is Chamshen Kangri (7,017m). Saser Kangri I (7,672m) is in the center, with Plateau Peak (7,310m) to its right. ***Divyesh Muni***

LADAKH | East Karakoram

SASER MUZTAGH: LAKNAK KANGRI, SOUTH FACE AND SOUTHWEST RIDGE

Driven by my desire to return to the Thangman Lungpa (valley), which I had partially explored in 2023 (*see AAJ 2024*), Sudeep Barve, Prajakta Ghode, Mahesh Kendurkar, Yogesh Umbre, and I formed a joint expedition organized by the Himalayan Club and Chakram Hikers, planning to attempt unclimbed Peak 6,496m (34°56'0.58"N, 77°38'15.99"E). If we found this unfeasible, there were many other objectives we could attempt.

After initially being sent back to Leh by a military check post at the start of the road to the Saser La—despite having the proper clearances and having traveled the same road one year earlier—we managed to get the requisite permission, and on August 1 our journey to the Thangman Lungpa continued. We spent three nights at an intermediate camp in the valley

before settling into base camp on August 6. We then split into two teams. One party climbed onto the ridge on the far (east) side of the north branch of the Thangman Glacier so they could look at the upper south flank of Peak 6,496m, while another climbed scree slopes up the south face to find a site for Camp 1.

Studying our photos from the day, we saw a possible route through the icy slopes above Camp 1, but it was riddled with crevasses. After stocking Camp 1 (5,670m), we spent the night there on August 10. Over the next two days, we sought a route up to the southwest ridge. Initially, Sudeep, Yogesh, our climbing Sherpas Phuphu Dorji, Phurten Bhutia, and Sangbu Bhutia, and I were defeated by gaping crevasses. On August 12, we tried a different line, climbing halfway up the face, then traversing left for about 100m to the lip of a vast crevasse. We followed this crevasse diagonally down to a spot where it narrowed and was crossable. This solved the puzzle, and we continued up steeply for 200m to the southwest ridge. We had fixed 500m of rope from Camp 1. The route to the top now looked feasible.

On the 13th, we shifted to a summit camp at 6,100m on the southwest ridge. Leaving at 5:30 a.m. on August 14 in windy conditions, we roped up and climbed the ridge, keeping to its south flank to avoid large cornices. We fixed 100m of rope on the final steep section and reached the top at 9 a.m. A clear sky allowed a panoramic view of most of the East Karakoram's 7,000ers. However, degradation of the glaciers in this region was alarming. There had been negligible snowfall the previous winter, which had left glaciers barren.

Like a golden eagle, this peak dominated the valley, so we decided to name it Laknak Kangri, the Ladakhi name for golden eagle.

—Divyesh Muni, *India*

Nya Kangri (6,496m GPS) from the south with the 2024 route up the south-southeast spur. The first ascent of the peak was completed after six prior attempts. *Nikolaos Kroupis*

NYA KANGRI, FIRST ASCENT, VIA SOUTH-SOUTHEAST SPUR

In July, I made my fourth expedition to unclimbed Nya Kangri (6,496m GPS, 34°37'38.48"N, 77°45'23.08"E), partway up the Arganglas Valley. Nya Kangri had received six previous attempts: in 2008 via the southeast face and south ridge by an Indian team; two attempts in 2016 by Indian teams via the south-southeast spur; in 2016 and 2022 by my two expeditions from the north side to reach the south-southwest ridge; and in 2023 by my expedition to the southeast face.

In 2024, Orestis Mitrou-Kintis and I

spent three days in Leh for acclimatization and then traveled to Sumur in the Nubra Valley. On July 14, we started from Tirit village (ca 3,300m) with three porters and trekked up the lower Arganglas Valley. After 12 hours we reached 4,580m, where we camped for the night. The next day, we reached our base camp at Phonglas (4,620m); this required a difficult river crossing a few meters upstream from Phonglas, where the river splits into three branches.

On the 18th, we ascended moraine leading to the glacier below the southeast face of Nya Kangri and camped at 5,430m. The next day, we explored the route ahead as far as the glacier and on July 20 set off from our high camp at 3 a.m. for a summit push.

Above 5,750m on the south-southeast spur, we found fixed ropes belonging to the 2016 expedition. Above 6,000m, the angle of the ice slope varied between 40° and 55°. We belayed 13 pitches to the summit, which we gained at 3 p.m. (We stayed three meters below the highest point, which was a large cornice.) We descended in nine rappels, leaving a single ice screw on the mountain, and returned to camp after a round trip of 16 hours. Two days later we were back in Tirit.

—Nikolaos Kroupis, *Greece*

LADAKH

HEMAR RI, NORTHWEST RIDGE

Acclimatizing for a trek in the Pologongka Group in August, Claudia Bäumler, 15-year-old Nina Bielefeldt, Hartmut Bielefeldt, and Nuhbu Gojing trekked from Kanji to the Spang Nala (valley) and climbed an easy peak on the east rim of the valley. The unroped ascent was by the northwest ridge and north ridge. They measured the top at 5,699m and, finding no sign of a previous visit, proposed the name Hemar Ri (34°03'46"N, 76°44'30"E), after a glacier just to the north.

—Information from Hartmut Bielefeldt, *Germany*

PEAK 6,124M, PEAK 6,128M, AND RALE

In September, Mayukh Banik, Sujit Kushe, and I, supported by Dorje Bhutia, Pasang (Paste) Bhutia, Pemba Bhutia, Angchuk Sherpa, Ang Tshering, and Lang Tshering, explored a group of mostly unnamed mountains east of Leh and just southwest of the Shyok River. From Karu, southeast of Leh, we drove north via Sakti, over the Wari La (ca 5,300m), and down toward the Shyok as far as Tangyar village and gompa (3,912m, 34°15'13.40"N, 77°52'20.28"E). On September 9, we set off up the valley to the southeast.

After a seven-hour trek, we set up base camp at 4,772m. Over the next two weeks, we established two higher camps and finally a summit camp at 6,071m, on the col between Peak 6,124m to the northeast and Peak 6,128m to the southwest. From here we climbed both peaks, finding evidence of prior climbers on Peak 6,128m. On September 29, we returned to the top of Peak 6,128m and continued along the ridge south and then east toward Rale (6,132m). At the summit, although a previous ascent is nowhere recorded, earlier climbers had built a massive cairn.

—Rajesh Gadgil, *India*

KHYAM LUNGPA: PEAK 6,050M AND PEAK 6,044M

In August 2023, while reviewing maps in Leh, I noticed the Khyam Lungpa (valley), which is northwest of the Tanglang La (5,328m), a pass crossed by the Manali-Leh Highway. What caught my eye was the proximity of several unclimbed 6,000m peaks within a ten-kilometer hike from the road near the village of Rumtse (4,300m), about 80km from Leh.

On August 20, I walked southwest into the valley and camped at 5,150m. The next day, I scrambled up the east face of a 5,885m peak that presented a perfect viewpoint for the upper valley. Several cairns were on top; their style of

Looking approximately south up the Khyam Lungpa from Peak 5,885m. Ama Chomo Nyug Ri (6,057m) is the peak prominent on the left, and Peak 6,050m is high on the right. Base camp was in the sunny valley in lower left. *Anindya Mukherjee*

construction was clearly traditional, not built by visiting climbers. While two main peaks at the head of the valley, Khyam I and II, had been climbed, in 2022 and 2012, respectively, there were nearer 6,000ers that were unclimbed. I asked an old friend, Gerry Galligan, if he would accompany me to the valley in July and August 2024.

By June, I was unable to control my patience and decided to make a quick trip to the valley with Aloke Kumar Das. On June 14, after three days of acclimatization in Leh, we left for the three-hour drive to Rumtse and the next day reached our base camp at 5,150m. On the 17th we moved to a higher camp at 5,350m to the northeast of Peak 6,050m (33°34'06.7"N, 77°39'00.4"E).

The morning of the 18th dawned crisp and clear as we set off for the east face of Peak 6,050m. Just before we reached the first gendarme on the north ridge, Aloke's crampon broke and he was forced to turn back. I continued alone up the ridge, both flanks falling sharply into the valleys below. It was a challenging traverse over gendarmes, interspersed with icy sections requiring an axe and crampons. After savoring the summit, I decided to extend the adventure by descending the south ridge and a southeast spur, which brought me back to the Khyam Lungpa. I had completed the traverse in nine hours at around AD.

In July and early August, I made two more ascents from this valley with Gerry Galligan and others (*see report below*), including the first ascent of Peak 6,044m (33°32'10.34"N, 77°40'35.43"E), which we traversed from east to west. A line up the north face of this peak attracted me, but for the rest of August I had guiding commitments in the Markha Valley. At the end of the month, I returned with Aloke, who would remain in support while I soloed the face.

On September 2, my crampons bit into the hard ice of the north face. After two hours, I reached the northwest ridge and traversed its remaining few hundred meters to the summit. I named the route Aloke Da (D) and descended to the glacier cwm where my friend was waiting. The journey that had begun months ago had come full circle.

—Anindya Mukherjee, *India*

KHYAM LUNGPA: PEAK 6,044M, EAST RIDGE

In August 2023, Indian mountaineer Anindya "Raja" Mukherjee discovered the climbing potential of the Khyam Lungpa (valley), and in June 2024 he made the first ascent of Peak 6,050m on the west side of that valley (*see report above*). I joined him in July to attempt Ama Chomo Nyug Ri

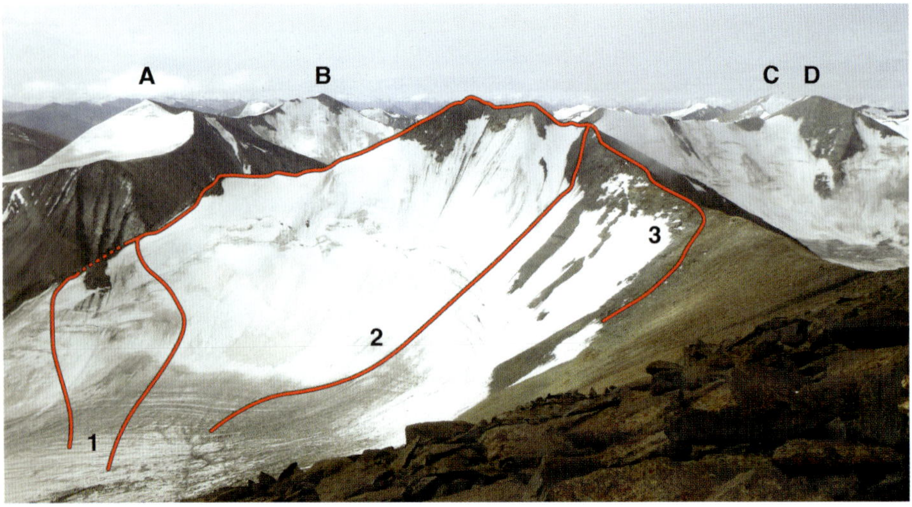

Peak 6,044m from Ama Chomo Nyug Ri to the north. (1) August 2024 routes to the east ridge, with descent by (3) the northwest ridge. (2) September 2024 ascent of the north face and northwest ridge. (A) and (B): UT Kangri I and II, climbed in 2020 by the Ladakh Mountain Guides Association. (C) Khyam I, climbed in 2022 by an Indo-Japanese expedition. (D) Khyam II, climbed in 2012 by an expedition from the Indian Statistical Institute. ***Divyesh Muni***

(6,057m, 33°32'46.36"N, 77°40'30.76"E, on some maps erroneously named Gyamshu). We had found no record of a prior ascent.

On July 30, after ferrying loads to a 5,629m camp in the valley east of Ama Chomo Nyug Ri, we began our climb up the east ridge despite threatening morning clouds. As we neared the summit, I saw a distinctly man-made cairn over a meter high. There was nothing for it but to admire the view in a bittersweet mood. We descended the south ridge to the saddle below an attractive 6,044m peak, then turned east down a scree slope to regain the tent. Our climb was about PD.

After a few days in base camp, Raja and I, along with Ashish Chanda, Lakpa Sherpa, and Neetu Singh, started to ferry loads for an attempt on Peak 6,044m. We set up a camp on moraine below the north cwm. The mountain looked impressive, with a long east–northwest ridge holding twin summit pinnacles, and a wide icefield on the north face cut by several long crevasses.

We set out in perfect weather at 6 a.m. on August 7. Ashish and Raja took a line on the far left side of the north face; Lakpa, Neetu, and I climbed a longer, steeper (50°–55°) line about 50m to the right. We regrouped on the east ridge and followed the shattered crest to the east top (the true summit). We were delighted to find no cairn. It was a sweet moment for me: another first ascent of a Himalayan 6,000er after many years without success.

We completed an east–west traverse of the mountain, descending along the northwest ridge, then down into the north cwm to regain our tent. We felt the grade of the route to be AD.

—Gerry Galligan, *Ireland*

RUPSHU REGION: THONGMETH KANGRI, NORTHEAST RIDGE

In a highly exploratory expedition to the Spiti-Rupshu divide, southwest of the well-known Tso Moriri (lake), a small group of Indian mountaineers made the first ascent of an unnamed 6,000m peak and explored the Monto Group in August and September 2023.

Rajesh Gadgil, Dilip Lagu, Rajendra Shinde, and support staff reached the end of a rough road, southwest of Tso Moriri, on August 14. They then trekked to a base camp at 4,985m (32°42'39"N, 78°05'50"E), established on the 19th. This is very arid terrain, and water supply became the main concern when making camps.

The Monto peaks—none of which have known ascents—lie on a ridge running north from the Spiti-Rupshu divide, and approaches from both the north and east were explored. With the eastern approach appearing the most promising, the team shifted to a suitable advanced base. Further inspection showed the face they needed to ascend to reach the highest peak—Monto I (6,331m)—was a rocky wall that would require rope fixing, rather than the snow and ice face they had expected. However, on the watershed ridge south of their camp stood unclimbed Peak 6,105m (32°37'28"N, 78°05'15"E), and this appeared far more accessible.

On August 30, they carried equipment southeast to a "summit camp" at 5,504m and the following night slept there. On September 1, Angchuk Bhutia, Pasang Bhutia, Sangbu Bhutia, Tshering Bhutia, Gadgil, and Shinde climbed icy slopes to the col (ca 5,750m) on the ridge east of the summit. They followed the snowy ridge southwest, easy at first then steeper toward the top, where they fixed some rope. All reached the summit at around 10:45 a.m. They named the peak Thongmeth Kangri.

—Lindsay Griffin, *AAJ*

LADAKH | Zanskar

CHILING II, NORTH FACE, ATTEMPT

In September and October, Michael Hutchins and I attempted to climb the 1,400m north face of Chiling II (6,253m, 33°49'3.62"N, 76°9'48.26"E). We turned back about 450m up the wall, finding the conditions to be horrendous, owing to poor rock and lack of ice. This was surprising, as the wall looked incredible, both in the images we'd seen prior to the expedition and in person. There is no doubt that, if it were in condition, Chiling II's north wall would be a worthy objective. Sadly, we suspect the conditions we found are typical, though admittedly we did not get very high.

The headwall on the unclimbed north face of Chiling II (6,253m). The 2024 team did not reach the headwall but found poor rock, sugar snow, and anemic ice below it. Describing the headwall runnels, Chris Wright wrote, "Maybe they were ice and maybe they were climbable, but we had no evidence to support this theory and plenty to discredit it." *Chris Wright*

During our expedition, we were able to confirm that the south-southwest ridge of Chiling I (6,349m, 33°48'43"N, 76°09'44"E) was indeed the route climbed in 1977 by Gino and Silvia Buscaini, who at that time were under the impression the mountain was named Z2 (*see AAJ 2019*). We extend thanks to the AAC's Cutting Edge Grant and the Mount Everest Foundation for support. A detailed report is at the *AAJ* website.

—Chris Wright, *USA*

Anja Petek on the east ridge of Lalung I during the first known ascent of the peak. ***Patricija Verdev***

LALUNG I, EAST RIDGE, AND OTHER ROUTES

Our all-female expedition of Ana Baumgartner, Urša Kešar, Patricija Verdev, and I (all from Slovenia) headed southwest from near the Pensi La with 18 porters on August 26 to climb in the Lalung Valley.

We had thought that our base camp would be at around 5,000m, but we soon realized this was unrealistic. After just three hours of walking, we found an excellent site at 4,100m, with clean running water. We checked higher locations but found only dirty water and unsuitable terrain. Our main goal was Lalung I and neighboring peaks, and the low base camp would add an extra day to the approaches.

The day after our arrival, we explored higher up the valley. It took an entire day to make a 20km round trip on moraine and glacial terrain, and, as the weather was poor, we didn't see much of the higher peaks.

On August 31, Patricija and I climbed a new route on a granite north-northwest face not far from base camp. This buttress, which starts at around 4,200m, lies on the south side of the valley and rises to Peak 5,332m (*Google Earth altitude; 33°51'28.47"N, 76°16'35.45"E*). [*A route had been climbed previously near the center of this face, ending at around 4,800m on the northwest ridge, by Indians Korak Sanyal and Spandan Sanyal; see AAJ 2018.*] The new route Connection (VI-) took 15 hours and involved around 1,400m of climbing.

Before moving up to an advanced base camp at 4,800m, we had a nighttime visit from a bear that sniffed around our tents for food. All four climbers were happy to relocate to a bear-free advanced base. Urša had difficulties with the altitude, however, so she and Ana returned to base camp, where they and our cooks and liaison officer had to deal with a full-on bear saga. After more than ten nighttime visits, resulting in Patricija's tent being ripped, heaps of food stolen, and the toilet tent demolished, they managed to scare off the bears with fire and enjoyed a few peaceful nights.

During this period, Urša and Ana climbed two more new routes on the north-northwest face of Peak 5,332m, ascending the right side of the face and finishing on the northwest ridge. On their first route, Bear Camp (800m of climbing, V-, eight hours), climbed on September 10, the two were hit by a snowstorm near the top of the face, forcing a long traverse right to the ridge. The second route, Calm Before the Storm? (670m of climbing, V+, six hours), climbed on the 13th, followed the planned line directly to the ridge.

Meanwhile, on September 9, Patricija and I left advanced base for the east ridge of unclimbed Lalung I (6,243m, 33°45'35"N, 76°14'13"E), camping a little way above the start. We'd had a forecast for a good weather window, but a snowstorm on the 10th forced us to set up our tent in the middle of the day and sit out the weather. The storm lasted all the next day, but the 12th dawned clear and we climbed late into the night.

Day five on the ridge required even more determination, and it wasn't until 1:30 a.m. that we settled down for a rest, not far below the top, having climbed the final difficult mixed pitches. In a moment of carelessness brought on by fatigue, we lost our tent poles to the wind and slept in bivouac sacks. The next morning was foggy with diffuse light, making it hard to navigate the remaining terrain to the summit. After some snow slopes, we reached the top at 9 a.m. on the 14th.

We proceeded with a long descent down the west ridge and then five rappels on the north face to reach the glacier at 6:30 p.m. It took another eight hours to reach advanced base. Next day, we descended to base camp. Just before stepping off the moraine, we saw three silhouettes—Ana, Urša, and Freni, our liaison officer—who brought smiles to our tired faces. We named our route Here Comes the Sun (M6+ AI5+). It gave around 2,000m of climbing.

Although the bear situation had calmed, we agreed it was best for both us and the animals if we left as soon as possible. We walked out on the 17th to the village of Tungri.

—Anja Petek, *Slovenia*

TOP: Lalung I (6,243m) from the north. The peak was traversed from left to right, up the long east ridge and down the west ridge and north face. *Patricija Verdev*

BOTTOM: Patricija Verdev following a mixed section on the second day of the ascent of Lalung I's east ridge. *Anja Petek*

EDITOR'S NOTE: *A good map and description of this area were published in AAJ 2019. The only documented previous attempt on Lalung I was in October 2022 when Innes Dean, Tim Elson, and Alex Mathie (U.K.) inspected the north ridge from the Lalung Valley, finding the ridge composed of frozen soil and loose rock (AAJ 2023).*

Tess Smith on the south ridge of Starikatchan during the 2022 attempt, when the climbers got within about 100 meters of the summit. ***Alan Goldbetter***

STARIKATCHAN, WEST FACE AND SOUTH RIDGE

The last bit of light in the sky faded quickly as we arrived on the summit of Starikatchan (5,904m). The wind swirled around us, and for a moment we sat, shivering, taking it all in.

In 2019, Tess Smith (USA) and I began our obsession with Starikatchan (H7 on the Sakamoto sketch map, 33°30'45.81"N, 76°43'29.58"E), west of Padum in Zanskar. We made our first attempt from the east, turning back due to poor conditions and unstable weather. We returned in July 2022 and tried to complete our line on the east face, then attempted to climb the south ridge via a line on the west face. Both attempts brought us heartbreakingly close, but the summit eluded us (*AAJ 2023*).

On July 13, 2024, we left our modest base camp at 4,600m in the Shimling Tokpo and reached the bottom of the west face. Climbing an obvious gully and ridge system at 2nd and 3rd class, we reached a bivouac spot just below the col on the south ridge, where the technical climbing would begin. The following day we climbed 300m of moderate slabs before reaching the crest of the ridge, where we either traversed or avoided gendarmes and crossed much moderate rock and snow to reach a headwall. Here, we found a perfect 5.7 splitter basking in the sun. It led to the top of the wall, and three short pitches took us to the peak's highest point, atop a griffon's beak–like formation. Visible were twinkling lights from the Doda (Stod) Valley villages to the east, some 2,000m below our perch.

After a few rappels in the dark, we bivouacked below the headwall and the next day reversed our route to a final five-star luxury bivouac at the bottom of the west face, where we were treated to an incredible view of the Starikatchan skyline meeting the Milky Way above.

Our 800m route was V 5.7 A1 40°. We would like to give special thanks to Matic Jošt for his inspirational report about this area in *AAJ 2017*, and to our lovely hosts at Skitpo Travel, whom we have the privilege of calling friends.

—Alan Goldbetter, *Finland/USA*

RANGTIK TOKPO: VAJRAYOGINI, NORTHEAST FACE AND NORTHWEST RIDGE

Zanskar attracted me because I had never visited the area and it is filled with unclimbed peaks. Various climbers I asked could not go, so I posted a short note on the Russian social network VK. In the end, four people accompanied me:

Bayarsaikhan Luvsandorj, a Mongol; Maxim Perevalov, a Ukrainian; Mikhail Pupeiko, a Belarussian; and Denis Sushko, a Russian now living in Thailand. I had no idea how capable they would be.

I like mixed lines, so we planned to arrive in the Rangtik Tokpo in June, assuming this would be a good time for such ascents. After a short period of acclimatization, we split into two groups. Bayar, Mikhail, and I opted for Peak 6,095m (33°27'47.35"N, 76°42'13.47"E), in the southwest corner of the Rangtik Glacier, by a route of medium difficulty. On June 11, we climbed from bottom to top in seven hours along the northeast face and northwest ridge. The GPS read 6,218m on the summit, and across the glacier to the northeast, Remalaye (6,278m, H5 on the Sakamoto sketch map) appeared to be of similar altitude. We called the mountain Vajrayogini after an important figure of Tibetan Buddhism, and the locals did not object.

TOP: Vajrayogini and the route of the first ascent via the northeast face and northwest ridge. The mountain was previously known as Peak 6,095m, but GPS put the summit at 6,218 meters. Immediately right is unclimbed Peak 6,005m. *Lea Goldberger*

BOTTOM: The snow-terraced south face of Chakdor Ri (6,193m), climbed by the southeast ridge in 2017. *Yuri Koshelenko*

At the same time, Maxim and Denis attempted Peak 5,820m, which we dubbed Potala. They tried the west-northwest ridge from the col between Potala and Shawa Kangri but retreated early due to Denis feeling unwell; the food cooked at base camp by our staff was not suitable for any of our stomachs and we suffered.

I next wanted to try the first ascent of Chanrasrik Ri (a.k.a. Chareze Ri, 6,080m, H2 on the Sakamoto sketch map), between Vajrayogini and Shawa Kangri. It had been attempted in 2018 by Italian climbers, but they stopped short of the true summit. [*This peak was climbed later in 2024; see report below.*] On the 15th, we chose a mixed line of around ten pitches but had to retreat due to Denis's health. There was no time for another attempt. I was impressed with the area and hope to visit in the future.

—Yuri Koshelenko, *Russia*

Traversing along the sharp ridgeline toward the previously unclimbed main summit of Chanrasrik Ri (formerly known as Chareze Ri). ***Elias Hangweyrer***

RANGTIK TOKPO: CHANRASRIK RI, SPARK TRAVERSE, AND OTHER ASCENTS

From July 9 to August 15, our team of three ventured to Ladakh. After a three-day journey, we reached the small village of Tungri in the Zanskar Valley, where we were warmly welcomed. With the help of local porters, we ascended to a base camp at 4,925m and subsequently spent 28 nights above 4,900m.

After an acclimatization phase, on July 21 we repeated the route Rolling Stones (Pellissa-Ricart, 2008; *AAJ 2010*) on Shawa Kangri (5,728m) as a team of three.

On July 23–24, Hangweyrer and Goldberger climbed the southeast face (D+, Dušič-Jošt-Žerovnik; *AAJ 2018*) of Remalaye/H5 (6,278m). They then traversed west toward a previously unclimbed top, which was later named Maytsak Ri ("Spark Peak," 6,060m, 33°28'46"N, 76°43'18"E) after consulting with locals. After bivouacking at a col at nearly 6,000m between the two peaks, the duo reached Maytsak Ri on the second day of the traverse. From the top, they continued 300m to the west and descended through a couloir leading to the westernmost section of the Rangtik Glacier. The Spark Traverse was D, UIAA V 60° ice. [*Editor's Note: The team did not summit Remalaye West (6,266m; AAJ 2018), which sits along the ridge between Remalaye and Maytsak Ri.*]

Following a rest day in base camp, Schneider and Hangweyrer attempted the vertical to overhanging northeast face of Chanrasrik Ri (6,080m, 33°27'41"N, 76°43'17"E; this peak was formerly known as Chareze Ri; *see AAJ 2024*). After climbing an A3 pitch in a prominent crack, they realized their intended style was too light and retreated. Since it was still early in the day, they scoped out a chimney system 60m to the left for a potential subsequent attempt. After four pitches up to UIAA V+, they descended to base camp.

On July 28, with a 3:30 a.m. start from their tent at the base of Chanrasrik Ri, Schneider and Hangweyrer repeated the route Jullay Temù (1,000m, UIAA V+ 70° ice, Limongi-Martinelli-Mosetti-Secchi-Vallata, 2018; *AAJ 2020*) and continued to the main summit of Chanrasrik Ri, completing the first ascent of the mountain. The Italian team in 2018 had climbed the ridge bordering the left edge of the northeast face, then traversed the sharp ridgeline southward, crossing over a central top before running out of daylight and bailing down the northwest face. Schneider

and Hangweyrer were able to continue south past the central top to the previously unclimbed summit of Chanrasrik Ri. They rappelled the west face and reached base camp by 11 p.m. [*Editor's Note: The Italian team's report in AAJ 2020 refers to the central top as the north summit (5,959m) of Chanrasrik Ri. In fact, there are three prominent tops along this ridge, so we are referring to the 5,959m spire, summited in both 2018 and 2024, as the central top. Both parties bypassed the northernmost pinnacle on the ridge.*]

The northeast face of Chanrasrik Ri (a.k.a. Chareze Ri). (1) Jullay Temù (Limongi-Martinelli-Mosetti-Secchi-Vallata, 2018). (2) Namyang MeJet (Hangweyrer-Schneider, 2024). The main summit, reached in 2024 via Jullay Temù, is hidden. At right are Vajrayogini, climbed earlier in 2024, and unclimbed Peak 6,005m. *Elias Hangweyrer*

At the end of July, we made two attempts on the northwest side of Jamyang Ri (5,800m), climbing three new pitches as a variation to Cunka (Dušič-Jošt, 2017), but our efforts were halted by poor rock and bad weather. On August 3, all three of us repeated the route Treasure of Zanskar (750m, ED+, Dušič-Jošt-Žerovnik, 2017) on Chakdor Ri/H8 (6,193m).

With the northeast face of Chanrasrik Ri still in mind, Schneider and Hangweyrer made a second attempt, this time in big-wall style. On the first day, August 6, they carried gear to the base of the wall and climbed the previously ascended chimney system. After a portaledge bivy in an overnight snowstorm, they started again at 10 a.m., climbing five technical pitches and fixing ropes for the next day. After another night at the same portaledge camp, they ascended the fixed ropes and climbed three additional pitches to reach the ridge on the left side of the face (the same ridge climbed by Jullay Temù). Having only planned to go this far, they rappelled their route and returned to base camp. They named the route Namyang MeJet ("Never Forgotten," 400m, 11 pitches, UIAA VII A2 60° ice). They placed a single anchor bolt.

The expedition exceeded all of the team's expectations. We thank the Deutscher Alpenverein and Österreichischer Alpenverein for support.

—Lea Goldberger, Elias Hangweyrer, and David Schneider,
Austria and Germany

The south face of Skarma Mindruk Ri (T16, 6,431m), above the upper Khapang Glacier, and the final section of the 2024 route, as seen from Col 5,836m. ***Matic Jošt***

CHHOGO TOKPO: SKARMA MINDRUK RI, ANTIMATTERHORN, SPAO RI, AND IBEX PEAK

In recent years, the peaks of Zanskar have seen increasing popularity with mountaineering expeditions. Despite this, there are still plenty of unclimbed summits from 5,500m to 6,500m.

With our liaison officer and support staff, Uroš Cigljar, Tilen Cmok, Boštjan Dečman, Nejc Škrablin, Tomaž Žerovnik, and I arrived on July 7 at base camp (4,482m, 33°23.984'N, 76°46.558'E) in the Chhogo Tokpo (valley), the eastern branch of the Haptal Tokpo. While several parties had visited adjacent valleys and climbed a few peaks on the watershed ridges with the Chhogo, the only prior reported climbing expedition to visit the Chhogo valley was an Indian-Romanian team in 2016 that climbed one peak and attempted another (*AAJ 2017*).

A very complex 6,431m mountain known as T16 (as designated by Kimikazu Sakamoto, who numbered the prominent peaks in his topographical sketches of the area) was our main objective. The lower south summit was climbed by Romanians Cosmin Andron and Cristina Pogacean in 2016, but the easiest approach to the main top (33°23'12.13"N, 76°48'45.67"E) appeared to lie up the south slopes above the Khapang Glacier, east of the Chhogo valley. The big riddle was finding a suitable passage from the Chhogo to the Khapang, and we devoted part of our acclimatization to solving this problem.

Aiming for a col on the ridge south of T16, we hiked up a side glacier, passing the route climbed by the Romanians, and climbed a 300m west-facing gully (300m, D+ M3 60°) to reach the col (5,836m). From there, it would be easy to descend to the gentle Khapang Glacier and traverse to T16's north peak.

The whole team returned to the col camp on the 14th, and the next day, in perfect weather, we climbed south-facing slopes above the Khapang Glacier and along the east ridge to the summit of T16 (600m, D+ 60°). Our expedition had been organized by a club from the Slovenian town Šentjur, so we named our route

Šentjurka (900m, D+). We later encouraged people in the nearest village, Tungri, to suggest a name for the peak, and they came up with Skarma Mindruk Ri (Skarma is "star," and Mindruk is a specific star in the constellation of Pleiades). Maybe the name will catch on.

In 2015, a British team climbed in the adjacent Korlomshe Tokpo, which drains to the south and east of these mountains, and attempted a "Matterhorn-like peak." Tomaž was keen to investigate, so on the 20th we two set off, moving up the main Chhogo Glacier, then turning east up a side glacier. We climbed to a col at 5,620m to the south of the Matterhorn peak, descended around 200m on the far side, then moved northeast to camp on the upper Korlomshe Glacier at 5,615m, nine hours after leaving base camp.

The next day, we climbed the east face and finally the south slopes to reach the summit at 9:30 a.m. (6,130m, 33°20.987'N, 76°47.273'E). We named the route Charlatan De Balkan (500m, D+ 60° ice) after an album by a popular Slovenian group. As the peak was absolutely nothing like the famous Swiss mountain, we named it Antimatterhorn.

In the meantime, Tilen and Uroš attempted the 400m west face of unclimbed Peak 5,435m, close to base camp at the end of the long west ridge coming from the south summit of Skarma Mindruk Ri (T16). After they had climbed around 250m (up to VI), Uroš was making a belay anchor when a large flake broke, injuring his right hand. The pair descended, and then, with other team members, went down to Padam for medical attention. Separately, Boštjan made the first ascent of a rock tower east of base camp, which he called Ibex Peak (5,321m). He climbed a straightforward 30° snow gully on the north flank.

By July 24, most of the team had left base camp. Although I've been climbing around 45 years, I don't have much experience with soloing, but I decided to try the north face of T9 (6,107m, 33°20'6.63"N, 76°47'5.93"E), which I had seen from the

TOP: Boštjan Dečman and Nejc Škrablin on the upper Khapang Glacier. (A) Unclimbed T11 (6,177m). (B) The ridge leading to unclimbed T13 (6,436m). (C) Col 5,836m, crossed to reach the glacier and Skarma Mindruk Ri (T16) from the Chhogo Tokpo. *Matic Jošt*

BOTTOM: Old and Abandoned on the north face of Spao Ri (T9, 6,107m). *Matic Jošt*

Antimatterhorn approach. I left base camp at 1 a.m. on the 25th, carrying two axes but no rope. The north face became icier and brittle the higher I climbed, but at 8:30 a.m. I reached the west ridge. The upper section of this ridge was rockier, but in one hour I was standing on the summit.

Deciding I didn't feel comfortable downclimbing the north face, I headed down a couloir on the southwest face to a neighboring glacier. Although I couldn't see all the way, it looked passable. Everything went well, and I was back in base camp by 3 p.m. Only Tilen and our cook were there to greet me, and all three of us descended to the village that night.

The locals suggested the name Spao Ri for the peak. It means "Brave Mountain."

I named the route Old and Abandoned (700m, TD II–III 75° ice). Why? Because I'm not young anymore.

The expedition is grateful to the Alpine Association of Slovenia for financial support. [*General notes on climbing in Zanskar, along with an extensive report on the 2024 expedition, with many additional photos, can be found at the AAJ website.*]

—Matic Jošt, *Slovenia*

The east face of Shingo South and the 2024 route. ***Subhajit Banerjee***

HIMACHAL PRADESH | Lahaul

SHINGO SOUTH, EAST FACE AND SOUTH-SOUTHEAST RIDGE

The Shingo La (5,090m) is a high pass on an old trekking route from Lahaul to Zanskar. More recently, the route has been converted to a motorable road. Close to the pass lie three peaks, often unofficially called Shingo East, West, and South. All are a little over 6,000m and have received multiple ascents. The first documented ascent of Shingo South was in 2002, probably by the northeast ridge. In 2015, Bill McConachie, from an Anglo-American expedition, climbed the southwest face and south ridge (*AAJ 2016*).

Our team planned a new route on this peak, and on September 4 we set up base camp near the Shingo La at 5,010m. After some acclimatization, we cached gear at 5,327m on the 7th and occupied Camp 1 there on the night of the 9th.

The next day, we climbed a rocky gully and broken terrain on the east face to reach the upper south-southeast ridge, fixing a total of 700m of rope. Heavy snowfall stopped movement on the 11th, but the next day, using the ropes, we moved up and camped at 5,856m. With scarce snow and water, we had to ration our water supply.

On the morning of September 13, we climbed 45°–60° snow and rock slopes on the south-southeast ridge to reach the rocky summit, arriving at 12:30 p.m. The mountain has two tops, and we found the higher to be 6,068m GPS (32°53'16.45"N, 77°8'43.25"E); a team climbing the northeast ridge will first reach a false summit of around 6,010m. We named the route Nirjala, a Sanskrit term meaning "waterless." We think it should be graded around AD.

The full summit team was Prakruti Alagudekar, Joy Das, Avantika Kekan, Sabyasachi Samanta, Subhendu Sikder, Tem Tapung, Shubham Thapliyal, our high-altitude porters Chandrapal Danu and Narendra Singh Danu, and me.

—Subhajit Banerjee, *India*

CHANDRA BHAGA RANGE, CB26, NORTHWEST FACE

Seven years ago, Michal Sabovčík and I started a project where we aimed to ascend a previously unclimbed mountain or route on each continent and then descend by paraglider. We did this in Antarctica in 2018 (*AAJ 2019*) and in Greenland in 2019. Although we then went our separate ways, the desire to finish the project continued. I tried in India, Pakistan, and Nepal, yet somehow the mountains always defeated me.

I returned to India alone in October 2024 and first focused on acclimatization, which, with a wing, can be rather less energy-intensive. It's great to sleep at altitude and in the morning glide down to the valley in ten minutes, instead of many hours of hiking

Paraglider view of the northwest face of CB26's south summit. Juraj Koreň flew to the mountain by paraglider, climbed the obvious snow and ice line on the left to the top, flew down to the glacier for a night in his tent, and then flew back out of the mountains. *Juraj Koreň*

downhill with painful knees.

Hungry for adventure, I packed light gear and flew around 40km to the northwest of Manali, heading first for a 5,300m summit at 32.3230°N, 77.06311°E, around 2.5km southeast of Hanuman Tibba (5,928m). I landed to the north at around 5,000m, left my tent, went up the north face of this peak, and skied down. After a night in the tent, I flew down to 3,800m for a rest.

On October 31, I set off flying 25km toward a preplanned goal, but from a distance I could see the face I wanted to climb was too dry and the peak too sharp for a takeoff from the top. I decided instead to aim for a summit at 32.3914°N, 77.44086°E and landed on the glacier to its southwest at 5,000m. [*This peak is CB26, or more explicitly the southern and highest top of CB26; that label is applied on some maps to the lower peak to the north. The peaks sandwiched between the Chandra and Bhaga rivers, south of Mulkila, are mostly referred to by numbers. The general feeling is that most or all of these have been climbed; however, there appears to be no recorded ascent of CB26.*]

I set off on foot for the northwest face, carrying the paraglider, a harness, a down jumpsuit, a stove, a liter of water, and skis. The face is about 600m, starting at 50° and rising to 70° before it reaches the northeast ridge. Ideal conditions took me to the top at 5,880m in late afternoon. After a short moment of joy, I started my descent. At high altitudes, the thin air increases the minimum takeoff speed, and it is difficult to run in deep snow—that's why I brought the skis. After a freezing night in the tent, I skied down the glacier until I found a suitable launch site. I was soon in the warmth of the valley.

I named the route In Honorum Alexandri (600m, WI3 70°). Mountaineers could say the peaks I climbed were too small, paragliding pilots could say I only flew a little, and skiers could say, well...it really doesn't matter. I achieved my goal of making a solo first ascent on this continent, and in addition I carried everything to the mountain with me. Not expedition style, not alpine style, but paragliding-alpine style. *Per ardua ad astra*!

—Juraj Koreň, *Slovakia*

UTTARAKHAND | Eastern Garhwal

The southeast side of Sundardhunga Khal (Sundardhunga Col), showing the 2024 ascent route and camps. On the right is Panwali Dwar (6,663m). ***Abhishek Das***

SUNDARDHUNGA KHAL: A FAMOUS PASS REACHED FROM THE SOUTH

Access to Nanda Devi's Inner Sanctuary has captivated mountaineers for more than a century. On the southern rim, Sundardhunga Khal (Sundardhunga Col, 5,520m, 30°17'10.7"N, 79°54'45.8"E) is the lowest point between Maiktoli (6,803m) and Panwali Dwar (6,663m), with the South (Dakshini) Rishi Glacier to the north and Sundardhunga (Maiktoli) Valley to the south. In 1932, the British Everester Hugh Ruttledge and Emile Rey, one of the foremost Italian guides of the time, inspected the south side of the col but were appalled by the formidable rock and ice wall of nearly 1,800m and retreated.

In September 1934, soon after their historic forcing of the Rishi Gorge to reach the Inner Sanctuary for the first time, Eric Shipton, Bill Tilman, Kusang Sherpa, Pasang Sherpa, and Ang Tharkay climbed glaciated slopes to Sundardhunga Khal and over two days descended the icefall and difficult ground on the south side to make the only crossing of the col to date. The problem of an ascent from the south remained.

In the 1980s, at least two attempts were made by mountaineers from West Bengal, then in June 2015 it was attempted again by Anindya Mukherjee, George Rodway, and Phurtenji (Lakpa) Sherpa. The Shipton-Tilman descent route looked unreasonable due to hanging seracs, so they tried a safer line farther to the right, then retreated at around 4,600m due to bad snow conditions. They planned to come back another year in October-November, when conditions would be better and the weather more stable.

The opportunity did not arise until 2022, when, toward the end of September, Lakpa and Mukherjee returned. By October 3, they had made Camp 1 on the face at 4,160m and identified a spot for Camp 2 at 4,580m.

Leaving early from Camp 1 on the 4th, they passed the Camp 2 site, below the first icefall, after two hours. Above, they crossed an avalanche-swept gully and mixed ground interspersed with rock bands sporting big, chunky holds. They reached a little rock ramp at 5,000m, and the way ahead looked more straightforward; they estimated another 1.5 hours to the col. However, they felt it safer to descend to Camp 2 and come back the following day to finish the job. Unfortunately, during that night and the next day, serac fall bombarded their climbing line. They decided not to push their luck and headed down.

On October 27, 2024, another Indian party, Abhishek Das and Thendup Sherpa, reached Maiktoli Base Camp at 3,908m, then made extensive reconnaissance and chose a line to the right of the 2022 attempt.

They navigated steep slopes of treacherous grass to place Camp 1 at 4,231m and stayed there the nights of the 29th and 30th while scouting the route ahead on more steep grass and loose rock. On the 30th, they placed Camp 2 at 4,917m and occupied it briefly the next day before setting out for the top at 2 a.m. on November 1. Climbing rock and crisp snow, they reached a ridge to the left (west) of the saddle at 11 a.m. and descended this to a col at 11:30 a.m. Glaciated slopes descended north from here into the Sanctuary. Their GPS showed an altitude of 5,653m. A direct ascent to this col would have been extremely dangerous due to rockfall and avalanche exposure.

About 200m to the west, Abhishek Das saw another col, which, based on his observations and Tilman's descriptions, he believes is the point where Shipton and Tilman's team crossed to the south. [*If one defines the likely 1934 crossing point as the true Sundardhunga Khal, then it would be the more westerly and lower depression. It is not possible to say with certainty, but it appears the 2022 attempt on the south wall was likely near the Shipton-Tilman descent route, while the 2024 ascent was farther to the right (east).*] As the two were running low on food at the high camps, they elected to descend directly to base camp, arriving at 11 p.m. the same day. An intense 21-hour effort had closed a long chapter in the storied history of this mysterious region.

—Anindya Mukherjee and Abhishek Das, *India*

TOP: The view north from Sundardhunga Khal into the Inner Sanctuary and to Nanda Devi. *Abhishek Das*

BOTTOM: The west face of Shipnoor, as seen from the long traverse to access the route. *Giripremi Club*

MAHARASHTRA | Sahyadri Range

SHIPNOOR, WEST FACE

The large, basalt west face of Shipnoor (a.k.a. Shipnur), near Ghatghar village in the Ahmednagar district, had never been climbed until January 2025. On their second attempt, members of the Giripremi climbing club reached the central west face by a long, exposed traverse, then climbed the face over several days, using fixed ropes and many bolts (470m, 6b+). Details are at the *AAJ* website.

—Information from Samiran Kolhe, *India*

NEPAL | Chandi Himal

Close to the summit of Angsi Dong Dong, looking southeast along the rim of the Angsi Glacier basin, which is in shadow behind the climber. Just to the right of the climber is Peak 6,013m, climbed by the left skyline ridge in 2024. The big peak in the distance, catching the sun, is Changla (6,563m), climbed by a Japanese expedition in 2010. ***Diogo Santos***

ANGSI GLACIER BASIN, FOUR FIRST ASCENTS

The Angsi Glacier basin lies in the northeastern part of the Chandi Himal on the border with Tibet. It was first reached by a British expedition in 2019, then again in 2023 by more British climbers, who made the first ascent of Ganglung Kangri II (*AAJ 2024*). Although the basin could be accessed quickly from the Tibetan side, this is politically impossible at present and a long trek in West Nepal is needed to reach it from the south.

After a flight to Simikot, Florian Büchting, Bas Mulder, Diogo Santos, and I trekked up the Chuwa Khola for six days to a base camp at 5,050m (30.321393°N, 82.087713°E), east of the Angsi Glacier, arriving on September 30. We knew from the 2023 trip report that there was an easy passage to the Angsi Glacier basin over the col between Peaks 5,936m and 6,254m. We also think it might be possible to access the basin directly from the lower valley farther to the west, but we did not explore this.

We established a camp in the basin, then on October 7 made the first ascent of Peak 6,013m (30°19'20.46"N, 82°2'13.53"E). It proved to be good acclimatization for the team, and we reached the top relatively easily (AD-) via the north ridge. Both the cold and altitude posed problems, giving us a good sense of the climbing conditions we should expect.

Back at our camp in the basin, we found that one of the tents had been flipped upside down by the wind. Two sleeping pads were lost, and one tent pole had broken. Bas and I decided to return to base camp, but Florian and Diogo stayed, and the next day made the first ascent of Ganglung Kangri I (6,256m, 30°20'33.43"N, 82°0'42.25"E) by the south ridge (AD). The granite on the lower ridge was high quality, but in the upper section it became loose and brittle. From the summit they traversed east to Ganglung

Kangri II (6,182m), completing the second ascent, and descended by the British route to the south.

After returning to the basin with a repaired tent, on the 12th, Bas and I climbed the north face of Peak 6,119m. It proved challenging due to powder snow and a general lack of ice, making good protection scarce. It was also bitterly cold, despite little wind. We descended the face by rappelling and downclimbing, naming our route Frostbound (D+). Bas suffered frostbite on one of his pinky fingers, and after a large blister formed, we decided to evacuate him by helicopter to Pokhara. There, it was confirmed he wouldn't lose the finger; he was moved to Kathmandu for further treatment.

On the 13th, Diogo and Florian climbed Angsi Dong Dong (6,171m) via the southeast ridge (AD+) and then traversed the mountain by descending the north ridge. They accessed the southeast ridge by a beautiful northeast-facing couloir and reached the summit at sunset. On the 15th, using the existing tracks on Angsi Dong Dong and Ganglung Kangri, I made a solo traverse of the two, following the frontier ridge and finishing with an ascent of Ganglung Kangri II. During this AD+ traverse, I had great views of Kailash and the steep north face of Ganglung Kangri I.

For our final climb, Florian and I attempted the attractive northwest side of Peak 6,222m (30°16'20.60"N, 82°6'58.55"E), a border peak south-southeast of base camp in the Changla Himal. Unfortunately, Florian contracted a sinus infection, and after an uncomfortable night beneath the face, he decided to go back. I continued alone but was stopped by a challenging bergschrund.

The next day, we began our return journey to Simikot. The weather during our stay had been generally good, with only two days of precipitation; the main difficulty had been the wind, which on some days reached 70 kph at 6,000m.

—Alexander Sternfeld,
The Netherlands

Frostbound on the north face of Peak 6,119m.
Alexander Sternfeld

NEW PEAKS OPENED IN 2024

In October, as part of a tourist development plan, the Nepal government announced it was opening 57 additional mountains for climbing expeditions. These range in altitude from just below 5,900m to a little over 6,800m.

The list includes many little-known peaks in West Nepal, Dolpo, and Mustang, which will be of great interest to exploratory mountaineers. There are also many subsidiary tops to climbed mountains: e.g., Chombu North (6,822m), a border peak a short distance north of the main summit of Chombu.

The peak list will need careful scrutiny by those aspiring to first ascents, as some already have been climbed, such as Pangbuk North (6,478m) in the Rolwaling and Nupchu (6,044m) in the Janak Himal.

Some peaks are confusingly named. Rongshar Ri II (6,492m) is more commonly known as Lunag West, while Pathibhara Northeast (6,857m) has always been referred to as Langpo South (and has been ascended twice). It is not to be confused with the 7,090m top close to the summit of Pathibhara (a.k.a. Pyramid Peak), which has for many decades been known as Pathibhara Northeast.

Download the list of 57 newly opened peaks at the *AAJ* website.

—Lindsay Griffin, *AAJ*

The northwest ridge of Patrasi II and traverse to Patrasi (P), seen during the descent from Tang Tang Pass into the Changda Valley. To the right, with its summit in cloud, is Kande Hiunchuli. ***Pasang Rinzee Sherpa***

PATRASI I, FIRST ASCENT, VIA NORTHWEST RIDGE OF PATRASI II

In the premonsoon season, Nepali guides Vinayak Jaya Malla, Pasang Kami Sherpa, and Pasang Rinzee Sherpa worked commercial expeditions to 8,000m peaks. After returning to Kathmandu, they enjoyed only a few days of rest at home before heading to Jumla in West Nepal, arriving on June 4. They were perfectly acclimatized for the adventure ahead: the first ascent of the highest summit of the Patrasi group, situated on the western rim of the Kanjiroba Sanctuary.

Aware that locals in this area would be heading to the highlands to collect yarsagumba (caterpillar fungus) for traditional Chinese and Tibetan medicine, and therefore porters would be hard to find, the three climbers brought four support members from Kathmandu. Neither the climbers nor support staff had previously trekked or climbed in the area.

Along with a local guide and three porters, the team drove to Pere (2,700m) on June 5, then walked four hard days via the Chaudhabise Valley to a base camp at 5,050m below the west side of the Patrasi group. Day three involved crossing Tang Tang Pass (4,950m, approximately 29°26'21.15"N, 82°30'22.44"E) and descending to an overnight camp at 4,100m in the Changda Valley, where they met an encampment of yarsagumba collectors.

At 8 a.m. on the 10th, they began their ascent of Patrasi. They first climbed a 200m snow couloir to reach the northwest ridge of Patrasi II (6,471m, 29°25'18.04"N, 82°35'5.70"E). After climbing 11 belayed pitches with rock to French 5a, and simul-climbing other sections, they reached 5,700m, where they were able to fashion a partial tent site. For safety, they slept that night in their harnesses.

The following morning, they left at 5 a.m. After another 11 pitches (up to M4) and a little simul-climbing, they arrived at 6,000m, where they decided to pitch their second camp at around 4 p.m. The climbing had been quite challenging in cold and windy conditions with intermittent snow showers. The rock was poor, and there were many places where protection points were 10m to 15m apart.

At 4 a.m. on June 12, the three set out for a long summit push. Following the corniced ridge, then crossing a section of hard blue WI3, they reached the top of Patrasi II, descended a little to a snow slope, then headed up onto the left

Steep ground on day two of the first ascent of Patrasi I. ***Pasang Rinzee Sherpa***

flank of the northeast ridge of Patrasi I (6,521m, 29°25'02.7"N, 82°34'59.6"E). They reached this summit at 4:35 p.m. in cloudy weather.

The descent was long and tiring, with muscles cramping toward the end of the day. Downclimbing and 15 long rappels (they climbed on 70m ropes) took them to the 6,000m camp. It was 9:30 p.m., and they didn't bother to cook, instead falling asleep very quickly.

On the 13th, it took the trio almost 11 hours to descend all the way to base camp. By the 17th, they were back in Jumla. All equipment and nondegradable waste was packed out, and they left only five snow stakes, ten pitons, and some cord on the mountain.

Commenting on the trip, Pasang Kami Sherpa said, "This expedition added an interesting chapter to my mountaineering journey. It was in stark contrast to my experience on 8,000m peaks, where fixed rope, oxygen, well-stocked camps, and support systems are the norm. Here, we were on our own, a small team carrying only essential things, making our own decisions, and adapting to whatever the mountain presented us."

For his part, Vinayak Jaya Malla said, "Let me tell you, for passionate mountaineers there's nothing quite like the pure joy of alpine climbing in one of Nepal's most remote areas. Far from human settlements and with no communication networks, one must be well prepared. Alpine-style climbing is a whole different game."

The team expressed gratitude to the Mount Everest Foundation for financial support.

—Lindsay Griffin, *with information from Vinayak Jaya Malla, Nepal*

NOTES ON THE PATRASI GROUP: *Three tops rise around a small, sloping glacier basin above 6,200m along the ridge to the northeast of Kande Hiunchuli (6,627m). Two are unnamed on maps, but the most easterly and lowest is referred to as Patrasi (Patrali on the HMG-Finn map). In AAJ 2015, it was suggested the other two be called Kande Hiunchuli Northeast I and II, but since that time a more logical alternative has been adopted, and all three peaks are now included in the Patrasi group: Patrasi I (or Main, 6,521m), Patrasi II (or Northeast, 6,471m), and Patrasi III (or East, 6,450m). Patrasi II was climbed in 1980, using 1,200m of fixed rope and two camps, by a Swiss team on the northwest ridge. Subsequently, three British expeditions failed on Patrasi II, as did the Anglo-Russian expedition reported in AAJ 2015.*

Sanctuary Peak (6,207m), in right center, from the southwest. The first ascent route climbed the glacier and finished up the left skyline ridge (west ridge). ***Yasuhiro Hanatani***

SANCTUARY PEAK, FIRST ASCENT, VIA WEST RIDGE

In 1996, a joint Shinshu University and Nepal Police expedition made the first ascent of Ratna Chuli (7,035m; *see AAJ 1997*). I was one of the team that reached the summit, gaining invaluable experience for my Himalayan career, all thanks to support from the university alpine club and its senior members. Due to the recent weakening of traditional mountaineering organizations, opportunities to take part in a similar "first Himalayan expedition" have become increasingly scarce. A new platform was needed, so I established the Himalaya Camp project, which gives climbers in their 20s and 30s the opportunity to attempt unclimbed peaks. I launched the first camp in 2015.

For the Himalaya Camp in the fall of 2024, Yo Hasigawa, Ai Hatakeyama, Yudai Hiratsuka, and Ayumi Matsumoto researched a number of unclimbed mountains and chose Sanctuary Peak (6,207m, 29°25'27.11"N, 82°37'25.89"E) in the Kanjiroba Sanctuary, the basins surrounding Kanjiroba (6,883m) at the head of the Jagdula Khola.

In his 2012 *AAJ* report, Paulo Grobel noted that "a small unnamed 6,207m peak, at the northeastern head of the glacial cirque between Kanjiroba and the Patrasi group, offered an elegant goal that we could accomplish in alpine style." Grobel's team did not attempt Peak 6,207m but did climb a 6,025m peak south of the Japanese Pass (5,831m) on the western rim of the sanctuary, which he named Sanctuary Peak. However, the true Sanctuary Peak, as listed on the Ministry of Tourism's permit list, is Peak 6,207m.

The four team members and I left Kathmandu on October 1 and arrived in Gauchaur (3,700m), where we would begin our trek, on the 7th. Our initial plan was to follow a trekking route shown on maps to Kanjiroba Base Camp. However, a local porter, who knew the area well, said it was too dangerous and that we should travel by the Jagdula Khola, the route used by earlier explorers of the Kanjiroba range (who had also found significant difficulties).

The second day of this trek was nerve-wracking. At one point, to descend a sheer slope to the valley floor, we installed five fixed ropes, and there were very worrying sections for our porters. The following day proved even more intense. A makeshift bridge of birch logs crossed the narrowest part of the gorge, and beyond that, more birch logs, leaning against a rock wall, provided the most terrifying ladder we had ever encountered. The lead porter negotiated all this while carrying a 30kg load. In the Himalaya one sometimes meets individuals who redefine the limits of human capability.

We were happy to reach Kanjiroba Base Camp (4,600m), south of the mountain, on the 13th. This area has been called Airport Plain, and the expansive flatland above the gorge could easily be used by a North American bush pilot.

On our first reconnaissance, we identified a route to Sanctuary Peak. A forecast of snowfall starting on the 20th caused us to accelerate our program and make a continuous ascent from base camp starting on the 17th. That day, we camped at an ideal spot on the moraine at 5,200m.

The next day, we chose a line up the right side of the glacier and navigated a route through crevasses to 5,500m before returning to camp. On the 19th, we left at 3:30 a.m. in perfect weather. We made steady progress, reaching the west ridge of Sanctuary Peak at around 6,000m.

Above lay a quintessential Himalayan challenge: traversing an arête of sugar snow with insecure snow-stake protection. This was the first such experience for some of the team, and progress was slow. I had not planned to take the lead on the climb, but I worried we might be too slow to summit. I took over, climbing quickly and carefully. At 12:30 p.m., after six pitches, we reached the top, or as near as safely possible due to large cornices. We cautiously descended the route as clouds gathered, and when we regained camp it was snowing.

It was deeply gratifying for the entire team to reach the summit together, a first in some time for our Himalaya Camp expeditions. Exploring West Nepal was inspiring, and the more I research the area, the more fascinating it becomes. I'm eager to go back.

—Yasuhiro Hanatani, *Japan*

NEPAL | Damodar Himal

KHUMJUNGAR, FIRST ASCENT, VIA SOUTH-SOUTHWEST FACE

The first ascent of Khumjungar (a.k.a. Khamjung, 6,750m, 28°53'19.65"N, 84°7'37.07"E) was undertaken by the "Project Together" team of Pur Bahadur Gurung and me, in December 2023. The expedition began in Kathmandu on the 15th.

On the upper glacier below Khumjungar. The route continued up the glacier to the low point in the photo, then ascended the steep south-southwest face, hidden behind the rock and ice buttress. *Prakash Gurung*

After a rugged jeep ride from Jomsom, we reached Tange village at 3,359m, then took four days to trek the Tange Khola valley to a camp at 4,800m, at the base of the glacier that flows northwest from the south side of Khumjungar. We established a high camp on the glacier at 6,060m, not far from the northwest base of the mountain. The overnight temperature here dropped to -20°C.

On December 21, we left at 4:30 a.m. and climbed the glacier, curving left to reach the bottom of the south-southwest face. This face had steep ice and crevasses, which required screw and snow-stake protection and belays. After only 4.5 hours and some precarious climbing along ridges, we reached the summit, where we were rewarded by fine views of four 8,000m peaks: Annapurna, Dhaulagiri, Manaslu, and Xixabangma (Shisha Pangma). We descended the same way and were back in Kathmandu on the 24th.

Employing pure alpine style during the winter season, the "Project Together" team set a benchmark for minimalist mountaineering and aimed to inspire more Nepali mountaineers to explore uncharted peaks. In the coming years,

Project Together will continue to focus on exploration and promoting zero waste in the mountains.

—Prakash Gurung, *Nepal*

HISTORICAL NOTES ON KHUMJUNGAR: *Despite half a dozen attempts and near misses, no team had stood on this summit until this ascent in December 2023. Khumjungar was reconnoitered by American climbers in 2007 and was attempted via the northwest ridge (to 6,195m) by a French team in 2011, by an unspecified route to 6,200m by Japanese in 2016, via the north face by another French team in 2017 (when Nima Sherpa is reported to have reached 6,600m), and via a line that was probably on the south-southwest face in the fall of 2023, by Americans who were turned back by bad weather on the summit ridge at 6,700m.*

NEPAL | Annapurna Himal

NILGIRI NORTH, WEST FACE AND WEST RIDGE, ATTEMPT

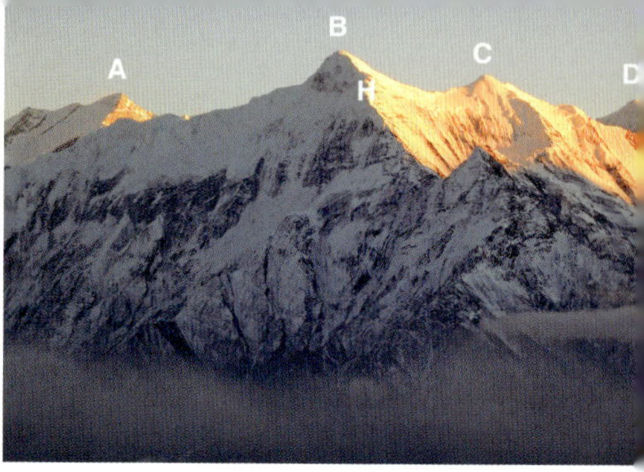

Evening sun on the Nilgiri massif. (A) Annapurna I. (B) Nilgiri North (the mountain's main top, 7,061m). (C) Nilgiri Central (6,940m). (D) Nilgiri South (6,839m). The west ridge of Nilgiri North divides sun and shadow, with the somber north face, partially climbed during the first ascent of the mountain, to the left. The 2024 attempt reached the west ridge from the opposite side and continued up the crest to a high point (H) at about 6,600 meters. *Damien Gildea*

In the fall of 2018, Tatsuya Aoki and I attempted the north face of Nilgiri North (7,061m, 28°41'21.22"N, 83°44'38.96"E), the highest of the Nilgiri peaks, retreating from 5,900m. We followed the original 1962 route up the rocky spur on the right side of the face to around 5,600m, then traversed left across a large hanging glacier until directly below the summit. This traverse was badly threatened by serac fall. We started up the face above, but the steepness, difficulty, and lack of reliable protection turned us back.

We returned in the fall of 2024, this time to attempt the west face, which, as far as we are aware, had never been attempted or even approached. First, we had to follow a valley from the Kali Gandaki to reach a 5,400m plateau below the face. No photos showed the valley floor, so we were unsure whether this was practical, and we wouldn't know if the face itself was possible until we were directly underneath it.

On October 1, we reached a yak-grazing pasture at 4,000m and established our base camp. For further acclimatization, we decided to climb to the 5,400m plateau. However, we were dismayed to find the way blocked by a steep rock wall capped by a serac barrier. Eventually we discovered a sheltered crack line on the right side and climbed this to where we could finally see the west face, which looked technically difficult and also full of avalanche runnels. We therefore decided instead to climb up left to a col on the west ridge at 5,900m and follow the ridge crest from there.

We began our attempt from base camp on the 9th, camping for the first night at 5,000m. We expected the route to the col to be straightforward, but we had to overcome much brittle rock. As we neared the ridge, the winds intensified, and we cut out a tent platform that was only just sheltered from the force.

The following day, the 11th, we climbed the crest to 6,200m, around the same height as the 1962 route reaches the ridge from the north face. We finished the difficult climbing the next day and arrived at 6,600m, having battled strong wind the whole time. In this section, we found one old piton about 25cm in length [*most likely placed in 1962 by Lionel Terray—see below*]. Around 400m of snow climbing remained, but Tatsuya was now suffering badly from the altitude, and we had to go down.

Although I am not satisfied with the result, we had a good climb on a facet of the mountain where there was no previous information. Someday, climbers will reach the top via the west face. It would be great if it was us.

—Takuya Mitoro, *Japan*

NOTES ON THE NILGIRI PEAKS: *The Nilgiri massif, north of Annapurna, comprises four tops, all of which have been climbed, but none more than a handful of times. The first ascent of Nilgiri North, the highest peak, took place in October 1962 when French alpinist and guide Lionel Terray led a small Dutch team (the first from this country to the Himalaya) up a difficult route on the north face (70° on ice flutes) to reach the west ridge between 6,200m and 6,300m. Terray, brothers Holger, Paul, and Peter van Lookeren Campagne, and Wangdi Sherpa reached the top. Their route is unrepeated.*

The unclimbed northwest face of Kajin Sara (5,772m). ***Paulo Grobel***

KAJIN SARA, EXPLORATION

The Kajin Sara is a small group of peaks to the south of Kajin Sara Lake, forming a ridge extending east from Lamjung Himal (6,983m), southeast of Annapurna II. The lake and peaks were "discovered" in 2019 by a Japanese group, and the three-day trek to the lake from Chame on the Annapurna Circuit is now promoted by local agencies.

In 2022, after an attempt on Lamjung Himal, the French guide Paulo Grobel and his team took a look at the Kajin Sara. He returned in 2024 with the aim of exploring the peaks' potential for technical training of Nepalese guides, and for small, discreet teams of Western mountaineers. (Most of these peaks are below 5,800m and can be visited simply by respecting trekking permit regulations.) Grobel's party climbed several summits of the Kajin Sara, but he has not documented any routes, in order to leave this compact area with a somewhat exploratory dimension.

Karma Himal from the west. The Devil's Ridge and Dema Hat are to the left. ***Paulo Grobel***

Kajin Sara Lake (named by the Japanese), at a little over 5,000m, is one of the highest in Nepal. The last couple of hours to the lake may be too rocky or snow-covered for mules, so in the fall of 2024, Grobel's party established base camp at 4,700m, where there is a hut.

A high camp, which the team used throughout most of their stay, was placed in a moraine valley to the east of the lake and just below the glacier coming down from a 5,772m peak they named Kajin Sara (28°28'55.16"N, 84°15'29.74"E). Farther west, on the long ridge extending from Lamjung Himal, is the highest summit of the group, named Chame (6,003m, 28°28'50.56"N, 84°13'36.88"E). To its west lies Lamjung Spitze (5,944m); the ridge then drops to Lamjung Pass (5,378m) in front of Lamjung Himal.

In front of Kajin Sara is the smaller summit of Chautari, which can be climbed en route to Kajin Sara via the northeast or west-northwest ridge. The west ridge of Kajin Sara continues to a summit of around 5,600m that is characterized by an elegant northeast snow arête, dubbed Cyrielle Ridge. The party was unable to discover a way to access this crest.

Farther west along the main watershed ridge lies Samaya Himal (ca 5,660m), with an elegant north ridge and an impressive, rocky east-northeast arête. Between this and Chame is the rocky Chame East (5,968m) with an impressive eastern aspect.

Northeast of the lake is Myabase Dada, a rocky summit of 5,422m. On the ridge running south from this to Kajin Sara are several rocky tops, useful for acclimatization. Kumari Peak has a snow ridge ending with a short rocky passage (PD-); farther south is the rock spire of Karma Himal.

At the southeastern end of the Kajin Sara chain lies the somewhat mysterious Toni Hagen Trail, its whereabouts at this point unknown. Nearby is a beautiful little snow summit marked as Namun Bhanjyang (5,496m) on some maps. (This is inappropriate nomenclature, as *bhanyang* means "pass.") There is no local name for this peak, and the team proposed naming it after Toni Hagen, the Swiss geologist who made a huge contribution to the exploration of Nepal. [*More photos and a satellite map of this area are at the AAJ website.*]

—Lindsay Griffin, ***with information from Paulo Grobel, France***

NEPAL | Peri Himal

PHUNGI, FIRST ASCENT, VIA WEST SPUR AND SOUTH-SOUTHWEST RIDGE

In post-monsoon 2022, three young Japanese climbers—Goto Kisuke, Adachi Masaki, and Kagami Taichi—attempted the west spur and south-southwest ridge of Phungi (28°49'48.29"N, 84°24'0.12"E), an unclimbed 6,524m peak southeast of Ratna Chuli, on the border with Tibet. The three Japanese retreated at around 6,150m in deep snow. [*This peak was opened for climbing in 2014 and should not be confused with Phungi Himal (6,538m), which lies east of Manaslu and was climbed in 2017; see AAJ 2018.*]

In the fall of 2024, our team of young Japanese university alpinists—Taiyo Ashizawa, Takuma Inoue, Masahiro Nakazawa, Ryoya Odaka, and I—completed

On the final section of the south-southwest ridge of Phungi (6,524m). The summit is behind the rocky tower. ***Fumiya Yokomichi***

the first ascent of Phungi by the same route that was attempted two years earlier.

For many on the team, this was the first visit to the Himalaya. We acclimatized gradually, reaching our 4,700m base camp on September 21, via the Phu Khola. We were initially pinned down by heavy snowfall but subsequently established Camp 1 at 5,000m and Camp 2 on the west spur at 5,500m. On October 3, we felt ready to make a summit attempt.

We were full of anticipation, but the mountain seemed intent on testing us, presenting one obstacle after another. The rock on the west spur up to 5,800m was brittle, seeming to require every ounce of our skill, courage, and luck. We overcame a snow face to reach what we thought would be the south summit, but instead we were faced with a vast field of crevasses.

After camping for the night, we set off for the top. At around 6,200m, we came upon a seven-meter knife-edge of ice, followed by a 15m drop that would require a rappel. As we'd left our fixing rope behind, retreat seemed the most sensible option. During the descent, we realized the west spur was much safer than we had remembered.

After three days at base camp, we made our second attempt. Rested and better acclimatized, we reached Camp 2 in only four hours. On the 11th, we climbed the west spur in just an hour, and by 6:30 a.m. we reached our cached gear on the south-southwest ridge. We continued up the crest to a small col at around 6,200m and set up camp in a relatively sheltered spot.

We left at 4 a.m. on the 12th, roped in two teams. The rappel beyond the ice knife-edge proved straightforward, but the rocky ridge that followed crumbled beneath our hands, and the snow arête that followed was terrifying. Takuma and Ryoya, who were head and shoulders above the rest of us in climbing ability, alternated leading in this section. We eventually reached a wider snow slope, from which we could see a rocky peak. However, when Masahiro reached it, he shouted down, "This isn't the summit, but let's keep moving, because there are no crevasses." I shouted back, "*Yo shiya*!" ("Hell yeah!"), the tension in my chest finally easing.

We arrived at the summit at 12:19 p.m. "We're not done yet," Ryoya reminded us, but we were all aware of that. By 6 p.m. we were back at our high camp, physically drained but elated.

Early the next morning, Masahiro, Taiyo, and Takuma ascended a top at the south end of the ridge, which was called Phungi South (6,342m). During the descent, as we all struggled below Camp 1 beneath enormous packs, Takuma looked at us and muttered, "It always ends like this." But the pain in my shoulders and legs was nothing compared with the pride swelling within my chest.

—Fumiya Yokomichi, *Japan*

Ondra Húserka approaching an ice smear during day three on Langtang Lirung's east face. The ice was bypassed on the left to reach the site of the pair's third bivouac. ***Marek Holeček***

LANGTANG LIRUNG, EAST FACE

The dramatic events of the days on Langtang Lirung are deeply etched in my memory. They belong to the wildest and most beautiful I have ever experienced in the mountains, but also the most painful.

Our small team arrived in Kathmandu in September and spent the initial days hanging around bars, as heavy rain blocked access roads. Once the roads were cleared, we trekked to Langtang via Gosaikunda and climbed Naya Kanga (5,863m) for acclimatization. On October 7, three weeks after arriving in Nepal, we set up base camp south of the Lirung Glacier at 4,500m, in sight of the huge, unclimbed east face of Langtang Lirung (7,227m).

On October 20, Ondrej (Ondra) Húserka (Slovakia), Ondrej Mrklovský (Czech Republic), and I made our first attempt, starting from a camp below the east face at 4,700m. When the sun rose, a warm breeze started to blow, and the effect was immediate. As if someone had opened a huge tank above us, stones and ice began to fall and we heard sounds like the growling of an angry dog. For 24 hours, we cowered under a small rock overhang while avalanches flew over our heads. After we reached base camp, Ondrej Mrklovský said calmly, "Mara, I'm not going up there again."

On the 25th, Ondra Húserka and I set out from advanced base for a second attempt. The climbing was difficult, with steep, air-saturated ice. We needed to move fast, and Ondra, in the lead, climbed brilliantly, like a motor mouse. At one point we were hit by a big avalanche that pummeled my head and shoulders. We began simul-climbing to move out of the dangerous central couloir and reach a sheltered bivouac site, at 5,500m, on a rocky spur—but not before a second avalanche hit Ondra on the head and gave me a Thai massage, unfortunately without any coconut oil.

The next day brought difficult climbing over smooth rock, followed by an icy couloir and more mixed terrain. We progressed slowly and bivouacked at 5,800m. On the 27th, we climbed to 6,300m. This day gave the most difficult climbing on the route, with a particularly taxing rock section to reach the central funnel. We were forced to place our tent on a slim rib. Ondra worried we could be swept away, but there was no better option.

Fatigue was beginning to take its toll as we headed right on steep ice the following morning. By late afternoon, the wind started to blow and both of us were shivering as we scanned the terrain for a possible tent site. Finally, behind one of the snowy curls at around 6,800m, we found a small cave. At least we could sit down and stretch our legs.

On the 29th, we reached the northeast ridge, atop the face, and bivouacked at 7,100m, taking all day to climb 300m. I had taken the lead, switching off my brain and counting steps as I plowed through powder snow. We both slept well at our nice, flat campsite.

The following morning was beautiful, with no wind. Knowing the top was close, we left everything except the rope and, moving together, reached the summit at 11 a.m. For around ten minutes, we were happy and had no worries. Then it was time to return to our tent, pack up, and continue down the northeast ridge. We eventually dropped onto the east flank and bivouacked at 6,300m. Below, a wild glacier descended toward the foot of the mountain.

Ondra Húserka climbing through broken rock on day one on the east face of Langtang Lirung, nearing the first bivouac site. ***Marek Holeček***

Cold and exhausted, we packed our frozen gear the next morning and started down again. In deep, avalanche-prone snow, Ondra, 60m behind me, kept the rope tight. At the top of a huge serac wall, I looked down at a view that filled me with horror. We had managed to zigzag between risks to this point, but now we would have to descend the face directly with at least four rappels. Prioritizing speed in this dangerous area, we chose to rappel simultaneously. At one point we were hit by a swarm of falling rock and ice, which made a crater in Ondra's helmet and caused him to bite through his lip. At last we reached a glacier plateau and hugged each other, as we felt we were out of major danger.

We continued down, circumventing or leaping crevasses. At around 5,500m, I drilled an Abalakov anchor and backed it up with one of our two remaining ice screws, then rappelled a short distance. I stepped over a narrow crevasse and walked a little way until I saw we would need to make another rappel.

Moving back up to below the narrow crevasse, I shouted to Ondra to start rappelling. A moment later there was a dull thump followed by strange rustling sounds. I rushed up to find the ropes disappearing into a narrow crack in the ice. The Abalakov had failed, and Ondra had fallen into the crevasse.

The east face of Langtang Lirung (7,227m). The left line shows the first ascent of the face, by Ondra's Star, in October 2024; the right line shows most of the descent. The route gained about 2,500 meters from advanced base camp at the foot of the face. The accident took place near the bivy site at far right, hidden behind the rock buttress. Kimshung Sar is the summit to the right. *Marek Holeček Collection*

I rappelled into the slot and located Ondra in total darkness, but I was unable to rescue him despite a struggle lasting hours. He had serious injuries, and they proved to be fatal. After confirming he had passed away, I regained the surface and got into my sleeping bag.

The next morning, I sent several messages, including one to Ondra's girlfriend, so she would receive the news directly from me. Then I left my sleeping bag as a marker and started down through a maze of crevasses and ice towers, again making short rappels. In late afternoon, I finally reached our empty base camp and, having a strong desire to talk to someone, changed into approach shoes and went down to Kyanjin Gompa.

The next day, I was taken by helicopter to locate the accident site and later flown to Kathmandu to deal with formalities. Ondra and I did not have time to think of a route name, so I will do that myself: Ondra's Star. [*On November 7, a strong Sherpa team was helicoptered to the accident site and was able to extract Ondrej Húserka's body by long-line.*]

—Marek Holeček, *Czech Republic*

KIMSHUNG SAR, SOUTH-SOUTHEAST RIDGE

Located immediately opposite the east face of Langtang Lirung, Kimshung (a.k.a. Tsangbu Ri, 6,781m, 28°16'19.74"N, 85°33'6.47"E) has a long south-southeast ridge between the Lirung and Kimshung glaciers, with subsidiary tops. The southern and lowest of these summits (28°15'40.42"N, 85°33'41.24"E) is around 6,320m and was given the name Kimshung Sar by the team that attempted it in 2024.

In 2016, the main summit of Kimshung had two attempts. Italians François Cazzanelli, Giampaolo Corona, and Emrik Favre tried the southwest face to south-southeast ridge, stopping at around 6,500m, a little below the crest, due to strong wind. The same year, two Swiss climbers, Philip Bührer and Alex Gammeter, tried an east-facing couloir from the Kimshung Glacier and reached a col of approximately 6,450m on the south-southeast ridge, where they retreated after finding the way ahead dry, with very loose rock. This same couloir was later attempted twice by Masha Gordon, with Yannick Graziani and with Jacques Sturm.

In 2024, Cazzanelli and Favre returned with six other Italian climbers. The team established base camp at 4,100m on October 14, then Camp 1 at the start of the Kimshung Glacier (5,400m) and Camp 2 (5,800m) toward the top of the glacier.

On October 27, Roger Bovard, Favre, and Stefano Stradelli left Camp 1 and climbed an east-facing snow slope up to the start of the south-southeast ridge, aiming for the southern top (Kimshung Sar); they felt this ridge was comparable to but a little harder than the Peuterey Ridge on Mont Blanc. At 2 p.m., 12 hours after leaving camp, they reached a rocky top about three meters lower and perhaps 100m distant from the highest point of Kimshung Sar. They were separated from this by a dangerously corniced arête, and they stopped there.

Roger Bovard, Emrik Favre, and Stefano Stradelli on the south-southeast ridge of Kimshung Sar, with the Kimshung Glacier below and, on the far side, part of the southwest face of Yubra. ***Damiano Levati***

The three descended the upper section of the ridge in half a dozen rappels, with sound anchors difficult to place. Realizing it would take too long to reverse the entire route, they headed down a couloir on the east face. After nine rappels they reached the glacier, eventually regaining their camp at 11 p.m.

On the same day, Cazzanelli, Jerome Perruquet, Francesco Ratti, and Giuseppe Vidoni left Camp 1, trudged farther up the glacier through deep snow in cold, windy conditions, and climbed the same couloir used by the 2016 Swiss team. The ascent was on snow up to 60°–70°. Just below the col, they found a piton from one of the previous attempts.

The four climbed two mixed pitches up the ridge toward the main summit of Kimshung, gaining about 80m in height. Although the terrain ahead did not look particularly difficult, the wind was now a real problem, blowing the ropes out horizontally. They turned around, making two difficult rappels to regain the col, followed by 12 rappels down the couloir, mostly from V-threads. They arrived back at base camp at 8 p.m.

After three days of rest, both teams were ready for a second attempt on Kimshung when they heard of an accident on Langtang Lirung (*see story above*). Two of the party went up to that advanced base camp, where they were told that Ondra Húserka had died and Marek Holeček was in trouble. Everyone went down to Kyanjin Gompa to organize a rescue, but this proved unnecessary when Holeček arrived later the same day.

—Lindsay Griffin, ***with information from Emrik Favre, Italy, and Rodolphe Popier, Himalayan Database***

NEPAL | Jugal Himal

The northwest face of Ganchempo (6,378m) and the route followed in November 2024. The climbers descended the standard route to the south-southwest. In 2023, Oswaldo Freire and Joshua Jarrín climbed a parallel line to the left. Various unauthorized ascents of the face are believed to have been made earlier. ***David Goettler***

GANCHEMPO, NORTHWEST FACE, DIRECT ROUTE AND TRAVERSE

Nicolas Hojac (Switzerland) and I left Kyanjin Gompa on November 15 and walked more than five hours to reach the foot of the glacier that descends west from below the northwest face of Ganchempo (6,378m). We camped there at 4,760m.

The next morning, at 3 a.m., we headed up the glacier to the foot of the northwest face. This took four hours.

Our original plan was to climb the mixed ground well right of the summit fall line, but on closer inspection we saw the ice was thin and fragmented. Instead, we continued up the glacier to a point slightly right of center of the northwest face and climbed directly up to the west ridge, just right of the summit. Conditions were very good, and apart from when we crossed the bergschrund, we only broke out the rope 60m below the ridge. Once on the ridge, it was only around 100m to the summit, which we reached in four hours from the foot of the face.

We spotted freshly fixed ropes to the south-southwest on the standard route, so we decided to descend that way and circle around the mountain to regain our tent. This took three hours. After a brief rest, we packed the tent and continued down toward Kyanjin Gompa.

The average inclination of our ca 700m route was 65°–70°. Maximum difficulties were found on several sections of 80°. [*See AAJ 2024 for another recent route up the northwest face. Several unauthorized parties in the late 20th century are believed to have climbed this face, but their route lines are not known.*]

—David Goettler, *Germany*

JUGAL I, FIRST ASCENT, VIA EAST-SOUTHEAST FACE

In the spring, a joint expedition from Korea and Nepal, led by Um Hong-gil and Lhakpa Sonam Sherpa, completed the first ascent of Jugal I (6,591m, 28°10'26.73"N, 85°48'59.13"E), north of Kathmandu. The expedition marked the occasion of the golden jubilee of the bilateral relationship between South Korea and Nepal, and was a collaboration between the Korean Alpine Rescue Association and the Nepal Mountaineering Association.

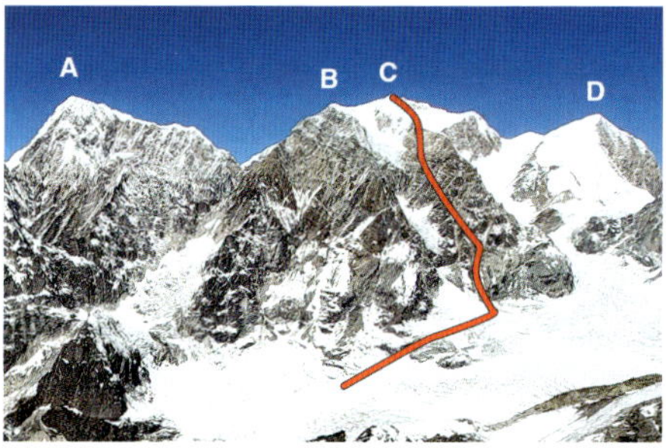

(A) Dorje Lhakpa (6,966m). (B) Jugal I south top (ca 6,510m, unclimbed). (C) Jugal I (6,591m). The 2024 first ascent by the east-southeast face, following a slender couloir through the rock, is marked. Behind and almost obscured by Jugal I is Leonpo Gang (6,979m). (D) Leonpo Gang East (6,733m). Jugal II (6,518m) is hidden north of Jugal I. *Tito Arosio*

A four-day trek brought the team to base camp at 4,700m, near the base of the Jugal Glacier. It was a full day's difficult hike from here to the foot of the mountain, so they set up an advanced base below the east-southeast face at 5,300m. Koo Eun-soo (climbing leader), Joung Je-gyun, Kim Dong-jin, Baek Jong-min, Um Tae-chul, and Byeon Joon-gi, along with high-altitude porter Dame Sherpa, fixed rope on the lower part of the mountain and set up camps. Lakpa Dendi and Lama Babu then fixed rope up to the summit slope at 6,300m, after which the whole team descended to base camp.

On May 2, Lakpa Dendi, Lama Babu, and Um Hong-gil left for the summit. They camped at 5,600m, then left at 12:30 a.m. on the 3rd. Lakpa Dendi reached the summit at 12:30 p.m., followed by Lama Babu and Um at 3:30 p.m. The same afternoon, Koo, Joung, Kim, and Baek climbed up to the top camp (5,600m), took a brief rest, then left for the summit at 11 p.m., reaching it at 8 a.m. the next morning.

Although the expedition had hoped to climb the adjacent Jugal II as well, they could see from high on Jugal I that the route over to Jugal II would involve complex terrain. They concluded it would be better to climb II separately, but did not have time to do so.

—Oh Young-hoon, *Korea*

The west-southwest ridge of Phurbi Chhyachu, showing (1) the 2024 Italian start and (2) the approximate line of the 1982 Japanese-Nepalese route, the first and only ascent of the mountain. A Czech team explored the face just to the left in 2024. *Tito Arosio*

EXPLORATION NEAR JUGAL V: *In April, four women from the U.K. set up base camp below Jugal V, accessed with some difficulty by the west side of the Jugal Glacier, as a landslide had made the east-side approach unfeasible. The goals were unclimbed Peak 6,200m on the frontier ridge and exploration of ski potential in the area, but snow conditions were deemed too poor for summit attempts. A detailed report is available at the AAJ website.*

PHURBI CHHYACHU, WEST-SOUTHWEST RIDGE, ATTEMPT

Drawn to Phurbi Chhyachu (6,637m) by its aesthetic appearance and sparse mountaineering history, Rosa Morotti and I aimed to repeat the original route on the west-southwest ridge in a light, alpine-style approach.

In 1982, a large Japanese-Nepalese expedition established three camps and fixed 2,000m of rope on this difficult ridge, and 16 climbers reached the summit over two days (*AAJ 1983*). The mountain had never been attempted before, and there has been no ascent since, although in 2023 a Spanish team almost completed a new route up the southeast ridge (*AAJ 2024*), reaching 6,570m.

From Kathmandu, we took a half-day jeep ride to the village of Bolde, then trekked for four days to a base camp at 3,900m.

Starting our climb on October 27, we discovered significant changes to the glacier at the base of the route. This necessitated climbing a difficult 400m variation start to the left of the original line, with sections of mixed climbing, ice, and inconsistent snow. Over four days, we progressed up the 1,600m route, encountering difficulties up to M5 80° ice. At approximately 6,200m, we encountered the sole remnants of the Japanese expedition: a single ice screw and a section of fixed rope.

From our top camp at around 6,300m, we planned to make a light push to the summit. Unfortunately, pulmonary edema forced me to stop here. Rosa continued alone and reached the start of the summit plateau at about 6,550m, where she turned back in deep snow, preferring to conserve energy for the descent. The summit was around one kilometer away.

Our descent was demanding and complicated by the scarcity of suitable ice for Abalakov anchors. After one and half days of rappelling, we finally reached the glacier.

—Tito Arosio, *Italy*

PHURBI CHHYACHU NORTHWEST FACE EXPLORATION: *In the fall, Marek Disman and Jan Kreisinger from the Czech Republic planned to climb the previously untouched northwest face of Phurbi Chhyachu, but seracs overhanging all potential routes deterred them. Instead, they tackled a mixed route to the right. After two and a half days of hard work navigating a challenging glacial maze of crevasses, seracs, and rock, they were unable to find a passable route.*

NEPAL | Rolwaling Himal

CHHOPA BAMARE, NORTHEAST RIDGE

Chhopa Bamare (6,109m, 28°3’32.05”N, 86°5’28.50”E) is the highest peak of the Pamali Range, a small subgroup in the northwest Rolwaling (east of the Friendship Highway between Zhangmu and Nyalam). It is a quiet area with almost no recorded climbing history, despite a relatively short approach.

Since the first ascent of the peak in 2019 (see *AAJ 2020*), by the southeast face and south ridge, there has only been one reported visit, in December 2023, when a group of Sherpas claimed to have made the “first ascent.” This was clearly not accurate, and both first ascensionists, Benjamin Billet (France) and John Kelley (USA), say the summit video provided by the Nepalese absolutely was not shot on the summit. [*It is thought they climbed a lower peak much farther south; see note below.*]

In the fall of 2024, Akitugu Konishi, Kotaro Kunimune, Yukio Ueda, and I initially planned to climb two independent direct routes on the southeast face. However, the face had far less snow than we expected, and the rock looked dangerous, as did the glacier approach. We quickly decided the only feasible route under the conditions was the northeast ridge.

From our base camp at 3,500m, we first established an advanced base at 4,000m and then, on November 2, climbed to Camp 1 (5,000m), close to the base of a couloir leading to a notch on the northeast ridge. For acclimatization, we climbed along the ridge toward the summit, traversing scree to avoid a rocky point we named Yak’s Back, then up a wall leading to the Dome at 5,450m. We returned to 5,250m, spent a night, then descended to base camp, where Yukio decided not to continue due to poor health.

The remaining three of us left base camp on the 10th with enough food and

The view from the flank of "Snow Peak" along the sharp northeast ridge leading to the summit of Chhopa Bamare (6,109m). ***Hiroyoshi Manome***

fuel for five to six days and arrived at Camp 1 by 2 p.m. The next day we regained our 5,450m high point—a vast plateau between the Dome and the subsummit we called Snow Peak—and made our Camp 2. The wall below the Dome gave nerve-wracking climbing on very poor rock.

On the 12th, we climbed six mixed pitches to the top of Snow Peak, descended a knife-edge snow ridge on the far side, then continued up the main ridge, which proved steeper than expected. We spent the night at 5,750m, just below a formation we called the Pinnacle. We were unable to pitch the tent and had to sleep in separate spots. Fortunately, although it was cold, there was almost no wind. In the morning, we took the bare minimum and headed for the summit.

The Pinnacle proved straightforward, but above lay a steep rock ridge. Up to this point, we had seen scattered remains of rappel anchors, but above was nothing. It seemed very likely an unknown party had turned back near here. [*These possibly were left by American John Kelley, who tried the ridge, solo, in December 2017.*] We continued to the upper wall, which gave the steepest and most difficult pitches of the route (M5). A slushy snow slope brought us to the summit, which we reached at 4:30 p.m. We were back at our bivouac by 8:30 p.m.

The next day, we reversed the ascent route and were off the mountain by 9 p.m. Due to the horizontal distance involved, the ups and downs, and the complex terrain, the route felt like proper "Himalayan mountaineering" more than alpine climbing. We named the route Tsumiki (a type of Japanese toy building block) after the fragile rock.

—Hiroyoshi Manome, *Japan*

PEAK 5,805M, FIRST ASCENT: *About five kilometers south of Chhopa Bamare, along the frontier ridge, is an unnamed snow summit of 5,805m (28°0'42.43"N, 86°5'7.24"E). On December 29, 2023, eight days after reaching their base camp, a Nepalese team comprising Lila Bahadur Basnet, Bhabindra Khadka, Sanjeeb Oli, Lakpa Geli Sherpa, Nima Gyalzen Sherpa, and Phurba Thile Sherpa made the first ascent of this summit, approaching up the glacier to the northeast and finishing up the north-northwest ridge. The climbers, belonging to two mountaineering/trekking agencies, aimed to add another suitable peak to Nepal's list of official trekking peaks and to promote a little-visited area.*

—Lindsay Griffin, *with assistance from Rodolphe Popier, Himalayan Database*

Beding Go (6,125m), with the northwest ridge, climbed in 2024, on the left and the southeast ridge, the original 2015 route, on the far right. ***Cian O'Brolchain***

BEDING GO, NORTHWEST RIDGE

On October 13, Pasang Kidar Sherpa and I teamed up to climb the northwest ridge of Beding Go (6,125m, 27°55'34.50"N, 86°23'25.84"E), which lies on the Nepal-Tibet frontier a little east of Gaurishankar (7,134m). Pasang is one of 14 IFMGA guides from the Rolwaling (the highest concentration of qualified guides from any region in Nepal). We completed an alpine-style ascent of this previously unclimbed ridge from a 5,100m high camp at the head of the Chhimugolche River, just west of Beding village.

It took us one day to ascend steep alpine tundra from Beding to a base camp at 4,875m in an area of talus. The site had been cleared by several previous parties attempting Dolma Kang (6,332m).

Our high camp was on snow near a series of glacial tarns, safe from serac fall from the southeast flanks of the frontier ridge. Above, broken rock led to the glacier at 5,150m. After a 30m section of 70° ice, we weaved through crevassed terrain to a glacial plateau at 5,490m, then climbed up the southern edge of the broad base of Beding Go's northwest ridge. Deep faceted snow slowed progress. We reached the crest of the ridge at 5,860m, where it is a true knife-edge.

With a 700m drop on the Nepal side and a 1,350m fall down the north face to Tibet's Rongshar Glacier, we moved with caution, staying close to the crest and trying to find the most supportive snow and avoid triggering avalanches. Snow stakes and other anchors proved to be of no use. After several short, steep steps (up to 90°) and a few false summits, we reached an undulating section of ridge at 6,070m.

Exposed shattered rocks, perched above the precipitous southwest face, formed the south edge of a sidewalk-width ridge. We gingerly made our way in the trough between this rock and the sharp snow ridge—the first time that we had found protection from the wind since sunrise. Crossing a final false summit, we treaded lightly up wind-hardened snow slabs to step onto the true summit a little after mid-day, eight hours after leaving camp. Evident were the old, fixed ropes from the 2015 original ascent via the south face and southeast ridge.

We descended our ascent route, mostly downclimbing, with the occasional rappel from Abalakov anchors on the sections of steeper ice, and reached our high camp at 4:30 p.m. We had a bite to eat, then continued for another hour to base camp. We named the route Friendship Ridge (TD AI3+).

—Danika Gilbert, *USA*

Chobutse (6,686m) and the 2023 route Just Breathe up the northeast pillar. On reaching the summit, the climbers descended left and then down the far side of the mountain, via the southeast face. The first ascensionists of the peak, in 1972, climbed the contorted glacier on the left to the broad saddle visible between Chobutse and Takargo (6,771m), then up the east side of Chobutse to the summit. *Wadim Jabłoński*

CHOBUTSE, NORTHEAST PILLAR

In October 2023, Maciej Kimel and I made the first ascent of the northeast pillar of Chobutse (6,686m), naming our route Just Breathe (1,600m, M5 WI4 R/X). The pillar had one previous known attempt, by Romanian Mihnea Prundeanu and Cypriot Kyriakos Rossidis, who reached 5,965m in 2019. The peak itself had no more than five ascents since the first in 1972, by a German team, via the northeast face and east-southeast ridge.

After a four-day (28km) trek, we made our base camp in the village of Na (4,200m), and after a brief rest, and with the help of two porters, established advanced base at 4,900m near the Rolwaling Glacier moraine.

We left here on October 14 and began climbing the pillar on terrain that reminded us of the Tatra at home. By mid-day we had reached our intended bivouac spot, so we kept climbing and eventually spent the night at 5,750m on a snow hammock. There was no option to pitch our tent, and we spent a cold, uncomfortable night, with spindrift pushing snow into our sleeping bags.

The next morning, we pushed on to reach an icy face covered with sugar snow. It was longer and in worse condition than expected, giving no opportunity for placing protection. We eventually found a snow cave inside a serac at 6,200m, and this flat, windless space allowed us to remove our harnesses and have a decent rest after the previous sleepless night.

On October 16, we set off with hopes of summiting and descending the same day. However, the terrain proved challenging, with technical climbing on a snowy ridge that had sections of 70°, icy overhangs, seracs, and unstable snow with no protection. Feeling the effects of altitude, we reached the summit at 3:30 p.m., took a quick selfie, and began our descent of the southeast face. This turned out to be far more complex and dangerous than expected, and we needed to bivouac twice before regaining base camp on the 18th, exhausted but safe.

—Wadim Jabłoński, *Poland*

Linkhu Chuli seen from base camp at around 4,700 meters on the Drolambo Glacier. Linkhu Chuli II (6,659m) is on the right, with the north spur, climbed in 2024, facing the camera. The descent was to the right. See the *AAJ* website for photos showing the lines of both routes in this report. *Yasuhiro Hanatani*

LINKHU CHULI II, NORTH SPUR; TAKARGO EAST, EAST FACE

After arriving in the Rolwaling in October, Connor Holdsworth, Jack Morris, Dave Sharpe, and Nathan White (all from the U.K.) established base camp on the 21st and an advanced base at 4,860m the next day. They then acclimatized by climbing Parchamo (6,279m), in preparation for two separate objectives.

Holdsworth and Sharpe planned to climb a new route on Takargo East and then continue up the long east ridge of Takargo South. Morris and White chose to attempt the impressive north spur of Linkhu Chuli II (Linkhu Chuli Nup, 6,659m, 27°48'19.80"N, 86°31'20.97"E), which divides the serac-torn north and northwest faces, providing a direct and objectively safe route through the chaos.

Linkhu Chuli II was first climbed in 1960, following the steep and difficult west-northwest ridge, by Alain Barbezat and Nawang Dorje Sherpa, part of a French expedition led by Robert Sandoz. The team established four camps above base camp. Another ascent of this route was claimed in 2019. Farther east, Linkhu Chuli I (6,749m) has been climbed only once, in 2013, by Ines Papert (Germany), climbing with Thomas Senf to their highest camp.

Morris and White left advanced base camp on the 31st, and after climbing the entry couloir to reach the base of the north spur, found sustained and technically engaging climbing, with limited options for bivouacs. On that first day, encountering loose and unprotectable rock on the crest, they bypassed it on the right flank, the climbing there forming the crux of the route, with one pitch of Scottish 7. After 16 hours of climbing, they bivouacked at around 6,150m.

After negotiating a steep central rock section, largely on the right flank of the spur, the pair pressed on, hoping the terrain would ease toward the summit. The opposite was true. Near sunset, they were faced with a compact, vertical rock buttress and were forced to traverse horizontally right for 100m, then cut a poor tent site at around 6,400m. They eventually got to bed at midnight after a 15-hour day.

The two started again at 7 a.m. on November 2, climbing largely on ice. At 2 p.m. they arrived on a northwest top and at

Jack Morris on the central rock section of the north spur of Linkhu Chuli II. ***Nathan White***

the junction with Linkhu Chuli II's original route on the west-northwest ridge. The main summit was just a couple of hundred meters away, but it was obvious that a big storm was moving in, so they chose to forgo it. Descending their route wasn't viable, due to lack of ice for anchors as well as loose rock and poor snow, so they headed down the west-northwest ridge, which until this point they hadn't really seen. After much downclimbing and rappelling through seracs, with a very cold bivouac at 6,200m, Morris and White reached the Trakarding Glacier a little before the bad weather moved in, and their advanced base in early evening on November 3. Within 24 hours, the Drolambo Glacier and the Tashi Lapcha Pass over to the Khumbu were impassable due to deep new snow.

Morris and White named the new route to the mountain's northwest top Dreaming of Rotisserie Chicken (1,400m, ED M6 AI3).

Holdsworth and Sharpe left advanced base camp two days earlier than the other British pair, on October 29, heading for Takargo East (6,132m, 27°52'22.18"N, 86°31'30.40"E). This summit was reached in 2013, via the northeast ridge, by Dawa Gyalje Sherpa, Nima Tenji Sherpa, and Tashi Sherpa, and again in January 2016 by John Kelley (USA), solo, via the south face.

Holdsworth and Sharpe crossed the Drolambo Glacier and climbed unroped up most of the east face (ca 600m). This was mainly Scottish 2/3, with a harder and looser step of Scottish 4 at the top. After spending that night very close to the summit of Takargo East, they awoke to find a set of snow leopard prints.

Two more days of climbing, mostly on loose rock and bottomless snow, but fortunately with good tent sites, took them along the east ridge of Takargo South (6,756m) until it met the main bulk of the mountain at around 6,200m. This was below the point where David Gottlieb and Joe Puryear had joined the ridge via the hanging glacier to the north during the first ascent of Takargo (6,771m) in 2010.

Holdsworth had been feeling rough for most of the ascent, and when specks of blood appeared in his vomit, it felt right to escape. On November 1, the pair rappelled the north flank to the side glacier below the east face of Takargo and returned to base camp on the 3rd. Up to their high point, they had completed around 2,000m of climbing, with cruxes of Scottish 5.

—Lindsay Griffin, ***with information from Connor Holdsworth and Nathan White, U.K., and Rodolphe Popier, Himalayan Database***

TENGKANGPOCHE, NORTHEAST FACE, SUNSHINE SPRING ROLL

Pat Perry Johnson and I arrived in Namche Bazaar on April 6. A week later, we attempted Kyajo Ri's southwest ridge but retreated 200m below the summit due to lack of time and deteriorating weather.

Disappointed but still full of motivation, we set our eyes on the northeast face of Tengkangpoche (6,487m). We moved to the Sunshine Lodge in Thame, and after a few days' rest with our gracious hosts, along with some local ice and rock climbing, we concluded the northeast face was quite dry, so we opted for a moderate line on the far left that linked ice and mixed terrain with long sections of snow, leading to the east ridge. We hoped this would give us the best chance to summit Tengkangpoche. [*The chosen line lies between Love and Hate, a route soloed by Nick Bullock (U.K.) in 2003, and Bullock's descent route a little farther left on the face. At that time, the face held more snow and ice.*]

After a bivouac at around 4,600m at the base of the route, we began climbing at 4:30 a.m. on April 22, navigating easy ice to the base of a smear on a clean rock face. Having been almost certain the ice on this smear would be too thin to climb safely, we were pleasantly surprised to climb it in two fantastic pitches at WI3+.

We continued directly up the northeast face, linking excellent sections of easy ice and mixed terrain with long stretches of steep snow. A final pitch of WI3 brought us to the east ridge. We bivouacked at 6,000m and endured a windy, sleepless night.

Clear weather allowed us to continue up the ridge the following day, encountering long sections of WI2/3 while traversing the south flank. There were a couple of tricky crevasses. We reached the summit in light cloud at 3:30 p.m. After a brief celebration and photos, we simul-climbed back along the ridge and continued our descent of the northeast face through the night, making 12 rappels via V-threads and rock anchors, and downclimbing long sections of snow. We reached the base of the route at 1:55 a.m. and were drinking hot coffee at Sunshine Lodge two hours later, excited at having spent two days on such a beautiful mountain.

We named our route Sunshine Spring Roll (1,500m, WI3+ M3) in celebration of the delicious spring rolls we enjoyed at the lodge, a place that will continue to live in our hearts. After a week and a half of rest, we returned to Kyajo Ri and, in a single push from our teahouse in Machermo, climbed up and down its southwest ridge in 23 hours and 23 minutes.

—Patrick Gephart, *USA*

LANGDAK, NORTH FACE, BANDE ORGANISÉE

After travel complications caused by intense flooding in Nepal, Antoine Rolle, Mathieu Stephan, and I reached Namche Bazaar on October 12. Another three days of trekking to the northwest brought us to our base camp at 4,560m on the Chhule Plain, north of Marlung in the Bhote Kosi Valley. Ascending the Chhule Valley to the west, then the Langdak Glacier, we reached the north face of Langdak (6,220m, 27°55'1.43"N, 86°33'40.65"E), our objective, and quickly identified a line that was not particularly exposed to objective risks.

We acclimatized on an unnamed 5,500m summit just in front of Langdak, then took two days' rest before walking the three hours to the foot of Langdak, where we bivouacked. We had time to fix the first two rope lengths (ice and loose snow) before going to sleep. The next morning, October 26, we climbed mixed terrain and snow of varying quality to an altitude of 5,640m, where a narrow bank of snow allowed us to pitch a tent. We were able to fix two ropes in the superb ice gully above before dark.

The following morning, having regained our high point, we were forced

Pat Perry Johnson climbing the thin ice smear that formed the crux of the new route on the northeast face of Tengkangpoche. *Patrick Gephart*

The north face of Langdak with (1) Bande Organisée (2024) and (2) the original route, soloed by Andy Parkin in January 2011. ***Antoine Rolle***

to use aid for a few meters on a pitch in poor condition. A beautiful gully then led to the upper couloir, which turned out to be more difficult than expected. At 5:30 p.m., we reached the top of the couloir and the col on the east ridge, setting up our bivouac at 6,140m.

At 7 a.m. on the 28th, we began climbing the easy ground above. One hour later, after a few mixed sections and the final snow slopes, we stood on the summit. The weather was perfect, allowing us to enjoy a fine panorama before starting down the standard route on the west ridge and southwest face. Rappelling the north face would have been quite complicated, because the route had several traverses, and poor rock and ice would have made it difficult to set up anchors. One hour later, we reached the upper Drolambo Glacier, which we descended painfully until 4 p.m. Our final bivouac was on the Rolwaling side of Tashi Lapcha Pass, where we used up our last supplies and gas.

The next morning, October 29, we roped up to cross the 5,753m pass, then put all the technical equipment in our packs and walked down to Thame. On the 30th, four hours of walking up the Bhote Kosi Valley took us to base camp. The loop had been completed. We called our route on the north face Bande Organisée (1,000m, 26 pitches from 30m to 70m, AI4+ M5 A1).

—Jérémy Fino, *France*

HISTORICAL NOTES ON LANGDAK: *In January 2011, Andy Parkin made the first ascent, solo, of the north face of Langdak, which he estimated to be around 850m high. The 2024 route starts left of the line climbed by Parkin, then joins it for the upper couloir. Langdak was the name given to the peak in spring 2014 by the Nepalese government. Before that, it had several names: Trident, used by the first ascensionists in 1952; Singkar, the name most commonly used by many Sherpas until around 15 years ago; and Rima Mancho, which was the name given to Parkin by local Sherpas. For more history of this peak, see AAJs 2012 and 2016.*

NEPAL | Mahalangur Himal – Khumbu Section

CHO OYU, SOUTH-SOUTHWEST RIDGE

At around 9 p.m. on June 7, a strong team composed primarily of Sherpas reached the 8,188m summit of Cho Oyu, completing the last major logical line on the mountain: the south-southwest ridge. The successful party was Chhangba Sherpa, Gelje Sherpa, Lakpa Temba Sherpa, Lakpa Tenji Sherpa, Ngima Ongda Sherpa, Tenjing Gyaljen Sherpa, and a 19-year-old Frenchman, Alasdair Mckenzie, who is attempting to become the youngest person to climb all the 8,000m peaks. (Cho Oyu was his 13th.) The ascent was carried out in siege style, with much of the route fixed to not far from the summit, and oxygen reportedly used from around 7,100m to the top and then on the descent to about 7,000m.

(A) Nangpai Gosum I. (B) Lungsampa. (C) Nangpai Gosum II. (D) Cho Oyu. (1) The approximate line taken by the 2024 expedition to the plateau and up the south-southwest ridge of Cho Oyu. (2) The south-southwest pillar of Lungsampa, climbed many times to reach the plateau in prior attempts on Cho Oyu's south-southwest ridge. *Damien Gildea*

The quest to climb the south-southwest ridge has been long. In 1981, a Japanese team tried to access the main ridge via the south-southwest pillar of Lungsampa (6,500m). After making the first ascent of this peak, they reached 7,120m on the plateau east of the main ridge. The same route was attempted in 1983 by Italian climbers, but they failed to get higher than 6,500m.

In 1987, an American team also climbed Lungsampa, then switched to the face much farther left, to the right of the south ridge of Nangpai Gosum I. They climbed to 6,700m but abandoned the project after a huge snowstorm. A few days after that storm cleared, there was a remarkable attempt by Hans Eitel, part of a German team, who climbed Lungsampa solo, then continued to the south-southwest ridge, reaching a high point of 7,400m. (He is generally credited with the first ascent of Nangpai Gosum II.) In 1989, Korean and Swiss climbers also were defeated on the Lungsampa route, and the following year a Soviet expedition established five camps and reached 7,600m before retreating in abysmal weather.

The ridge was left alone until the winter of 2021–2022. The Chinese side of the mountain was closed that year, causing a huge loss in income for Nepalese agencies and Sherpas. Ostensibly looking for a route from Nepal that they could manage with clients, commercial operators considered the south-southwest ridge. A strong team of Sherpas took up the challenge and, using the 1987 American line up the face right of Nangpai Gosum I, reached around 7,600m. In the autumn, more Sherpas returned and, using the same approach, got as far as 7,300m. Autumn 2023 saw a five-member Russian team use the Lungsampa approach and reach 7,350m.

In late May 2024, another Sherpa team, from the Seven Summit Treks agency, placed a Camp 3 at around 7,000m on the plateau after climbing the Nangpai Gosum I route, then forced the route up the south-southwest ridge as far as 7,625m. However, they had run out of fixed rope and enough oxygen for a summit attempt, and they needed a rest. They returned to base camp. Meanwhile, the very strong Gelje Sherpa (K2 in winter, etc.) was in Kathmandu after guiding an Everest ascent. As he had made a previous attempt on the route, he was asked to help and immediately accepted.

With Gelje, a few other fresh Sherpas, and 1,000m of rope, a team set out from base camp on June 5 and climbed directly to Camp 3. The next day, they crossed the kilometer-wide plateau and made Camp 4 at 7,200m. On the 7th, they left in the dark and negotiated the first crux, a steep couloir with loose slabs and rockfall, at 7,500m, where the route breaks out onto the south face. On the second crux, a final rocky headwall, they overcame sometimes waist-deep snow in a couloir, managing to complete the difficulties before exhausting all their rope. Above, easier slopes led to the summit, which they reached at 9:10 p.m.

Descending through the night, they regained Camp 4 at 6 a.m. on June 8 and base camp by 10 p.m. that day. The five-kilometer-long ascent had a vertical gain of 2,500m. Above 7,400m, the difficulties were sustained on snow, ice, and mixed terrain.

—Lindsay Griffin, *AAJ*, and Rodolphe Popier, *Himalayan Database*

KYAJO RI, NORTHEAST AND EAST FACE, BUTTERFLY EFFECT

After trekking four days to a base camp above the village of Machermo, we spent the next five days acclimatizing, reaching

Seen from a belay on the east face of Kyajo Ri, cloud bubbles up from the Dudh Kosi (a.k.a. Gokyo) valley. *Michał Król*

an altitude of 5,600m. Our plan then was to descend to Machermo for a rest, but the weather forecast suggested otherwise. An ongoing window, followed in just a few days by poor conditions, made us decide to start the mountain action immediately.

Early in the morning of October 31, Maciej Kimel, Mariusz Madej, and I started up the northeast face of Kyajo Ri (6,186m), following a line to the right of Stealing Beauty (1,050m, 6b A2 M6; *AAJ 2014*). We planned to climb alpine style and not use aid.

On the first day, we climbed about halfway up the face. Right from the start, the wall was very steep, and we knew the only relatively comfortable bivouac spot would be at around 5,600m. After 15 pitches with demanding mixed and rock climbing, we arrived at this shelf 12 hours after leaving the ground. It turned out to be quite small and uncomfortable, not allowing more than a few hours of interrupted sleep.

The next day, we started up soft snow and after a while arrived at the central part of the wall, which offered excellent climbing on high-quality vertical granite. The difficulties were significant, but the climbing went smoothly, and after 14 pitches we reached a comfortable ledge at around 5,900m.

We spent the night in our sleeping bags, without a tarp or tent, and the next morning set off for the summit, which was 300m above. We climbed up to the east summit, thinking that traversing from there to the main top would be a formality. We couldn't have been more wrong. The connecting ridge was sharp and jagged, and required more technical climbing. Nevertheless, at 10:30 a.m., and after a total of 34 pitches, we reached the top and a breathtaking panoramic view.

We knew the descent would be serious. We returned to the east summit, then started down the southeast ridge (first climbed in 2006). After five rappels and downclimbing we bivouacked at 5,700m. The next day was the last one with fine weather. We got up at dawn on November 3 and after more rappelling reached our base camp around noon.

A few hours later, we had made it down to Machermo, exhausted, dehydrated, but happy. Sadly, this happiness was ultimately overshadowed by the tragedy of Ondrej Húserka, a friend who had died on the descent from Langtang Lirung (*see story above*). We dedicated our ascent to him and believe he is watching over us from a better place. We named our route Butterfly Effect (1,150m, 6b M6). The climbing is generally independent of Stealing Beauty but intersects with it at around 5,700m.

—Michał Król, *Poland*

Kyajo Ri (6,186m), seen from the northeast. (1) Southeast ridge (5.9 AI3, Hobby-Kear, 2005). (2) Stealing Beauty (6b A2 M6, Belousov-Kopteva, 2013). (3) Butterfly Effect (Kimel-Madej-Król, 2024). (4) Attempt on the northeast face (Fortune-Rowe, 2011). (5) Attempt ending on the north ridge (Bonino-Meli, 2009). (6) North ridge (UIAA III+ M6 AI4+, Hák- Holeček, 2018, climbing mostly on the east side of the crest). *Ben Dare*

EDITOR'S NOTE: *This new route starts up a 2011 attempt on the northeast face by New Zealand climbers, but where those climbers moved right onto the hanging glacier, the Polish climbers continued left to terrain on the right side of the east face. A line here had been attempted several times by Dutch parties and German climbers. The highest point reached by these teams was at the base of the headwall, at around 5,800m.*

HUNGCHI TRAVERSE

NEW ROUTE UP THE WEST FACE AND FIRST ALPINE-STYLE ASCENT

By Symon Welfringer, *France*

When you go on an expedition to the other side of the world, things rarely go to plan. Our ascent of Hungchi was unexpected.

Charles Dubouloz and I arrived at our 5,060m base camp in May, hoping to establish a new route on Gyachung Kang (7,952m). However, during our acclimatization I fell ill with a nasty case of bronchitis.

I took a week's rest and plenty of medication. Meanwhile, Charles attempted the southwest ridge of nearby Hungchi (7,029m), spending three days alone and reaching around 6,200m. [*A Japanese expedition used this route to make the first ascent of the mountain in 2003; see AAJ 2004.*] Independently, both of us had spotted a new line on the west face of Hungchi, and this quickly became our Plan B.

Following Charles's return, we had three days of rest, after which he was still a little tired. I was back up to about 80 percent. We had a forecast for half a weather window.

We set off from base camp on May 16, and after four hours of walking over moraine, camped at 5,300m. Our line was toward the left side of the west face, and would require a 1,300m ascent to reach a small depression on the northwest ridge at around 6,580m. [*The northwest ridge was first climbed from the Tibetan side, in 2006, by a Japanese expedition.*] There was no possibility of a good bivouac on the face, so we needed to climb to the ridge in a single day.

We set off at 5 a.m. the following morning. I was in worse shape than Charles, so he took the lead more often. Conditions were good, with no clouds or wind, but the 12 hours on the face felt like the sporting performance of a lifetime. At

Hungchi from the west, showing the traverse (left to right) and bivouacs of the May 2024 ascent. The left skyline is the northwest ridge, first climbed in 2006; the climbers reached the ridge at a similar point, but from the far (Tibetan) side. *Damien Gildea*

the shoulder, I was exhausted and had a headache, and Charles had to set up the tent. At that moment, Charles doubted we would continue, but the next day was his birthday. Who could refuse him the gift of a summit?

We barely ate, and inevitably the night was bad, but the next morning's sunshine boosted our motivation. Those last 400m up the technically moderate snow ridge took us a full six hours. At 1:30 p.m., we reached the summit. It was snowing, the wind had strengthened, but Charles was now 35.

We elected to descend the steep southwest ridge, which Charles had previously attempted. It turned out to be complex, with unreliable snow that allowed almost no opportunity for rappelling. We hoped to drop to 6,300m for the night, but got no farther than 6,700m, where it was snowing hard and our headaches were only just beginning to dissipate. We managed to drink but didn't eat anything, and the tent broke during the night.

In the lower section of the new route on the west face of Hungchi. *Symon Welfringer*

On the morning of the 19th, we told ourselves we had to be at base camp that evening, because the forecast for the 20th was super ugly. Reluctantly, we decided to abandon the tent to go lighter. We descended to below 6,500m, at which point we could see barely two meters ahead, and we knew from prior observation we had reached the most complex section of the ridge.

To our right was a 1,200m face with seracs: We didn't have enough gear—or a shield—to descend that way. The map indicated the east face on the left was "only" 700m to the glacier. We hadn't seen it, but we took this option, beginning a series of rappels from Abalakov anchors. With no idea whether there would be dangerous seracs or loaded slopes ahead, our anxiety about hitting a dead end was palpable. However, fortune smiled. A few hours and less than 15 rappels later, we were trudging down a steep snow slope at 6,000m.

It took a further three hours after reaching the glacier to walk south and then west around the mountain through a chaos of blocks and boulders. At around 8 p.m. we struggled into base camp. We named our route after the French song by Saez: "Le Cavalier sans Tête" ("The Headless Horseman," 1,700m, ED). [*Hungchi had only been climbed three times before, all with extensive use of fixed rope and camps. The alpine-style ascent by the French pair was also the first traverse of the mountain.*]

Khangri Shar (6,792m) from the southeast. The glaciated slopes and couloir leading directly to the col between Pumori (on the far right) and Khangri Shar have been attempted by a number of teams, including a Korean pair in 2024 that reached the col but did not continue up the ridge. ***Korean Khangri Shar Expedition***

KHANGRI SHAR, SOUTH COULOIR AND EAST RIDGE, ATTEMPT

Khangri Shar (6,792m, 28°1'10.86"N, 86°48'52.81"E), which lies on the Nepal-Tibet frontier between Pumori and Chombu, is a difficult peak with no recorded ascent. It was brought onto the permitted list in 2002 and has been attempted a handful of times. The south face is steep and predominantly rocky. To the right, complex glacial terrain and a couloir lead to a 6,459m col that marks the lowest point on the ridge connecting Khangri Shar and Pumori. Climbers have also remarked on an elegant southeast spur rising directly to the summit—this would give a difficult route.

Multiple teams have attempted the glacier and couloir route, generally using fixed ropes, and most reported being stopped by dangerous conditions. None reached the Khangri Shar–Pumori col. (*See details at the AAJ website.*) However, in the fall of 1990, the couloir was climbed to the col by a team of Americans attempting the west ridge of Pumori.

In April 2024, An Chi-young, who has completed many ascents in the Himalaya, and Woo Seok-ju spent three days climbing the southeast face to the 6,459m col. The two negotiated a brittle rocky face of about 500m and then complex glacial terrain with numerous crevasses, often climbing unroped. In late afternoon on April 14, they reached the col and camped. From there, they could see that the east ridge had a 200m section of rocky pinnacles followed by 800m of sharp corniced arête.

Unfortunately, Seok-ju was tired and unwell, so the two decided to descend to base camp for a rest. This took two days, and when Seok-ju's condition worsened, they abandoned further attempts.

—Oh Young-hoon, *Korea*

AMA DABLAM, WEST FACE, CHEGI

In the autumn, Nikita Balabanov and I started a long-term project on Makalu, aiming to establish a new route in alpine style. Before departing for Nepal, we assessed the odds of success for our first go at just five to ten percent. And, as usual, the mountains had their own agenda. Two days after we reached base camp, a storm delivered 1.5m of heavy, wet snow. Trekking to advanced base camp (5,700m) became a two-and-a-half-day ordeal in high-altitude boots rather than a single day in running shoes. Our plans for Makalu unraveled quickly.

Nikita mentioned a mixed line he'd spotted years ago on Ama Dablam's south face. Skeptical but intrigued, I agreed we should check it out. What followed was anything but simple: a grueling trek over Sherpani Col (6,100m) and Amphu Lapcha Col (5,900m) in unseasonably snowy conditions. Finally, we arrived at Ama Dablam base camp.

The south face? Bare rock. No ice, no mixed line. Our attention shifted to the west face—a spur on the left side. A quick internet search confirmed there were no prior ascents of this line to the northwest shoulder. [*The lower part of the line identified by Balabanov and Fomin appears very similar to one started by a team of*

Korean climbers in 1988; they escaped left to the northwest ridge just below the steep rock bands in the middle of the face and descended. However, during their first two days on the face, the Ukrainians reported they did not see any old ropes, pitons, or other signs of previous climbers.] After a rest, we set off on October 27. That night, we bivouacked at 5,100m below the glacier.

Above the bergschrund, at 5,500m, the real climbing began. Mixed terrain, well-frozen early in the day, turned treacherous by afternoon as water streamed down the face. Progress slowed, and when we found a good snow mushroom at 5,800m, we stopped early, at 2 p.m., to bivy there.

Day two brought a rock barrier at 6,000m, with challenging moves requiring bare hands. By late afternoon, we reached the northwest ridge, bivouacking at 6,200m. Here we joined the 2000 British route, which we more or less followed to the top.

Snowy ridges above the shoulder tested our patience on day three. The leader climbed unprotected pitches of sugar snow, then dug a cave and sat in it for a belay stance. Another bivy followed at 6,400m. Day four featured ice gullies on the headwall, culminating in a couloir. Rockfall delayed progress until nightfall, when temperatures dropped and conditions improved. By late evening, we reached a serac bivy 50m below the summit.

On the morning of October 31, we summited Ama Dablam (6,812m). Clear skies, no wind, and—rare for this iconic peak—no other climbers. We descended via the normal route, navigating the chaos of commercial teams, and returned to base camp that evening.

We named our partial new route Chegi (1,600m, ED M5 AI4 80°) in memory of a friend of Nikita's killed in Ukraine. Despite the setbacks on Makalu, we discovered beauty and purpose on a peak we'd never planned to climb together.

—Mikhail Fomin, *Ukraine/Slovenia*

TOP: Steep mixed ground on the west face of Ama Dablam. *Nikita Balabanov*

BOTTOM: The west side of Ama Dablam, showing (1) the northwest ridge, (2) the Korean attempt (1988), (3) Chegi (2024), mostly following prior routes above the shoulder, and (4) the southwest ridge. Other routes on the face are not shown. *Alex Buisse*

The Sharphu Peaks from the east. (A) Sato Peak. (B) Sharphu III. (C) Sharphu V. (D) Sharphu I. (E) Sharphu II. (F) Sharphu VI. The Korean expedition in 2024 reached the broad Sato–Sharphu III saddle from this side, then continued up the ridge to Sharphu III's foresummit. ***David Bacci***

NEPAL | Ohmi Kangri Himal

SHARPHU III, ATTEMPT BY SOUTH-SOUTHEAST RIDGE

On October 30, a Korean expedition led by Jo Moon-yong, with three Sherpa climbers, claimed to have made the first ascent of Sharphu V. This claim was bolstered by a summit certificate from the Nepalese government.

However, no credible evidence exists to confirm the successful ascent of Sharphu V. Their purported summit photo fails to show climbers standing on top of any peak; they are grouped below a large rock tower, and Jo mentioned a big rock formation at the very top, which they were unable to climb due to lack of aid gear.

Closer examination of their photographs has shown the Korean team approached from the east up the Namphumba Glacier and climbed a relatively steep mixed wall to reach the broad pass between Sato Peak and unclimbed Sharphu III (27°43'50.29"N, 87°54'17.78"E). From here, they followed the gentle, south-southeast snow ridge of Sharphu III to a foresummit (the large rock tower in the photo). Beyond lies another pointed snow summit considered to be a little higher, though this may not have been obvious to the Korean team from their vantage point.

—Oh Young-hoon, *Korea*

SHARPHU PEAKS, STANDARDIZING NOMENCLATURE AND ELEVATIONS: *The Sharphu group is a collection of peaks on a north-south ridge to the west of Kambachen village, forming the watershed between the Ghunsa and Yangma valleys. Over the years, there has been much confusion over the naming of the individual summits in this group and their relationship to each other, including in the AAJ.*

For consistency among the AAJ, the Himalayan Database, and the Nepalese government, we will define the main summits—from north to south—as follows: ***Sharphu IV*** *(6,172m), summited in 1962 by Japanese climbers, who gave it the name Nupchu after the glacier to the southeast.* ***Sharphu VI*** *(6,076m), unclimbed but attempted from the north.* ***Sharphu II*** *(6,328m, Tanga II on some maps), climbed in 2018 by an American-Lithuanian team.* ***Sharphu I*** *(6,433m, Tanga I on some maps), climbed in 1963 by Japanese.* ***Sharphu V*** *(6,158m, Tanga III), unattempted.* ***Sharphu III*** *(6,220m, called Marson on some maps, after a pass of that name to the west), attempted but unclimbed.* ***Sato Peak*** *(6,164m), attempted but unclimbed. On the ridge northwest of Sharphu VI stands the smaller peak of Tha Nagphu (5,980m), which has been climbed.*

All heights cited here are from the HMG-Finn map and Himalayan Database but do

The photo that started it all: the northeast face of Pandra, seen from Janak East in October 2013, showing (1) Peine Plancher (2017), (2) A Piece of the Sun (2024), joining the 2017 route, and (3) the Taniguchi-Wada attempt (2016). In center, in the distance, is the Tibetan side of the Makalu-Lhotse-Everest group, while on the far left is part of Chamlang. The peak at far right in the middle distance is Chabuk (6,792m). ***Hiroshi Hagiwara***

not agree with the elevations used by the Nepalese government, which for some peaks are dramatically inflated.

The Nepalese Mountaineering Association (NMA), in collaboration with the Ministry of Culture, Tourism and Civil Aviation, has created an online portal of Nepal's peaks to aid with permits and other matters, and this portal's list of coordinates for the six Sharphu peaks agrees, approximately, with the nomenclature above. However, it lists Sharphu I at 7,070m and Sharphu III as 6,885m—some 600m higher than the actual elevations. The 7,070m altitude for Sharphu I came from the successful 1963 team, which claimed the altitudes assigned to these peaks were far too low. They are not.

These exaggerated heights presented a problem in 2022 for an Italian team that planned to attempt Sharphu III but was informed a few days before leaving for Nepal that the ministry's higher altitude figure would require a permit far too expensive for their budget. They went elsewhere.

—Lindsay Griffin, *AAJ*, and Rodolphe Popier, *Himalayan Database*

NEPAL | Janak Himal

PANDRA, NORTHEAST FACE, A PIECE OF THE SUN

"Mr. Hagiwara, what mountain is this?" The question was asked by Kei Taniguchi as she looked at a picture taken by Hiroshi Hagiwara, editor of *Rock and Snow*, in 2013. The photo clearly showed the unclimbed northeast face of Pandra (27°51'56.34"N, 87°59'24.96"E), measured at 6,673m in 2002 by the first ascensionists (the HMG-Finn map has an erroneous height of 6,850m).

In 2016, Taniguchi attempted Pandra with Junji Wada, retreating from two-thirds height (*AAJ 2017*). On return to Japan she wrote, "I've opened Pandora's Box. I will definitely go back to check what's inside." Tragically, a month later, she fell to her death from Mt. Kurodake.

I interviewed many people to compile a book about Kei's life, called *A Piece of the Sun*. In the final chapter, I hoped to incorporate a scene in which some of us, including Wada, climbed Pandra. However, Wada was seriously injured just before

Early on day two of the ascent of the northeast face of Pandra, climbing part of the three-pitch Pandra Great Icicle. ***Suguru Takayanagi***

our team was due to leave Japan, and the expedition was postponed. Finally, in 2024, eight years after Kei's accident, Suguru Takayanagi, Hiroki Suzuki, and I went to Pandra to complete her route. Wada had become a family man, starting a new life.

Just 20 minutes into the start of our trek from Sekatum, a landslide occurred. We ran for our lives, but our kitchen helper was hit and died instantly. "Isn't Himalayan climbing just the ego of developed countries?" I wondered aloud to Suzuki, then worried for the next three days about whether we should go ahead with the expedition. However, our sirdar implored us to continue. We arrived at our 5,100m base camp on October 12.

The approach to advanced base at 5,300m on the west side of the Chabuk Glacier had changed significantly in eight years due to global warming: Much of the ice had gone, unstable moraine made walking difficult, and the northeast face of Pandra looked far drier than in the pictures taken by the French in 2017. [*In October 2017, French climbers Mathieu Détrie, Pierre Labbre, and Benjamin Védrines completed the first route up the northeast face: Peine Plancher (1,200m, WI6 M6; see AAJ 2018).*]

After acclimatization, we left advanced base for Pandra at 7 a.m. on October 25. It took three hours to reach the foot of the wall, after which we climbed to a bivouac site at 5,500m, where we pitched the tent using a snow hammock. The climbing to this point, following the line taken by Taniguchi and Wada, had involved crumbling rock and brittle ice.

On day two, we climbed three pitches of excellent, steep alpine ice, dubbed the Pandra Great Icicle. Above, a couloir with poor protection and belays cut through the center of the face, and at 5,800m we made our second bivouac.

On the 27th, we headed directly toward the summit. [*From around this point, or below, Taniguchi and Wada traversed to the north spur; the 2024 team continued direct and joined the line of the 2017 French route, which came in from the left.*] At around 6,000m, the French party had found a pitch of M6. Takayanagi, who is about ten years younger than us, onsighted that pitch easily—he should achieve great things in the Himalaya. Suzuki took the lead and brought us to a bivouac beneath a rock outcrop at 6,200m. We were able to pitch the tent properly—but only just.

The next morning, we left our bivouac gear and headed for the top. Takayanagi climbed an overhang that was much more difficult than the M6 the day before. We then climbed ice and difficult sugar snow, with little meaningful protection, to reach a snow cave after dark at around 6,500m. We shivered through the night in just the clothes we were wearing.

With Suzuki in the lead, it took only 30 minutes to reach the top. Suzuki shouted, "Whoa, we did it!" I've been climbing with him for 20 years, but this was the first time I'd heard a serious roar. The weather was perfect. Our GPS recorded 6,665m.

By 4 p.m. we had returned to our snow cave, and the following day we rappelled to the base. We named our route A Piece of the Sun. It will continue to burn in our hearts and guide us toward greater mountains.

—Akihiro Oishi, *Japan, with help from Kaoru Wada, Hiroshi Hagiwara, and Rodolphe Popier*

NORTH FACE DIRECT

THE FIRST ASCENT OF PHOLE IN THE KANGCHENJUNGA HIMAL

By Hidesuke Taneishi, *Japan*

The ridge extending west from Jannu crosses three summits as it descends toward the Ghunsa Khola valley. The first two, Sobithongie (6,652m) and Phole (6,645m; both altitudes from the HMG-Finn map), are close together and separated by only a shallow depression. Indeed, some maps refer to them as one peak: Pholesobi. Much farther west is Kyabura (6,294m). All three were opened for climbing in 2002, but until 2023 none had received a serious attempt. [*There are rumors that Sobithongie was attempted or climbed from the north around 20 years ago, but these are unconfirmed.*] In a book written by the Japanese expedition that made the first ascent of the northwest face of Jannu, in 1976, Sobithongie-Phole is described as a "rocky head of hopeless rock and ice."

Hiroki Yamamoto on mixed terrain at 6,500 meters on the north face of Phole. *Hidesuke Taneishi*

The North Face Direct on Phole (6,652m), seen from Merra Peak. The summit immediately left is Sobithongie. Jannu is just out of the picture to the left. *Hidesuke Taneishi*

Hiroki Yamamoto and I attempted the north face of Phole in autumn 2023, but due to illness we had to descend from around 6,200m (*AAJ 2024*). We returned in October 2024 for another attempt. The north face is so steep that tents cannot be pitched except in the middle section, using a snow hammock. Like the Americans who climbed the north face of Jannu in autumn 2023, we used portaledge-like G7 Pods.

We arrived at Kangbachen (4,100m) on October 9 and used a lodge there as our base camp. We acclimatized on Merra Peak, directly opposite our mountain. The American and French teams that tried Jannu East in the autumn had previously acclimatized on Merra, and we used their tent sites.

On October 26, Hiroki and I left base camp for our attempt on Phole with a little less than 30kg of gear on each of our backs. We climbed 1,000m over moraine and glacier to establish an advanced base at 5,050m, below the north face. We then took two days to break through the lower face, where protection was difficult to arrange. The ice was too brittle to take screws, so we excavated rock protection from under the snow. It was so steep that we were nervous about making long runouts. During the bivouacs, spindrift from the upper face swept over us all night and even got inside the Pod. Our clothes became wet and then froze, making us very uncomfortable.

On the 29th, we crossed the lower-angled middle section and reached the upper face. Next morning, we started up the initial steep wall, finding very thin ice. However, unlike the lower part of the face, the ice in this section was quite solid, and at the crux we were able to use micro-nuts and Tricams for protection. The climbing was like that in Alaska or Chamonix, and we enjoyed it.

On October 31, we left the Pod and headed for the top. From base camp we had seen a chimney going directly to the summit. Now we could see this above us, but to reach it we had to climb a 100m rock wall. This was the second crux. In places the wall exceeded 90°, but cams, nuts, and screws were sound, and we were able to climb comfortably. We then ascended the icy chimney, followed by a sugar-snow wall with no protection. We broke through the cornice above and exited onto the ridge just below the summit.

Hiroki, standing next to me, shouted in joy, "We've done it!" We congratulated and embraced each other. Then we climbed upward for 30 seconds to stand on the summit. It was 5 p.m. Illuminated by the sunset, Jannu was stunningly beautiful. It was also clear that Phole, where we stood, was higher than Sobithongie, despite what the map says. Our altimeter registered more than 6,650m, and we judge Phole's elevation to be around 6,652m.

After five minutes we started down, vowing to each other that we would get down alive. We regained the Pod at 8 p.m.

The next day, November 1, we descended the rest of our route, mostly by rappel but with some downclimbing. We used Abalakov anchors in the upper face and Tricams, pitons, slings, and nuts in the lower part. After almost 30 rappels, we reached the foot of the face at 7 p.m. The name of the route is simply North Face Direct (1,500m, ED+).

Hiroki Yamamoto descends from the summit of Phole. Jannu (Kumbhakarna, 7,710m) catches the setting sun, with the north face in shadow and the west pillar facing the camera. *Hidesuke Taneishi*

China

XINJIANG | Tien Shan

On Dry Martini, with the eastern arm of Paradise Lake and unnamed peaks behind. ***Zhen Wang***

PARADISE LAKE, DRY MARTINI AND OTHER ASCENTS

As the proverb goes, you won't know how big China is until you arrive in Xinjiang. The long journey to Paradise Lake proves this saying is accurate.

Paradise Lake (a.k.a. Akekule Lake, 3,050m, 42°34'48.77"N, 82°23'32.68"E) lies on the Wusun Ancient Road, a former north-south migration route across the Tien Shan that is now a highly popular yet serious trek of about 120km. The lake is nearly surrounded by unnamed 4,000m peaks, some of them glaciated and all apparently unclimbed until 2024.

A few years ago, Yang Guang showed me a photo of the area. I was shocked: Towering limestone walls surrounded a turquoise lake, green grass, and herds of sheep and cattle. He had not climbed there but was keen to go. COVID-19 prevented it at that time, but we decided to try in 2024, choosing the best time of year for this area: early July to early August. Accompanying us was regular climbing partner Hongshu Qui and longtime climbing photographer Zhen Wang.

The lake can be accessed from the north by flying in a sightseeing helicopter for around 30 minutes or taking an off-road vehicle for around six hours, then walking for another five hours. We chose the latter. This hike involves seven or eight river crossings, requiring wading or riding a horse. There are organized camping areas at the lake, but due to the passage of many tourists, the environment has been damaged, and garbage is rife. Another problem of this area is the unstable weather: In our 20 days, there was only one period of 48 hours without rain.

While the rock on the high alpine peaks is not good (*see related report below*), the lower rock walls are of an unusually high-

ABOVE: Looking southwest across Paradise Lake (a.k.a. Akekule Lake). (A) Peak 4,539m, climbed in 2024; see story on next page. (B) Peak 4,359m, unclimbed. (C) Peak 4,171m. (D) Peak 3,700m, showing the line of Dry Martini, climbed in 2024. *Expedition Photo*

RIGHT: Unclimbed walls near Paradise Lake. The rock is limestone, generally of high quality at lower elevations. *Zhen Wang*

quality alpine limestone, and there are hundreds of excellent boulders scattered around the alpine meadow. The area is currently open to climbing, providing you register in advance and your climbing plan is approved by the local authorities (*see the AAJ website for more information*).

On the west bank of the lake stands a cluster of rock peaks rising to around 3,800m. We chose the nearest and smallest (approx. 42°35'13.09"N, 82°22'37.93"E) and spent ten days putting up Dry Martini (450m, 11 pitches, 5.11a) on the southeast face. The route has a mix of bolted and traditional protection, and we completed the ascent on July 23. On the last pitch, Zhen turned to Yang and said, "How long have you been looking forward to reaching this summit?" Yang replied, "Twelve years. The first time I saw a picture of this face was 12 years ago."

We also created a number of sport routes, from 5.9 to 5.12, and some boulder problems of V2 (we had not expected boulders, so carried no pads). Our climb was just the beginning. I believe that as time goes by, more rock climbers will come here and open new routes, making Paradise Lake a destination for climbers from across China and even from around the world.

—Zhiming Wang, *with assistance from* Zhan Fang, *China, and* Xia Zhongming, *Germany*

Foreshortened view of Peak 4,539m from the east, showing the glacier climbed during the first ascent. The climbers continued up the southeast ridge to the top. ***Expedition Photo***

PARADISE LAKE, PEAK 4,539M, NORTHEAST GLACIER AND SOUTHEAST RIDGE

Deng Tao, Li Bo, and Zhang Xinyi arrived at Paradise (a.k.a. Akekule) Lake in August, with part of a group aiming for the glaciated 4,000m peaks around the lake, all unnamed. (*See report above for an introduction to Paradise Lake.*) Peak 4,539m rises to the south-southwest of the lake at 42°32'40.27"N, 82°22'3.83"E.

The three climbers established their base camp next to the lake at 3,050m and on August 14 they moved toward Peak 4,539m and camped at 3,450m, where they could see a logical route to the top.

The next day, they left at 10 a.m. and quickly reached the glacier that rises to the southwest below the rocky east face of the peak. As they put on crampons, a falling rock hit Deng. While the rockfall didn't stop the ascent, later medical examination showed one rib was broken. Deng led up bare ice at 50°–65°, placing intermediate protection as the others followed simultaneously. Higher, when they reached more crevassed terrain, they began belaying. They didn't find a place flat enough to bivouac until 9 p.m., when they discovered a small crevasse at 4,350m in which they could spend the night.

At 10 a.m. on the 16th, they left their bivouac gear and continued to the southeast ridge, finishing through a three-meter-wide, hard-ice couloir between rock buttresses (25m, 75°). The ridge itself was loose and broken. (Though from a distance the rock here looks like granite, it is actually a sort of poor metamorphic stone formed by the recrystallization of limestone.) Fifth-class climbing took them through exposed terrain to a final 40m pitch of 5.6. At 4 p.m. they were standing on the two-meter-square summit.

They descended by making three rappels on the ridge, one in the ice couloir and two more on the icy slope, to reach the bivouac site. They then continued down into the night, reaching the 3,450m camp at 2:30 a.m. on August 17. During this descent, much of it in moderate to heavy rain, Li's left hand was broken by rockfall. With help from other members of the team, all three walked through the stormy night to reach base camp. The climbers named their route Knockin' on Heaven's Door (1,100m, D 5.6 AI2+ 60° snow).

—Lindsay Griffin, *with information from Zhan Fang, China, and Xia Zhongming, Germany*

XINJIANG | Kunlun – Aksai Chin

Khan Yalik (6,700m, labeled as Oierlizuoke in this report) from the East Karakash Valley. The November 2024 attempt on the northwest face is marked. An earlier ascent climbed the face farther right. ***Ed Hannam***

OIERLIZUOKE (KHAN YALIK), NORTHWEST FACE, ATTEMPT

In 2024, my company, Feeding the Rat Expeditions, obtained the first permits to visit the Chinese side of K2 since 2011. However, in October, immediately before our planned departure, the permits were unexpectedly suspended, for reasons only described as "military." Eager to help, the Xinjiang Mountaineering Association laid out other options that would fit the logistics we already had in place. One of the offerings was the Aksai Chin region, which we grabbed before they changed their mind.

We settled on the East Karakash mountains of the northern Aksai Chin. These are probably the highest mountains in all of the Aksai Chin, though the only named peak is Oierlizuoke (6,700m, 35°50'51.11"N, 79°34'29.57"E). This area has a number of summits around 6,500m, but climbing here had never been formally allowed. [*The mountain described here is better known as Khan Yalik and was climbed in 1996 and possibly earlier. Most sources use the name Oierlizuoke or Qierlizuoke Feng for a 6,802m peak that is 22km northwest of this mountain. See the AAJ website for more information about historical ascents in this little-known range.*]

Benji Brennan and Sam Wieske (Australia), Alex Tang (China), Tom Rospabe (France), Marco de Vecchio (Italy), and I acclimatized to 5,300m in the Tibetan ranges of western Sichuan, then flew to Kashgar in mid-November and drove to a point south of Oierlizuoke. Following the East Karakash River, we made multiple carries over several days to a base camp at 5,200m.

In the upper reaches of the river, the mountains rise around 1,600m. Oierlizuoke is a narrow, dorsal-fin ridge running northeast-southwest, with the southeast and northwest faces both rising from glacier basins.

We attempted the central northwest face rising above the East Karakash Glacier. Our line was a snow and ice runnel, starting about 500m above the glacier. The gradient began at 45°, then steepened. The climbing was not technical, and as the temperature never got anywhere close to rising above freezing, rockfall was minimal.

Our high point was on November 29 at around 6,000m. At base camp, temperatures had already fallen below -30°C inside tents (around -25°C during the day). Our equipment was up to the task, but the weeks above 5,000m were starting to wear. We retreated and then drove more than 4,000km home to Chengdu.

—Ed Hannam, *Australia*

TIBET | Himalaya

BUZZER BEATER

THE FIRST ASCENT OF 7,221-METER KARJIANG

By Xia Zhongming, *with information from Liu Yang, China*

By his definition of a mountain versus a subsidiary top, mountaineering statistician Eberhard Jurgalski lists the Himalayan peak Karjiang (7,221m, 28°15'36.94"N, 90°38'41.94"E), near the Tibet-Bhutan border, as the 97th-highest mountain in the world. Of the unclimbed main summits on this list, only Apsarasas Kangri I (7,243m), Lapche Kang II (7,250m), and Gankar (Kankar) Punzum (7,575m) were higher. On August 13, Karjiang left the "unclimbed" list, as Chinese alpinists Liu Yang and Song Yuancheng stood on the summit after a three-day climb.

The Karjiang group and nearby Kula Kangri massif stand about 165km southwest of Lhasa. A team from Japan climbed the main summit of Kula Kangri (7,554m) in 1986, and the east and central

ABOVE: On the lower part of the southwest face of Karjiang. ***Liu Yang Collection***

OPPOSITE PAGE: The southwest face of Karjiang (7,221m), showing the line and bivouacs during the first ascent of the mountain. ***Liu Yang Collection***

summits fell to another Japanese expedition in 2002. Karjiang has three summits: a south or main peak; a central peak (Karjiang II, 7,216m); and a northwest peak (Karjiang III, or Taptol Kangri, 6,824m). Japanese climbers attempted the main summit in 1986 (a different expedition from the one above) but found it too difficult; they then made the first ascent of Karjiang II via the northwest ridge. A Dutch team also tried the west face of the main summit in 2001, failed, and climbed Karjiang III.

Liu Yang had been attracted to Karjiang for several years, but as a university lecturer, he only had the summer holidays of July and August available for expeditions—not an ideal season for attempting this mountain. Nonetheless, Liu and Song Yuancheng, with a photographer and two hired staff, arrived in Lhasa in mid-July, and on the 24th they trekked up the glacier flowing north from the Kula Kangri and Karjiang groups to reach a base camp at 5,800m. It was lower than they wanted, but the porters would go no farther. Their subsequent reconnaissance proved unfruitful, as the upper mountain was shrouded in cloud. Some of the team suffered from altitude illness, so they all returned to Lhasa.

On July 30, the team was back in base camp. Starting out at around noon the next day, Liu and Song climbed up the southwest face of Karjiang and camped beneath a serac at 6,350m. On August 1, they reached 6,650m and camped again beneath a serac. An overnight storm dropped one meter of fresh snow, but the following day the two continued upward for another 250m, then spent two hours cutting a tent platform. Again, it snowed all night, and, experiencing headaches the following morning, the two descended to base camp.

ABOVE: Looking south across Pumo Yumco lake at 5,000 meters. (A) Karjiang II. (B) Karjiang. (C) Kula Kangri East. (D) Kula Kangri Central. (E) Kula Kangri West. (F) Jiexiang Group (6,672m, unclimbed). ***Liu Yang Collection***

LEFT: Liu Yang and Song Yuancheng in the crevasse bivouac at 6,900 meters. ***Liu Yang Collection***

Back in Lhasa for another rest, they felt convinced they could climb the face with a three-day weather window. Their best option proved to be around August 11–12, when only eight centimeters of snow was forecast to fall.

After returning to base camp on the 10th, they set off at 2:30 the following morning and started up the southwest face at 5 a.m. This time they chose a line close to the rock wall left of their previous attempt. They simul-climbed to 6,550m—the first part comfortably icy, the second through deep snow—and used a small, natural ice cave for a bivouac site. It was too small to pitch the tent, so they slept with the tent fly draped over them.

Snow fell overnight but stopped at 5 a.m. on August 12, and they climbed to a large crevasse under a serac at around 6,900m. Again, they were forced to sleep with the flysheet draped over them, as the tent poles broke due to the cold. The next morning, they left their gear and climbed 100m to reach loose mixed terrain with unreliable protection. By 2 p.m. they had gained the summit ridge, where they turned right and moved together for 55 minutes to the highest point.

Starting the descent of their route in a whiteout, they were unable to find ice for the first rappel and resorted to a buried pack lid as a makeshift snow anchor. Four rappels from Abalakov anchors in thin ice, followed by difficult downclimbing, got them back to their high bivouac site under the serac. They were exhausted but opted to continue. Following their ascent route down proved difficult in snowfall and bad visibility, and from time to time they were hit by spindrift avalanches. However, at 5 a.m. on the 14th, they made it to the glacier.

The moraine below was now covered in more than half a meter of fresh snow, and they were forced to crawl down it. They reached base camp at 9:30 a.m., having taken 4.5 hours to cover 1.5km. The snow had prevented porters from returning to base camp, so the two climbers left their gear for later collection and continued down to meet their friends, who drove them to Lhasa. They arrived there at 4:30 a.m. on August 15, just in time for their flights home. Their 11th-hour success prompted them to choose the route name Buzzer Beater (1,300m, AI3 M4 70° snow).

(A) Nobgyar North, (B) Nobgyar, and (C) Zhuqing from the northwest, showing the 2024 ascent (left) and the descent of the rock buttress directly below Zhuqing, along with the first three bivouacs. ***Zhan Fang***

ZHUQING, NORTH RIDGE VIA WEST FACE OF NOBGYAR NORTH

The highest of a cluster of peaks in the northern Shaluli Shan, separated from the well-known Chola Shan by the G317 Highway, is Zhuqing (5,849m on Chinese maps, 32°2'25.95"N, 98°49'1.06"E), named after the town nine kilometers to the north. [*Zhuqing has become the accepted spelling in publications written in English. However, a phonetic interpretation of the Tibetan name would be Zhiltroen.*] There was no recorded ascent in this group until August 2023, when Qiyun Fu and I climbed the south face and southeast ridge of Zhuqing East, measuring its altitude at 5,722m (32°2'16.98"N, 98°49'11.6"E). We had hoped to continue to the main summit but ran out of time.

The following month, Yongpeng Fu and Xinyue Cao climbed Sejong (5,816m, a summit southwest of Zhuqing; *see AAJ 2024*).

I returned in February 2024 to try Zhuqing via an approach from the north, but the weather prevented an attempt. I then asked Wenkai Zhong to try Zhuqing with me in the summer.

Using three porters and three motorbikes, we headed south from Zhuqing town on August 3 to reach our base camp at 5,050m. The next day, we climbed up the rocky west face of Peak 5,737m (Nobgyar North, spelled Nobyugya in *AAJ 2024*) to a height of around 5,500m, where we bivouacked. In the lower section we didn't belay, but higher there were two pitches of 5.9.

The following morning, we climbed the upper ice slope (50°), with the second jumaring and carrying most of the load. We reached the summit of Peak 5,737m at 4:20 p.m. and continued along the ridge in the direction of Nobgyar. To the north-northeast, 1,800m below us, we could see the elaborate Dzogchen Monastery, just south of Zhuqing town. We bivouacked on a large, flat boulder on the ridge.

August 6 dawned clear, and in two hours we reached Nobgyar, which we measured at 5,777m. Continuing south, we simul-climbed until the final rocky section of Zhuqing. Here, a section of M3/4 led to the summit, which we measured at 5,804m. In all, the traverse from Nobgyar North covered one kilometer.

Rather than return the way we'd come, we decided to rappel about 500m down the rocky west face, a nearly disastrous decision. A couple of rappels from Abalakov anchors got us to the top of the rock wall, where progress was greatly hindered by several stuck ropes—in one case requiring Wenkai to retrieve the ropes manually and downclimb very difficult rock. Rockfall hit us and damaged the ropes. We made an unplanned bivouac, with little food or fuel, on a narrow platform at around 5,500m.

On the morning of the 7th, we experienced more stuck ropes, loose rock, and poor anchors, and had to descend on partially cut ropes until our 12th rappel from the summit dropped us into the bergschrund, from which we descended to a final bivouac site in a snow scoop.

The weather was still sunny on August 8, and we traversed a two-kilometer crevasse maze to base camp and then returned to Zhuqing town at 4 p.m. It rained cats and dogs the day after we left the valley, as if to demonstrate how close we were to a situation that would have given us no way back.

We named our ascent Remembering Yueshuai (700m, D- 5.9 AI2 M4). Yueshuai Song had been my climbing partner since I started alpinism in 2022, but he was tragically killed in a rappel accident on Xuebaoding in May 2024. The late Dongdong Yan, one of the most renowned Chinese alpinists of his time, once remarked that the best way to honor someone is to remember them, so they are never too far away.

—**Zhan Fang, *China***

CHOLA RANGE, PEAK 5,560M; ZHUQING RANGE, PEAK 5,538M AND PEAK 5,590M

In August 2023, Haoyu Wen and I went to the northwestern Chola Shan in search of easily accessible summer ice. Our objective was a peak about three kilometers southwest of the Cho La Mountain Tunnel (4,378m) on the Sichuan-Tibet Highway (G317). The peaks in this area are sharp granite towers and rise to an altitude much higher than designated on available maps. (Our objective was 5,489m on the map, at 31°53'08"N, 98°55'52"E, but turned out to be around 5,560m.) I flew a drone toward the west face of our objective and saw that the top section was a vertical rock wall.

The 2023 route up the west face of Peak 5,560m (GPS) in the northwestern Chola Shan. The snow slopes below the face were reached by climbing to a saddle off the bottom of the picture from the northeast (left). *Xueer Yu*

After camping, we climbed the northeast ice face, unroped much of the way but belaying sections of AI2. After 300m, we reached a ridge connecting our summit to a large rock tower to the north. We followed the crest south to an area of snow-covered crevasses at 5,470m. We couldn't see the final west-facing wall, but assumed it would be difficult, so we retreated.

Haoyu returned in July 2024 with Qiyun Fu and ascended the same route, though this time it was misty and they belayed most of the ice. Reaching the final, steep west face in the afternoon of July 25, Haoyu led the first pitch. At the top of this section, she realized the weather was quickly turning bad and there would be no time for Qiyun to follow. She soloed the last 30m of 5.9 to the summit, then immediately began rappelling. A horrific rainstorm hit the pair, making the descent tough and cold. The 450m route was 5.9 AI2.

During my 2023 trip, I had tried to find an approach from the south to peaks in the Zhuqing Range. I went to the Shengxian (a.k.a. Shenwonlu) valley and was amazed by the proliferation of giant granite boulders and rock walls. I returned in 2024 with Haoyu Wen, Qiyun Fu, and Peifeng Xie, but the monks living in the valley told us the approach to the glaciers, which they had done in the past, had recently been destroyed in a flood. As I was quite satisfied with our earlier ascent of Gangga I (*see report below*), I decided to return to Chengdu. The other three crossed the flooded boulderfields and reached the mountains.

On August 5, all three climbed Peak 5,538m (32°1'38.78"N, 98°51'10.12"E) via the north ridge, accessed from the southwest. The grade was around PD+ (5.6 50° ice).

They then moved base camp farther east, and on August 7 climbed Peak 5,590m (32°0'32.03"N, 98°52'0.57"E) via the north face, accessed from the west. The grade was around AD (AI2+ 70°), and the climbers measured the summit altitude as 5,529m, which they felt was more accurate than the map height. This area offers good potential for alpine ice and rock routes.

—Xueer Yu, *with information from* Haoyu Wen, China

TOP: The 2024 route up the north face of Peak 5,590m (map height; measured at 5,529m), Zhuqing Range. *Peifeng Xie*

BOTTOM: Unclimbed granite west of Peak 5,538m in the southeast Zhuqing Range. *Peifeng Xie*

DAPU MOUNTAINS, DAPU II AND PEAK 5,410M; GANGGA RANGE, GANGGA I

During the summer of 2024, Haoyu Wen and her various climbing partners made the first ascents of six peaks in the northern Shaluli Shan (*see related report above*).

In the first week of July, Haoyu and I, with two trekkers, traveled to the Dapu group of mountains, aiming to reach some colorful lakes we'd seen on a satellite map. We drove along the G317 Sichuan-Tibet Highway to reach the entrance to the Banchang Gou, a valley that heads southeast and gives access to the southwest side of the main Dapu peaks. From where we left the vehicles, we rode horses through swamps and bushes for 12km to reach the lakes at

ABOVE: The Dapu peaks from the south. From left to right: Dapu III, II, and I. The 2024 team climbed the glaciated face of Dapu II. ***Xueer Yu***

LEFT: Gangga I and the route of the first ascent on the upper west face and ridge. ***Xueer Yu***

4,800m. I was surprised, at this time of year, to see WI2 ice near the treeline.

We camped by the glacier to the south of Dapu II (5,472m, 31°39'34"N, 99°33'23"E), and the next morning, Haoyu, Jun Ma, and I climbed to the summit via the glacier.

Several days later, Haoyu came back to this valley with Zixuan Huo, Jiajun Jiang, and Meiying Zhou to climb a rocky pyramid to the south of the valley: Peak 5,410m (31°38'07"N, 99°30'05"E). [*On Google Earth this is a tiny summit of around 5,300m, which, due to its sharpness, has lost altitude on the satellite imagery; 5,410m was the measured altitude.*] This is the highest summit in the area to the south of the Dapu mountains. The four climbed the north ridge, with 5.4 rock and some mixed.

Later in July, Haoyu, Qiyun Fu, and I decided to attempt unclimbed Gangga I (5,688m), southwest of Ganzi. We quickly discovered that the approach road from the south had been damaged by flooding, so we took a 35km 4WD road from the west, which I had discovered during the Dapu trip. This gave a smooth ride to a farm southwest of the mountain. With the help of a few locals, we established base camp at 5,000m below the west glacier.

The next day, we carried heavy packs up 50° ice slopes, which were exposed to rockfall, toward the west ridge. Haoyu and Qiyun climbed unroped but set up a rope for me on the steep section. We arrived on the ridge at 2 p.m. and put up the tent, but before retiring for the night we fixed a rope across a crevassed area above.

We set out at 4 a.m. on August 1, crossed the crevasses in the dark, and continued up the icy face above, moving together. Haoyu took the lead, placing screws and snow stakes as intermediate protection. We crossed over a foresummit of 5,650m, then followed a broad snow ridge to reach the main summit, on which we arrived at 9 a.m., and where I unfurled an LGBTQ pride flag. Qiyun and I descended by downclimbing and rappelling, while Haoyu downclimbed and removed all the anchors. [*Editor's Note: Although ascents of smaller peaks in the Gangga range have been recorded in the AAJ, this was the first known ascent of the highest summit.*]

–Xueer Yu, *China*

SICHUAN | Qionglai Shan

The west face of Seerdengpu (5,592m), approximately 850 meters high. Prior to 2024, the peak had only been climbed once, by the northeast ridge (Johnson-Kellogg, 2010). The west face had been attempted at least eight times without success. ***Griff***

SEERDENGPU, WEST FACE, WILD CHILD

In 2015, when I first saw Seerdengpu (5,592m) from the west, I never thought that one day I would stand on the summit. The ca 850m west face was one of the great unclimbed walls of Siguniang National Park and had been attempted many times, notably by American Pat Goodman. In 2013, with Matt McCormick, he made unsuccessful attempts on three different lines, then later another attempt with Marcus Costa, and another, more toward the southwest, with David Sharratt. Costa made another attempt with Enzo Oddo. The face had also been tried by Russian, Australian, Polish, and Chinese teams. Loose terrain and objective danger appear to have been a common problem.

Until 2024, Seerdengpu had only one ascent. In 2010, Dylan Johnson and Chad Kellogg (both USA) climbed the northeast ridge. Prior to their ascent, four parties had attempted the north face.

I first tried the west face in August 2021 but chose a poor line and retreated after 80m. In 2022, I changed to the previously attempted line on the right side of the wall (the line attempted by Costa and Goodman,

The line of Wild Child on the upper west face of Seerdengpu. The route had a total of about 1,200 meters of climbing. ***Griff***

as well as the Russian and Chinese teams). I retreated after 350m. Over three weeks in July 2023, I only reached 200m up the same line. I returned in August 2024.

Unable to get an official permit, I had to work alone, as porters did not dare provide service. [*Because of this, the author is using an alias.*] I entered the valley several times as a tourist, each time carrying a 40-liter bag. In the end, I ferried a total of 75kg of equipment from the road in Shuangqiao Valley to my base camp at 4,500m.

After the initial 170m of the face, which is 5.7, the route enters a gully. It is always wet. Some previous attempts had failed due to the volume of water, and in 2015 Costa and Oddo tried this route in January, finding the gully nicely frozen but the rock above dangerously loose. They retreated from the Russian high point. I kept mostly in the bed of the narrow gully, which was wet and loose, but easier (5.8 C1+). I made my first portaledge camp at the top of the gully at around 5,100m.

On the first day above the portaledge, I climbed 80m at 5.9 C1+. When I rappelled to the ledge that evening, I found two holes in the fly, one of them large. A small bag on the ledge had also been hit and damaged. The next day, I climbed up left on loose but easy rock (5.6), found a site for my next camp, and spent all the following day moving my equipment to Camp 2 (5,250m).

On August 24, I aided a horizontal crack and took the only fall of the route. I retreated and took a different line, a corner with a thin crack that evolved into a chimney. It was a brilliant 60m pitch at 5.9+ C2. (I suspect it would go free at 5.11 or 5.11+.) Above this, I traversed left using all my 70m rope, then went back to the portaledge for the night. I found it difficult to sleep due to the cold, and perhaps the excitement of being close to the top.

On the 25th, I regained my high point and continued up at 5.8 C1+. That day I dropped an ascender, a Camalot, and a sling. I realized that I was losing concentration and needed to be more careful. That night, I didn't get to sleep until 3 a.m. I was sick and cold. I left Camp 2 again at 8 a.m. on August 26—a total of 27 days since I first started ferrying loads from the road. I reached my high point at 11 a.m. and climbed for a further 150m to the top of the face. From there I walked 200m over ice and boulders to reach the highest point of the mountain, at 2:55 p.m., for its second ascent.

Unfortunately, just 50m before reaching the summit, a loose boulder fell onto my left foot and broke a toe. As I started back down, it began to rain. Four hours of rappelling through rain and sleet took me back to the portaledge. My foot was painful and didn't look good, so I decided I should get off the mountain the next day and called friends to let them know.

On the 27th, I threw some gear and the portaledge off the wall and rappelled from 11:30 a.m. to 5:30 p.m., reaching base camp that day. A few days later I was in a Beijing hospital, having an operation on my toe. My friends later collected my gear from base camp.

I named the route Wild Child. It has around 1,200m of climbing up to 5.9+ C2. I did not carry a bolt kit, but there are five bolts in the initial gully, all installed by a 2014 Chinese team for rappel anchors. Higher, there is one bolt at Camp 1, thought to have been installed by the Russian team.

—Ma Fang, *China*

Thailand

KRABI PROVINCE | Ao Nang

DREAM WALL, FUN DEE

For most climbers, the town of Ao Nang is simply a launchpad to the famous Tonsai and Railay bays. However, Ao Nang has its own burgeoning climbing community bursting with life, some already classic sport climbs, and new routes going up regularly.

In March 2024, Kiwi expat and local developer Dave Hood and I set our eyes on the biggest wall in town: the Dream Wall. (When I say "in town," I mean that you can walk there from any hostel on the main strip.) After a few weeks of legwork, I was able to establish a relationship with the families who own the nearby resorts, and they gave us their blessing to access the wall. Now we just had to climb the 150m wall of steep, "melting" limestone from the ground. Trad climbing isn't common in Southeast Asia, so our rack was limited. It consisted of seven hand-me-down double-length runners and an old funkness wire for slinging tufas, a half rack of nuts, a couple of hooks, and three removable bolts.

Dave insisted on taking the first pitch, which featured a thick 30m vine that hung a body length from the wall—he was certain it would hold body weight and act as an easy shortcut. Dave frogged his way to the top of the vine before the late-season heat could even give me the belay sweats. We continued climbing free on high-quality rock, with a few major runouts. Around 140m up, we reached a massive tufa-blob ledge. I aided the overhang above by drilling removable bolts, slinging a tufa, and hooking pockets for about 15m until the quality of the rock dramatically worsened just below the jungle summit, a standard occurrence on these karst formations. We fixed ropes down the wall, and later I returned to bolt the entire route with titanium glue-ins, with occasional help from Kiwi expat Dennie Vester and American Christian Womack.

The finished route has five pitches in the 5.10 range on very solid and enjoyable limestone, with a wildly exposed last pitch at 5.12a. (Climbing the Tarzan vine on the first pitch is no longer required.) We called the route Fun Dee (150m, 5.12a), or ฝันดี, which translates to "Sweet Dreams." This is the first significant multipitch route on mainland Krabi. In Thailand there is always a chance that access to a crag could be revoked. Thankfully, the local climbing organization, Krabi Bolting Fund, is maintaining good relations with the neighboring locals.

—Dakota Walz, *USA*

The six-pitch Fun Dee (5.12a) runs up the center of Ao Nang's Dream Wall. *Dakota Walz*

Sam Smoothy peers down Aoraki/Mt. Cook's north face during one of 2024's ski descents. ***Will Rowntree***

ANNUAL ALPINE SUMMARY

Warm, settled weather in the early summer of 2024 led to a steady stream of activity in the ranges of the lower South Island, with many of the more noteworthy climbs taking place on the lower-elevation peaks of Otago and Fiordland.

In January, Sooji Clarkson made two trips into the Humboldt Mountains to climb new lines on the northeast face of Somnus (2,293m). Clarkson and Penzy Dinsdale ascended the right-hand of the two prominent buttresses on the face, which they named Somnthing (700m, 16/5.8). Clarkson returned with Ruari Macfarlane to climb Battle of the Somne (400m, 19/5.10c) up a smaller rib on the far right edge of the face. Both of these routes are to climbers' right of the original Northeast Buttress route (Dare, 2014).

Farther north, in the Huxley Range, Joe Collinson and Maria Koo ventured into Canyon Creek, off the Ahuriri Valley, to climb a six-pitch route on the southeast outlier of Point 2,082m. Blue Moon (22/5.11c) follows the crest of the buttress on the southern aspect of the outlier peak. [*The online report also describes new rock routes above Milford Sound.*]

Following a relatively quiet winter, the spring kicked off with a flurry of activity among the higher peaks of the Southern Alps in Aoraki/Mt. Cook and Westland Tai Poutini national parks. On rock, Michael Lehmann and Justin Wimmer climbed a new route on the west face of Lendenfeld Peak (3,194m). The Fiend (125m, 22/5.11c) starts ten meters right of The Mutant (McCartney-McFarlane, 1995) and climbs solid red graywacke sandstone up one of the steepest sections of the wall.

The main highlights of the spring undoubtedly came from the skiing sector, though, with impressive descents on some of the country's highest peaks.

At the end of September, visiting Canadian skier Christina Lustenberger teamed up with Sam Smoothy to make the first ski descent of Mt. Vancouver

(3,309m), north of Aoraki/Mt. Cook. Starting out north along the summit ridge, they descended a steep couloir on the northeast face to the upper Linda Glacier.

Not long after, Smoothy and Will Rowntree made the first descent of nearby Mt. Teichelmann (3,144m) via a line on the east face. The pair then joined Lustenberger and Frenchman Guillaume "Gee" Pierrel to make a rare descent of the Bowie Couloir on the north face of Aoraki/Mt. Cook (3,724m); they skied the face in its entirety, including the upper portion of the Zurbriggen Ridge from the base of the Summit Rocks. Lustenberger and Pierrel, with Ross Hewitt, then skied the Syme Ridge on Mt. Tasman (3,497m).

Lustenberger and Pierrel then embarked on a trio of first descents over a period of four days. They started with Mullet Direct, named in memory of Mike Gardner, on the southeast face of Dixon Peak (3,004m), above the north end of the Grand Plateau; this roughly follows the line of the original southeast face climbing route (Biggs-Duff, 1973). Back on Mt. Vancouver, they skied a line they called Uncle Pete down the steep snow slopes and hanging glacier of the standard east face climbing route (Barley-Forsyth, 1950). Finally, on October 17, they made the first ski descent of the Jones Route (Murray Jones, 1973) on the 1,000m east face of Aoraki/Mt. Cook's middle peak. They called the ski line Hunter's Moon.

The line of Hunter's Moon, a ski descent of the 1,000-meter east face of Aoraki/Mt. Cook's middle peak. The Jones Route, followed during the ascent, climbs right of the rocks in the middle of the face. ***Mathurin Vauthier***

During the same week, Emily Jones, Petrouchka Steiner-Grierson, Mathias Gruber, and Connie Henderson made a quick second descent of Lustenberger and Pierrel's line on Dixon before turning their attention to Silberhorn (3,300m). Here, they made the first descent of a line down the skier's left side of the south face, largely running parallel to the Silberhorn Arête.

Moving to the western side of the Main Divide, Lustenberger, Rowntree, and Smoothy made the first ski descent of Douglas Peak (3,077m). The trio climbed the northeast ridge, then made one rappel from the summit before skiing the east face. They traversed the upper Forrest Ross Glacier to climb the east ridge of Glacier Peak, then descended the west face back to Pioneer Hut.

Returning to the Grand Plateau, Rowntree and Smoothy climbed Mt. Dampier (3,440m) by the south ridge from Green Saddle, en route to making the first ski descent of the peak via the west face. They then traversed out from north to south over Harper Saddle to Empress Hut. After resting for a day at the hut, they climbed and skied a new direct line down the east face of La Perouse (3,078m), making the third ski descent of the face and the second full descent from the summit.

Slightly to the north, Beau Fredlund and Ross Hewitt claimed the first ski descent of the aesthetic Central Spur on the Spencer (west) Face of Elie De Beaumont (3,109m)—nicknamed Dragon's Back by the pair.

The spring wasn't all about skiing. In November, in the Darran Mountains, Daniel Joll and Tanja de Wilde made three trips to the granite Charismatic Wall of Point 1,655m. Their DJ Wild (24/5.12a) follows the first seven pitches of Uprising (2018) before continuing straight up where Uprising moves right. Joll and de Wilde added 16 pitches, with a mix of technical face climbing, overhanging cracks, and friction slabs.

—Ben Dare, *New Zealand*

Looking back to Mt. Strachan from the final skin up Mt. Dechen on day three of the traverse. ***Anna Keeling***

HOOKER RANGE: HIGH-LEVEL SKI TRAVERSE

Ruari Macfarlane is visionary when it comes to unclimbed and unskied lines in New Zealand. Our idea for a ski traverse of the Hooker Range was to begin at Aoraki/Mt. Cook and cross the Main Divide at Barron Saddle (1,992m) via the Scissors (2,239m). From there we would drop to the headwaters of the mighty Landsborough River to access the Hooker Range and ski five of its main peaks. The end point would be the Paringa River in South Westland. The total distance would be about 90km, with 11,000m of gain and loss, in very remote country with no easy escape routes. As far as we knew, the Hooker Range had not been traversed on skis.

On October 12, Ruari, Troy Forsyth, and I made a late dash from Mt. Cook Village, climbing 1,000m to Mueller Hut to begin the journey. The next morning, we skied to the south with dust on crust providing a fast descent to the Mueller Glacier. Our first crux was crossing the broad Scissors snow slope on the Main Divide. Ruari set a brilliant track, and eventually we donned crampons to reach the Scissors ridge. We could see the Hooker Range, our ultimate goal, to the west of us, and the snowline was an ideal 1,100m. We dropped into the subalpine for a swim in a glacial lake before crossing the Landsborough River in late afternoon. There, we collected a bucket of extra food that Ruari had stashed in the summer.

Each of our days on this tour began with a long climb back into the alpine in running shoes (often including river crossings). Transitioning back to ski boots provided daily relief.

Townsend Glacier was our first foray onto the Hooker Range. The 600m climb felt arduous with transalpine packs. Unable to traverse the ridge west toward Whitcombe Peak (1,887m) due to an impassable crown wall, we descended 1,000m back to the south, skiing on cooling corn, and walked five minutes to a perfect campsite under a full moon.

The next day, we skinned and cramponed up a steep east-facing ridge next to Whitcombe Creek and the Fettes Glacier, which allowed convoluted access to the Zircon Glacier, and eventually the summit of Fettes Peak (2,451m). A seven-meter crown wall from a glide-slab avalanche was nervously negotiated via a narrow, skiable ledge. The ski off the south side began perfectly and remained so for miles until rockfall crossed our descent couloir to Zora Creek. A small corner and a tiny ice runnel gave passage with aluminum crampons, a 45cm ice hammer, and skis stashed on packs. I inched down this 50m M3 section, trying not to kick out the ice sliver. There were no anchors for rappelling, just muddy shale. We crossed Zora Creek barefoot in the dark and camped immediately.

Day three began with an ascent west to Mueller Pass (1,445m) and on to Mt. Strachan's (2,561m) northeast ridge. Traversing south from the ridge, we skinned 800m up the Strachan Glacier and cramponed the last 50m to the summit. Another crux awaited: the steep descent west to the Edison Glacier. A rollover hid the terrain below, but a runout was visible via a fast velvet snow surface. We hopped across glide cracks and bergschrunds, then booted, traversed, and skinned southwest to the Strachan-Dechen col. Travel was surprisingly fast on Mt. Dechen's (2,643m) upper slopes, and we skinned to the summit as the sun set over the Tasman Sea.

We descended to the west and then southwest, dropping 1,650m to the Ōtoko River. The start of this descent, on the vast McCardell Glacier, felt like skiing a volcano. The next 1,000m passed through the Eye Tooth Falls, a wide couloir. Huge schist walls loomed through the jungle mist on either side as we skied into endless and complex avalanche debris. We hit the river flats at 900m just as it got dark.

On day four, the initial scramble south and upriver to Lower Ōtoko Pass went smoothly—one of us scrambled to the top of a schist boulder and hauled up all the packs, taking care not to tangle our skis in the subalpine scrub. There was a committing river jump and steep cramponing to reach Mt. Hooker's east ridge, and a steep, flat-light couloir to ski into the Hooker Glacier.

Hiking up to Lower Ōtoko Pass, en route to Mt. Hooker. *Ruari Macfarlane*

After a nine-hour ascent, we stashed our overnight gear in a hole before the final 500m skin and crampon up Mt. Hooker (2,640m). Thick rime coated the summit rocks. We almost circumnavigated the peak to reach the mountain's northwest side, then Ruari launched into the final 50m of steep rime to the top; Troy and I opted to skip it, feeling less comfortable climbing this terrain with one stumpy ice tool. We descended a steep couloir southwest to another subalpine camp in upper Murdock Creek.

On day five, a weak northerly system arrived, which meant no visibility for our planned direct line down the west side of Mt. McCullaugh (2,226m), which we summited from the southeast. Instead, we traversed south around the peak by GPS and booted east over the Buttress (1,870m) to Tunnel Creek's west side. Eventually, we emerged soggy through the clouds and into a green and gold world.

After a comfortable night under a great rock slab at the bush line, we rallied southwest down a steep, forested ridge to Tunnel Creek Hut and spent a night there. On day seven, we hiked for two hours to meet a jet boat at the Paringa-Ōtoko river junction for a fast exit to the West Coast highway. Ruari, ever the purist, walked the whole way.

—Anna Keeling, *New Zealand*

IN MEMORIAM

Many of these tributes have been edited for length. The complete text and additional photos are at the *AAJ* website: *publications.americanalpineclub.org.*

DAVID BREASHEARS, 1955 – 2024

JIMMY CHIN

David Breashears, who died at his home in Massachusetts on March 14, at age 68, had an outsized influence on many people's lives, including mine. His endeavors as an incredibly bold and visionary climber and alpinist were legendary. He also was a devoted human rights advocate, a spokesperson for climate issues, and a visionary filmmaker who broke trail for the rest of us who followed in his footsteps. For some of us, literally. Among many notable films, David's *Everest* would become the highest-grossing IMAX film of all time. It was a cultural phenomenon for an entire generation and transported an entirely new audience to the rarefied world of the high Himalaya.

Born in Georgia, David came to prominence as a climber after his family moved to Colorado, where, as a teenager, he made bold roped and solo ascents, including the 1975 onsight first ascent of Perilous Journey, near Eldorado Canyon, a route now considered 5.11 X. Early expeditionary climbs included the second ascent of Ama Dablam, in 1979, as part of a filmmaking team, and the 1982 first ascent of the north face of Kwangde, also in Nepal, with Jeff Lowe.

David achieved his greatest fame as both a mountaineer and filmmaker on Everest: He climbed the mountain five times and made other attempts, including three expeditions to the Kangshung Face; he guided Richard Bass to the top in 1985 to complete Bass's Seven Summits quest; and he and his IMAX team helped save lives during the 1996 disaster on the mountain.

For many of us, David wasn't just a visionary climber and director, but also a loyal friend: complicated, charismatic, confident yet vulnerable, occasionally mischievous, always exacting in his standards, whether it was directing a film, leading an expedition, or putting together a meal. He was deeply intelligent and a ferocious advocate for the environment and other causes. (David's nonprofit GlacierWorks raised awareness of the effects of climate change in the Himalaya.) He always made an impression when he walked into the room, with the glint in his eyes and that million-dollar smile—maybe it wasn't so much a smile as a smirk, like he knew something you didn't know, which was usually the case. That's the David I remember: larger than life in one moment and deeply thoughtful and caring the next.

I can honestly say I would not be where I am now if it were not for the belief David had in a young dirtbag climber trying to make his way through the world. In 2004, David invited me to climb Everest and work on a feature film with him, Ed Viesturs, Veikka Gustafsson, and Robert Schauer. I will never forget getting that call: I was so nervous and intimidated that I failed to respond when he asked if I'd like to join the team. There was a pause and he just said, "Well, think about it." I picked my jaw up off the floor and stammered, "Yes, I would really like to join your expedition."

When I met him in Kathmandu, I was starstruck and a little terrified. I decided then and there I would never disappoint this man. I can honestly say I have never worked harder on any job than that Everest trip, before or after. David taught me how to approach major productions on serious expeditions, and the attitude and ethos required to pull off incredibly challenging and complex projects in good style. I noticed that he always led from the front. He elevated those around him. These were lessons I've carried with me throughout my career.

I still look up to David and what he achieved in his extraordinary life. But mostly I am grateful for his belief in me, grateful to him for being my friend. David's legacy will live on through the people he inspired throughout our community. You will be dearly missed, my friend.

—Jimmy Chin

MICHAEL GARDNER, 1991 – 2024

"To live till you die is to live long enough."
—Lao Tzu

Dear Michael, your life wasn't nearly long enough for us.

Heavy shock and grief swept our community on October 7, 2024, with the tragic news that Michael had fallen at a hanging bivy while attempting a new route on the north face of Jannu East (7,468m) in Nepal. This was his second attempt to climb the face with his longtime climbing partner and close friend Sam Hennessey. Michael came to rest there, but his spirit soars on.

Michael shared the Lao Tzu quote above on social media after his last annual pilgrimage to the site of his father George's death on the Grand Teton in 2008. Mike was only 16 years old when his father died. In the remaining 16 years of Mike's precious life, he didn't waste a day.

Since he was young, I watched Mike grow up with his beautiful family. Michael's dad was my close friend, mentor, and climbing partner; his mother, Colleen, is a close friend and a soul sister. Michael always had the remarkable presence of an old soul, paired with exuberant youth and a joy of living—infused with perma-stoke—that was magnetic. He carried that forward for three all-too-short decades, not just shining but beaming his light far and wide.

Most remarkable, and what I will always hold dear, was Michael's presence in every moment, the kindness he had for all things great and small, and his bright smile (mustache and mullet included) that lit up every space he shared.

Mikey walked, climbed, skied, and skateboarded the Earth he cherished with grace and humility. His passion and zest for living life to the fullest, combined with his natural athleticism and confidence, enabled him to reach his ultimate potential with trusted partners in the wildest places, inspiring us to no end. He thrived on shared adventures with gifted partners, with minimal resources and high levels of commitment.

Over a period of seven years, Mike and Sam set new standards for light and fast alpinism, often with skis on their backs. Their visionary tactics in climbing big alpine routes in ski boots was as impressive as their athleticism in shredding variable mountain snow conditions with only 60mm underfoot. A series of feats in Alaska Range ski alpinism culminated in 2021 with an extraordinary 64-hour traverse of Denali: With Adam Fabrikant, Mike and Sam climbed the Cassin Ridge, then made the first ski descent of the Northwest Buttress, descending 10,000 feet to exit via the Peters Glacier onto the tundra, where they switched out ski boots for tennies and made numerous bone-chilling glacial river crossings on minimal calories to complete their grand traverse.

In addition to being a great alpinist, Michael was a talented guide who in a very short career guided 12 Denali climbs, six Vinson Massif climbs, and over 150 ascents of the Grand Teton. He skied and climbed on every continent and spent five seasons in competitive freeskiing, with consistent podium finishes. He was named one of the 20 best skiers in the world under age 18 by *Powder* magazine. Mike loved competitive skijoring, and after only one season, he proudly won the coveted big belt buckle after landing a backflip midcourse at his hometown event in Ridgway, Colorado.

At the young age of ten, Mike's skateboarding talent landed him his first sponsorship. He always attributed his athleticism and success in life to his skateboarding experiences, which he shared with humility and depth—in eloquent words and stunning photos—in publications and on social media. His bold, expressive, and eloquent style reflected his passion and love of life.

More than all of his other accomplishments, those who knew Mike recognized that he had mastered being human. With heavy hearts we go on, all the better for sharing the path, a rope, turns, and stoke with Michael. As we attune to his expansive unconditional love, we'll meet him again, cheering us on as always. Like so many, I'm grateful to have loved and been on the receiving end of Michael's abundant love.

"It is not the length of life, but the depth of life."—Ralph Waldo Emerson

—Angela Hawse

FRED GOLOMB, 1924 – 2024

Dr. Frederick Golomb often said, as his children recall, "I'm the luckiest man in the world."

Depending on which way things went at several major junctions, Dr. Golomb might well not have survived to say it.

As a young man raised in the Bronx, already a skier, he eagerly enlisted in the 10th Mountain Division corps, yet in the Army Specialized Training Program he scored so high on an aptitude test that he received the opportunity to attend Yale University (class of 1945) and the University of Rochester Medical School (finishing in 1949). In World War II he did not go overseas, where nearly 1,000 from the 10th were killed and many more wounded.

In 1953, Dr. Golomb served in Korea as chief of surgery in the 44th MASH unit. In 1954, as he tended to a wounded soldier in the field, his hand and leg were injured in a grenade explosion that he was fortunate to survive. Golomb received a Purple Heart.

He also was invited by Charles Houston as expedition doctor on the tragic, legendary 1953 expedition to K2. Says Phil Erard, a longtime friend of Golomb, "He told me his hospital work prevented it." Nearing the summit on K2, the climbers were pinned in a storm, during which Art Gilkey, age 26 and a close friend of Golomb's, fell ill with thrombosis. As his teammates tried to rescue him, Gilkey was swept away and the others nearly suffered mass disaster, saved only by Pete Schoening's famous boot-axe belay.

JAMES GOLOMB

Golomb's mountain experience was varied and broad. In August 1948, he climbed the Grand Teton with Dick Emerson, and the two were first to suss out a rappel into the Upper Saddle, a version of the now standard descent. In the early 1950s, he climbed in the Gunks with Gilkey, Hans Kraus, Bonnie Prudden, and Fritz Wiessner.

In the summer of 1951, while on a geology-research expedition with the scientist and mountaineer Maynard Miller, Golomb did several first ascents on the Juneau Icefield in Alaska. He named a 7,000-foot peak Everlast (58.783801N, -134.158670W), after his father's boxing-gloves company. He was an AAC member from 1952.

In 1954, home from Korea, Golomb wed Joan Schneider, enjoying a long marriage until her death in 2011. Fred had a long climbing partnership with his son, James, a neurologist at NYU, where his father had completed his residency and also practiced—they overlapped there for 14 years.

"We were really best friends," says James. He describes his father as methodical, a calculated risk-taker, good-humored, and ever optimistic, typically saying amid poor weather, "I think I see a little bit of blue up there. I think it's breaking up."

The two climbed in the Gunks and in New England, the Rockies, Cascades, and mountains of Alaska, and they did annual ski mountaineering trips to France for nearly two decades. Fred continued ski alpinism well into his 80s, and at 87 took up paragliding. In 1981, he and James attempted a 6,700-meter mountain in the Barun Valley of Nepal.

Golomb taught his daughter, Susan, who is a prominent New York literary agent, to ski at age three, and he "was proud and thrilled," Susan says, when she "caught the bug" and climbed in the Gunks.

Professionally, Golomb was a revered surgeon who participated in milestones in medical history. At Johns Hopkins, he worked with Dr. Alfred Blalock to address heart issues in newborns. Golomb became director of NYU's chemoimmunotherapy division and was a pioneer in melanoma treatment. He trained in plastic reconstructive surgery, devising a Z-plasty operation drawing on his experience at the 44th MASH. Susan remembers him saying once that he had "made someone a belly button."

Somehow he found time for many other interests: He was an offshore yachtsman, a windsurfer and a kayaker, and he raced a Porsche. He made a film about his lifelong love of the mountains. He often said, "I am a surgeon in New York, but I climb mountains for a living."

"My father had no regrets," Susan says. "He did everything he wanted to do, he knew he was loved, and he really cared about the alpine world."

—Alison Osius

TM HERBERT, 1936 - 2024

On March 23, 2024, my hero passed away. TM Herbert was the quintessential Yosemite climber.

Born in Utah, TM grew up in Southern California, and found climbing in 1957, when he was in his early 20s, and it became his lifelong passion. He started at 5.0 at Tahquitz and worked his way up to the hardest grade at the time of 5.9.

TM moved to Berkeley, California, and spent much of the 1960s in Yosemite Valley. He had the great fortune to be one of the Golden Age climbers; it was an era when the walls had many unclimbed lines waiting for a team brave enough to attempt them prior to the advent of rescues. The first ascents of El Capitan's Muir Wall, with Yvon Chouinard in 1965, as well as the West Face of El Capitan in 1967, with Royal Robbins, were two of his finest achievements.

By 1969, he had graduated college and started a family with his wife, Jan. I was the eldest of their two boys. The family moved to the foothills of the Sierra, and TM worked as an elementary school

teacher. Most weekends of the spring and fall were spent in Yosemite Valley, and during the summers we lived in either Tuolumne Meadows, where he guided for Yosemite Mountaineering School, or the Tetons in Wyoming. Christmas vacation was in Joshua Tree.

During the 1970s and '80s, TM climbed with the Stonemasters in the Valley, the last of his small tribe from the '50s and '60s to continue climbing. He kept climbing into the 2000s and continued the tradition of sitting around a campfire and telling stories. Every summer weekend, he would drive to Tuolumne, park at the guide school, and bivy in the back of his car. Throughout his 60s and into his mid-70s, he soloed South Crack on Stately Pleasure Dome, as well as Cathedral Peak. Hundreds of climbers have come up to me with the story of an old man with a hat and a great sense of humor who had passed them.

When TM stopped climbing, he continued to visit Tuolumne, hiking, bird-watching, and telling stories. Alzheimer's slowly set in, and he moved to an independent-living facility and then a group home. He continued his daily walks and maintained his jovial nature. Two weeks before his passing, he introduced me (his son) to the home's staff as his twin brother.

What does TM stand for? It is the name on his birth certificate. He would tell you it stood for "Tough Mother." I will tell you it stands for Tuolumne Meadows. He was an authentic Yosemite climber for over five decades. Hours before he passed, as I sat with him, he stared at a poster of Yosemite on the wall. He said, "That is the most beautiful place I have ever been." He talked about how much he loved being a Yosemite guide. I told him he was my hero. He will be dearly missed.

—Tom Herbert

CHRIS JONES, 1939 – 2024

During his and Chris Jones's fifth night on the 5,000-foot north face of North Twin in the Canadian Rockies, George Lowe's mind raced, aware the two might not be able to go up or down.

At 3 a.m., as Lowe wrote later, Chris asked, "Are you awake?"

"Of course!" Lowe said.

Lowe's account in the 1975 *AAJ* continued: "We are overdue tomorrow. Rescue? Chris talks of people who waited and perished. The basic toughness in him that is so critical in a climbing companion comes out. We will keep going until we are absolutely stopped."

The pair did only two major climbing trips together, but one of these—to North Twin in 1974—resulted in an enormous milestone in alpinism. Another trip, in 1973, included the Supercouloir on the north face of Deltaform in the Canadian Rockies and the first ascent of the south face of the Devils Thumb in Alaska. Jones already had climbed many big faces in the Rockies: He established new routes on the north faces of Mt. Assiniboine and Mt. Edith Cavell, in 1967, with Yvon Chouinard and Joe Faint; the north ridge of Mt. Columbia with Gray Thompson, in 1970; and the north face of Kitchener, with Thompson and Jeff Lowe, in 1971.

GEORGE LOWE

The north face of North Twin was not climbed again for 11 years, until David Cheesmond and Barry Blanchard did a stunning separate line. Blanchard wrote in the 2002 *AAJ*: "I'll suggest that, in 1974, the route that George and Chris opened on the north face of North Twin was the hardest alpine route in the world."

Born and raised in the United Kingdom, Jones moved to America in 1965, at age 25, as an employee of IBM. (He was to work in software development, taking many leaves for climbing.) He spent the summer of 1967 in Camp 4, Yosemite, and pulled off the first free ascent of Serenity Crack (5.10d) with Tom Higgins. But it was in the mountains that he really left his mark, with new routes from the Sierra to Alaska and South America.

After the first ascent of the northeast face of Yerupajá in Peru, in 1968, with Dean Caldwell, Paul Dix, and Roger Hart, Jones wrote humorously in a "C.V." account of his climbing: "By now I had the conviction that I could attempt the most challenging alpine routes anywhere in the world; this may have overplayed my hand, but commitment counts for a lot."

1968 was also the year of the storied Funhog expedition, in which Jones joined Yvon Chouinard, Dick Dorworth, Lito Tejada-Flores, and Doug Tompkins for a monthslong road trip to Patagonia, where they climbed the southwest ridge, a.k.a. the California Route, of Fitz Roy, for the third ascent of the peak. Jones co-authored *Climbing Fitz Roy, 1968: Reflections on the Lost Photos of the Third Ascent*. His widow, Sharon Ponsford-Jones, says, "I believe Chris considered Fitz Roy and North Twin to be his most meaningful climbs."

George Lowe, in a eulogy at Jones's memorial, praised his friend for his sharp intellect and for being analytical, sincere, and wryly humorous.

Jones was a lover of classical music, opera, art, and travel. His history book *Climbing in North America* (1976) influenced a generation of American climbers. In it, he wrote: "The mountains are not just masses of rock and ice. They are places where people have struggled, laughed, dreamed, and sometimes died."

Post-climbing, Jones and his wife lived in both France and Glen Ellen, California. He took up cycling with a passion, riding with his local clubs, usually 30 to 50 miles, three times a week. Ponsford-Jones says her husband had begun a memoir when he fell ill.

Jones wrote in his "C.V.," "I followed my dream and was richly rewarded. I left nothing on the table; I gave it my all."

—Alison Osius, *with help from George Lowe*

ARMANDO MENOCAL, 1941 – 2024

"Let me say it," he whispered through a grin. "You're young, and you'll have plenty of time to blow things up in the future. I should handle this one."

We were discussing a difference of opinion in climbing policy, much as we had done for the last 30-plus years. Armando and I were a bit hawkish on the particular subject, but as usual, he had a lesson for me as an activist. In this case, I learned: "You can't show anger very often, so make sure you pick those moments when it will count."

I would continue to listen and learn from him until a few weeks before his passing in October 2024. A year and a half earlier, Armando had stopped by our home in Lander, Wyoming, for an evening. He'd complained that he was having difficulty getting his cardio up to its usual place. Two weeks later he called us, having just seen a doctor and then a specialist. Lung cancer. He never smoked and always took care of himself, but no one can fend off bad luck.

Armando Menocal was born into a Cuban American family in Miami on March 31, 1941. He attended the University of Florida and then George Washington Law School. After finishing law school, he moved to the Bay Area to work in civil rights litigation, making weekend forays to Yosemite and the higher peaks of the Sierra.

I met him in 1989. He was this friendly, funny old guy (but not as old as I am now) who had a huge amount of traditional climbing experience, but, unlike many older climbers, he was willing to embrace the sport climbing movement. The American climbing community had been broken in two by the opening of clean, crackless faces with rappel-placed bolts. When the American Alpine Club's old guard refused to allow their Access Committee (which Armando had been asked to form) to support sport climbing, he challenged them. They fought for years, sometimes screaming in open meetings, and eventually Armando left.

"I'm starting a new nonprofit to support all forms of climbing," he'd said over the phone. "And it's going to need help from a lot of people. Can I count on you?" Of course, I was in.

As he led the effort to create the Access Fund in 1990, his legal career in California was winding down. The new nonprofit would be based in the climbing hub of Boulder, Colorado, but Armando didn't want to live there and instead began spending summers and falls in Jackson, Wyoming. That's when we began climbing together regularly, as well as meeting for beers at the Brew Pub and watching Monday Night Football, together with a small cadre of climbers who cared about that sport. We both worked as "guest guides" at Exum, the status giving us the right to be more selective about our assignments. Somehow, Armando and I worked together more often than not.

I remember him reaching out to me in the spring of 1998. "I want to talk to you about a project I'm assisting Chris McNamara with," he'd said. "Its sole purpose is the replacement of aging fixed anchors." I recently spoke to Chris about the creation of the American Safe Climbing Association. "He was huge for the ASCA!" Chris exclaimed. "I was like 18 years old and knew next to nothing. He put together all the legal work for the organization."

Armando's will to work for the climbing

community was unmatched, and his legal expertise and experience as an activist were exactly what was needed. When the Access Fund and ASCA were strong enough to stand without his tutelage, Armando went on to create Acceso PanAm to assist climbers in Latin America. For his work on behalf of climbers, the AAC awarded Armando and Access Fund co-founders Rick Accomazzo and Randy Vogel with Honorary Memberships in 2020.

Exploring his Cuban heritage, Armando traveled to the island in the late 1990s and learned about the climbing potential of Viñales, where he became a leading supporter of route development and local climbers. He also met the woman, Laura Rodriguez, who would become his wife—though not without a fight, as Armando was banned from travel to Cuba for more than a decade. They eventually married in Florida, and eventually he won the right to return to Viñales.

Armando Menocal's warm and gregarious personality helped to draw hundreds of us to work for the rights of climbers. He was my friend, partner, and mentor. But despite all the time we spent talking about access and bolt replacement, it is his laughter I will remember the best. He was upbeat and happy, and his smile warmed any room.

—Sam Lightner Jr.

JOHN WILLIAM MIDDENDORF IV, 1959 – 2024

CAMERON M. BURNS

On July 28, 1992, John Middendorf and Xaver Bongard reached the summit of Great Trango Tower, a massive shield of rock in the Karakoram. They had spent the previous 18 days climbing the east face, fighting poor weather and never-ending objective hazards. Mostly unscathed, the two spent three days rappelling the 4,400-foot, 33-pitch route. Predictably, they were soon household names in the climbing community. One of the few Grade VIIs on Earth, The Grand Voyage was also one of the biggest rock climbs ever done.

For Middendorf, the celebrity was more than appropriate. He had climbed dozens of walls all over the globe, establishing new routes and fast times, and was only midway through a very productive outdoor life.

John Middendorf was born in New York City on November 18, 1959, and lived in Connecticut for the first ten years of his life. His father, J. William Middendorf II, was a military man, financier, and diplomat who worked on Republican presidential campaigns and had appointments under three presidents. His mother, the late Isabelle Paine Middendorf, had trained as a nurse but left that career to raise John and his four siblings.

Middendorf spent three preteen years in Holland with his family—his father was named ambassador to the Netherlands in 1969—and his teenage years in northern Virginia. He was first exposed to climbing when his parents sent him to a mountaineering school near Telluride, Colorado. Through the early to mid-1970s, Middendorf climbed at East Coast crags, including ice climbs in New Hampshire.

In 1978, he made his first trip to Yosemite with friend John Ely and became acquainted with the climbing landscape that would shape his entire life. He attended Dartmouth in New Hampshire for two years to study engineering, but in 1981 transferred to Stanford, closer to his newfound home. After earning his degree, he was offered a spot on the rescue team and moved to Yosemite for an extended stay. Between 1981 and 1986, he fired off dozens of wall routes—new routes, speed records, and solo adventures, many of them first winter ascents, first one-day ascents, fastest ascents, and on and on.

In 1986, he joined longtime Valley climbers Steve Bosque and Mike Corbett for a winter attempt on Half Dome's south face. A storm nearly killed all three as the route became a waterfall and falling water and snow crushed their primitive portaledges and their bodies. They eventually were helicoptered off. The south face would've been Middendorf's 40th big-wall route in the Valley. Instead, it became a turning point.

Middendorf began reinventing the portaledge and formed A5, a company that designed and developed wall-climbing gear. Having moved to Flagstaff, Arizona, Middendorf suddenly had easy access to the desert country of the Four Corners, and he explored the area, making first ascents of about 20 towers. His new base also afforded trips to Zion, which was still wide open for new routes. Middendorf and friends did a handful of new, hard walls in the Grade V–VI range, including the stunning southwest buttress of Abraham. He also climbed a new Grade VI on Mt. Hooker in the Wind River Range with Steve Quinlan.

In 1997, he sold A5 to The North Face, then dabbled in several creative and scientific outlets, including surveying, a newspaper job, and river guiding. He met his future wife, Jeni, in 2007, while guiding the Grand Canyon. They were married and had a son, Rowen, before moving to Australia in 2009. Rowen's sister, Remi, was born in Tasmania.

Middendorf continued climbing, and in 2010 he became active in the push to save ancient forests in Tasmania. Having already received a master's degree in architecture from Harvard University, he studied fabric architecture at the University of Sydney and founded a new portaledge company, D4. Members of the Bob Brown Foundation, a Tasmanian environmental organization, used his portaledges—the successors to heavy plywood platforms—for tree-sitting disruptions of the logging of ancient trees for wood chips. His particular interest was the Takayna/Tarkine wilderness in northwest Tasmania. He made all his designs open-source, so that anyone with some scissors, fabric, tubular aluminum, and rudimentary sewing skills could copy his designs.

As a writer, Middendorf published dozens of articles and several books on wall climbing. He also did probably the most significant research into the development of climbing gear that any single researcher has ever undertaken; the research was published in 2023 in two volumes called *Mechanical Advantage: Tools for the Wild Vertical.*

Middendorf died unexpectedly in his sleep while visiting family in Little Compton, Rhode Island, on June 21, 2024.

"John was a delightful character who loved the world's wilderness," Bob Brown said after his passing. "Our foundation is shocked by his sudden loss. We are grieving for his wife, Jeni, and young family." Middendorf was awarded the prestigious Deni Greene Award by the foundation posthumously.

—Cameron M. Burns

DAVE REARICK, 1932 – 2024

Pioneering free climber, mathematician and teacher, long-distance cyclist, master woodworker, self-taught classical guitarist, aspiring astronaut, and entertaining storyteller Dave Rearick died on August 21, 2024. He was born in Illinois, raised in Florida, and as a young man spent summers at the YMCA camp in Estes Park, Colorado, the gateway to Rocky Mountain National Park. He loved to tell how, still a teenager,

NPS PHOTO OF BOB KAMPS AND DAVE REARICK (AT RIGHT)

he snuck out of camp with a friend and scrambled to the summit of Longs Peak via the north face, arriving back at camp many hours overdue. Later that summer, they returned to Longs with a hatchet, a few pitons and carabiners, and a 50-foot rope and climbed the technical east face, returning to camp after midnight.

Early in his climbing career, Rearick climbed in the Gunks, where he learned from Hans Kraus, Jim McCarthy, and Bonnie Prudden; in the Tetons, where he met John Gill; and at Stoney Point, where he met Bob Kamps. These partnerships with some of the best climbers of the time hastened his rise as a climber. He did the north face of the Grand Teton with Kamps and made the second ascent of the Totem Pole in Monument Valley, Utah, with Tom Condon and TM Herbert.

After earning a bachelor's degree in physics at the University of Florida and working for a defense contractor on Long Island, Rearick migrated to Southern California to earn a doctorate at Caltech. There, he joined the ranks of climbers who were advancing the art of free climbing at Tahquitz and Yosemite. He made the first ascent of The Vampire at Tahquitz—including some 5.10 free climbing—with Royal Robbins in 1959. He and Robbins did the first free ascent of the East Chimney of Rixon's Pinnacle in 1960, the first 5.10 in Yosemite. The pair also made the third ascent of the Northwest Face of Half Dome.

In 1960, authorities at Rocky Mountain National Park lifted a long-standing ban on attempting the Diamond on the upper east face of Longs Peak. This coveted wall had been in the sights of at least two Colorado climbers, Dale Johnson and Layton Kor. But they were out of town, and the California team of Rearick and Kamps got to the head of the line. Over two days in August 1960, Rearick and Kamps made the first ascent of the most prominent and direct line on the Diamond, now called simply D1.

The following year, Rearick took a faculty position in the Mathematics Department at the University of Colorado in Boulder. He continued to climb at a high level for the next 20 years, one of the early climbers who focused solely on free climbing. Rearick made notable ascents in Eldorado Canyon (first free climb of T2 with Bob Culp in 1962); at Castle Rock (free ascents of Coffin Crack and the third pitch of Athlete's Feat with Pat Ament); in Rocky Mountain National Park (Sykes' Sickle on Spearhead in 1958); in the Sedona, Arizona, area (The Mace with Kamps and Herbert in 1957); and in the Utah desert.

Rearick eventually gave more of his time to cycling, and he had some heroic adventures. His garage was filled with road bikes, many of them vintage European models. He often rode through Colorado and Utah to climb peaks, sometimes round-trip from his home. He was among the first to do what's now called the Longs Peak duathlon (bike and hike up Longs Peak, then hike and bike back home).

The last climb I did with Dave Rearick was in August 1985, the 25th anniversary of his D1 ascent. We climbed the North Chimney below the Diamond and sat on Broadway for at least an hour, absorbing the immensity of our surroundings. I am sure Dave was reliving that unforgettable day, 25 years earlier, when he and Kamps were in the same place, preparing for the climb of their lives.

—Bill Briggs, *with Pat Ament*

RUPLEY FAMILY

JOHN ALLEN RUPLEY, 1933 – 2024

John Rupley died on July 20 from pulmonary arterial hypertension and cardiac failure, the result of chemotherapy-induced pulmonary fibrosis. A leading American alpinist from the 1950s through the '70s, he also was a productive researcher and teacher at the University of Arizona, a gourmet cook, and a competitive pistol shooter.

Well over six feet tall, with the physique of an NFL linebacker and a calm, fact-driven personality, John added great strength and endurance to his climbing parties. Over three decades, he made many first ascents in the Washington Cascades, Canadian Rockies, Alaska, Shawangunks, and the Tucson-area crags of Arizona.

Born in Brooklyn, he moved with his family to San Francisco when he was six and then to Guatemala City when he was ten, following his father, who was an executive for W.R. Grace. John returned to the United States at age 13 and attended the Hill School in Pennsylvania, followed by an undergraduate degree from Princeton and a Ph.D. in biochemistry at the University of Washington in Seattle.

At UW, he met Ila Ruud, who became his wife of 64 years and a lifelong climbing partner. They married in 1960 and moved to New York for John's postdoctoral fellowship at Cornell; John taught Ila to climb during weekend trips to the Gunks and a honeymoon in the Alps.

John had started climbing at the Gunks during his second year at Princeton, meeting fellow student Jim McCarthy and becoming a frequent climbing partner of Hans Kraus and later Fritz Wiessner, beginning lifelong friendships.

One reason John chose the University of Washington for graduate studies was proximity to the extensive nearby alpine terrain. There, he began climbing with Fred Beckey, Don Gordon (Claunch), Tom Hornbein, Hank Mather, Herb Staley, and other top alpinists of those days. He had a productive climbing partnership and friendship with Beckey that lasted until Fred's death in 2017.

In 1961, John and Ila moved to Tucson, where John served as professor in the Department of Chemistry and Biochemistry at the University of Arizona until retiring in 1998. His new job led to a climbing sacrifice, as he withdrew from the 1963 Everest expedition, of which he was an initial member, to focus on his work. His research in molecular biophysics led to significant contributions to the understanding of the role of water in enzyme activity and protein structure. He delighted in mentoring graduate students and postdoctoral associates.

Though he couldn't go to Everest, John immediately saw the climbing potential of Mt. Lemmon near Tucson, and he and Ila began putting up new routes. Climbing for both joy and training for mountaineering, they didn't name or grade routes or record their many adventures. Needing reference points, later climbers and authors named the Rupley Towers, The Rupley Route, The Lost Rupley Route, Rupley 1, Rupley 2, etc. Consequently, John and Ila's names are etched in stone on Mt. Lemmon.

I met John in 1974 when he and Fred Beckey organized a trip to attempt the unclimbed northeast ridge of Mt. Clemenceau, one of the high peaks in the Canadian Rockies west of the Columbia

Icefield. We became close friends on that trip, and my wife, Eloise, and I often visited John and Ila in their spacious adobe home.

After retiring from the university in 1998, John developed two new interests: gourmet cooking and competitive pistol shooting. Unable to escape his scientific inclination, he pursued both with precision and attention to detail.

In a note to Eloise and me a day after John's death, Ila aptly described his love of the mountains: "John really thought of himself as an alpine climber. He left the Gunks to truly move into the 'real mountains.' Rocks are nice, but the whole package of weather, ice, glacier knowledge, high altitude, the route-finding chess game, the isolation—all that was a much more satisfying world for him. And he loved the sweet air, the quiet, the fellowship and fun with his buddies. It was joy."

—Gray Thompson

SYLVAIN SAUDAN, 1936 – 2024

Out of Western Europe in the late 1960s and early '70s, a new form of alpinism was dawning: that of skiing down—after climbing up—terrain formerly thought of solely as climbs. While names such as Vallençant and Baud soon captured the imagination with their 60° descents and peddle-hop turns, they weren't the first of the modern extremists. That appellation perhaps best falls to a Swiss ski instructor and mountain guide named Sylvain Saudan.

Saudan was born in 1936 and raised near Verbier, Switzerland. As a child of the Alps, he was on skis from an early age, reportedly "skiing to school" and no doubt involved in the skill-building snowplay of mountain kids everywhere.

As the years rolled, Saudan grew into an unmistakable visage, with neck-length black hair brushed rearward from a prominent forehead, often sporting a jaunty Swiss ski instructor's pin centered on his chest. He took up a career as a helicopter ski guide in the Bugaboos of British Columbia, eventually shifting his focus to the Kashmir region, where he founded Himalaya Heliski.

Perhaps Saudan was distracted by the mass quantities of powder available via his helicopters. It wasn't until 1967, at 30 years old, that his reputation as the "skier of the impossible" took root. Among other inaugural descents in the Alps, that year's feats included the Spencer Couloir on the Aiguille de Blaitière and the Whymper Couloir on the Aiguille Verte. Both runs defied opinions as to what was "skiable."

In 1971, Saudan's quest for the steeps brought him to the United States, where he made the first descent of Mt. Hood's Newton Clark Headwall, a complex route with a lengthy 50° crux. Saudan's use of a helicopter to reach Hood's summit somewhat diminished his accomplishment (climbing is as much a part of ski alpinism as the descent), but the route was nonetheless impressive, and being a masterful self-promoter, Saudan was greeted by an eager press at the base of the mountain.

As word of Saudan's descents spread through the tiny community of North American ski alpinists, the effect was observable. In the spring of 1971, Bill Briggs made his first descent of Wyoming's Grand Teton and Fritz Stammberger skied the north face of North Maroon Peak in Colorado. Both events were seminal.

Over the ensuing years, two more of Saudan's descents stand as highlights of progression. On Denali, in 1972, he skied the Messner Couloir, what's now one of the most sought-after—yet elusive—ski descents in the world. Ten years later, he aced the denouement of his career with a first descent of 8,080-meter Gasherbrum I (Hidden Peak).

When the "skier of the impossible" passed away at age 87—from a heart attack, at home—more than one ski mountaineer couldn't help but think: *How do you do what Sylvain did and last all those years?* Skill, chutzpah, plenty of luck? Or, could it be as simple as Saudan's answer in a 2016 interview by Bernhard Scholz: "I never skied down anywhere if I wasn't sure!"

—Louis W. Dawson

LOU WHITTAKER, 1929 – 2024

Lou Whittaker, a world-renowned mountaineer and guide, passed away at his home near Mt. Rainier on March 24. "Big Lou" was 95.

Lou grew up in Seattle alongside his identical twin brother, Jim. The twins began climbing with the Boy Scouts at age 12, then joined The Mountaineers and the Explorer Scouts climbing group. After practicing at Monitor Rock in West Seattle, Lou, Jim, and their brother Barney did their first alpine climb in 1943: the Tooth, near Snoqualmie Pass. The twins climbed Rainier in 1945, at 16. At 18, according to RMIguides.com, Lou had climbed all the major peaks in Washington, and by 19 he and his brother began guiding on Rainier. That year, 1948, they also joined the Mountain Rescue Council.

Standing at six feet, five inches, the twins were recruited by Seattle University on basketball scholarships, but both preferred Rainier guiding and ski patrolling at Stevens Pass. Upon graduation, in 1952, Lou and Jim were drafted into the army, during the Korean War, and sent to a Signal Corps detachment in California. In January 1953, the two arrived at Camp Hale, Colorado, to train members of the 10th Mountain Division for missions in alpine conditions.

In 1954, the twins returned to Seattle, where their lives, which had been largely shared until this point, diverged. Jim became CEO of the REI Co-op and was the first American to climb Everest, summiting with Nawang Gombu Sherpa. Lou, who was invited on the Everest trip but ultimately declined, was defined by his lifetime connection to Rainier.

Lou served as the chief guide under Rainier's main concessionaire for 14 years while also working at Osborn & Ulland, a prominent Seattle outdoor outfitter. He opened Whittaker's Chalet, a ski and mountaineering store in Lakewood and ran it from 1962 to 1972, while still climbing and guiding, then purchased the guiding concession on Rainier and co-founded Rainier Mountaineering Inc. (RMI Expeditions) in 1969 with Jerry Lynch. He was a leader in developing the guiding profession, with, as RMI wrote in a statement upon his death, "many of the world's premier mountaineers benefiting from Lou's tutelage." His son Peter took charge of RMI in the late 1990s, and son Win guides for RMI.

Lou also climbed in Alaska, the

Himalaya, and the Karakoram. In 1982, he led a strong team that attempted a new route on the north side of Everest. With him was Washington's Jim Wickwire and RMI guides including Eric Simonson, Marty Hoey, Phil Ershler, George Dunn, Joe Horiskey, and Larry Nielson (who was to become the first American to climb Everest without supplemental oxygen). Hoey, age 31, a beloved RMI guide on pace to become the first American woman to climb Everest, died in a fall at 26,600 feet.

In 1984, Lou returned to Everest and led the first American ascent of the north side of the mountain. (Phil Ershler summited alone.) At age 60, Lou led an expedition that made the first American ascent of Kangchenjunga. He wrote about his adventures in *Memoirs of a Mountain Guide.*

Upon retiring, Lou and his wife, Ingrid, who had worked for Whittaker's Chalet, at RMI, and up at Camp Muir, lived in both Ashford, gateway town to Mt. Rainier National Park, and Sun Valley, Idaho. Lou was involved with many organizations, including as a founder and member of the board of Crystal Mountain ski area; he and Ingrid were part of the Nisqually River Council and Nisqually Land Trust.

Lou's philosophy on life was simple: "When it comes down to dying," he once said, "I want to know what it is like to have really lived."

—Adapted, with additions, from tributes published by The Mountaineers

CONTRIBUTORS

The following international climbers who passed away in 2024 wrote many articles and reports for the *American Alpine Journal*. Here, we offer brief tributes to these friends and contributors.

ARCHIL BADRIASHVILI not only was among Georgia's leading alpinists, he also contributed immeasurably to the world's knowledge of Georgian alpinism and the Caucasus Mountains, with many in-depth articles in the *AAJ*. A physician and mountain guide, Badriashvili died in a fall from Shkhelda in the Caucasus precipitated by a lightning strike. (*See also the story on page 98.*)

JOHN CLEARE, a British photographer and author, captured memorable images of rock climbing and mountaineering from the Old Man of Hoy to the Eiger and the Himalaya. He wrote and edited many books, including *The World Guide to Mountains and Mountaineering*, which is still useful to *AAJ* editors 45 years after it was published, and he himself climbed throughout the world.

MARTIN FEISTL fell during a free solo in the mountains of the Austrian Tyrol in May. Feistl was a wide-ranging climber whose many new routes in Greenland in 2023 were highlighted in two *AAJ* reports. Capturing both his ethics and his drive, one of these began, "In every part of [our] expedition to the Mythics Cirque, we placed the 'how' above the 'what.'"

TOMAS FRANCHINI, a guide from the Brenta Dolomites of Italy, died in a fall from a bivy site on Nevado Cashan in Peru. Franchini's reports appeared frequently in the

AAJ for over a decade—from Patagonia, Peru, India, China, and the Karakoram, including solo new routes on big peaks in China and Pakistan.

EVGENY GLAZUNOV from Russia died during the descent from a solo winter attempt on Ak-su in Kyrgyzstan, having climbed the extremely difficult Chaplinsky Route on the north face. Glazunov described numerous new routes on the granite peaks east of Lake Baikal in several recent *AAJ* reports.

ONDREJ HÚSERKA, one of the leading lights of Slovakian alpinism, died in a crevasse fall while descending from the first ascent of the enormous east face of Langtang Lirung in Nepal (*see page 304*). Húserka's new routes ranged from the Tatra Mountains to Patagonia and Kyrgyzstan; he wrote about a new route on Phaalkan Meenaar in India for *AAJ 2023*.

VITALY "RAGE" KOMAROV, a Kazakh climber and ski mountaineer, died in an avalanche on Tuyuk-su at the start of the 2023–2024 ski season. Komarov accomplished many new routes and first ski descents, and published a skiing guidebook in his home country. For *AAJ 2018*, he wrote about the first ski descent of Talgar Peak (4,973m), with American Brody Leven.

KEITA KURAKAMI died on Mt. Fuji in his home country of Japan as a result of a preexisting heart condition. Kurakami was a bold and adventurous rock climber whose achievements included a roped solo free ascent of the Nose of El Capitan. In *AAJ 2017*, he wrote about the first ascent of the Moai Face on Mt. Mizugaki, a 5.14a with huge runouts. (*See also the story on page 84.*)

KAZUYA HIRAIDE AND KENRO NAKAJIMA died in July during an alpine-style attempt on the west face of K2. One of the strongest alpine partnerships of recent times, the two Japanese climbers made many first ascents in Pakistan, including the north face of Tirich Mir in 2023, the northwest face of Karun Koh in 2022, the south face and southeast ridge of Rakaposhi in 2019, and the northeast face of Shispare in 2017, all of which they described in *AAJ* stories. Hiraide earned the first of his three Piolets d'Or for the first ascent of the southeast face of Kamet in India, with Kei Taniguchi, in 2008.

NECROLOGY

In addition, we remember the following AAC members who passed away in 2024.

Jon Anderson
Burt Angrist
James Baker
George Basch
Jeffrey Benfield
Alan Durfee
Jeremy Freeman
James Gehres
Stanley Goldberg
John Harkness
Roger Hedlund
Mihaela Gabi Ianoși
Robert Linck
Austin Mallet
Janel Mathews
Gurdon Miller
John Reilly
Manel Casanova Rutllant
Mary Jane Sainsbury
Robert Schuster
Dr. Michael Wiedman
Warwick Williams
T.C. Price Zimmermann

BOOK REVIEWS

Edited by David Stevenson

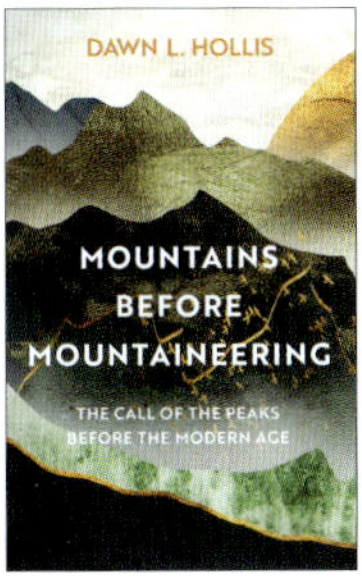

MOUNTAINS BEFORE MOUNTAINEERING: THE CALL OF THE PEAKS BEFORE THE MODERN AGE
By Dawn L. Hollis (The History Press)

OTHER EVERESTS: ONE MOUNTAIN, MANY WORLDS
Edited by Paul Gilchrist, Peter Hansen, and Jonathan Westaway (Manchester University Press)

Ghosts haunt the pages of mountaineering history: names of the innumerable dead recounted in litanies of loss; blank spaces between the lines, recalling those forgotten, silenced, or erased. And there are also what historian Daniel Lord Smail refers to as ghost theories: "old ideas that continue to structure our thinking without our being fully aware of their controlling presence." In *Mountains before Mountaineering*, Dawn Hollis describes how Smail's concept applies to her research on early European climbing history: "It seems to capture exactly what I keep coming up against: an idea so old and so oft-repeated that it has taken on the status of fact, its real origins long forgotten."

For Hollis, that mistaken "fact" is the myth that almost no one perceived the beauty of the Alps, let alone enjoyed climbing them, until the arrival of the Romantics and British mountain tourists. Her book—along with *Other Everests: One Mountain, Many Worlds*, edited by Paul Gilchrist, Peter Hansen, and Jonathan Westaway—is part of a growing effort to uncover errors in past histories and to reveal how these distorted narratives impact views of mountaineering today. Read together, the books trace the arc of a particular delusory vision that began in the Alps and spread across the mountain world.

For decades, best-selling authors and respected scholars have quoted 17th-century European descriptions of the Alps as "boils" and "warts," evoking images of perplexing ugliness and fear. "This is a compelling vision," Hollis acknowledges in *Mountains before Mountaineering*. "It is fascinatingly strange to imagine a time when the overall view of mountains was so at odds with that of today, and deliciously tempting to cast ourselves as having a special relationship with mountains, unknown by our ancestors.... It is also...*wrong*."

As Hollis deftly proves, the myth leaves out accounts of pre-18th-century alpine adventurers longing to prove themselves or to encounter marvels, naturalists delighting in mountain wildflowers, religious seekers hoping to get closer to the heavens, and scholars insisting that peaks were God's ornaments on Earth. Most of all, the myth neglects the experiences of people who lived among the Alps: guides who led travelers over snowy passes, hunters who chased chamois from ledge to ledge, and herders—mostly women—who led cattle to high pastures. It was local people, Hollis shows, who started to develop many fundamental practices of mountaineering, from early crampon use to glacier travel and crevasse rescue.

For a long time, *mountaineer* meant someone who dwelled in the mountains. As Victorian climbers adapted the word's significance to describe only their identity, they emphasized their status as heroes of mountain tales above the "porters" and "guides" who enabled their ascents, as well as other villagers who'd explored the heights before them. By claiming to have invented mountain climbing, the Victorians propagated additional myths that haunt us: a belief that a love of peaks can be cultivated best by "modern" elites, rather than shared by people from all backgrounds; an assertion that outsiders can know mountains better than local residents might; and an insistence that a "true mountaineer" climbs for "purely" recreational motives, discounting the rich variety of reasons that people have climbed and continue to do so today.

One ghost theory thus propagated others that spread beyond the Alps, restricting ideas about what kinds of protagonists count as "real" climbers and whose mountain stories matter.

The editors of *Other Everests* likewise begin with images of ghosts, evoking the invisible creators of footprints on the world's highest peak. Since the early 20th century, as they note, many casual readers of classic Western mountaineering tales would have assumed such tracks usually belonged to white men on their way to complete a grandiose, heroic ascent. Yet in the 16 essays of this volume, some of the best international mountaineering scholars demonstrate that the phantoms of Everest aren't always the ones we're conditioned to expect.

Sifting through archives and oral histories, the *Other Everests* writers uncover figures frequently absent from dominant accounts, as if buried under windswept drifts of snow. The "fleeting detail" of a monk folding a white *khata* ceremonial scarf in John Noel's 1922 Everest film hints at the missing scene of the avalanche deaths of seven local staff. Images of female expedition workers and mountaineers re-emerge from lesser-heard stories and old photos—such as the faded picture of a Sherpa woman bent under one of the heavy loads of the 1953 Everest expedition.

Turning to the present day, contributors describe how Sherpa outfitters, guides, and mountaineers have started to reclaim their side of Everest as a "Nepali mountain," while inequalities persist. Through access to social media and modern communications technologies, Sherpas have found wider audiences for counternarratives that disrupt stereotypical tales and restore their own voices. And as scholar Ruth Gamble recounts, the vision of Chomolungma (the mountain's Sherpa name) as a sacred summit has persisted—beneath the widespread image of a commodified "Mt. Everest."

The collection of essays evokes, as the editors hope, "a plurality of perspectives, a world of multiple or alternative" peaks—an abundance of once seemingly invisible mountains crystallizing into overlapping, radiant forms. Yet as our climate crisis accelerates, the topographies of all these "Other Everests" are at risk of loss once more. Countless writers in the past have described high peaks as "sublime." Today, contributor Yvonne Reddick observes, the snows of the South Col themselves are *sublimating*, vanishing into thin air.

When I first heard Hollis present her research at the 2015 Thinking Mountains conference, historian Maurice Isserman congratulated her: "Now, we need to rewrite all our books." That same year, I asked the anthropologist Pasang Yangjee Sherpa how she thought mountaineering literature should evolve. Her response, quoted again in *Other Everests*, now resonates even more deeply: "The story should be about the existence of multiple stories and about bringing them to light.... It should involve shifting our focus from one-way-of-being to recognizing the multiple-ways-of-being."

A decade later, *Mountains before Mountaineering* and *Other Everests* have joined a swell of books creating new bodies of mountain literature beyond the limits of the old canon, from the award-winning histories by Bernadette

McDonald, Nandini Purandare, and Deepa Balsavar, which restore stories of Pakistani and Sherpa expedition staff, to genre-pushing works such as Elizabeth Bradfield, CMarie Fuhrman, and Derek Sheffield's *Cascadia Field Guide*, which elevates plants and animals as worthy heroes of alpine tales.

Amid rising ecological disasters, both *Mountains before Mountaineering* and *Other Everests* suggest, we need to break free of the "ghost theories" that merely promoted accounts of summit conquests by a privileged few—and to expand the boundaries of our empathy until we recognize the stories of all people and all living things in the mountains, including the land itself. As a Ladakhi woman, Dolma, told anthropologist Karine Gagné (cited in *Other Everests*): "To care for the glacier, you have to see the glacier, you have to know the glacier, like you know a friend."

—Katie Ives (*adapted in part from the author's articles in Alpinist issues 88 and 73*)

TOBIN, THE STONEMASTERS, AND ME, 1970–1980: REMEMBERING TOBIN SORENSON, THE BEST CLIMBER IN THE WORLD
By Rick Accomazzo
(Stonemaster Books)

Much the way nature abhors a vacuum, historians seem to hate unlabeled epochs. A chunk of American climbing history seems to have been left without a title. It's the bit between the end of the "Golden Years" (roughly the mid-1950s through the late '60s) and the time since sport climbing took over in the mid-1980s. That is, the period from about 1970 to roughly 1983–84.

Though unnamed, this was certainly an important period in climbing history, and it was characterized by some of the most impressive ascents that ever happened in the Western Hemisphere—hard free climbing, sketchy protection, and very limited use of permanent anchors. It melded with the hippie music and the dropout motif of the day—and the incredible amounts of drugs being consumed.

These guys and gals (the guys were numerous; the gals few—folks like Lynn Hill and Mari Gingery) did things their own way and pointed the way forward. Somehow, sport climbing subverted what should have been hard traditional free climbing's brilliant adulthood—hard trad would take a hit for several decades. (Though it's been revived, thankfully.) In the 1970s and early '80s, the guys and gals pushing the sport called themselves the Stonemasters, and their influence was felt not just in California but all over the continent.

Now, Rick Accomazzo, a central figure of the Stonemasters (these days a retired lawyer in Boulder), has written a book describing his life with that group and the life of Tobin Sorenson.

Compared with his Southern California brethren (a band of well-meaning misfits), Tobin Sorenson was a different egg. His life was anchored to religion. He swore off drugs and alcohol (he thought beer "taste[d] like piss"), and he climbed in the name of the Lord. In the early 1970s, he blitzed through Southern California, then Yosemite, setting a high bar with nearly every climb. Then he got into alpinism and rocked the world.

Accomazzo sums up his case for labeling Sorenson "the best climber in the world" at the end of the 1970s: "In the span of one year, starting in August 1977, after a long layoff, he climbed the hardest Alpine walls in Europe, putting up four new routes (including two on the fabled great north faces), the first alpine-style ascent of the Eiger Direct, and the third winter solo of the Matterhorn north face.... He had climbed the hardest Yosemite routes in near-perfect style at a time when Yosemite Valley contained the most difficult rock climbs in the world. Finally, in the same year, he dipped his toe into high-altitude climbing and succeeded in a bold, on-sight free solo ascent of 20,981-foot Huandoy Norte. In the next two years he bounced from daunting first winter ascents in Canada, to first ascents on sunny Australian cliffs that surpassed the existing grades, to impressive technical alpine first ascents in New Zealand."

One of the best things about *Tobin, the Stonemasters, and Me* is how it shows the huge influence Southern California (specifically Tahquitz) had on climbing in Yosemite Valley. After all, the "Yosemite" decimal system was invented at Tahquitz, as were many other climbing ideas and styles, and certainly many of Yosemite's best climbers—including Sorenson—cut their teeth at Tahquitz.

The Stonemasters meticulously explored Southern California, then came to Yosemite and changed the game in free climbing and the notions of speed, style, and boldness. There's a reason Jim Bridwell, John Long, and Billy Westbay stand so proud in the famous photo of them in front of El Cap—they earned it. Indeed, there's a reason the Stonemasters' logo—a lightning bolt adopted from Gerry Lopez's line of clothing, jewelry, and surfboards—gets rescrawled on the Midnight Lightning boulder problem every year. You have to be a master of stone to do the problem.

In recounting Stonemasters lore, Accomazzo's fine work belongs alongside a couple of other books—George Meyers's *Yosemite Climber* (1979) and John Long and Dean Fidelman's *The Stonemasters: California Rock Climbers in the Seventies* (2009)—and it does worthy service to anyone wanting to label that magical epoch by describing the playgrounds and, more importantly, the players.

Tobin, the Stonemasters, and Me is one of the best reads I've had in a long time, and it puts the shine on what it means to be a climber. And—a nod to the designer—it's a beautiful book to hold and behold: gorgeously designed, wonderfully illustrated, sumptuously packaged. They put some ducats into this one.

Go with the flow, man, and embrace the style, the boldness, and the sheer thrill of the Stonemasters era.

—Cameron M. Burns

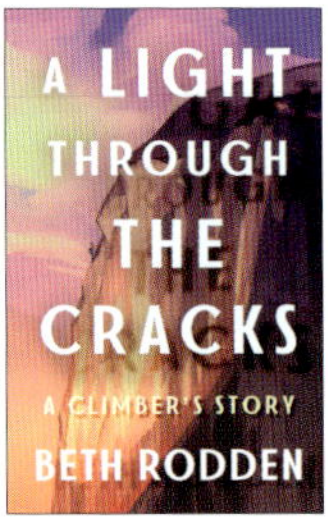

A LIGHT THROUGH THE CRACKS: A CLIMBER'S STORY

By Beth Rodden (Little A)

Beth Rodden's memoir recounts her harrowing kidnapping in Kyrgyzstan, in 2000, and the famous climber's long struggle with recovery and search for identity within the sexist, uber-competitive world of professional rock climbing.

Readers may start this book looking for a page-turner about a dramatic kidnapping, and Rodden delivers with a detailed account of her ordeal, but she also guides her readers through a much quieter yet more universal experience—that of living with and healing from trauma. To this reader, at least, it did not feel coincidental that the language of Rodden's captivity closely mirrors the feelings she describes later in the memoir about her tenacious drive for recognition and respect in a male-dominated climbing culture. The parallel between the two threads is ultimately the book's power: For female athletes, captivity takes many forms; battles are fought not just against gravity but against identities assigned to Rodden without her consent or prompting.

To write a compelling memoir, one needs more than just a good story; the author also needs the literary skill to tell it well. Rodden's prose is detail-driven, almost diary-like, but never feels indulgent or overdramatic. Though she is generous and vulnerable in sharing her experiences, the memoir doesn't feel like a sordid tell-all; Rodden handles her words with care. Her descriptions root the reader in a fully embodied experience; we feel as if we are there with Rodden, experiencing events and emotions alongside her. Rodden is a flawed protagonist who makes mistakes, but she offers us such an intimate window in that it's easy to stay with her, to root for her even when—especially when—she is most hard on herself. Readers looking for a more highbrow, literary prose style may not be fully satisfied with *A Light through the Cracks*, but this memoir never billed itself that way, and in the publishing world of athlete-turned-author, Rodden holds her own space.

A Light through the Cracks is organized into three chronological sections exploring Rodden's formative years with partner and eventual husband Tommy Caldwell and their kidnapping, then their notable climbs together, and finally their divorce and Rodden's remarriage, the birth of her child, and her reconciliation with her climbing career. As is true with the lived experience of trauma, the kidnapping foregrounds the memoir, shaping—and, for a time, controlling—Rodden's emotions and perspectives of the world. This narrative structure also has the effect of making the later descriptions of difficult climbs hit harder; the reader distinctly feels that gravity has become stronger for Rodden, and she fights toward literal and figurative ascent from very real demons, some from the kidnapping and some set loose from a climbing culture beyond her control.

In the final section, there is a sense of reconciliation without concession with this sport that has given Rodden so much but also tried, unsuccessfully, to tear away her self-worth. Rodden becomes "just Beth," not a kidnap victim or the former wife of a famous climber, but someone strong and assured enough to walk alongside their ghosts and keep climbing, in every sense.

—Rebecca Young

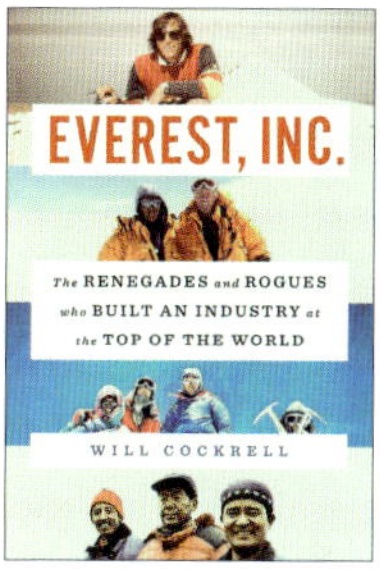

EVEREST, INC.: THE RENEGADES AND ROGUES WHO BUILT AN INDUSTRY AT THE TOP OF THE WORLD
By Will Cockrell (Gallery Books)

Will Cockrell wanted to know how, after a mere 394 climbers reached the summit of Chomolungma in the 39 years leading up to 1992, that number exploded to roughly 11,500 people over the next 32 years. Or, as he puts it: "How did a peak that was at first unclimbable, then downgraded to simply suicidal, become one that thousands of people could scale?" In telling the story, he touches on the dividing line that makes people either infatuated with summiting this mountain or disgusted by what the critics call "the circus."

Everest, Inc. is in the category of climbing books that are not about an individual attempt or climb but more a profile of a region or mountain, such as Heinrich Harrer's history of the north face of the Eiger in *The White Spider*. On Chomolungma, the very nature of the audacious goal of guiding climbers unskilled in high-altitude mountaineering safely to the top and back has turned the mountain into a business setting, and Cockrell's focus is on these guiding ventures and their competition. The companies are the personalities here, at least as much as the climbers themselves.

Cockrell provides refreshing insight into the approach and values of the guides on Chomolungma. He advocates for them, giving numerous examples that reaching the top is not their primary goal; rather, they find an intrinsic reward from helping others reach what might have otherwise been unattainable. There is a greater degree of "hand holding" in an attempt on this mountain, and Cockrell contrasts this with the traditional guides of rigid European and Canadian schools, and the less structured American tradition (though both focus on teaching increasingly complex skills and emphasize gaining experience). On Chomolungma, the nature of high-altitude climbing, supplemental oxygen use, and acclimatization rotations put the mountain and its 8,000-meter peers in a unique category. It is difficult to fairly compare the approaches to guiding, Cockrell notes, when lower mountain experience is less applicable.

Chomolungma today elicits two extreme viewpoints: It's either the site of one of the world's greatest adventures, where one can stare down death, or it is a crowded and commercial amusement park that is the antithesis of adventure. It comes down to values and which approach you value more. Cockrell's respect for the commercial guiding companies and their guides is not expressed in a vacuum, even addressing the views from critics like Jon Krakauer.

Everest, Inc. doesn't break a lot of new ground—the stories of the dawn of Everest guiding and the creation of the companies that followed have been told in other books and articles—but Cockrell effectively consolidates the information. He also has applied his journalism skills and accumulated knowledge of commercial guiding from his work at *Men's Journal* to the story; he interviewed contemporary guides, business owners, and new Nepali entrants to the "industry" to bring different perspectives.

This book says "company" too many times for a reader like me who is looking for stories of people in wild places and on adventurous climbs. I will put it on a different shelf than my climbing books, perhaps next to *Endurance* by Alfred Lansing, which is used as a text in some business schools—just as *Everest, Inc.* might be one day, too.

—Andrew Szalay

A PLACE AMONG GIANTS: 22 SEASONS AT DENALI BASECAMP

By Lisa Roderick (Di Angelo Publications)

A Place Among Giants is not only a fresh perspective and certain-to-be classic of mountaineering literature, but also a love story involving the author, Lisa Roderick, and the Alaska Range, her husband, climber Mark Westman, and the thousands of unique personalities she interacted with during her 22 seasons as Denali's base camp manager.

A Place Among Giants is a memoir of a unique life—the kind that only a few strong women have experienced. As the manager of Kahiltna base camp, Roderick spent more than two decades safely coordinating thousands of planes full of climbers and tourists in and out of the Alaska Range. (Many were flown by her brother, Paul Roderick, who runs Talkeetna Air Taxi.) Each page in this book exudes the reverence she has for this vast and wild place of sprawling ice and towering mountains. It would seem impossible to portray the enormity of North America's grandest peaks within the confines of a book, but as I flipped through these pages, I could feel the wind on my cheeks and the pre-climb nerves twitching, just as if I were stepping out of my tent in the predawn twilight on the Kahiltna.

Roderick's book delves into the relationships she formed with close friends, some of whom died while reaching for lofty dreams. She also details funny anecdotes that have become legendary around base camp, such as the time she humbled an angry Russian climber into compliance with a few choice words when he tried to intimidate her. Then there's the time a non-climber snuck onto the glacier and stalked a guide up the West Buttress, dragging only a pink wheeled suitcase and baffling the many climbers who passed her. "It's the big one," she said when a group of tourists asked which mountain was Denali.

Sprinkled throughout are tales of legendary rescues and bar-setting feats of alpinism. Roderick addresses her worry as her alpinist husband progresses to bigger and more dangerous Alaskan routes, and she opens up about her own feelings of vulnerability and self-doubt, adapting to a midlife diagnosis of hypothyroidism, and the loss of far too many friends in the climbing community.

A Place Among Giants is a fantastic read from someone who has arguably spent more time in the Alaska Range and knows it in a different way than anyone else probably ever will. While Roderick frequently notes that she felt small among the surrounding mountains, she undoubtedly has left a lasting impact on the Alaska Range and on many of those who encountered her there.

—Clint Helander

SURVIVAL IS NOT ASSURED: THE LIFE OF CLIMBER JIM DONINI
By Geoff Powter
(Mountaineers Books)

Hats off to Geoff Powter and Jim Donini for teaming up to tell Donini's life story in *Survival Is Not Assured*. The story is beautifully written and captivating, as it not only describes many of Donini's legendary climbs but also takes the reader into the depths of his personal life.

Powter gives the reader insights into Jim's formative years—before climbing—that even Donini's close friends may not have known. Donini's time as a Green Beret cultivated his drive to complete a mission with trust and dedication to his comrades. In his foreword for the book, Michael Kennedy describes Donini as "a person who values friendship above all else."

Powter powerfully and vividly recounts the story of Donini's attempt on the north ridge of Latok I in Pakistan in 1978, as part of the famous team that included Kennedy, George Lowe, and Jeff Lowe. They climbed alpine style up into the edge of survivability, abandoning the climb just pitches from the summit because of Jeff Lowe's illness. Powter also recounts the near-fatal accident and complicated, high-risk rescue of Malcolm Daly as he and Donini attempted an unclimbed route on Thunder Mountain in the Alaska Range. Daly would survive but lose his leg as a result.

These stories are interlaced with chapters about Donini's personal life in which the reader learns more about Jim's heart-wrenching losses within his family. *Survival Is Not Assured* takes on a deeper meaning as Powter deftly weaves the threads of Donini's accomplishments with his failures; the book is not merely an account of three decades of serious climbing, because it also captures the bond of partnerships, family, and friendships in and out of the mountains. Powter takes us to the Alaska Range with Donini and Jack Tackle in a way that paints the relationship of these alpinists as chosen family in a majestic temple, where life can be felt in pure and simple terms.

For all the mountains have given to Donini, he has given back to the climbing community through his work with the American Alpine Club and other organizations. In Donini's words, "Our lives are short, and we need to live in the present and be all that we can be to the ones we care about; we also need to celebrate the love and beauty that those no longer here were able to give us." This book is a gift, and my only complaint is the pages turned too fast.

—Kirsten Kremer

HEADSTRAP: LEGENDS AND LORE FROM THE CLIMBING SHERPAS OF DARJEELING
By Nandini Purandare and Deepa Balsavar
(Mountaineers Books)

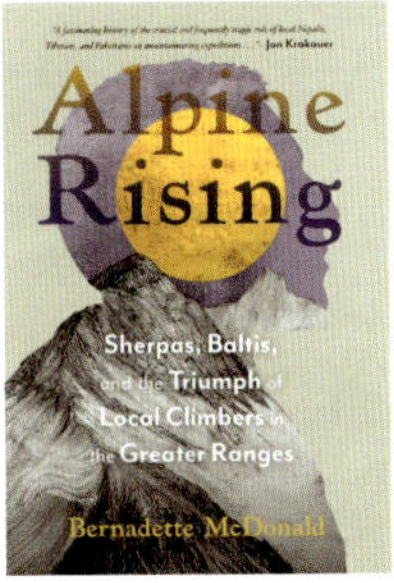

ALPINE RISING: SHERPAS, BALTIS, AND THE TRIUMPH OF LOCAL CLIMBERS IN THE GREATER RANGES
By Bernadette McDonald
(Mountaineers Books)

I have been waiting for these books all my life. As someone whose every school-age vacation was spent walking in the Bengal/Sikkim/Garhwal/Kumaon Himalaya and as an absurd girl who tried to read everything she could lay hands on, I desperately wished, even as I read extraordinary books by extraordinary mountaineers from around the world, that I had greater access to the stories of the people whose food, music, architectures, languages, religions, color palettes, and ethics composed my days.

The very few indigenous narratives that existed—Tenzing Norgay's or Ang Tharkay's, for example, notwithstanding their mediation by translators and co-authors—seemed like exceptions proving the apparent rule that mountaineering ambitions, innovations, and accomplishments were the proper domain of white and usually male climbers. And that mountaineering was a proper exercise of the colonial drive: that human beings naturally relate to mountain landscapes with a sense of entitlement and dominion. The backbone of all Himalayan mountaineering that has ever existed—who carried the food and fuel infrastructure; who cooked; who ran the communications on foot; who provided the rescues—was in plain view for me but missing from the literature.

Despite its subtitle lightly evoking "legends and lore," Nandini Purandare and Deepa Balsavar's *Headstrap* is based on solid archival research: painstaking perusal of nearly 100 years of Himalayan Club records, hundreds of hours of conversation in over 150 interviews, and, importantly, a decade of thinking and writing by two remarkable storytellers. *Headstrap* is an uncovering of some of the complexities, dreams, fallibilities, leadership, and sheer grit of the single most influential demographic of climbers in the highest mountains of our planet. Here, some of the greatest legends of mountaineering—Ang Tharkay, Pasang Dawa Lama, Ang Tsering, and Tenzing Norgay—emerge as people with their own profound realities of needs; explained and unexplained ambitions; camaraderies of the trail; heroisms and lapses of extenuating circumstances; glories of recognition; lonelinesses of success; and dreams of better futures for their children.

Structurally, the book situates the cultural history of the climbing Bhutias, especially Sherpas, of Darjeeling in three parts, usefully ranging from 1) the 19th century's imperial Trigonometrical Survey of India (in the course of which a Bengali named Radhanath Sikdar first calculated the tallest mountain on Earth into record in 1852), to 2) the "Darjeeling dream" that brought so many inhabitants of Khumbu to Darjeeling with the promise of employment throughout the 20th century, to 3) post-independence neocolonialism that continues to beset mountaineering in the subcontinent today. This political history of the region is well known but has seldom been so succinctly rendered. More valuably, this story has never been told with clear exposition of the colonialist-capitalist underpinnings of all the botany, anthropology, geology, commerce, medicine, and "development" in the area.

There is also a meta-critical awareness with which Purandare and Balsavar exercise their listening (for theirs is ultimately an oral history) and then transfer it to the page so readers can *hear* these remarkable stories. The facts sometimes change between tellers. But—and perhaps therefore—the truth remains. Dozens of unforgettable moments emerge, including, among many others: 1934, year of desolations on Nanga Parbat, when Joan Townend, then secretary of the Himalayan Club, realizes the importance of creating meaningful records of Darjeeling's "for hire" climbers; 1945, when Ang Lhamu agrees to marry her late cousin's husband, Tenzing Norgay, and to look after his two young daughters; 1945, when Ani Lhakpa Diki "waits and waits" for her partner to return from a reconnaissance expedition to Kangchenjunga and is finally given $36 as compensation for her husband, then leaves her nine-month-old in the care of her three-year-old while she puts her load-carrying headstrap back on to earn subsistence for the family; and ca 1976, when Ongmu Gombu is dropped off for her first day at school by her father, Nawang Gombu, for whom this simple parental activity becomes a "big thing" because "he didn't go to school."

The book also tells the story of post-colonial (with the hyphen in the sense of after colonialism) Darjeeling climbing. The creation of the Himalayan Mountaineering Institute was famously facilitated by Nehru, the first prime minister of India, following the success of Edmund Hillary and Tenzing Norgay and capitalizing on interest in mountaineering in 1954: "The Institute trains young men not only to climb Himalayan peaks, but also creates in them an urge to climb peaks of human endeavor." With its express emphasis on "young men"—a curious emphasis in a democracy otherwise aspiring toward such equality that universal adult suffrage was enacted in 1949, a mere two years after political independence in 1947—the Institute relegated itself to being a future boys' club. And with its first—and every subsequent—principal being a member of the military, the Institute similarly constrained itself to assault-oriented stagnations of the art of climbing.

The same despicable colonial drive that made of Chomolungma (as the mountain was known by Bhutias) or Sagarmatha (as it was known by the Nepalese) an "Everest" (so named after an imperial surveyor who never set eyes on the mountain) similarly kept the stories of some of the world's most accomplished climbers as a footnote of sorts in mountaineering history for over a century. Purandare and Balsavar's book goes a terrific way toward balancing the record. But a longer way yet remains for these very important stories to be told as fully or as contextually as possible. Among the things that should come next is the trove of mountaineering history that Bhutias and Sherpas themselves carry, and which, should they choose to share in their own voice, we should read with care.

Until then, this book should be required reading for all visitors to the Himalaya, just as the first action items incumbent upon everyone even thinking of climbing in the area should be to 1) somehow contribute to better maternal and infant care in the area and 2) contribute to better insurance for Himalayan climbers and support staff.

With *Alpine Rising*, Bernadette McDonald continues her transformative contribution to mountaineering literature in the 21st century. Rich in another set of interviews—so much so that the interviewers and translators Saqlain Muhammad and Sareena Rai arguably function as authorial collaborators for this volume—McDonald's book does characteristically vivid and meticulous work of bringing the motivations, dreams, losses, flamboyances, and achievements of "local" climbers to light. With less cohesion but with ample detail, this book also tells the story from the beginnings of

Himalayan mountaineering to this day. In McDonald's clear writing, stories of two distinct communities of climbers—of the Nepalese/Indian/Tibetan Himalaya and the Karakoram, respectively—emerge in conversation with one another.

Valuably, this is one of the first books in English to document stories of certain Karakoram climbers from the earlier 20th century—starting with the first Nanga Parbat expedition in 1932—to the present. The author, who brought us the magnificent *Freedom Climbers* (2011), again brings to narrative an entire community of mountaineers whose political and socio-economic realities condition their climbing. This time, the story feels unfinished. I dare to hope this is because McDonald's next project is a history of Pakistani climbing, especially in the Karakoram.

The book's greatest achievement is in McDonald's willingness and ability to demonstrate the distance between the very planets that Himalayan mountaineering's employers and employed hailed from throughout the 20th century. One of the most stunning stories is that of the egregious (non)leadership of Fritz Wiessner, who in 1939 managed to alienate and then lose track of most of his team on K2, and then also dispatched and lost a phenomenally strong rescue team—the upper reaches of the rescue being unconscionably, if unsurprisingly, composed solely of Sherpas. Three Sherpa climbers, Pasang Kitar, Pasang Kikuli, and Phinsoo Sherpa, were lost. None of the reports resulting from the expedition had time or space for the families of the Sherpas who died. And this is not the only story of vast discrepancies in outcomes. Notwithstanding the subtitle's promise of tales of "Triumph of Local Climbers in the Greater Ranges," the book holds necessary space for the sufferings, non-recognitions, griefs, and continued prayers of the climbers who gave so much of themselves to the high mountains, and those of their partners and children who still hold the vast emptiness of the losses.

A remarkable high point rounds out the story of the triumphs: the winter ascent of K2 by ten Nepalese climbers in 2021. Rightly, that story has been and continues to be told mainly by its protagonists. What is ultimately at stake, McDonald reminds us, drawing on Tashi Sherpa's words, is respect. "The mountains are about mutual respect," Tashi Sherpa says. And "climbers from Nepal and Pakistan deserve all the respect they are finally getting," writes McDonald. "Respect is worth celebrating." [*The full version of this essay, exploring these topics in greater depth, is at the AAJ website.*]

—Amrita Dhar

THE COLOR OF EVERYTHING: A JOURNEY TO QUIET THE CHAOS WITHIN

By Cory Richards
(Random House)

Cory Richards has been a prolific 21st-century alpinist, high-altitude mountaineer, and adventure photographer. From being the first and only American to summit an 8,000-meter peak in winter to being National Geographic's 2012 Adventurer of the Year, Richards's success in climbing and photography made him a public figure around the world, even live-streaming his 2016 ascent of Everest without supplemental oxygen via Snapchat. In this memoir, Richards relates the expeditions that built his career, but not from the angle that often typifies mountaineering literature. It is the examination and admission of his own culpabilities—which led him to an "early retirement"—that make up the marrow of the book.

Richards uses a broken timeline and braided-narrative structure to piece together the road that took him to—and also away from—the Greater Ranges. From his earliest memories, Richards experiences severe trauma in his home, and as a young adult slowly and painfully unravels a diagnosis of bipolar disorder. He experiences homelessness, drug use, and sexual assault at an age when most would be concerned with their math test in sixth period. After a few years of repeatedly running away from private institutions for troubled teens, always to be returned, Richards begins to climb again, like he had with his father as a boy. Climbing leads him to photography, which will stabilize and shape the course of his life for decades to come.

While Richards examines the roots of his trauma to understand his own motivations, the memoir is also a deep reflection on identity and how one's perception of their identity can drive them to ends they might not desire. As any climber who has committed significant time to their craft knows, ours can be a selfish pursuit. I believe the same may be said for the life of an artist, and at his core, Richards is an artist. The passion and obsession he poured into mixed routes and high altitude are only exceeded by his ambition as a photographer. The two crafts always intertwined and embedded with his identity, to the point that he began to question his own self apart from his crafts. It is Richards's commitment to and control of his craft, now through memoir, that permitted him to admit the motivations and shortcomings of his previous identity.

Richards gracefully navigates the consequences of his failed relationships and addictions with prose that employs brevity to capture complex experiences. Through examination of his furious rage as an adolescent, infidelity in his marriage, contentions around prioritizing mental health in climbing, and honesty about his past sexual misconduct, brought to light through the #MeToo movement, Richards lays himself out on the page with unfailing exposure. As when leading a delicate mixed pitch, he does not take the easy way out. He continues on, admitting his faults with grace and conviction, and without blaming his mental health for the pain caused to others.

Reading this memoir of someone who has lived chaotically up to the very edge of life, I appreciated the refreshing perspective that we are responsible for ourselves, the good and bad, without denying the complexity of simply existing.

—Wade Dittburner

In Brief

Avalanche Dreams: A Memoir of Skiing, Climbing, and Life, by Louis W. Dawson (Best Peak Press). A poignant look at a feral youth in 1970s Colorado and "the struggles for meaning in the world of extreme alpinism," by the author of *Wild Snow*.

Dixon, Descending: A Novel, by Karen Outen (Dutton). Two brothers attempt to become the first Black Americans to summit Everest. Note that the first Black American to summit Everest was a woman, Sophia Danenberg, in 2006.

The Lions of Winter: Survival and Sacrifice on Mt. Washington, by Ty Gagne (Tmc Books). The dramatic story of New Hampshire rescuer Albert Dow, who lost his life in an avalanche while searching for lost and frozen Hugh Herr.

Outsider: A Life with the Elephants and Mountains of Africa, by Iain Allen (Vanguard). A page-turning memoir from one of Kenya's most renowned climbers and guides.

Secret Plans: Vol. III; 40+ Years of Cartoons for Climbers, by Tami Knight (Tellwell Talent). Climbing is serious but also absurd—no one is better at showing us how to laugh at ourselves than Tami Knight.

Tap Dancing on Everest, by Mimi Zieman (Falcon Guides). Zieman's memoir describes her time as medical support for the four-person Kangshung Face of Everest team in 1988.

INDEX

COMPILED BY EVE TALLMAN & RALPH FERRARA

Mountains are listed by official and variant names. Indexed photographs are in bold type. Ranges, geographic locations, and maps are also referenced.

C

D

T

U

V

W

X

Y

Z

THE AMERICAN ALPINE JOURNAL 2025

American Alpine Club

AAJ

INTERNATIONAL GRADE COMPARISON CHART

SERIOUSNESS RATINGS

These often modify technical grades when protection is difficult

PG-13: Difficult or insecure protection or loose rock, with some injury potential

R: Poor protection with high potential for injury

X: A fall would likely result in serious injury or death

YDS=Yosemite Decimal System **UIAA**=Union Internationale des Associations D'Alpinisme **FR**=France/Sport **AUS**=Australia **SAX**=Saxony **CIS**=Commonwealth of Independent States/Russia **SCA**=Scandinavia **BRA**=Brazil **UK**=United Kingdom

Note: *All conversions are approximate. Search "International Grade Comparison Chart" at the AAJ website for further explanation of commitment grades and waterfall ice/mixed grades.*

YDS	UIAA	FR	AUS	SAX	CIS	SCA	BRA	UK	
5.2	II	1	10	II	III	3			D
5.3	III	2	11	III	III+	3+			
5.4	IV-	3	12		IV-	4			VD
5.5	IV IV+		13		IV	4+			S
5.6	V-	4	14		IV+	5-		4a	HS
5.7	V		15	VIIa		5		4b	VS
5.8	V+	5a	16	VIIb	V-	5+	4 4+	4c	HVS
5.9	VI-	5b	17	VIIc			5 5+	5a	E1
5.10a	VI	5c	18	VIIIa	V	6-	6a	5b	
5.10b	VI+	6a				6	6b		E2
5.10c	VII-	6a+	19	VIIIb		6+			
5.10d	VII	6b		VIIIc	V+		6c		E3
5.11a	VII+	6b+	20	IXa		7-	7a	5c	
5.11b		6c	21			7			
5.11c	VIII-	6c+	22	IXb	VI-	7+	7b		E4
5.11d	VIII	7a	23	IXc			7c	6a	
5.12a	VIII+	7a+	24				8a		E5
5.12b		7b	25	Xa	VI	8-	8b		
5.12c	IX-	7b+	26			8 8+	8c		
5.12d	IX	7c	27	Xb			9a	6b	E6
5.13a		7c+	28	Xc			9b		
5.13b	IX+	8a	29			9-	9c		
5.13c	X-	8a+	30			9	10a		E7
5.13d	X	8b	31	XIa	VI+		10b		
5.14a		8b+	32				10c	7a	E8
5.14b	X+	8c	33	XIb		9+	11a		
5.14c	XI-	8c+	34	XIc			11b		E9
5.14d	XI	9a	35				11c	7b	
5.15a	XI+	9a+	36	XIIa		10	12a		E10
5.15b	XII-	9b	37		VII		12b		E11
5.15c	XII	9b+	38	XIIb			12c		
5.15d	XII+	9c	39						